SACRED CONTRACTS

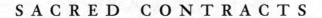

Sacred Contracts

AWAKENING YOUR

DIVINE POTENTIAL

Caroline Myss

HARMONY BOOKS  NEW YORK

Published by Harmony Books, New York, New York.
Member of the Crown Publishing Group.

Random House, Inc. New York, Toronto, London, Sydney, Auckland
www.randomhouse.com

Harmony Books is a registered trademark and the Harmony Books
colophon is a trademark of Random House, Inc.

Printed in the United States of America
Design by Barbara Balch

Library of Congress Cataloging in Publication Data
Myss, Caroline M.
Sacred contracts : awakening your divine potential / Caroline Myss.
1. Self-actualization (Psychology)   2. Goal (Psychology)
3. Archetype (Psychology)   I. Title.
BF637.S4 M97 2001

158.1—dc21

2001039486

ISBN 0-517-70392-0

10 9 8 7 6 5 4 3 2 1
First Edition

For my father and my brother Joseph—
my family in Heaven

CONTENTS

ACKNOWLEDGMENTS

I could not have written this book had it not been for the unfailing support of Peter Occhiogrosso. A superb author and scholar of world religions, Peter provided me with his support both as a writer and as a vast resource of information. Consolidating workshop research that I had gathered for fifteen years while creating an archetypal tool for personal inner work became an undertaking that required a "mind mate," and Peter was that person for me. His constant support as a professional, and his emotional support as a dear friend, became a spiritual resource that I came to depend on through every month of the journey of birthing this book. I can never thank him enough.

Leslie Meredith, my brilliantly talented editor and loving friend, guided this text with her genius, insight, and ever-present lead pencil. I have never known an individual as gifted with guiding the incarnation of another person's vision as Les is, and no gift is more generous. She is a master of editorial "tough love," and I have come to rely on every thread of her skill for the creation and completion of all of my books, this one most of all. Once again, without her, this book could not have been written. Les is one of the dearest Sacred Contracts that Heaven has provided for me.

My gratitude flows abundantly to Ned Leavitt, my agent, who has been one of the guardians of my work since we began our partnership years ago. I also thank Linda Loewenthal, my editorial director, and Chip Gibson, my publisher, for their continual faith in this project. To Clarissa Pinkola Estés, my dearest *Madrina*, my love and thanks for always being available to me through every phone call with her boundless, warm, and caring heart and generous jewels of wisdom and guidance. My love and appreciation for Donald Meshirer cannot be measured. His love and devotion got me through every difficult moment of this project. My love and gratitude go to Penny Simon, a forever friend who also happens to be one of the most dedicated publicists that an author could have on her team.

C. Norman Shealy, M.D., Ph.D., has been my professional colleague and loving friend for seventeen years. Through him I refined my skill as a medical intuitive, and for the past nine years he has worked with me in the classroom, teaching this material to students. I can never describe how much Norm has helped me in my work. His commitment to bringing the vision of Sacred Contracts to fruition was, for me, like having a backup spinal cord. He provided to this book his natural genius for generating original ideas and insights. His energy for long hours in the classroom and his dedication as a brilliant teacher have inspired thousands of students to pursue the depth of their Sacred Contracts. I will never have another creative companion in my life like Norm. My Contract with him is truly larger than this life.

There are so many other people who all deserve my gratitude. My dearest friend, Mary Neville, has helped me construct every stage of my professional life. Her loving support as a friend and her guidance as a professional is a constant inspiration to me. I owe her a debt of gratitude that words cannot communicate. To Judy Haskett, my assistant, my deepest love and gratitude for holding down the fort. To David Smith, my business partner and wise friend, my lasting thanks for contributing his creative genius to my endeavors. And to my cousin Colleen Daley who did an exceptional job of artistically crafting all the illustrations in this book—thanks, cousin.

The list of personal friends who have contributed their help along the way is a long one indeed. I especially thank Jim Curtan for being the consultant on identifying archetypes in films. His former career as a manager to actors was invaluable. My thanks to Lynn Bell and Chandra Sammons for helping me amass information on fairy tales and myths. I also want to thank Ron Roth and Paul Funfsinn for the grace they contribute to my life and to my work. To Michael Gluck, all my love for your endearing companionship and constant outpouring of love and optimism. To you, I am so lovingly grateful. And to my dear friend Peter Shaw, my love and gratitude to you for years of generous support of my work and of our friendship.

But most of all, I want to thank my family—especially my mother, my brother Ed and my sister-in-law Amy, along with my nieces,

Rachel and Sarah, and nephew, Eddie—whose devotion and love carried me through every single day. They are Heaven's special blessing to me.

Finally, I would like to thank all of the people who contributed their life stories to the pages of this book, particularly Mickey Magic. Their journeys have provided the backbone for this material. Without the help of these individuals who so generously shared their pains and triumphs, this book could never have been written.

AN APPRECIATION

I first met Caroline almost two decades ago, and we have been work-ing together ever since. I was particularly impressed then with her belief that we each have a Sacred Contract to learn to use power wisely, responsibly, and lovingly. When Caroline began elaborating this concept of a Sacred Contract in our own workshops and for this book, she began to see energy in the form of archetypes. Gradually, it became clear to her that archetypes are the forces responsible for our learning the use of power.

Carl Jung is generally credited in the modern world as having introduced archetypes, although the idea had been espoused originally by Plato. Jung did first develop the concept of the collective uncon-scious, the ever-present sum of all experiences that the human race has acquired throughout history. These experiences appear in all ages and all latitudes, but also appear in individual dreams, fantasies, visions, and ideas.[1] Beyond these seminal ideas, Jung actually described a rather limited number of archetypes. He elaborated in detail only: Shadow; Wise Old Man; Child and Child Hero; Mother (Primordial and Earth); Maiden Anima (Female Pattern); Animus (Male Pattern). Each of these, he says, has a multitude of variations, and they change and evolve constantly. They are fluid and cannot be rigidly classified. According to Jung, archetypes provide the foundation for our person-ality, our drives, feelings, beliefs, motivation, and actions.

Jung emphasized that his was only an "introduction" to an under-standing of archetypes and that others would take this work forward. Indeed, many authors, psychologists, and philosophers have written insightful, valuable, in-depth descriptions of various archetypes. Until now, however, there has not been a cohesive overview and in-depth

1. Carl Gustav Jung, *The Structure and Dynamics of the Psyche (Collected Works of C. G. Jung, Volume 8)*, edited and translated by G. Adler and R. F. C. Hull, (Princeton, N.J.: Princeton University Press, 1970).

use of archetypal psychology. The work of Caroline Myss in *Sacred Contracts* brings our understanding and use of archetypes to a remarkable new level. She truly moves the entire field of psychology and archetypes into the twenty-first century.

Some eight years ago, I had the unique privilege of working with Caroline for three days in developing my own archetypal charts, a process that you will learn in this book. We spent three full days analyzing not only my basic twelve archetypes but also their movement and interaction in three different phases of my life. Those three days were totally transformational. At the end of them, I felt as if I had been taken apart, gently and lovingly, cell by cell, and put back together. My psychological and physiological state has never been the same. For over six months after that three-day experience, I went through what is often called a Kundalini experience, with the most vivid and powerful archetypal dreams I have ever had. Periodically, further integration continues to take place.

Shortly thereafter, when we introduced this system to our first class, I stated that I believed that Sacred Contracts would become a powerful diagnostic and therapeutic tool. My faith and belief in this system has grown consistently as we have worked with hundreds of students. In *Sacred Contracts*, you will explore your archetypal relationships with your career; finances; use of power in general; human versus divine justice; abandonment; sickness; family; sexuality; creativity; relationships; death; and victimization; and you'll reflect upon the meaning of archetypal energies as they influence the twelve categories that contain every aspect of human life. Archetypal insights will also direct your spiritual development as you learn to fulfill your divine potential. Ultimately every archetype is merely an individual expression of one Universal energy pattern, which is our connection to the Divine. The power of Caroline's Sacred Contracts system is now being made available to you. I trust that your exploration of your real Self with this unique spiritual tool will be as fun and enduring as mine. Thank you, Caroline!

—C. NORMAN SHEALY, M.D., PH.D., *Professor of Energy Medicine, Holos University Graduate Seminary; Founding President, Americana Holistic Medical Association; President, Holod Institutes of Health, Inc.*

from "The Trial by Existence"
by Robert Frost

And from a cliff-top is proclaimed
The gathering of the souls for birth,
The trial by existence named,
The obscuration upon earth. . . .

And the more loitering are turned
To view once more the sacrifice
Of those who for some good discerned
Will gladly give up paradise. . . .

And none are taken but who will,
Having first heard the life read out
That opens earthward, good and ill,
Beyond the shadow of a doubt. . . .

Nor is there wanting in the press
Some spirit to stand simply forth,
Heroic in its nakedness,
Against the uttermost of earth. . . .

But always God speaks at the end:
"One thought in agony of strife
The bravest would have by for friend,
The memory that he chose the life;
But the pure fate to which you go
Admits no memory of choice,
Or the woe were not earthly woe
To which you gave the assenting voice."

And so the choice must be again,
But the last choice is still the same;
And the awe passes wonder then,
And a hush falls for all acclaim.

And God has taken a flower of gold
And broken it, and used therefrom
The mystic link to find and hold
Spirit to matter till death come.

'Tis of the essence of life here,
Though we choose greatly, still to lack
The lasting memory at all clear,
That life has for us on the wrack
Nothing but what we somehow chose;
Thus are we wholly stripped of pride
In the pain that has but one close,
Bearing it crushed and mystified.

INTRODUCTION

The oldest wisdom in the world tells us we can consciously unite with the divine while in this body; for this man is really born. If he misses his destiny, Nature is not in a hurry; she will catch him up someday, and compel him to fulfill her secret purpose.

SARVEPALLI RADHAKRISHNAN
(president of India, 1962–67)

We all want to know why we are here. What is our mission in life? Those people who know it are easy to spot: their lives shine with meaning. Their perception of their life's purpose gives them the strength to live through the rough times as well as to enjoy the good. Many people, however, are confused—or completely in the dark—about their reason for living.

Through my years as a medical intuitive—someone who can "read" a person's internal physiological condition intuitively, rather than by physical examination and diagnosis—I have frequently been asked, "Why am I sick, and how can I heal?" Even more often and more insistently, I'm asked, "Why am I here? What is my real purpose? What should I be doing with my life?" This lack of self-understanding and direction is a health problem itself, in a sense, for it can lead to all sorts of emotional stress, including depression, anxiety, and fatigue. And when these stresses or negative emotions become entrenched, they can contribute to the development of an illness. It's not only your mind that wants to know your mission—this knowledge is vitally important to your body and spirit as well.

A confused or directionless life has other consequences. Lack of knowledge of your mission can become a destructive force in your relationships. As the late theologian, mystic, and Harvard professor Howard Thurman often said, there are two questions that we have to ask ourselves. "The first is 'Where am I going?' and the second is

'Who will go with me?' If you ever get these questions in the wrong order, you are in trouble."[1]

Without self-understanding, without aim, we can hurt others around us as well as ourselves. If we don't have a clear sense of how to see the "bigger picture" when things go wrong, we are not able to respond appropriately to events or people. A man named Philip once told me that he would probably still be happily married, if he had only had a better sense of what he should be doing and where he belonged. He had been frustrated for years and his chronic discontent took such a toll on his wife that she finally left him. Even after his divorce, however, Philip was unable to make the kinds of changes in his life and career that he needed to make. "The problem with change," Philip told me, "is that one change is never enough. Once the process starts, you can't stop it."

He is right, of course, and yet as the renowned Jungian psychologist James Hillman once said, "You have to give up the life you have to get to the life that's waiting for you." If Philip could have seen where he was going, he would have been able to act more appropriately. He would not have been so self-involved, and he and his wife would both have been better off. But he could not find a way to get himself on track.

After helping people find and use their inner compass for more than seventeen years, I have come to believe that this absence of spiritual and emotional orientation has become epidemic. Besides being a personal problem for many people, it is also a global concern: from a cosmically practical point of view, what good is it to the universe to have a planet filled with souls who have no idea whatsoever why they are here or what they are supposed to be doing?

When people asked me how they could "fix" or heal their lives, how they could find the right direction in which to head, I often would direct them to pray for guidance. But as valuable as prayer is, I wondered if there was not some other definite way or process by which they could bring clarity to their lives and find their purpose. No one can see everything in advance, of course, but if we had a way of looking at the symbolic meaning of our experiences, we would be more prepared to face and accommodate the inevitable changes. Rather than fight change—and build up emotional scar tissue—we would be able to choose to see events in a different light, accept the changes, and get on with our lives.

Given the personal and global significance of knowing our mission, why has it been so difficult to find out what it is? How can we best search and inquire? Why do some people find their mission easily while others struggle for a clue? How can we get better at figuring it out?

For our own good, each of us needs to learn what our mission is, because the details of how we live our lives accumulate to create health or illness. As I discovered after conducting more than eight thousand medical intuitive readings in those seventeen years, "our biography becomes our biology"—which I wrote about in *Anatomy of the Spirit*. In other words, the little troubles and major traumas that we go through take up residence and live in our bodies and affect or block our energy. So it stands to reason that the further we stray from our true mission in life, the more frustrated we will become, and the more out of sync our energy will be.

By coming to know your mission, you can live your life in a way that makes best use of your energy. When you are working well with your energy, you are also making the best expression of your personal power. I call this living in accord with your Sacred Contract.

In my intuitive readings I have been able to help people work more consciously with their energy by spotting the traumas or other life events that have lingered in their energy fields. When I bring these memories back up into their awareness, they can often see how they have lost their energy or power through their overidentification with these wounds or experiences. Once they see these "energy leaks," they can proceed to call back their spirit. While this remembering can be helpful, most people can already recall such major experiences without my help. But where I believe that I have genuinely assisted people is by helping them identify and interpret the underlying patterns of thoughts and beliefs that color their memories. In these sub-patterns lie the interpretations and meanings that you assign to your experiences. These interpretations become cellular memories and carry the emotional energy charge that affects your biography and consequently your biology.

When you remember, for example, that you excelled in math at school, that memory of success might have a positive, inspiring effect on your body and mind. But if your success in math caused resentment or alienated you from jealous friends or siblings, it will also carry a negative emotional charge. Perhaps this negative charge attaches itself to every subsequent success, and you begin to associate guilt with achievement. Say, however, that your experience of these emotional complications actually prepared you to face later challenges. Rather than being angry at those jealous friends or siblings, you could become grateful for their contribution to your life training. By reading your own energy, by becoming aware of the lens through which you see your world, you can change your mind and change your life.

In detecting the emotional charge in your biography, you can begin to see how the fragments of your history have worked together in ways that have affected your past, your present, and the state of your health. This perspective is what I call *symbolic sight*. Seeing your life in broad strokes and bright pieces allows you to redraw your conception of your future and fill in the fine, interpretive lines more consciously. Symbolic sight enables you to get back your energy or spirit and heal emotionally, spiritually, and sometimes even physically. Symbolic sight will be an important method of working with your energy to bring your Sacred Contract into focus.

When I read someone symbolically, I see his energy—in all his individual roles—streaming out and around him. Yet I simultaneously see him as a unified sum of all his parts. And I also see him as a single cell connected to a greater matrix of energy. In my readings my subjects become human holographs. Their overall energy pattern is reflected in their individual cells, just as our individual souls hum actively within a kind of global soul comprising all life on the planet. Our words, thoughts, deeds, and visions influence our individual health just as they affect the health of everyone around us. As vital parts of a larger, universal Spirit, we each have been put here on earth to fulfill a Sacred Contract that enhances our personal spiritual growth while contributing to the evolution of the entire global soul.

Our life's mission, or Contract, cannot be defined or measured simply by our external life, however. Your purpose is not only your career or hobby or romantic relationship. A Contract is your overall relationship to your personal power and your spiritual power. It is how you work with your energy and whom you give it to. It is also how much you are willing to surrender to divine guidance. Although a Contract is not the physical details of your life, you can use those details to figure out what your Contract is. Your life is composed of many facets that shimmer and reflect both your physical and your internal energy. In attempting to grasp the whole of this reflection, you can discern and define your mission. Just as each fragment of a hologram contains the entire image, your mission is reflected, although maybe from a slightly different angle, within each of these many individual energy rays.

Still, it takes practice to learn to see the larger picture in these fragments, to learn to add them together to get the sum of your mission. Discovering your Contract is bound to give you surprises. You're going to have rugs pulled out from under you and realizations that rock you. But in the process you will learn how to see symbolically, how to manage your personal power, and how to fulfill your Sacred Contract.

In my previous books *Anatomy of the Spirit* and *Why People Don't Heal and How They Can*, I explained some of the ways that energy works, how it organizes itself around our seven emotional centers, or chakras, and how you can learn to read your energy and hone your intuition to see where your spiritual and physical disruptions or diseases originate. I taught how and why energy could become blocked or distorted and how this blockage—which is often connected to unfinished business in the past—could be cleared so that you could heal. Usually the emotional or spiritual healing was tied into learning the lesson of the emotional center or centers involved in the illness. Sometimes the lesson was the illness itself, and learning to work with that form of energy brought insight into the mental and emotional changes that needed to be made.

After many thousands of readings, I came to the conclusion that an organizing principle even greater than the interplay of the chakras is shaping the energy within each of us—and shaping our lives as it does so. I began to identify universal forms of cosmic intelligence that are directly involved in the day-to-day organizing of our lives. In fact, with every reading that I did after 1989, what I could only call an archetypal pattern stepped forward out of the details and fragments of each life and assumed a definite shape, offering clear insight into that person's psyche and why her life was as it was. These patterns, often ancient in origin, populate our minds and lives in ways that affect us deeply. Yet we are generally unaware of them. These patterns of intelligence are archetypes, dynamic living forms of energy that are shared in many people's thoughts and emotions, across cultures and countries.

During one reading about ten years ago, for instance, while I was looking for emotional data in a woman named Laura, I almost dismissed an energy "hit." While it didn't seem significant to me at the time, I saw a pair of eyes flashing an imperious, hypercritical "look." I mentioned this image to Laura, who said that her husband always looked at her that way—judgmentally, as if he were the Master and she the Servant. Indeed, Laura herself always had a "look" too—one that silently begged for approval from her husband. Yet to Laura her husband's condescending glances were the energy symbol of their painful marriage.

After we spoke, Laura went to several women's support groups, and eventually she understood that she could not wait for her husband's permission to be who she was or who she wanted to become. She realized that she was allowing her husband to make her feel inadequate and powerless, and that his condescending glances symbolized his attitude that she was not his equal. She also sensed that he was so afraid she would leave him that he had to keep her disempowered— or metaphorically "barefoot and pregnant." In time they went into counseling together and were able to make changes that kept their marriage alive while allowing each of them to grow together.

Seeing herself enmeshed in the energy pattern of Servant and Master allowed Laura to break that pattern and become her own master. In working with this archetype, she was also able to perform a greater service. Laura came to embody what is positive in the Servant, by serving a greater good, helping her husband see beyond his fears, and changing her marriage for the better.

Learning to read the archetypal patterns that influence your energy is the natural complement to working with the energy of the chakras. Just as the energies of your chakras work together to provide a map of physical and energy information, the collective body of your archetypes produces a view of the governing forces of your psyche and soul. This interrelationship of forces explains why I was able to move so naturally from reading the energy of chakras to reading the energy of archetypes. The energy body that surrounds you, which is created by the chakras, contains all the data of your biology and your biography, so it makes sense that this energy would manifest in patterns of archetypes that affect your life.

So to work with these big energies, these archetypal patterns, you have to step away from your life, step up and back from the detailed brush-strokes that make up your energy self-portrait, to see the whole picture. Working with your archetypes involves seeing your life in symbols at the center of a panoramic vista. From this vantage point you are able to take into account all parts of your life. You don't just focus on the major events or significant wounds.

In the 1990s I began teaching seminars on these archetypal energies. As my students learned to identify their archetypal patterns, then link the characteristics of each archetype to crucial behaviors and relationships, they often got instant clues to their life's mission. The energy of the archetype and its manifestation in our psyches and lives is so pervasive and intimate that no part of our lives exists separately from at least one archetypal pattern. Usually no fewer than twelve are our constant companions. Each has a story to tell you; each brings with it the power of the world myths and legends in which it has figured over time, and the energy of the patterns of belief and behavior out of which it was created.

Archetypes are the architects of our lives. They are the energy companions through whom we can learn to understand ourselves, as Laura did. These psychological, emotional patterns—how we live and whom we love—can lead us to a profound understanding of our purpose. Their energy can connect us to our higher Sacred Contract—to our greater mission on the planet. As I saw in my reading of Laura, there are no insignificant relationships. Every experience that we have contains purpose and meaning. Each event, each person in our lives embodies an energetic fragment of our own psyche and soul. Our individual spiritual task is to recognize and integrate all of them into our awareness so that the greater pattern of our mission can shine forth in its full dimensions.

This realization eventually became the genesis of this book. In *Sacred Contracts* lies a process that helps you to discover and integrate the fragments of your psyche. It is a guide to intense self-examination for the purpose of finding your individual archetypal companions, and working with them to realize your life's mission and Sacred Contract.

Moreover, this book is an introduction to a mystery school. It's the study of a different sense of time and space that we inhabit through our relationships, which are really our Contracts with other people. The language of this mystery school is one of spiritual alchemy. With it we'll learn to transform heavy physical relationships and emotions into spiritual gold. This process involves prayer and contemplation, and it also requires examining all the fragments of your life experiences and relationships. You'll be researching your archetypes' energy chemistry—how they express and assert themselves in and through your life. By discovering and working with your individual archetypal companions, your connections to the cosmic forces directing your life, you will consciously affect the course of your life.

You are about to embark on a journey into the archetypal dimension of life, a dimension of consciousness that contains all of us collectively and yet somehow also individually. For although the way you express your archetypes is unique to you, these energies correspond to the archetypes of other people in your life. They interact. Everyone has a Child archetype, for example, and so the inner Child in you connects you to the inner Child within everyone else. Learning to read your own archetypes allows you to read other people's archetypes as well. And it provides you with a better capacity for understanding and connecting with your loved ones, family, friends, colleagues—even strangers.

Carl Jung believed that archetypes live in a collective unconscious through which all souls are connected. The collective unconscious holds the energy of all who have participated in an archetype through the ages—the stories, myths, legends, and prototypes. Their stories and histories, briefly offered in the Appendix at the end of this book, can help you identify which archetypal energies most influence you. Knowledge of archetypes in turn helps you to understand why certain relationships have been necessary in your life and why you have had to take on specific duties that either surprised and delighted you or seemed burdensome and destructive. You learn again and again in working with archetypes that everything has its role, regardless of how painful or joyful it may be.

After you have determined your archetypes and worked with them for a while, the accumulation of insights they give you will tip you into a greater revelation: your mission emerges in its purest form. "I was born to serve God's poor," declared Mother Teresa. Before she could state that, however, she faced enormous difficulties and endured harsh criticisms that were necessary so that she could intensify her resolve, her social skills and contacts, and her spiritual growth. Even though the antagonists in her youth tried her courage and seemed to impede her progress, in truth they served her most by refining her purpose. For instance, the first two religious orders that Mother Teresa entered made her discontented, because neither was founded to do the charitable work she was being guided to do. She eventually founded a new community of her own to serve the needs of the poor—as well as her Sacred Contract.

This book, then, is a product of my wanting to share with people my insights about our individual and collective life purpose over nearly two decades of working with the energies of the human spirit. It presents a new language of spiritual interpretation to help you become fluent in understanding yourself and your life's mission. You'll first learn about the "nouns" of your psyche—your archetypal spiritual companions. You'll also see how their energy works in your life—the "verbs" of archetypal energy and manifestation—and how their actions express your mission in small and big phrases. You'll eventually learn to build bigger and bigger verbal pictures of your own life until out of it all emerges a whole, profound new view of your full potential, your purpose in life, and your higher Sacred Contract.

Sacred Contracts is an interactive book. You are meant to respond to the stories and teachings in a way that will help you understand the nature and purpose of your Contracts and the role played by your personal archetypes. So please get yourself a journal or notebook in which to write observations and associations that come to you as you read these chapters. I'll be asking you to remember intuitions and other glimmerings you've had of people you were meant to meet and things you were meant to do. And beginning with Chapter 5, you will need to keep a record of your answers to a series of questions, as well as insights and impressions that will arise when you begin exploring your archetypal patterns. If possible, dedicate one notebook just to the information and insights you develop in working with this book, and use it as you continue to work with your archetypes and Sacred Contract.

By developing symbolic sight and archetypal language, you will grasp the whole of your life with a level of spiritual clarity that can heal the emotional and spiritual wounds you have accumulated and fill you with awe that your life is also of great importance to everyone you encounter. It becomes possible for you to trust that everything that is meant to come your way will arrive in due time, that you will be with the right people at the right moment, and that divine guidance endlessly flows into your soul. It can't be otherwise: we manage our Contracts, but the Divine takes care of the Sacred.

CHAPTER I

What Is a Sacred Contract?

A contract isn't about saying what you meant. It is about meaning what you say.

OLIVER WENDELL HOLMES
(1809–94, physician, poet, and humorist)

When I was a young girl, my father always told me, "I don't care what you do when you grow up, so long as you're a nurse or a teacher." I can still remember my fury when he would say that, because I was interested only in writing. The very idea of teaching school was out of the question. Yet today, in spite of all my efforts to avoid life in the classroom, I am a teacher—of workshops, of theology, of motivation—and what's more, I love it. I feel distantly connected to the nursing part of my dad's directive too, through the healing effects my work has had on many people.

My father passed away in 1989, and in the early 1990s, as my mom and I were discussing my work, I said to her, "Well, he won after all." Then I realized that Dad hadn't "won" some sort of game or struggle to control what I did with my life. My Contract had won. My father had been able to glimpse aspects of it, as many parents can, although their vision is often clouded by their own expectations and wishes for their children. Even without knowing about archetypes, Dad had seen something in me that evoked his understanding of the greater function and meaning of a nurse and teacher, and he related it to the career choices that were common for young women at the time.

Still, my Contract does contain the archetypes of the Teacher and Healer, which have manifested through the events of my life, even though I have never formally studied healing or teaching. My higher education has been in journalism and theology, but my work in medical intuition simply "happened." I did my first intuitive reading almost by accident, and then another, and another. Word spread through the neighborhood, and soon I was doing ten to fifteen a week. My growing reputation led to invitations to lecture on my work, which in turn led to invitations to teach workshops.

The most extraordinary feature about how I learned energy anatomy was the precision with which my education was organized. Again, it simply "happened." Within a period of seven to ten days, three people with the same illness would approach me for help. Each one would prove to be coping with similar but slightly different life problems that had contributed to the development of their illness. By the time I read all three individuals, I felt I had grasped the major energy stress factors behind their conditions. Shortly after I completed one trio, another three people in quick succession would contact me for help. Again, each would prove to have the same illness. Gradually my understanding of energy anatomy led me to realize that our biography becomes our biology.

Once I understood that principle, my education seemed to move in another direction. Whereas my previous readings had focused on assessing an individual's physical and emotional chronology, I suddenly began to perceive images that had no apparent connection to the person. In reading a woman who wanted to understand her neck pain, for instance, I got the image of a pirate in her energy field. She was a housewife from the Midwest, so this information meant absolutely nothing to her. Yet while subsequently undergoing relaxation and visualization exercises with a hypnotherapist, she also sensed the pirate energy in her field. She "saw" him slashing her throat with his sword. Curiously, she also felt more positive associations, including wild lawlessness and liberated sexuality. These conflicting impressions of the pirate energy indicated to her that she was being choked or controlled by her life circumstances while yearning for a freedom that she could not consciously voice.

Reading another woman a short time later, who complained of severe arthritis in her hands, I kept seeing the image of an artist. When I mentioned this, however, she was baffled, insisting that she had no artistic talent whatever. Nonetheless I suggested that she take up pottery as therapy for her arthritis. She began by making simple clay vases and in time flowered into a gifted potter who now produces artistically sophisticated pieces.

Finally, while reading an Australian salesman named Jimmy who had been seriously depressed for several years, I saw a strong actor in his energy field. But Jimmy had never done any acting even though he did want to, because, he said, he was still "in the closet" and was afraid that if he acted, it would "come out" that he was gay. He was, in fact, already acting—as if he were straight—but the blocking of his talent and identity had made him implode emotionally. A few years later I was thankful to hear from Jimmy that he had pulled out of his depression and now acts in summer stock. He takes his stage work seriously, and he is no longer hiding his sexuality.

When these odd images first began to emerge, they seemed so disassociated from the people I was reading, so off, that I felt that I had somehow lost my intuitive accuracy. Yet these readings ultimately proved helpful for every person. Then one day in 1991 everything fell into place for me. I was listening to a conversation between two women in one of my workshops. Within five minutes of meeting, they had exchanged the ordinary details of their lives, such as where they lived and what kind of work they did. After the basic physical details, they then spoke about what life experiences had brought them to a spiritual workshop. Suddenly they found a life pattern they shared, an energy link that was immediately noticeable in their heightened response to each other. Their children were grown, their marriages were happily established, and they had arrived at a natural transition point in their lives—they were tired of being everyone else's "servant." Now they wanted to serve themselves. Retired and liberated, they wanted to pursue their own interests and to develop their own spirits.

As I listened to these kind souls describe the pattern of their lives, I was seeing through their conversation to its symbolic level. As good mothers and marriage partners, they had acted in behalf of others for most of their lives, but having accomplished this early mission, they were now striking out on their own, as the Servant of myth and legend must. When the biblical Joseph was sold into slavery by his brothers, for instance, he bided his time and did the work requested of him through many years of service. But then he used his singular gifts as a dream interpreter to earn his freedom and become a great leader in the land—going from Servant to Master.

All of a sudden the vivid but mystifying images that I had been getting in my recent readings made sense. The Pirate, the Artist, the Actor, and the Servant were not part of the individual, physical chronology that I had been used to reading. Rather, these images were a part of each person's spiritual chronology, a personal mythology that had begun even before they entered their physical lives. These images were archetypes, energy guides that could direct people toward their spiritual purpose, their Contracts.

The mythic lightbulb that got turned on that afternoon has stayed on ever since. From that point on, every reading I did opened with an evaluation of a person's spiritual chronology, the archetypal patterns that express themselves through his personality and life experiences. And just as trios of people with the same physical illnesses had contacted me for intuitive readings, people with the same archetypal patterns began contacting me in a relatively short period of time, though spread over months rather than days. Some of my first readings, for example, were for several people who had the Wounded Child archetype, a pattern of emotional scars from childhood. Then I met a few who had in common a dominant Victim archetype. Just as before, each of these people reflected slightly different aspects of these archetypes as a result of their individual personalities and life experiences.

As I began to work purposefully with the archetypes in my readings and to teach them in my workshops, I gained further insights about how they function within our psyche. When Jung proposed his theory of the collective unconscious, he defined it as mainly populated with countless psychological patterns derived from historical roles in life, such as the Mother, the Trickster, the King, and the Servant. Along with our individual personal unconscious, which is unique to each of us, he said, "there exists a second psychic system of a collective, universal, and impersonal nature that is identical in all individuals." This collective unconscious, he believed, was inherited rather than developed. I have observed that some archetypes step out from the backdrop of this great collective to play a much more prominent role in people's lives, and that each of us has our own personal alignment of key archetypes.

Through a process of research, reflection, trial, and error, I ultimately concluded that a unique combination of twelve archetypal patterns, corresponding to the twelve houses of the zodiac, works within
each of us to support our personal development. These twelve patterns work together in all aspects of your life. They can be particularly
vivid and perceptible in your problems or challenges, or in the places
where you feel incomplete. And they can be particularly useful in
healing painful memories, or redirecting your life, or finding a way to
express your untapped creative potential.

In a sense each archetype represents a "face" and "function" of
the Divine that manifests within each of us individually. Humanity has
always given names to the many powers of Heaven and tried to identify
the qualities inherent within each. The multifaceted archetypal power
of the feminine, for example, expresses itself within forms as diverse
as the Virgin Mary and Mother Nature. The ancient Romans and
Greeks saw universal feminine powers in the characteristics of Athena
(the goddess of counsel), Venus (goddess of love), and Sophia (goddess
of wisdom). The Hindu culture of India gave the Goddess names
embodying different attributes of divine motherhood, such as Lakshmi (prosperity), Durga (fertility), Uma (unity), and Kali (destruction/
rebirth). It was as if God had to separate into many different aspects in
order for us to begin to approach that power. Yet once it was named,
we could invoke it and assimilate it and express it.

Archetypal patterns awaken in us our own divine potential. They
can liberate us from the limitations of our thoughts and feelings. They
can help us shed light on the dark or little-known corners of our souls
and amplify our own brilliance and strengths. Archetypes are a source of
emotional, physical, and spiritual power and can help us free ourselves
from fear, although sometimes, as we first get to know them, a few of
them may initially unleash fears within us. Our spiritual challenge with
any archetype—or fear—is to face it and recognize the opportunity it
presents to learn its inherent lesson and develop an aspect of personal
power. With an archetype that we perceive as difficult or even malevolent, our task is to acknowledge it, overcome whatever weakness it indicates, and work to make its divine potential our own.

The goddess Kali, for instance, is the energy of destruction. She
has the power of the Saboteur archetype, which is present in all of us.

But what is the other side of destruction if not rebuilding and rebirth? In symbolic or Contract language, the Saboteur archetype can trip you up if you do not face its considerable power, but you can also use its energy consciously to dismantle areas of your life that you need to face or fix or heal. There are always two sides to every archetype, and both can be made to work to your advantage.

We tend to perceive ourselves and our universe as either good or bad, internal or external, me or you, right or wrong, symbolic or literal, joyful or sad. Our strengths and fears divide our spirit into polarities—into a duality, in Eastern terms—which is why faith and doubt wage eternal battles in our psyches. By identifying and working with our archetypes, however, we can learn to consolidate the faces of our spirit and bring its power into our daily life to direct our thoughts and actions. These energy guides help us act mindfully and honorably; they help us manage our power and live up to our divine potential.

I myself have found that the archetypal work I have done with each reading has contributed to my own spiritual growth and development. The experiences and insights I've had together with people I've read have helped me refine my skill as a medical intuitive, furthered my awareness of my archetypes, and even helped me through my own difficult times. I have come to believe that my encounters with my students, my workshop attendees, my readers, and so many other people are anything but casual. Like the extraordinarily organized way in which I had learned energy anatomy and was later led to read archetypal patterns, divine order makes itself known in all areas of our lives.

Sacred Contracts and Your Divine Potential

On the day the mythic lightbulb went off in my head and I saw that archetypes are part of a person's spiritual chronology, I also realized that they are so ancient that they must predate our physical birth. Our archetypal inheritance is prehistoric, primal. It comes from our own energy origins in the Divine, which is also the source of our Sacred Contract—the guided plan for our life. We co-create our Contract with divine guidance, and it includes many individual agreements—or subcontracts—to meet and work with certain people, in certain places, at certain times. For that reason, I will be using the plural *Contracts* interchangeably with *agreements* throughout this book. Both terms represent the earthly commitments, the tasks you have been assigned, and the lessons you agreed to learn in this incarnation in order to fulfill your divine potential.

The experiences and relationships you are meant to have are with your parents, children, close friends, and any people with whom you share a passion for something. These people—as well as your adversaries—are in your life because you made an agreement with them prior to this lifetime to support each other's spiritual growth. Indeed, every relationship and experience is an opportunity for you to grow and transform your life. Some relationships may even offer multiple opportunities. In every one you will have to choose how to exercise your own power.

As I stress in all my work, choice *is* your greatest power. It is an even greater power than love, because you must first choose to be a loving person. For example, take the simple matter of someone apologizing to you for having spoken thoughtlessly or hurtfully. In that one instant, the power of transformation rests entirely with you. You can transcend the density of your anger and choose to forgive, transmuting that instant into an exchange that restores energy to both of you. Or you can repress your divine nature and cause that potential opportunity for healing to become a contaminated energy transaction. Choosing to act in accordance with your divine potential consolidates the power of your many "faces," your inner and outer worlds.

Your divine potential can often be heard speaking to you through your conscience, which lets you know when you have acted inappropriately. We all have felt the heavy, gut-wrenching sensation of guilt when we have judged another, broken our word, or passed up an opportunity that came our way. If you look closely at this feeling, you can sense that it is the result of repressing or acting against your divine potential. Conversely, you can also recognize the feeling of cellular harmony and health that comes from acting with love, compassion, generosity, and friendship.

Acting through your intuition, your divine potential always alerts you to "look alive" when you are in the midst of a "choice point," a significant "Contract moment," or a recognition of someone with whom you have an agreement. Because each contractual relationship in your life is carrying a fragment of your spirit, just as you carry a fragment of others' spirits, when you feel strong energy responses to a person or place or in a situation, it is because you have come upon a part of your spirit that lives outside of your being. The atmosphere around you and within you becomes heightened. Your emotions and pulse race more rapidly, and your reasoning either becomes clearer or heads into a fog bank. Your body transmits noticeable physiological responses. As I tell the people in my workshops, if you were to stop in the midst of these types of responses and immediately read your surroundings symbolically, you would interpret the events or relationships occurring in that moment from an entirely different plane of reality. You would notice your inner Warrior emerging, for example, in the form of your temper. Or you would sense the Lover filling your senses as you merge with the seductive tranquillity of an evening sunset.

Your divine potential also speaks to you through your dreams. It is a desire to get more out of life, but not just accomplishments or material gain (although these things can sometimes manifest as part of fulfilling your potential). Your divine potential is the fullest expression of your spirit; it is discovering the depths of your capacity to create and to express love, compassion, forgiveness, generosity, and wisdom. Your divine potential becomes more audible as you release your need to know why things happen as they do. It becomes more perceptible as you decide to look beyond the physical plane of life, past what the Hindus and Buddhists call *maya*, or illusions. Never revealing its full measure at once, your potential motivates you to discover the greater purpose and meaning of your life. You are not born knowing how great an artist or how powerful a healer or how stalwart a friend you could be in this lifetime. You are not born knowing how deeply you can love and care for another. You have to learn to act with courage, self-confidence, and faith. These are potentials you need to discover within yourself. These are spiritual qualities that must be earned.

Like heroes in a mythic journey, we are meant to struggle to make the right choices. Our divine potential calls us to rise above the Self's basic needs for survival in the physical world. We're called to grow beyond our Self. But we can't grow spiritually only by using our intellect. Divine order and divine logic are different from earthly logic and reason and cannot always be perceived by our minds. Think of the many scriptural stories or myths in which the Divine revealed itself in full: When the Lord appeared on Mount Sinai, he told Moses to warn the people not to look on Him or they would perish. Saint Paul was thrown from his horse and temporarily struck blind by a vision of the risen Christ. The elephant-headed Hindu deity Ganesha's human head was burned to cinders when his mother, Parvati, invited the god Shani to look at him, forgetting in her pride the destructive power of Shani's gaze. These accounts indicate the deeper truth that divine consciousness is not easily apprehended by our human faculties.

This is where your archetypes can help you. To fulfill your divine potential and even to resolve the many issues of daily life—like power plays at the office or the healing of past injuries—you must enlist a higher plane of consciousness. You must get beyond reason to where you can "see" and "understand" the symbolic or greater meaning of the experiences. Your archetypes are your guides into this realm of symbolic perspective. Your quest for meaning is in itself a form of spiritual practice. Questions such as "Why have I been born?" and "How do I find the voice of God within me?" are in fact spiritual invocations, prayers that are answered not in words but through experience. These questions activate your divine potential, energize your archetypes, and compel you to complete your agreements, or Contracts, with other people.

To be able to see symbolically, to act appropriately on your intuitions, takes practice, and the purpose of this book is to help you develop these skills. I cannot think of a more valuable contribution that you can make to your spiritual health than learning to understand your Sacred Contract as it is written in your own archetypal language. By learning to identify your energy patterns, you will be able to gain a much greater vision of the meaning and purpose of your many experiences and relationships. When you can symbolically read the content of your life, you can make dramatically better choices. When your life plans are suddenly interrupted, you can choose to view that event as a "Contract intervention" rather than as a crisis. What symbolic vision gives you above all is choice—the choice to see events as arbitrary and antagonistic, or as blessings that are part of a plan in which you have some say. Symbolic vision helps you understand the daily questions that arise for you as well as the spiritual unfoldment of your life.

Balancing Fate and Free Choice in Your Sacred Contract

In other cultures and at other times, people have envisioned their Sacred Contract as the action of fate, the grace of God, or the accumulated karma of past deeds. Fatalism about life and love leads some to say, for example, "It was just his time," or "They were meant for each other," or "It was the work she was born to do." Modern scientific culture tries to attribute such events to genetic predisposition, to cause and effect, or to chance. Eastern cultures, which have studied the interior processes of the psyche and spirit longer and more intensively than the West, have evolved a belief in a continuum of lifetimes rather than a single life followed by eternal reward or punishment. According to the laws of karma, just as your actions in this life plant seeds that ripen and bear fruit in future lives, so your current lifetime reflects your past deeds. Although the Eastern system of karma (and reincarnation) is considered to be overseen by gods or a greater energy, our rewards and punishments and the rate at which we evolve spiritually are all based almost entirely on our own efforts.

The West has tended to favor a mixture of fatalism and divine order. Greek and Nordic mythology paid homage to the three fates who spin, weave, and cut the thread of life. Ancient Mediterranean and Middle Eastern societies relied on soothsayers, oracles, and astrologers to help them discern the course of their lives as already determined— or "written in the stars." The Western monotheistic traditions that arose in the Middle East assigned much power to the role of God in determining our destinies, while still placing a large burden on individuals to follow God's laws or reap the consequences. The Protestant doctrine of predestination preached by John Calvin and others in the sixteenth century, however, tipped the balance entirely in God's favor. According to their beliefs, our purpose in life is to fulfill the duties and responsibilities that God has assigned us, but because human nature is essentially corrupt, we cannot achieve salvation (the reward of Heaven)

except by the grace of God. Moreover, to the Calvinists, God has pre-
destined certain people to receive that grace and not others, leaving us
dependent on a kind of luck controlled by the Divine, which has
already decided our fate. Acting morally is all but reduced to a form of
hoping that one is already among the elect.

To help you share in my own vision of Sacred Contracts, I use
comparisons from both Eastern and Western beliefs about the relative
roles of fate, free will, and divine will. Yet I believe that we have a
deeply intimate relationship with the Divine and a very impersonal
relationship with cosmic order. The laws of the universe such as cause
and effect and magnetic attraction apply equally to all. The orbiting of
the planets and the timing of the tides take care of themselves, and I
do not have to think about them. We actually embody the laws of the
universe whenever we exercise our power of choice: I make a choice,
and it has a consequence, regardless of who I am. Yet I can influence
the quality of that consequence if I am mindful in my intention. This
fact that we can determine our own motivations reflects our intimate
connection with the Divine. My intentions do not change the laws,
because all my choices will still have consequences. But if my motivations are compassionate and sincere, the consequences are more likely
to be positive. And a single action can result in an inestimable cascade
of physical, emotional, and spiritual effects.

As part of our intimate relationship with the Divine, It prods us
to learn lessons and work on our spiritual growth in ways that we
may consciously resist at times. That may sound like a contradiction—
if we have co-created our Contract with the Divine, why would we
resist or ignore It? We do because, before we're born, we forget the
particulars of our agreements. We have to remember our purpose
by taking action and searching for it. This is not as difficult as it
may sound, because when you are living in accord with your Contract,
you usually know you're on the right path. We all slip off the right path
at one point or another, however—perhaps when we are trying to take
the path of least resistance, as the nuns who taught me used to say.
Ironically, what seems to be the path of least resistance can be the more
arduous in the long run if you are acting against your Contract.

Ultimately, we make choices every day—consciously and unconsciously—that implement the terms of our Contract, keeping us on the

path or getting us back on the path. We can also choose to enlist the aid of archetypes, spirit guides, and even the grace of God through prayer and meditation to attempt to fulfill our agreements more expeditiously. If you do not choose to believe in a literal prebirth contract, or in reincarnation, or even in the power of grace, you might want to view your life metaphorically, as a journey you have agreed to take. In past-life regression therapy, for instance, patients are invited under hypnosis to reenter the events of previous existences. Yet the leading proponents of this method have shown that the vivid stories people uncover about themselves during regression do not need to be viewed as literal events in order to be emotionally beneficial, but can be seen symbolically. People who "remember" past-life wounds, beliefs, revelations, and family histories invariably feel that they have gained from the insights these memories provide into their own unconscious and their life situation.[1]

You can also think of your Sacred Contract as your own unique contribution to life around you that arises from your particular set of circumstances, relationships, and family. Whatever interpretation you choose, the extent to which you can decode your Contract will depend on your willingness to accept that everything we do is for a purpose far greater than we will ever know, that every deed you do affects your life and others' for good or ill. As Thich Nhat Hanh teaches, we "inter-are." To believe in an invisible order, a divine or implicate order, as quantum physics calls it, or the order beneath the disorder that chaos theory describes, is a healthier, more interesting choice than seeing no meaning in life whatsoever.

Discovering and working with your archetypes and other elements of your Contract will change your view of your own destiny. You will bring new meaning to your life and move from seeing it as random and haphazard to accepting that it is carefully planned and directed, with you as an active participant.

Transformational Agreements

Liza, whom I met at a workshop in Seattle, went through a radical life change that her work with her Sacred Contract enabled her to envision in a transformative way. Every one of her life's plans was overturned by a serious accident, which many people would consider a tragedy, but Liza ultimately realized that the heavens were redirecting her for a reason. Although at first her rational mind refused to accept the changes in her life, Liza came to see everything as leading her to fulfill her divine potential.

At the time I met Liza, I had been researching the subject of Contracts for about seven years. The topic for the workshop was "Sacred Contracts and Archetypal Language," and during the break Liza asked if she could speak with me about her life. She had been in a car accident when she was twenty-six that had left her partially paralyzed on the right side of her body. At the time she had been working as a high school gymnastics teacher and soccer coach, so this injury obviously changed her life dramatically. As we talked, I did a reading on her, and among the numerous impressions that I received from her energy system was the persistent and prominent image of Humpty Dumpty falling off his wall.

I asked Liza, who was then thirty-one, if she related to the Humpty Dumpty children's rhyme, or if she had liked it as a child. "You know, when I was around eight years old," she said, "I had a dream in which I saw myself getting on a small boat on this big river. I wanted to get off that boat because I wanted to be on one of the huge ocean liners that were also on that river, but I was told that this was my boat and that I had to learn to travel in it. After the accident I commented to my mom that I had fallen off the wall like Humpty Dumpty, and she said that I had to work very hard at putting the pieces of my life back together again. I suspect now that the boat I didn't want to get on in that dream represented the physical challenge that I would have to work with in this lifetime."

Liza told me that after her injury, she had left the shattered pieces of herself, like Humpty Dumpty, lying on the floor for months. Then she had a dream about the same boat and river, only now the boat was moving in circles. She realized that this was because of her paralysis, which meant she could row with only one arm. "I recognized that I had to make a decision about whether I would learn to row that boat or drown in my despair," she said. "I also realized that I could never trade it in for another one, even though I longed to. I decided to do whatever it took to master that tiny vessel of mine."

Liza's physical limitations actually led her to do things that previously she would not have considered. "The first thing I had to do was to shift the image I held of myself. While my body could no longer move at the pace it could before the accident, I was still in charge of the speed at which my mind, heart, and spirit could travel. Accidents are no accident, I decided, and I ultimately came to believe that there must have been a reason why the heavens gave me this boat. And so I went into prayer one afternoon. I imagined myself in that boat, and I dropped the oars into the water while praying, 'Okay, you row.'"

Liza made a point of saying that this act of surrender was very difficult to maintain. She would awaken in the mornings drenched in sweat from the extreme anger that arose in her while she slept. She also endured numerous periods of depression. "People who have not experienced traumas or disabilities do not realize the full extent of what they mean," she said. "Your entire world changes, including your friendships, dreams, possibilities for marriage, and potential to have children. It's not just your body that has been reduced in what it can do—all the plans you had for your life are changed. And the fears you have to confront are phenomenal, beginning with, How will I survive now?" Yet Liza made the choice to respond positively to her crisis, because she wanted to assert more authority than the accident over the shaping of her future.

During her recovery Liza promised herself that she would be open to any new options that the universe brought into her life. Six months after the accident, she was back teaching again, but as she said, "My heart was no longer in it. I felt incredibly inadequate, and I also could not shake the feeling that the rest of the faculty felt that I no longer had the stuff of a great athletic coach. As a result, I knew I would have to find something else to do. But I didn't know where to begin to look."

Almost a year after returning to her job, Liza received an invitation to speak to an organization that helps physically disabled children and young adults in gymnastic programs. She immediately accepted and shortly afterward was helping these children develop gymnastic skills. She volunteered her services in the beginning, because she wasn't sure if she could really help any of the kids or if the organization would consider adding another person to its payroll. But by the end of the school year, she had become an employee. When she and I spoke, she was still working there.

"I don't consider what I do a job," she said. "Now I can see that all I do, and what I had to go through to get here, not to mention what may be waiting for me in the future, are aspects of my Contract. My accident, if you want to call it an accident, made me confront myself and my relationship to life. I had to rely on the strength of my faith to get through this, and my faith wasn't that strong when this happened. During my recovery, I felt dark emotions I didn't know I had in me, such as jealousy at other people's ability to walk. The hardest thing I ever had to do was to work my way through these feelings and to come out the other end a person who still saw potential in her life. Prior to my accident I used my will to make my life work, but now I had to rely on the strength of my spirit.

"Today I am able to give more of myself to these kids than I ever contributed as a high school teacher. They need all the inspiration, hope, and self-esteem I can offer them, as well as what I can teach them physically. They make me feel that everything I have been through and everything I do is of the greatest value. I understand their frustration, their fear of getting by in the world, their despair over the quality of life they might have. I know what they are living inside, and I can help them cope with that part of their lives because I've been there, and revisit there on occasion. But I am also proof that everyone's life is of the greatest value, regardless of the shape of one's body. The key is to learn to row the boat you've been given."

In her efforts to come to terms with the dramatic way in which her life path was changed, Liza completely redefined her understanding of her life's purpose. After the workshop she wrote to me, "Like most people, I used to think that the purpose of my life was to do something special, like be a good gym teacher. So when that 'something special' was taken from me, I also felt that my purpose in life was gone. But I learned that my concept of a life's purpose had been extremely limited. Had my accident not happened, I would never have been introduced to the option of thinking of my life as being guided by a Contract. I would never have seen my life's purpose as something I was supposed to be rather than do. Now I can co-script everything about who I am."

Grace and Charism

Liza's recovery was made possible by many things—her mother's encouragement, her willingness to listen closely to her dreams, and a few "breaks" that came her way. Her decision to turn over the job of rowing her boat to God might seem, to you, like a simple act of determination and will—or perhaps even one of frustration. But I attribute it to something entirely different: an infusion of grace from the Divine that allowed her to open herself to the healing forces of the universe and recognize her own great potential.

The nature of grace and how and why we receive it have long been questions for Western philosophers and theologians. I see grace as a form of vital energy that descends to us from the Divine, the Western equivalent of what the Indians call *prana* (literally "breath of life") and the Chinese, *ch'i. Ch'i* has several different meanings, including air, breath, temperament, and strength, but it generally refers both to the vital energy that is circulated through and stored within the body and the breath itself—two aspects of *ch'i* considered to be inseparable. This vital energy is often viewed as an impersonal force emanating from the magnetic energy source of the universe; according to Taoist belief, it flows directly from the North Star and the Big Dipper. The key difference between the Eastern and Western conceptions of this vital force is that Easterners believe they can facilitate the flow of *prana* and *ch'i* through meditation and physical exercises, including breath control, yoga, and qigong.

Although most Westerners believe that grace flows to us from the Divine, Western religion itself is divided about precisely what opens the tap. Some believe that we need grace for our spiritual health and ultimate salvation yet are completely dependent on God to bestow it on us—an outlook that would seem to diminish the role of free will. Others believe that we are entirely dependent on our own efforts to achieve salvation, but they find it difficult to explain those sudden, unexpected infusions of energy and insight that are capable of completely turning our lives around for the better. Some Christians believe that grace is a spiritual supplement that is given to us when we request it through prayer or earn it through the use of sacramental rituals. Others believe that grace flows from God to us without being requested, just as it flows into the heart of an infant who is baptized, or works as a kind of secret force in the heart of a sinner that leads him to repent.

However and whenever it comes to us, though, most people believe that grace enhances our life-force, providing us with strength, protection, and courage in times of need. It has the potential to heal illnesses and bestow blessings. I believe that we can earn grace through prayer, meditation, and other spiritual practices that increase its presence within us. But I also believe that there is a divine form of grace that provides us with spiritual stamina and direction and that flows into us in times of need whether we ask for it or not. This divine energy is your *charism*, a unique expression of grace that empowers you to fulfill your Sacred Contract. The word *charism* comes from a Greek root meaning "gift." It derives from ancient Christian theology, where it denotes a special divine endowment bestowed on believers as evidence of the power of God's presence in their lives. One's charism was thought to be a gift of proof that the Divine was intimately present in the work one was called to do in this lifetime. (This meaning survives in our use of the word *charisma*.)

Sometimes we are not immediately aware of having received a gift of grace until we see its effects in our lives, as Liza did. But at certain times we may experience an *epiphany* (from Greek roots meaning "to manifest"), a sudden illumination of our intimate union with the Divine. During an epiphany, your relationship to God is transformed from one of doubt or fear into one of deep trust. You suddenly understand that everything in your life has occurred by divine intention, by the grace of God. People have described their epiphany experiences to me as the sudden ending of the inner chaos and lack of direction or significance they felt. Through a sudden infusion of charism, your inability to make sense of life's challenges, coupled with the emotional weight of feeling as if you are living without purpose or direction, is transformed into the knowledge that each moment in your life is divinely ordered.

Charism can even make its way into our lives when we are not consciously asking for it. A woman named Cindy told me that she finally made contact with her charism while she was having coffee in a bookstore. "As ridiculous as this sounds," she said, "I was reading a story in a local paper about two people who were getting married that weekend and how they had met. It was very romantic, and it made me feel very lonely. I started to slip into that dark place of self-pity in which you tell yourself that none of that kind of magic ever happens to you. My thoughts drifted to my place in the divine scheme of life, and I decided that I was a fairly insignificant player in this world. Then suddenly I had an insight that penetrated my body, mind, and spirit simultaneously. It was as if a spotlight had been turned on, making everything and everyone in my life shine as brightly as my eyes could handle. Even people I wasn't fond of looked lovely to me.

"During that experience I was given a sort of life review in which I recalled every emotion I had ever had with each person in my life. At the end of that process, I knew that I would recognize that energy flowing in me for the rest of my life. When the whole experience was over, I was left with an indescribable sense of connection to God that made me feel that I had always been guided and that I was not alone."

The energy that Cindy felt surging through her during her epiphany in the bookstore is her charism, which she now recognizes "as God's voice within me." Mystics from Saint Teresa of Ávila and St. Ignatius Loyola to Sri Ramakrishna and Sathya Sai Baba have also felt this presence of the Divine at work in them. The Hindu temple priest and visionary Ramakrishna, for instance, had visions of Muhammad, Jesus, and the Buddha, after which he embraced Islam, Christianity, and Buddhism—an extraordinary practice in nineteenth-century India. As a young man in the early sixteenth century, Ignatius Loyola was more interested in courtly life and military exploits than in the clerical life that his father wanted for him. While recovering from a leg wound received in battle, Ignatius read the lives of Saint Francis and Saint Dominic, and suddenly he experienced an exhilaration and energy that led him into the spiritual life. His book of mystical practice, *The Spiritual Exercises*, is still used by laypeople seeking to enhance their own awareness of the Divine within.

With the decline of monastic life today, mystics are often a part of mainstream society. Your own search for your purpose in life makes you a similar seeker of God's presence—and a candidate for an infusion of grace. Even if your experience of charism is not as dramatic or immediate as Cindy's—or Ramakrishna's and Ignatius Loyola's—you should be alert for its workings within you. Your passion to know the individual nature of your spirit, for instance, is nurtured by your charism. Your charism is also the energy through which the uniqueness of your spiritual identity is revealed to others, the equivalent of your own spiritual trademark. As this grace helps you to know yourself, you then channel it to others. And the reverse is also true. The energy that you intuitively sense in the people around you is the essence of their charism.

Groups as well as individuals have their own charism. Tribes and other forms of community life have a collective grace by which they identify their unique spiritual purpose. Rituals and ceremonies that are derived from a group's particular focus draw on their charism for guidance; they are also a means through which the group can discern whether someone desiring to become a part of that group is appropriate. One Christian monk told me, "Our charism as a community is to serve God through dedicating our lives to prayer. In the cloister we see everything we do as part of a group devotion to bring the Spirit into the lives of those in need on this earth. If a person desires to join this community, his individual charism needs to be aligned to that of this group. Without that unity that person would not be able to survive the rigors of this life. He would not be fed by the special grace that comes to our group—not because it is denied him but because his spirit requires a form of sustenance that is simply not present in our community grace."

Some people do try to ignore this divine grace, even as it flows into them. When I was a young girl in parochial school, the nuns loved to talk to us about our "vocations." To them, of course, a vocation meant only one thing: a calling to the religious life. They made plain that we always had free will and could refuse the calling, but that we would never be as happy or fulfilled as we would if we had followed our vocation. Although I feel it was wrong for them to pressure us to join a religious order, I would agree that failing to acknowledge your charism, vocation, or Contract can make life more difficult and less fulfilling. As Gregg Levoy writes in his book *Callings*, vocations can be many things:

They may be calls to do something (become self-employed, go back to school, leave or start a relationship, move to the country, change careers, have a child) or calls to be something (more creative, less judgmental, more loving, less fearful). They may be calls toward or away from something; calls to change something, review our commitment to it, or come back to it in an entirely new way; calls toward whatever we've dared . . . ourselves to do for as long as we can remember. . . .

Unfortunately, we often simply tune out the longings we feel, rather than confront and act on them. Perhaps we do not really forget our calls but we fear what they might demand of us in pursuing them. Anticipating the conniptions of change blocks us from acknowledging that we do know, and always have known, what our calls are.[2]

In some ways, this book is itself an emanation of grace that came to me in a series of unexpected insights. As Joseph Campbell said to Bill Moyers in *The Power of Myth*, when you write a creative work, "you yield yourself, and the book talks to you and builds itself. To a certain extent, you become the carrier of something that is given to you from what have been called the Muses—or, in biblical language, 'God.' This is no fancy, it is a fact. Since the inspiration comes from the unconscious, and since the unconscious minds of the people of any single small society have much in common, what the shaman or seer brings forth is something that is waiting to be brought forth in everyone." In that sense I want you to view this book as an opportunity to evoke and recognize your own charism, muses, and insights—to get in touch with those longings and hidden vocations that will add so much more to your life once you learn to acknowledge them.

To the extent that you are able to acknowledge and accept the grace and guidance that come your way, your life will become more rewarding. Seeing life symbolically means always looking for the larger and deeper meaning in any event. That view transcends the physical plane and, especially at moments of stress or confrontation, allows you to rise above whatever is happening and see it in the context of your entire life—as your spirit guide, for instance, might see it.

Even if you have not felt the presence of a spirit guide or the suspicion that you are living an assignment that was given you before birth, you may have noticed certain recurrent patterns of problems or events in your life. Perhaps you have trouble with your parents, or troubled relationships with other men or women. Perhaps you have repeated illnesses or difficulties in your career. Or perhaps your life as a whole is fine, but you feel that you are missing something. You may need to try to see these things from a different perspective. To do this, you need to be sensitive not only to your physical environment but also to the planes of awareness where the landscape is more symbolic than literal. One such plane with which we are all familiar is the realm of dreams.

Flying Home

Since the earliest days of written history and probably long before, dreams have provided a symbolic pathway to our hidden fears and desires. By revealing to us the language in which our psyche speaks, dreams illuminate not only the dilemmas or opportunities that we may be facing right now but also the very way our soul visualizes those situations. Sigmund Freud, who called dreams "the royal road to the unconscious," Carl Jung, and many others since have all presented elaborate methods for interpreting dreams through their complex symbolic imagery. But the key to some dreams lies in a simple understanding of the meaning of a central image.

Over the past eighteen years, for instance, I have had a series of related dreams that all revolved around one consistent image: an airplane taking flight. The first dream featuring this airplane occurred in 1982, when I was at a tremendously low point in my life. Just a few years before, I had been getting increasingly disillusioned with my work as a journalist. Then one day I was given an assignment to cover a workshop on death and dying by Elisabeth Kübler-Ross. The level of suffering in that workshop, and the astonishing way in which Kübler-Ross was able to help people devastated by the death of a loved one, inspired me to return to school to study religion and mythology. But the postgraduate degree in theology that I earned didn't help me find my niche any more than my B.A. in journalism had. Two years after leaving graduate school, I was struggling to find a clear direction for my life. Working as a secretary in the department of pharmacology at Northwestern University, I could not figure out where I was going.

I felt as if I were living on a pendulum that was oscillating between worlds. My spiritual studies lifted me up, but then I was swung back to earth and the panics and fears of ordinary life. I became stuck in a deep depression that began to feel like a thick mental weight, kicking off what would become a decade of severe migraine headaches. After months of this dark time, I reached the point at which I said to a friend, "I've got to do something. A part of me is dying, and if I don't do something soon, I will die." I meant it. I felt that I had lost my trust in life itself, even though at the same time I still completely trusted that God would somehow lead me through it all. I was living in a psychologically and emotionally contradictory state, which made me even more desperate.

Then I had a very unusual dream. Jung might have called it a "big dream." I was the only passenger in a small but high-powered jet plane. My plane was still on the ground, idling in what looked like a stall in a barn that held a number of other planes in similar stalls. Each of the other planes took off in succession, as they were meant to, but my plane continued to wait for permission from the control tower, while I grew angrier by the minute. Finally I relayed a message to whomever was sitting in the control tower: "Hey! What about me?"

"Turn your motor off," came the reply. "We're holding you until the skies are safe for your journey."

My plane was in a "stall" just as I was stalled physically, emotionally, personally, professionally. Yet the control tower, which to me even in the dream represented God, sent the message that I was cared for and watched over. Still asleep, I became saturated in the feeling that God was in His Heaven and all was right with my world.

When I awoke from that dream, I was content to wait for my appropriate time of departure. I lost my desperation to find a concrete direction for myself. Every part of my life looked different from that moment onward. I was being watched over; there was a plan for me that was already in motion behind the stillness and frozenness of my external life.

Buoyed by the reassuring message in my dream, I decided to enjoy the emptiness of purpose in which I was floating. My job as a secretary provided everything I needed to survive in the physical world. I had a paycheck as well as the precious gift of time to do whatever I wanted after work. I had no heavy professional assignments hanging over my head, no deadlines, and no stress from not being able to do my job well. I had a liberated life. I was free to spend time with friends and family, and I enjoyed life in a carefree way that I have not been able to do since.

Because I had absolutely no private agenda or ambitions within the political and financial organization where I worked, I could not have cared less if I lost my job. I had no desire to achieve any rank or privilege among the group of professionals with whom I worked, and this made me feel happy. Although in the eyes of the scientists for whom I worked I had nothing, I actually had everything. These scientists gave me my first education in how awful human beings could become and act when motivated by insecurity and ambition. Competing for grant money, promotions, and power, the scientists were held captive by their fear of others' success. When I went home each evening, I left on my desk everything related to my work, but they went home with briefcases filled with the weight of work and fear.

In that occupation I learned one of the most spiritually productive truths that I now rely on each day of my life: when you do not seek or need external approval, you are at your most powerful. Nobody can disempower you emotionally or psychologically. This spiritual security gave me a liberated feeling that was practically euphoric. It made me appreciate why the famous line "to thine own self be true" in Shakespeare's *Hamlet* is considered a spiritual commandment. You cannot live for prolonged periods of time within the polarity of being true to yourself and needing the approval of others. At some point you will realize that you are doing harm to yourself by being what you think you should be so that someone approves of you. In the language of a Contract, compromising who you are to gain the approval of another is a very precise example of giving away a piece of your spirit. Eventually you give away more and more of yourself until you have no strength or sense of self left. I understood then that manipulation is the art of making another person's spirit dance for personal amusement, and only through honoring oneself do we become strong enough to refuse to dance. My airplane dream led me to a freedom from my own mental weight, depression, and anxiety about my future and purpose. Indeed, within a few years I met a couple who shared my growing interest in human consciousness, and they invited me to join them in starting a publishing company in New Hampshire.

Thirteen years later my life had changed dramatically. I had become a professional medical intuitive, teacher, and author. In 1995, when I started work on *Anatomy of the Spirit*, I had another airplane dream—the first since the initial one in 1982—and it proved to be the next in a series. The airplane became the specific symbol or archetype, not unlike a private phone number, that would be used in my dreams to get my attention. Each airplane dream was a direct communication from the Divine. The airplane signaled that I was following the right course, one that had been laid out for me and that I had somehow agreed to.

Each dream also measured the progress I was making toward completing my flight plan and getting a book off the ground. At the time of the dreams, I was feeling that I had not yet reached the depth of the message I wanted to communicate in *Anatomy of the Spirit*. I was walking around it, so to speak, but had not yet seen its full meaning. In the first dream of the "Anatomy" sequence, I was running through an airport to catch a flight, but the plane left without me. Sometime later I dreamed that I was about to board my flight when I was paged on the loudspeaker and a voice told me, "Please pick up the white phone." I knew that if I answered the page, the plane would leave without me. Nevertheless I decided to take the call. As I lifted the receiver of the white wall phone at the airport, I turned around to see my airplane take off, just as I knew it would. I expected to hear a voice when I put the phone to my ear, someone who would give me the direction I needed on my book. But there was no voice on the other end of that receiver. I hung up the phone, turned to face an empty airplane gate, and left the airport feeling that I had been abandoned.

In the next dream I made it onto the plane, only to be told that there was no seat for me and I would have to get off. The heat of humiliation flushed over me as I looked at the faces of hundreds of people staring at me as if I had invaded their "air space." Air, for me, represented the astrological element of the mind, and I took the dream to mean that I was traveling through conceptual territory where I did not yet belong. Shortly after that dream, I was still frustrated that I had not yet found the core message of *Anatomy*, but as I was lecturing to a group of twenty-eight students, I turned to write something on a white flip chart and instantly "downloaded" an image that merged three great mystical traditions and their biological implications: the seven chakras of the East, the seven Christian sacraments, and the ten sefirot of the Tree of Life from the Jewish Kabbalah. In less than a second, I received, I understood, I accepted, and I started the book over again.

During the next dream in this sequence, I finally was able to board my plane. I spotted an empty seat way back in coach, but as I was heading for it, I noticed the flight attendant looking for me. I tried to avoid her, and on reaching my seat I slid my body as low in the seat as possible and covered my face with a magazine. But it was too late. We had made eye contact, and it was evident that I would not be allowed to stay on board. Besides, even in the dream I had come to the realization that I simply could not hide from anyone. Had I been meant to be in the seat, I would have been allowed to stay. But it had someone else's name on it, and nothing I could do would change the fact that I was not scheduled to be in that seat. I was despondent. I thought that I was finally doing what I was supposed to be doing. And I was extremely eager for the manuscript to be finished.

That was the problem, I later figured out. I was too eager. The manuscript would be completed on time, but not in my time, and I still had a great deal of work to do on it before it would be accepted. Ideas and insights that had seemed to me self-evident needed fuller development to become airborne, and so I wasn't being given the green light just yet.

After many more months of refinements, the manuscript was finally accepted. As I was waiting for it to be published, I had the final airplane dream connected to that book. Once again I boarded the plane and spotted the same empty coach seat where I had sat on the previous flight. I quickly slipped into the seat, buckled up, and held my breath, waiting for takeoff. My heart was racing in the dream, and my body was shaking with anxiety. And then it happened again: the flight attendant spotted me. Just as I was preparing to grab my carry-on and climb out of my seat, she said, "Why don't you take your belongings and come with me, because there has been a mistake." I followed her down the aisle thinking, Whatever could the mistake be this time? But we passed the exit door of the plane, and she led me directly into first class. "Here you go," she said. "This is your seat. You've earned it." Following those words, I was given a bottle of champagne, and the plane took off.

I did not have another airplane dream until I started work on this book, *Sacred Contracts*. I hadn't been making much progress on the manuscript, and once again I was sinking in emotional quicksand. The dream began with me walking into an airline office in which I found myself applying for a job. For the first time, however, I was aware of the name of the airline: Aer Lingus, the Irish company. I was waiting in line at the ticket counter along with a truly oddball assortment of people. I wondered what I was doing there, and once I figured out that I was applying for something, I was convinced that I did not qualify. When it was my turn to hand in my application, the gruff woman behind the desk grabbed it out of my hand and walked into a back room. I stood there waiting for what felt like an eternity until she reemerged.

"All right, then, you've got the job," she announced. "Now get on that plane."

"But I don't have any clothes, or money, or even a passport," I said.

"That's too bad," the woman said sternly. "Either leave behind everything you have, or you can't get on the plane."

"But," I said, "some things are very precious to me."

She was unmoved. "Either you get on that plane with nothing, or you stay here."

I looked at all of the people boarding the plane, none of whom was carrying any luggage, not even a handbag, and I told her that I needed time to get my things together. How could they do this? I wondered. How could they get on that plane with no luggage? When I protested once again that I didn't have any clothes or money, the woman replied, "Everything you need will be provided. You'll be met when the plane lands."

All I can remember thinking then was, I hope the clothes they have for me are the right size—and I'd prefer designer clothes. At that moment I heard my name being paged, and I saw the white wall phone from my earlier dream. I knew from experience what would happen if I picked up that phone. The flight was almost fully boarded now, and the woman with the stern voice repeated her warning. "Either you leave everything behind and get on that plane now," she said, "or you stay here and move backward."

As I ran through the gate and onto the Aer Lingus jet, I thought, Why am I doing this? I don't live in Ireland. I don't know who these people are. I don't know where I'm going. I'm going to a foreign place. I somehow knew that the questions I had been asking were not mythical or hypothetical. They were profoundly spiritual questions: Do you really want to take flight in the second half of your life? Are you willing to let go of everything to do so?

After boarding that flight, I found that the seats in the first-class section, to which I was once again escorted, were arranged in rows like a movie theater, facing the cockpit, which had enormous glass windows like the ones in the film version of *20,000 Leagues Under the Sea*. Looking out, I had a panoramic view until we entered an enormous fog bank. Frustrated at the lack of a view, I started to get out of my seat, but the flight attendant told me to stay where I was. I insisted that I wanted to see the pilot, but she answered simply, "That isn't allowed." I knew I had to trust that I'd get out of the fog eventually, just as I knew that I must have answered yes to those earlier questions. But I still didn't know exactly what I had said yes to.

Even though it was a dream, the decision to get on that plane felt like the single most terrifying choice I'd ever made. And with good reason, as it turned out. That latest dream marked the beginning of a cycle of wrenching personal losses during which I was separated from close friends, family, and business associates, either through literal death or by a painful parting of the ways. I was at the grand turning point, the halfway mark in my life. I felt as though I were living in a field of death, having to let go of so much and so many that I loved so dearly, including an older brother, who passed away during this deep, excruciating period of spiritual excavation. Strangely too, I was scheduled to teach a ten-day workshop in Ireland the day that he died, and indeed after his memorial I flew to Shannon Airport—and the final leg of my journey was on Aer Lingus.

Yet even in the midst of my hell, this dream brought comfort to me, because it forecast that I was about to fly into a new, more rewarding place and experience. Despite what all these airplane dreams portended, they were ultimately reassuring to me. They told me again and again, in no uncertain terms, "You are flying the right path." They also said, "You still need direction; you still need to make choices; you still have to meet the unknown; and we're still checking your attitude." But they said it so lovingly that I never awoke in fear—despite the fact that within the dreams themselves I often felt anxious, abandoned, or confused.

As I labored on my new book, the significance of this dream and the ones preceding it became increasingly clear to me. I knew that I was being supported, that the universe would not let me get too far ahead of myself or fail to get where I was supposed to go. A big part of its meaning was that I knew that the dream was also about the book itself. Even the name Aer Lingus suggested that the vehicle I was traveling on had to do with language, with expressing the ideas in the book that I had been struggling to get airborne. It also assured me that the plane had a destination and that a greater force was at work, a force that had reserved a seat for me and expected me to be on board.

Although I had never given up hope of God's help, I hadn't expected it to come through the vehicle of my own dreams. I had never really paid much attention to my dreams or even read books about their interpretation. Yet they had provided me with the most extraordinary guidance through difficult times in my life. They had also helped me to let go of an old view of myself as undirected and unsure, and to begin to see a different shape to my life. Even if I hadn't believed in God, my dreams would have made me rethink that position.

The dreams reinforced my belief that events take place by design, that our life is laid out in steps and stages arranged in such a way that we always have the opportunity for spiritual transformation, which is the ultimate goal of working with your Contract. Spiritual transformation results when you move from seeing things strictly in physical, material terms to seeing that there are reasons why things happen as they do—that there is a greater plan behind them. Your Sacred Contract allows you countless chances to grow and change, dependent only on your willingness to pick up the subtle clues and cues that appear along the way. Dreams, intuitions, apparent coincidences, and "chance" encounters are just a few of the cues that will lead you on the path to genuine transformation.

The Goal of Spiritual Transformation

Most of us would probably admit that changing our lives for the better—as well as helping other people—is part of the reason we are all on earth in the first place. Without the potential to learn, to grow, or to be a force for good, life would be a pretty stagnant affair. Knowing your Sacred Contract allows you to see how apparently random events and encounters—whether positive or negative—are actually part of a life script that provides you with countless opportunities for spiritual transformation.

A common misconception about spiritual transformation is that it must be initiated by a trauma or tragedy of some kind—a serious illness, the loss of a loved one, a financial or personal catastrophe. Most of us find it difficult to believe that a major shift in perspective can be motivated merely by the contents of a book or subjects discussed over lunch with friends. But as I learned from speaking with Sharon, a reporter whose specialty was hard news, life changes can be catalyzed by the most apparently accidental encounters. "Reporters are cynics by nature," she told me. "You have to be somewhat cynical, or you'll be too easily seduced by the stories people tell you. When I started my career, my ambition was to write great human interest stories. But I especially liked the dramatic, political stuff. Well, one day I was sent out to cover a police officer who was volunteering his time to speak to kids in inner-city schools about the dangers of handguns and drugs. My first impression was that he was on a public relations mission sponsored by the local police department to get them some good press coverage. I met him in the morning, and we spent the day going to three schools. His sincerity and genuine interest in kids was making me nervous, because I realized that I was falling for this guy. By noon, I could not have cared less about this story. All l wanted to know was if he was married."

Somewhere in her interview with Bill, Sharon asked him how his wife felt about his volunteering efforts. "When he told me he wasn't married, I could barely hold my tape recorder without shaking," she said. "I was terrified that my emotions were beginning to show, so I kept asking him more about his motives. Then he told me that he just felt drawn to helping kids have a better chance at living a good and productive life."

When Sharon asked if Bill's motivations for doing this work were spiritual, he brushed off the question. "I guess you could think of it that way, but I don't see why you would find that necessary," he said. "I'm more interested in why one person who spends five hours a week volunteering his time is so 'unique' or 'amazing' that it even qualifies as a newspaper story. That suggests how rare we find the act of volunteering some part of ourselves to others."

Sharon decided to write her article from that point of view, investigating the question as Bill had posed it. Her story generated such an enthusiastic response that she and Bill were asked to come on a local talk show, then radio programs. "Pretty soon we were holding open forums discussing what motivates people to help others," she said. "This avalanche of response changed my attitude about what I wanted to do as a reporter. I decided that I wanted to specialize in doing stories about people I call the Sacred Minority. I interview people who give of their time and people who have reasons for believing that no amount of help or giving would make any difference in life. I would never admit to my co-workers that I consider what I do now a spiritual mission, but actually I do. I am reporting about how human beings relate to each other's spirit and their own power to create change."

Putting it into symbolic language, Sharon acknowledged that all of her work and all of the people she encountered represent the Contract she made in life. That extended to Bill too, since their "chance" meeting did lead to marriage and two kids.

Sacred Contracts and Human Relationships

Bill and Sharon clearly had a Contract with each other. The Turks might call it kismet—one's destiny or lot in life—and the Jews, be'shert—Yiddish for "destined to be your beloved." They were not meant to be together merely romantically, although that's certainly part of it. Above all they were meant to work together on issues and problems that went beyond their personal lives. In their development of transpersonal qualities, they would be led to achieve a kind of spiritual transformation. That kind of work can be intimate and loving, but at times it can also require blunt honesty. In his lovely book *Anam Cara* (a Gaelic phrase meaning "soul companion"), John O'Donohue talks about the Buddhist tradition of the *kalyana-mitra*, or "noble friend." Your noble friend, he says, "will not accept pretension but will gently and very firmly confront you with your own blindness. No one can see life totally. As there is a blind spot in the retina of the human eye, there is also in the soul a blind side where you are not able to see. Therefore you must depend on the one you love to see for you what you cannot see yourself."[3]

Because life is complex and there is so much to "see"—about ourselves, the world, and the Divine—we have Contracts with many people in our lives. Imagine that upon incarnation, each soul splits into countless fragments that move instantly into the exploration of the global soul. You know when you meet people who radiate something that is deeply attractive to you, and you may feel "empty" when they are gone. The popular term *soulmate*, applied to one's ideal romantic partner, doesn't begin to capture this truth; in fact, we all have many soulmates who play very different roles in our life. Perhaps *noble friend* is a better term. These are the people you are not simply destined but are *required* to meet. And no matter how many opportunities to meet with them escape you, if you have a Contract you *will* meet up eventually, perhaps many times, until you complete any unfinished business in the exchange of your souls.

A woman named Jill told me that she had dated a man in college with whom she was deeply in love, yet she turned down his marriage proposal because she felt that she had not yet explored life on her own as an adult. She realized that she was sitting, as she said, "dead center in the middle of my heart," loving her boyfriend but also madly in love with her desire to travel and to live her twenties as a free spirit. "Either way, I knew I was going to be hurt and filled with regret, so I chose the path that would empower me the most. I knew that, had I married then, I would have eventually felt as if I had shut down. The choice I made gave me the potential of opening up, so I truly ended up feeling that I had no choice but to say no to marriage."

Although Jill's former love was never far from her thoughts, her memories did not cause her the same degree of sadness she might have experienced had she suppressed her desire to travel. Fifteen years after they had parted, however, "destiny or fate or my Contract brought us back together," she recalled. "I was home, the phone rang, and it was Andy. He had run into old friends, asked about me, found out that I had never married, and bingo—we began to see each other again. We were obviously meant to be together. We just had to do a few things in between."

I cannot prove, in the scientific sense of that word, that even if you attempt to avoid a meeting that you are "contracted" to have with someone, it will eventually take place. But we seem to have an ingrained belief in destiny. There's an old story from the East, called "Appointment in Samarra" (on which John O'Hara based his famous novel), that tells of a master who sends his slave into the village on an errand. While in the village, the slave encounters the figure of Death and is so frightened by it that he runs to the next village, Samarra, to hide. On hearing that his slave has disappeared, the master goes to town and confronts Death. "Why did you scare my servant?" he demands.

"Actually," Death replies, "I was not trying to scare him. I was only surprised to see him here, because I'm scheduled to meet with him tonight in Samarra."

From a symbolic point of view, as well as from the traditional position of much of Eastern religious thought, no one is in your life by accident. Having said that, however, it is apparent that some people weigh in more dramatically than others. The intimate relationships of your life, such as your family, friends, mates, lovers, close working partners, and even your adversaries are all part of your agreements to learn certain lessons on earth. But because your Contract includes the whole of your life, some other relationships that appear to be either brief or casual cannot be written off as insignificant.

I can still recall a brief exchange with a high school English teacher who cornered me after class one day to offer me some advice on both my writing style and my attitude. At the time I was carrying on a love affair with the Theater of the Absurd—playwrights including Eugene Ionesco, Samuel Beckett, and Harold Pinter—and my literary contributions to this class reflected my infatuation. Because of my lack of training, as well as a few other missing links in my appreciation of classical English, my work was one step above disaster. My teacher kindly offered me a piece of advice—one sentence long—that reshaped my appreciation for education across the board for the rest of my life. "You know, Carol," she said, "in order to write anything well, even the presentation of absurdity, you have to learn the laws of English like a master, so that you can break them like an artist." As a teen, I had thought that being creative meant absolute freedom to do anything you want; but in that moment she taught me that real creativity is based on a solid foundation of knowledge and discipline. I must have agreed to meet this wise teacher, because she changed my whole understanding of artistic and literary creation.

Conversely, you've probably had the experience of trying to make a relationship "happen" with another person, but try as you might, the bond never does come to be. There are people you are meant to be with, and there are people who, no matter what you do, will not be a part of your life. Similarly, some people may be trying to bang down the door of *your* life, but regardless of what they do to please you or to get your attention, you are not open to embracing them. None of us belongs in everyone's life. One clue I can offer in helping you determine whether someone belongs in your life is to become sensitive to what I call the "animation" factor. By my definition, *animation* refers to a kind of electricity that occurs between two people when the energy of life kicks in, as it does for lovers who absolutely adore each other. (When I discuss the role of chakras in Chapter 6, you'll learn how to pick up other clues based on these subtle inner energy centers.)

The absence of electricity between people is as obvious as its presence. Without electricity nothing will bridge the gap between you and forge a connection. You may be able to establish a temporary bond, but unless that flow between you and another person is natural, the bond you are trying to establish will be unsteady and full of static.

Animating connections can also include relationships with people for whom you have an immediate dislike or with whom you fall into an instant pattern of power plays. In those cases, you can be sure that you also have something to learn from them, although it may be more challenging than mutual attraction. Carlos Castaneda said that the people from whom we often learn most in life are the "petty tyrants"— the ones who push our buttons and make us see in them the very qualities we most dislike about ourselves. Gurdjieff often played that role with his own disciples, having them spend the entire day digging an enormous hole in the ground, then telling them to fill it in.

In terms of your Contract, the petty tyrants in your life are as helpful and significant as your most beloved noble friends. You have agreements to work with both because they each have something to teach you about yourself that you cannot learn anywhere else.

CHAPTER 2

Contracts of Myths and Masters

Your Contract, along with all the subcontracts that constitute it, is not an end in itself. It is a means to an end, a plan to help you develop your divine potential. Think of your Sacred Contract as a life course in which you are meant to learn many lessons. When you start out exploring any course, it's best not to become overly concerned about defining it in a single sentence or narrowing its purpose to a single lesson. It will take you a while to be able to say that you were born for one specific purpose, as Mother Teresa did, since you will be trying to uncover many agreements and learn many lessons that your mission contains.

The idea that we have life lessons and "tasks" that we are assigned to complete is an ancient one. Dr. Clarissa Pinkola Estés, in *Women Who Run with the Wolves,* tells the story of Vasalisa and Baba Yaga, an archetypal tale that she dates back to the prehistoric horse-Goddess cults—even earlier than classical Greek mythology.[1] Vasalisa is a young girl whose mother is dying. Before she passes, however, the mother gives Vasalisa a tiny magical doll to guide her. "Should you lose your way or be in need of help," her mother says, "ask this doll what to do. You will be assisted."

After the mother's death, Vasalisa's father remarries a widow with two daughters who are, as in so many fables, cruel to Vasalisa because she is sweeter and more beautiful than they. Hoping to get rid of her, they deliberately extinguish the fire that warms their house and force her to go into the forest to get coals from the old witch Baba Yaga. To find her way through the dark, menacing woods, Vasalisa reaches into her pocket and consults the doll, who tells her the right way to go at every fork in the road.

When Vasalisa finally locates the old witch and asks for fire, Baba Yaga tells her that she can have it only after the girl performs several seemingly impossible tasks for her, including separating the mildewed corn from the good corn and retrieving millions of poppy seeds from a pile of dirt. While Vasalisa sleeps, her doll completes the tasks. The tiny doll hidden inside a pocket symbolizes every woman's need to use her intuition when making difficult, fine distinctions in judgment. Just as our dreams can help us solve our problems if we pay attention to them, so can our still small voice within. The fresh and mildewed corn, poppy seeds, and dirt represent what Estés calls "remnants of an ancient healing apothecary," which also symbolizes healing the mind and spirit with the help of intuition.

After Vasalisa completes the tasks, Baba Yaga gives her a skull with fiery eyes to take home and relight the hearth. Vasalisa returns triumphantly and with this "inner" fire restores the life-giving flames to the home. By morning, the fiery skull has burned the cruel step-family to cinders.

As Estés aptly points out, this is a story about the power of intuition, specifically about power handed from mother to child. "Over generations," she writes, "these intuitive powers became as buried as streams within women, buried by disuse and unfounded charges of disrepute. However, Jung once remarked that nothing was ever lost in the psyche." Women can rediscover and act on their inner powers. Men too grow detached from their natural intuitive powers and need to become reacquainted with them, as Vasalisa's father had to awaken to the evil he had unwittingly brought into his home. We all must be mindful of inner thoughts and our actions so that they do not lead us to hurt ourselves or our loved ones.

The frightening journey that Vasalisa agrees to go on and the tasks she undertakes are her path to power and self-realization—her Contract. She and all of us are meant to learn to rely on our little doll, our inner voice and self, the intuitive sense of where to go and how to proceed in life with all its dangers and demands. Ultimately, as in the classic Hero's Journey of mythology described by Joseph Campbell, Vasalisa returns home with something of great value to both herself and her tribe. Her willingness to accept her Contract and learn from it sets her up in a position of personal power and invulnerability from external influences.

Like Vasalisa, you too will have many tasks to fulfill in many aspects of your life. Your Sacred Contract, your mission in life, cannot be reduced to just one thing—one job, one relationship, one goal. To help you grasp the full extent of your Sacred Contract and its agreements, it might help to compare them to a simple business contract.

In short, a Sacred Contract is an agreement your soul makes before you are born. You promise to do certain things for yourself, for others, and for divine purposes. Part of the Contract requires that you discover what it is that you are meant to do. The Divine, in turn, promises to give you the guidance you need through your intuition, dreams, hunches, coincidences, and other indicators.

Legal contracts hold us accountable for the multiple terms and clauses that are part of the overall agreement. Even in taking out a mortgage to buy a house, for example, you are required to do more than simply make a monthly payment. You have to keep the house and property in good repair, pay taxes, insure it, and usually, in order to accomplish all this, deal with numerous other parties. You also agree to abide by the law of the country and state in which you sign the agreement or take out the mortgage.

Your Sacred Contract too subjects you to the laws and order of a greater state—that of the Divine. The whole of creation, in fact, follows rules that govern and maintain the flow of energy and life, from the law of gravity to those of thermodynamics. From the earliest days of civilization, humanity has been given rules to follow and has accepted the need to abide by them. Among the most widely accepted of these, which can be considered subclauses of your Sacred Contract, are the Ten Commandments.

Even before Yahweh handed those codified rules to Moses, however, He had made other covenants with Noah and Abraham, promising to protect their offspring and help them prosper if they met certain terms. For the first time the scriptures used the word *covenant*, a term that originally meant a legally binding agreement between two or more parties—in essence, a contract. As a visible symbol of His covenant, God put a rainbow in the sky to remind Himself to uphold His end of this agreement. In return, he required that Noah and his descendants "be fruitful and increase in number." More significantly, Yahweh commanded not only that they procreate but also that they respect the sanctity of life, saying that "from each man . . . I will demand an accounting for the life of his fellow man. Whoever sheds the blood of man, by man shall his blood be shed; for in the image of God has God made man." God established His covenant with Noah and his descendants "and with every living creature that was with you—the birds, the livestock and all the wild animals, all those that came out of the ark with you—every living creature on earth" (Gen. 7–9). In other words, we are to be stewards and caretakers of the planet.

God later established a similar covenant with Abraham, offering to preserve and multiply his offspring in exchange for Abraham's agreement to have all the male children of his people circumcised. Although both Abraham's and Noah's Contracts were established in what we might call the spiritual realm, they specified particular terms of action in the physical world, compliance with which would yield great benefits to all parties.

Here are some other comparisons between earthly and Sacred contracts:

- In a legal contract, two parties agree to participate in some task, or to hold themselves accountable to the same commitments, for a mutually beneficial reason.

    In a Sacred Contract, an individual and the Divine commit to a mission that promises to expand that individual's spiritual consciousness as well as further the expression of the Divine on earth.

- In a secular contract, you commit to doing what you must to fulfill the terms of the contract legally. You may also agree to work with subcontractors or obtain raw materials you need to complete the agreed-on tasks.

    In a Sacred Contract, the Divine guarantees that all materials or energy that are essential to the completion of your task will be provided. These provisions can include anything from receiving necessary earthly capital to being guided into certain relationships or developing an illness.

- A legal contract holds you responsible for the quality of the project or product. You warrant that you are qualified for the task.

  Although you have everything you need within you to fulfill your Sacred Contract, you will not be provided with everything you want. You will probably have to learn that you have the inner resources to do what you need to do. You will have to learn your strengths and capacity to push yourself beyond your apparent limitations.

- In a business contract, work is offered in exchange for some kind of support, usually financial, often in the form of an advance or binder. Some contracts provide regular payments throughout the term of the contract as certain subclauses are fulfilled. You may be promised certain future bonuses, such as royalties, residuals, or stock options, and you may receive certain secondary advantages, including on-the-job training, expenses, insurance, and other fringe benefits. In addition to financial remuneration, one party may offer to help in other ways. In a deal between a writer and a publisher, for example, the publisher may also agree to promote your book in a number of ways, with advertising and a publicity tour.

  In a Sacred Contract, your payment is in spiritual capital— in insight, purpose, self-understanding, and the attainment of spiritual attributes such as compassion, selflessness, and faith. Your Sacred Contract is supported by divine guidance, what we might call a "heavenly bank account" on which you can draw for inspiration and energy to complete your assigned tasks. In addition, you may receive unexpected infusions of grace from time to time to help you complete your tasks.

- Although a legal contract can be broken, there are often severe consequences, including legal and financial penalties, which can extend for years.

A Sacred Contract is a learning process and therefore cannot be broken. It commits you to developing your inner consciousness and your understanding of how to work with forces greater than your own personal will. Our personal and spiritual growth benefits others around us. We learn, among other things, that we are here to help each other. Because a Contract is an opportunity to empower your spirit, you are bound by higher laws to pursue that process. You are often given more than one opportunity to complete a learning process. Each time you try to avoid an opportunity or challenge, the consequences become more severe.

- If conditions change over the course of a business contract, you may be able to renegotiate its terms in good faith. If, for example, your expenses exceed expectations for reasons beyond your control and keep you from fulfilling your agreement, you may be able to request some form of financial relief. Professional athletes, among others, renegotiate long-term contracts if their market value is perceived to have increased significantly.

As you progress in understanding the terms of your Contract and what you have agreed to learn, you may discover that what you thought was a Contract to develop your personal potential— to become better at your work, say—is actually a Contract to expand your divine potential. Although your Contract hasn't changed, your understanding of it can, and it may feel to you like a renegotiation. The Spanish philosopher Miguel de Unamuno once wrote that as humanity suffers on earth, God suffers with us (which is, after all, the root meaning of compassion). Although we have agreed to certain terms, it may be that those terms evolve as we evolve, and that even the Divine doesn't know exactly how things will turn out.

- A legal contract includes elements of choice. You are free to decide how to follow through with the terms of a contract, as long as those terms are met by the agreed-on date. If I'm under contract to deliver a manuscript by January 1 of next year, it doesn't much matter whether I write one page a day in my spare time or take several months off to work intensively on the whole thing. I can write it by hand, type it, or work on the computer, as long as the final result is coherent and adheres to the subject matter that was promised.

A Sacred Contract also includes the element of choice. For all that the Divine provides, you have complete choice about whether to view the provisions as blessings or as burdens. You may choose to delay meeting the terms, but you can't avoid them altogether.

As a temporal example of how choice works, imagine that, before you were born, you agreed that in this life you needed to learn to master the use of a knife. Prior to your birth, your guide offered you a piece of wisdom: "If you grab the blade first, you will cut yourself, you will bleed, and it will take you a long time to heal. You will be angry with your knife, and thinking that it is a weapon, you will use it to harm others. If, however, you grab the handle first, you will think of this knife as a tool, and you will use it to make wonderful creations, as a cook, sculptor, designer, or surgeon. Either way, once you come back to the heavens, you will have mastered the use of this knife. But the choice of how you do it, and with how much suffering, is in your hands—literally and symbolically."

You can choose to learn by wisdom or by woe. Consider, for example, that learning the power of forgiveness is essential to your spiritual path. Learning forgiveness indicates that you have someone to forgive, so, say that you need to forgive your parents for pressure they put on you or demands they make of you. Or maybe you need to forgive a boss who fired you from a job in which you were financially secure but emotionally unfulfilled and unhappy. These people are playing a role in your life that is necessary for you to figure out. Through your interactions with them you will learn about your purpose. You have to make a conscious choice whether to forgive them. Without a doubt the choice to forgive is a greater challenge than remaining resentful, but this more difficult path will bring you peace and spiritual wisdom. Resentment, though appealing to our sense of righteous indignation, comes with a high price in the long run—it is harmful to your physical, mental, and emotional health. When you choose *not* to forgive your parents, employers, and other supposed adversaries, you isolate and alienate yourself from others and from the world. You trap yourself in an unhealthy energy pattern that can even lead, ironically, to making you eventually dependent on others through illness or other life circumstances. Refusing to accept a spiritual task such as forgiveness is a painful way to learn, but learn you will. And if you refuse the lesson, you will encounter it again and again—and next time.

Contracts in Myth

There are a number of historic precedents for the belief in Sacred Contracts. The world's scriptures recount God speaking directly to many people, from Adam, Noah, and Jesus in the West to a wide range of seers and mystics in the East. Yet the Divine also sends extraordinary spiritual messengers to get our attention and insure that we abide by His plan. Messengers who provide guidance and support from the heavens include figures such as the angel Gabriel, who plays a key role in both the Gospels and the Quran, as well as a wide range of anonymous guardian angels, spirits, sylphs, *jinn*, asuras, faeries, and "little people." Spiritual messengers form the basis of much of the world's religious literature, from the Angel of the Lord who spoke to Abraham, Jacob, and Muhammad to the angel Moroni of the Mormons. They relay blessings, warnings, wisdom, and requests to those on earth, either directly through voices and apparitions or indirectly through dreams or insights that flash through our consciousness "out of the blue."

Many people have shared stories with me about divine encounters with angels in which they received profound guidance, comfort, or instructions about how to proceed with their lives. And many people describe angelic interventions in which they are given a warning about something or someone in their lives. I had such an experience years ago while on my way home from work one evening. As I was driving down a main highway in Chicago, I heard a very clear voice tell me, "Slow down. A red truck is going to run the stop sign at the next street." I immediately stepped on the brake, and as I did, a red truck raced through a stop sign not ten feet in front of me. Only then did I realize that something beyond my own intuition had warned me.

Messengers also bring news that is less dramatic but no less life-altering. The 1991 movie *Grand Canyon* is a wonderfully rich depiction of everyday angels and life-altering interventions. Written and directed by Lawrence Kasdan, the film weaves together several plots in which apparently innocent synchronicities bring people together in ways that change their lives. One of the main characters, Claire, played by Mary McDonnell, finds an abandoned baby under a bush when she goes on her daily run and slightly alters her usual route. She is convinced that she was meant to find and care for this baby and says so to her skeptical husband, Mack, played by Kevin Kline. "Some kind of connection has been made," she says, "and it has to be played out." When Mack tries unsuccessfully to change her mind and then tries to end the discussion by saying that his head hurts, Claire refuses to allow it, saying memorably, "It's just an inappropriate response to get a headache in the presence of a miracle."

Mack later recalls a miracle of his own. One morning when he was about to cross a busy Los Angeles street, a hand reached out and suddenly pulled him back to the curb. Just then a bus rumbled by right in front of him, and he realized that his life had been spared, an event, he says, that "literally changed everything for me." Looking around, he sees that the woman who grabbed him back from the curb is smiling and wearing a Pittsburgh Pirates cap. The Pirates happen to be Mack's favorite team—he even named his son after Pirates great Roberto Clemente—and he realizes that this cannot be simple coincidence. "That's not your usual thing at nine A.M. on Wilshire Boulevard—a woman in a Pittsburgh Pirates baseball cap," he says. "It's a little suspicious."

The events in the film remind me of the true-life story of Maureen, a newly married woman in her early thirties who developed a tumor in her ovaries and had to have a hysterectomy. Realizing that she could never bear children plunged her into a depression so intense that both her parents and her husband feared that she might attempt suicide. Besides her own grief over the loss of her ability to conceive, Maureen feared that her marriage would eventually disintegrate, because she knew how much her husband wanted children.

"I had believed from the time I was a child that I was meant to be a mother," she told me when we met some years later. "I could not imagine a future other than as a wife and mother. After the operation it was as if my life had ended. In fact, a part of my life did end. I no longer felt the same about anything. I remember going out with my mom about three months after the surgery and spotting a woman with twin girls, two years old and absolutely darling. I had never felt such envy and rage. I wanted to run up to her and shake her and tell her she was living the life I was meant to have."

Then one night Maureen had a visitation from an angel. "Even though I was asleep," she said, "I was also awake. It's very difficult to describe my state of consciousness. I saw this beautiful angel sitting at the foot of my bed. She asked me, 'Why are you so sad?' I told her that I had made a mistake in taking on this lifetime. This was not what I wanted, and the pain was too great. She replied, 'There is no reason for you to feel such despair. I've come to tell you that tomorrow you will meet your son.' I looked at her and replied, 'That's impossible.' But she said, 'Oh, is that so? You have not made a mistake in accepting this life. And your passion to be a mother was not given to you to cause such pain. Your agreement is meant to be fulfilled differently than you expected, that's all.'" Then the angel told her to go back to sleep.

The next day felt like a "dream fog" to Maureen, who did not remember her dream when she first awoke. She wasn't sure what had happened, except that she sensed something was different. "The phone rang about ten in the morning," she said. "A friend of mine named Lynn, whom I hadn't spoken with in a long time, called to tell me that she was now running an adoption center. I couldn't bring myself to tell her what I had been through but just listened as she explained that she found her work both satisfying and heartbreaking. 'I mean,' she said, 'we are now looking for a home for this sweet little baby boy whose mother doesn't want anything to do with him.'"

Instantly Maureen replied, "I'll take him! He's supposed to be with me. He is my son."

Lynn paused and said, "Okay, let's start the paperwork. That must be the reason I thought about calling you."

"Then the dream exploded into my mind," Maureen told me. "It wasn't a dream. My angel had really come during the night to bring me the message that I was about to have a baby. I just had no idea I was pregnant."

Without a doubt we are surrounded by our angels, invisible beings of light who guide us through the mysteries of our lives. Maureen did have a Contract to be a mother, and when the time was right, the "delivery" took place.

Ancient cultures believed that angelic messages came from a higher source—God or gods, who have a history of communicating such warnings and requests. Several of these cultures were shaped in part by their belief in a system of cosmic order imposed by a deity. In their universe individuals were expected to serve the will of that god or at least to be under his supervision. The Aryans who invaded India and established the Vedic religion (the forerunner of Hinduism) in the Indus Valley around the second millennium B.C. called their god of order Mitra. In Persia, which had been invaded by other groups of Aryans, this same deity was called Mithra. Centuries later, the ancient Romans called him Mithras. Common to all three conceptions of this god-force was the belief that all humans had contracts with Heaven and were obligated to abide by these contracts. In his book *Mithras*, D. Jason Cooper writes that the contract offered by the Aryan Mitra was not between equals, but Mitra was a just lord. Both sides had certain obligations. "Mitra oversaw the affairs of his worshipers. He established justice for them. In return, his worshipers had to be upright in their dealings with others. Mitra was thus 'lord of the contract.'"[2]

According to the *Rig Veda*, the oldest sacred text of India, Mitra (whose name derives from an Indo-European root that translates as both "friend" and "contract") was a fair God who took care of his followers. As the Lord of Justice, however, Mitra determined punishment as well as reward, and so expected people to complete all of the tasks assigned to them in an honorable manner. Because Mitra oversaw the activities of all humanity, he was also called the god of ten thousand eyes, able to observe and hear from his place in the heavens every conceivable action, from conversations held in small corners to participation in mass social rituals. Mitra was everywhere, a constant reminder to his devotees of the need to be and do what the gods expected of them. For all that, Mitra was not a threatening god but

one whose power lay in creating order and balance. Although he punished wrongdoers, he also had the capacity to forgive repentant
humans, perhaps (along with Yahweh) the first god who rewarded
penitence.

Within the Persian culture, Mithra also oversaw the contracts of
humankind. In a *yasht*, or hymn, dedicated to Mithra in the Zoroas-
trian scripture known as the *Avesta*, he is frequently referred to as "the
one who calls people to account." Like Mitra, Mithra was considered
a moral god, judging contracts not only between individuals but
between nations as well. Mithra punished those who broke their
agreements, did not fulfill obligations, and lived immorally. His punishments could include anything from the curse of a disease to death
from a weapon. Mithra supported a well-organized, fair government
and acted destructively toward people in power who harmed their
own people. Mithra was also thought to be the judge of those whom
commoners could not judge—their kings and other lofty rulers. No
human being was above his wrath. It was Mithra who established truth
as supreme among his worshipers.

The ancient Indians, Persians, Greeks, and Romans were not the
only peoples who believed that the gods watched over humans, kept
accounts, and controlled human destiny. One of the principal deities
of Norse mythology, for instance, is Var, the goddess of contracts and
marriage agreements. Var is said to listen to marriage vows and com-
pacts made between men and women and to take revenge against any
who break their vows. In the Mesoamerican region around the turn of
the second millennium, the Toltecs and Aztecs worshiped a god
named Tezcatlipoca. Associated with destruction (like the highly regarded Indian deities Shiva and Kali), Tezcatlipoca ruled the night sky,
moon, and stars. He presided over the cosmic ball court, which the
Aztecs saw as the constellation of Gemini and where the gods played a
game to set the fate of humankind.[3] Tezcatlipoca was also the protector deity of slaves and punished anyone who harmed them. His name
means "Smoking Mirror," and as a master of black magic, he was often
depicted with a black stripe across his face or a black mirror made of
obsidian or hematite on his chest, in which were reflected all the
thoughts and actions of humanity.

From the historical records of Mitra/Mithra, we cannot tell how people were supposed to recognize their life contracts or how they might have been revealed to them. Perhaps those contracts obligated people to a certain class, or perhaps a contract was thought of as a way of participating in a lifelong mystery that unfolded one step at a time. Nor is there any clear indication that people believed that their contracts had been agreed to prior to birth, or that they had any role or freedom in choosing their life's work. To find the earliest known account that addresses those subjects, we have to look to Greece in the fourth century B.C.

In Book 10 of *The Republic*, Plato gives a rich, detailed description of the stages of entry through which a soul must go before incarnating on earth. Some scholars believe that Plato was simply using what is known as the myth of Er, which closes *The Republic*, as a poetic metaphor to back up his argument for living a virtuous life. Yet the myth actually bears a striking resemblance to reports of contemporary people who have had near-death experiences or who have recalled disembodied spiritual experiences that they believe happened before their birth.

The Er of Plato's tale was a Greek soldier who returned to consciousness some twelve days after he appeared to have died on the battlefield. Awaking on his own funeral pyre (in a scene reminiscent of an Edgar Allan Poe short story), Er tells a remarkable tale of what he witnessed during the time he was suspended between life and death. As Plato relates the story through the voice of Socrates, Er found himself in a kind of way station between Heaven and earth, where souls were passing from one plane to the other. The dead were waiting to be judged and assigned to their reward or punishment, while other souls prepared for their journey to earth. In one great meadow, souls awaiting their return to earth went before the three Fates: Clotho, who spins the thread of life; Lachesis, who determines its length; and Atropos, who cuts it off. Plato then writes:

When Er and the spirits arrived, their duty was to go at once to Lachesis; but first of all there came a prophet who arranged them in order; then he took from the knees of

Lachesis lots and samples of lives, and having mounted a
high pulpit, spoke as follows: "Hear the word of Lachesis,
the daughter of Necessity. Mortal souls, behold a new cycle
of life and mortality. Your genius will not be allotted to you,
but you will choose your genius; and let him who draws the
first lot have the first choice, and the life which he chooses
shall be his destiny."

After this prophet makes his announcement, he lays out many
possible life scenarios among the souls waiting to incarnate and
advises them to choose from these "samples of lives." Plato informs us
that "there were many more lives than the souls present, and they
were of all sorts. There were lives of every animal and of man in every
condition," including tyrants.

> [A]nd there were lives of famous men, some who were
> famous for their form and beauty as well as for their
> strength and success in games, or, again, for their birth and
> the qualities of their ancestors; and some who were the
> reverse of famous for the opposite qualities. And of women
> likewise; there was not, however, any definite character in
> them, because the soul, when choosing a new life, must of
> necessity become different. But there was every other qual-
> ity, and they all mingled with one another, and also with ele-
> ments of wealth and poverty, and disease and health; and
> there were mean states also.[4]

Plato makes it clear that while some of those choosing their lot in
life were newly minted souls from Heaven, many others had lived
before, and their choices were influenced by previous lives. Odysseus,
for example, was so disenchanted about ambition from his endless
striving that he opted for the life of "a private man who had no cares."
Jungian psychologist James Hillman offers a cogent summary of
the final stage of Plato's story in his book *The Soul's Code: In Search of
Character and Calling*. "When all the souls had chosen their lives
according to their lots," Hillman writes,

they went before Lachesis (lachos = one's special lot or portion of fate). And she sent with each, as the guardian of his life and the fulfiller of his choice, the genius (daimon) that had been chosen. . . . Lachesis leads the soul to the second of the three personifications of destiny, Klotho (klotho = to twist by spinning). . . . Under her hand and her turning of the spindle, the destiny of the chosen lot is ratified. Then the genius (daimon) again led the soul to the spinning of Atropos (atropos = not to be turned, inflexible) to make the web of its destiny irreversible. And then without a backward glance the soul passes beneath the throne of Necessity, sometimes translated as the "lap of Necessity."[5]

Before entering life on the earth plain, however, the souls marched to the Plain of Forgetfulness, a barren waste with no trees or vegetation, and then were required to drink from the River of Unmindfulness. As they drank, they forgot everything that had just transpired. The reason the gods ask us to do this should be obvious: if you know ahead of time exactly what's going to happen in your life, actually living it will seem as exciting as watching a replay of last year's St. Patrick's Day Parade. How would you ever bring yourself to begin a relationship with someone who you knew would lie to you and abuse you, yet from whom you needed to learn a valuable lesson? How would you be able to bear counting the days when your loved ones would die?

The problem of living with even some foreknowledge of one's future dilemma was brought home for me in a private consultation I gave to a man named Paul, who was in a serious state of depression. As I read Paul's energy "file"—the information encoded in his energy centers, or chakras—I was struck by its lack of a conventional sense of personal history that is typically present in the people whom I read. Instead, the information I was picking up was quite vague, leading me to speak only in—for me—frustrating appraisals such as "You sort of feel as if you can't make any choices in life and stick by them," or "It seems you almost get something started and then you just drop it." Paul had none of the substance that I can detect in people who have accumulated life experience and "cell memory." He was, in a sense, psychically empty, so providing him with any kind of direct and clear information was impossible. The only semiconcrete image that I got was of Paul in discussions with "people," but I could not relate these interactions to his depression.

After I confessed my frustration to Paul, he opened up and said that actually one image was very useful to him, because I had validated certain memories that had long troubled him. Paul could recall a number of incidents that had happened to him before he had "descended" into physical life. When I pressed him to be more specific, he astonished me by saying that the "people" with whom I had seen him in conversation were actually two "beings of light" whom he vividly remembered had helped him create the elements of this lifetime—before he was born. As in Plato's story of Er, Paul had been presented with an array of choices and was urged to shape his life's mission based on events and influences from previous lives, obligations that he needed to fulfill to be able to help others in their spiritual development, personal debts he owed, and some new experiences that he was allowed to select. All of the events and relationships that he chose, with the help of his spiritual advisers, were woven together around one major path. The beings had been very specific about certain events he was meant to be a part of, adding that the details of getting to these events would be taken care of from their end. Paul felt he had been introduced to a kind of "support group"—a celestial version of AA, or Archetypes Anonymous—that sounded a lot like the archetypal patterns I had just begun to identify in my workshops and readings.

Although Paul said that numerous details had been organized and explained to him, he could not recall most of them. He did remember that he had been given choices about some of the events that he would need to "attend," and that he was told that he was under contract to learn tolerance, among other skills of the soul. Paul was also asked in what way he would like his learning to take place and was offered three options. After choosing one, he was aware that in spite of the predetermined plans, there were still blank "creation spaces" that would be filled in by the choices he made during his life. It all sounded a little like choosing your college curriculum: decide on a major, take the required courses, and then pick a few electives for fun.

Sadly, though, Paul didn't seem to be having much fun. The only thing he was sure of was that before descending from the energy plane of life to the physical plane, he had been told to take a drink from a river similar to Plato's River of Unmindfulness. But because Paul did not want to forget everything that had just taken place, he decided not to drink the waters. In his words, he "jumped the river" and "slipped onto a ribbon of light" that led directly into his mother's womb. As it turned out, his decision to flout the directions he was given had dreadful consequences. Because of his resulting larger-than-life memory, he had never felt grounded on earth, and consequently he could not function in the real world, where he had trouble choosing to do anything, for fear that some part of him knew ahead of time that it wouldn't work out.

"I abdicated any power of choice I had by refusing to forget," Paul said. "I'm drowning alive in the feeling that I have no power in any matters of my life. I should have agreed to forget, because that would have given me options in my life."

Paul said he was destined to live the first life that he saw, that even though we have "places to go and promises to keep," we still have to choose how our challenges or opportunities will manifest. It may be, for instance, that you need to go through a certain experience—say, being passed over for a promotion—so that you'll discover what you really need to do. But if you knew before taking a job that you were going to end up in a dead end, you might have a lot of trouble showing up in the first place. As a result, you wouldn't get to have the kind of inner revelation that can only come from finding your back up against the wall. Paul felt frozen into inaction by the constant sensation that he knew what would happen in any given situation.

Although Paul's story was unusual, I suggested that he try to have faith that he actually still had his power of choice but was just so stymied by his extraordinary memories that he was unable to recognize it, since the gift of choice cannot be taken from anyone. Whether or not Paul had actual memories, he may have been using them as an excuse for not living his life to the fullest—as a metaphorical inability to act decisively—which would be enough to depress anyone. Nonetheless, the parallels with Plato's story are intriguing.

Whether we take Plato's and Paul's fascinating stories on the level of reportage, myth, or metaphor, we can derive some valuable lessons from them. Plato makes clear that the choice of our "lot in life" is a cooperative effort with the Divine. Through a series of aides or messengers, including the "prophet," the three Fates, and our personal "daimon" (a kind of guardian spirit), the Divine offers us a selection of possible lives. Each life will vary in nature and length, but it is up to us to choose the individual setting with its attendant challenges. Our social and economic station in life, our physical appearance, health, and genetic predisposition are all part of the package. We even have the option, it appears, of choosing "mean states," including a life of selfishness and megalomania.

But the key to the myth as well as the metaphor is that these potential "lives" are essentially templates with no "definite character." We each supply the specific character as we interact with the lives and challenges we have contracted for. In the Platonic scheme, then, free choice is an ongoing process that begins from the point at which we select the terms of our life, and it continues through our last action on earth. We are truly in control of our fate. "Virtue is free," writes Plato, "and as a man honors or dishonors her he will have more or less of her; the responsibility is with the chooser—God is justified."

That very freedom can seem daunting—as if we are "to freedom condemned," as Jean-Paul Sartre put it in the title of one of his books. Even if we accept the principle of divine grace and guidance, we are still likely to long for some specific road map, some guide to our own Contract. I believe that we can find that road map in part by examining the lives of some of the world's great spiritual masters, who, however high their level of realization, walked the same earth as we do and faced many of the same doubts and fears.

Contracts of the Masters

The Hebrew Bible, known to Christians as the Old Testament, together with the Christian New Testament amount to an extensive documentation of God's contractual agreements with the people of Israel and later with the followers of Jesus. Indeed, the English word *testament* itself refers to a legally binding agreement, as in "last will and testament." In the opening chapters of Genesis, Yahweh makes an agreement with Adam that he "may eat freely of every tree of the garden," except for the tree of the knowledge of good and evil. "For in the day that you eat of it," Yahweh says, "you shall die." Adam and Eve fail to keep their agreement, and they suffer the consequences: death and foreknowledge of death. According to Rabbi Harold Kushner's intriguing theory, Adam and Eve were not actually punished for eating from the tree of knowledge but simply entered the world of human self-consciousness that separates us from the animals, who don't have to make the kinds of moral and ethical decisions that are integral to thinking people's lives—or to a Sacred Contract.[6] But the fact that Adam and Eve's troubles began when they did not uphold their end of an agreement with the Divine shows the importance with which our Western spiritual ancestors endowed Contracts. And God's Contract with Noah, as we have seen, provided for nothing less than the survival and flourishing of the entire human race.

Adam, Eve, and Noah are clearly metaphorical figures who represent reinterpretations of the creation and flood myths of ancient Mesopotamia, which the ancient Hebrews would have assimilated into their culture along with a respect for law and order. But Abram, later called Abraham, must to some extent have been based on a flesh and blood character, the founder of the Hebrew race and religion. His detailed, personalized story, and those of other spiritual leaders who founded many of the world's great traditions, represent compelling manifestations of a Sacred Contract in action.

The wisdom of men such as Moses, Jesus, Muhammad, and the Buddha shines through all mythic overlays and religious dogmas. The truths that they embodied in their lives transcend cultures and personal beliefs. You needn't be an orthodox Christian to believe that you should love your neighbor as yourself, for instance. Nor do you have to be a Buddhist to acknowledge that the craving, hatred, and ignorance that derive from seeing ourselves as essentially separate from all other beings are the major source of suffering in our lives.

Regardless of the masters' traditions, their teachings speak to us because they lived actual physical lives. They also confronted universal challenges on their paths to self-awareness and to comprehension of the power they carried inside them. Each of them had to awaken to the full measure of his Contract—they were not born enlightened. Their teachings are blueprints for what our spirits need to do to make the transition from seeing life in physical terms to understanding the purpose and meaning of life on a symbolic level.

Many of us believe that if only we were smarter, more dedicated, or holier, we would know what we were supposed to be doing on earth because then God or the universe would enlighten us about our real mission. We mistakenly believe that the great spiritual leaders, such as Abraham, Moses, the Buddha, Jesus, and Muhammad, had their Contracts spelled out for them. Yet none of these figures truly saw his Contract early on. Their life paths were *not* obvious but required that they *develop* the trust and stamina to surrender unconditionally to the will of Heaven. As a rule, that doesn't happen to a child or an adolescent or even a young adult. Nor does it happen all at once. We develop faith and other abilities in stages, and our progress becomes most obvious in midlife. Still, some people do acquire insight in a single rush, an epiphany. For instance, otherwise ordinary people who have had near-death experiences report a sudden awakening, after which they become conscious of their life as part of a larger plan, and they live it differently from that point forward. In the Hindu tradition, spiritual and nonspiritual people alike have reported an extraordinary surge of energy, known as a kundalini awakening, that shoots up the spine to the crown of the head and often transforms the focus of their lives to spiritual service.

These ancient spiritual leaders—as men—came face-to-face with God and truth. In their humanness these prophets, as well as numerous other saintly men and women, felt confusion and fear as they learned the meaning of their tasks. Guidance was often given to them when they needed it, but they still often doubted themselves and felt abandoned, even despairing, as they sought to fulfill their mission, which some of them learned quite late in life. Each struggled with his ego and each was tested, some several times, to determine whether he could finally connect with the divinity within him. Collectively, their lives form the archetypal prototype for the process of how a Sacred Contract is revealed. We'll go through the five stages of a Sacred Contract in the next chapter, but first let's examine some of the themes or soul "tasks" that appear in these stages.

Four of the prophets went through a renunciation of their previous life and identity and were "reborn" with a new identity. Each also was renamed to recognize this spiritual attainment. A ritual soul-naming occurs when an individual can no longer be recognized as his normal self by the society he serves, when he has evolved beyond his human function into an eternal Self, a universal leader or embodiment of a greater truth. Abram became Abraham when the Lord sealed their covenant. Jesus became known as the Messiah and after his death as the Christ ("the Anointed One"). Following his spiritual transformation, Siddhartha Gautama became the Buddha ("the Enlightened One"). And Muhammad son of 'Abd Allah came to be known as the Prophet.

A soul-naming also represents a conscious fulfillment of the necessary tasks of service—the Sacred Contract. The individual has come fully into his power, even though he has not yet completed his Contract or life. From that point on, he or she operates only from the power of the soul and speaks only with the voice of the soul. So the soul is given its own name. The ego or former self is no longer dominant but becomes a servant-companion, a vehicle through which the soul communicates messages from the Divine.

Orphans and Expatriate Heroes

As Joseph Campbell writes in *The Hero with a Thousand Faces*, "the really creative acts are represented as those deriving from some sort of dying to the world."[7] The archetypal Hero's Journey described by Campbell, Sir James G. Frazer's *The Golden Bough*, and others always begins with a process of separation or alienation from the tribe, followed by a series of difficult challenges that the hero must meet alone. The journey culminates in a descent into the abyss of self-doubt and a loss of faith in the Divine, but then results in a vital transformation and a renewal of trust, which in turn leads to a revelation of some new knowledge, insight, or wisdom. The hero then returns to the tribe and imparts this insight—or tries to, since heroes, like prophets, are not always welcome in their hometown. Their presence unsettles us and makes us aware that other truths and lives exist beyond our physical routines. Yet we fear the disruption that pursuing our divine potential would create, even though our everyday comfort will be disrupted if it is standing in the way of our Contract.

When you become conscious of your Contract, as opposed to living it in an unconscious way, you go through a painful process of severance, similar to the Hero's Journey, because you are no longer part of the tribal mind. "For whosoever will save his life shall lose it," Jesus said. You have broken away from the general mind-set, and the group is likely to perceive your individuation—like anything new or different from the status quo—as a fundamental threat to its own unity. Ironically, as in the case of these great teachers, severance from one's personal tribe can lead to something beneficial to the survival of the universal human tribe. The great mystics—Abraham, Moses, the Buddha, Jesus, Muhammad—all shared a common fate of abandonment and separation from their tribe early in their mission, and this alienation or exclusion was essential to the completion of their Contract. Abram left the ancient Sumerian city of Ur and set out for Canaan, then later was compelled by famine to make a sojourn in Egypt. "Go from your country and your kindred and your father's house to the land that I will show you," the Lord told him.

Another key figure in the Hebrew Bible, Moses, was an orphan who was forced to flee Egypt after killing an Egyptian in an act of rage. After God appeared to him in the burning bush, Moses begged not to be made the leader of his people, insisting that he had none of the requisite qualities.

Jesus' own parentage was questioned by his neighbors, since Mary was pregnant when Joseph married her. As a perceived bastard, or *mamzer*—the child of a woman impregnated by someone outside of the community—Jesus would have been without a voice in his local congregation. "No bastard shall enter the assembly of the Lord," the Torah commands (Deut. 23:2).[8] When he returned to his hometown of Nazareth after his enlightenment to teach, Jesus was met with a cold reception by the contemptuous locals, who said, "Isn't this the carpenter? Isn't this Mary's son and the brother of James, Joseph, Judas, and Simon? Aren't his sisters here with us?" But later when Jesus was preaching and was informed that his blood family was listening outside, his response was "Who are my mother and my brothers and my sisters?" Looking around at those sitting near him, he indicated that *they* were his family. Although many of the people of Israel followed Jesus and his teachings, the leaders of his own religious tradition for the most part rejected him and his message. His outsider status would mark Jesus throughout his public ministry.

In marked contrast to the humble, shadowy origins of Jesus, the Buddha was born into a wealthy and powerful family in the foothills of the Himalayas; had he remained at home, he would probably have become a tribal leader and a great warrior. Legend holds that on the birth of Siddhartha Gautama, the Buddha-to-be, an astrologer told his father, Suddhodana, that the boy would become either a universal monarch whose chariot wheels would roll across the land or an enlightened one who would set in motion the wheel of the Dharma— the great truth that would alleviate humanity's suffering. Suddhodana preferred the first possibility, but despite his best efforts he could not keep his son from discovering the world of suffering and death outside of his opulent palace.

Although married with an infant son, Siddhartha determined to leave behind home, family, inheritance, and tribe and embark on a Hero's Journey in behalf of humanity. He became a voluntary orphan to search for truth and explore his inner self. Drawn to the saffron-robed figure of a wandering monk who appeared serene amid the suffering of the world, Siddhartha shaved his head and went looking for a spiritual teacher. According to tradition, he studied with two of the leading meditation teachers of his day and practiced extreme asceticism with a small group of like-minded seekers. Yet in time Siddhartha rejected both the conventional meditation and the asceticism of the forest monks along with the established priestly religion of the Hindu Brahmins, once again orphaning himself in order to discover his own path. Like Jesus, he returned from his journey with something of great value to the tribe.

The Prophet Muhammad's father died before he was born, and his mother died when he was only six, leaving Muhammad under the protection of his uncle, Abu Talib. Although he was cared for, to be without parents in the tribal society of seventh-century Arabia left one vulnerable both financially and physically. Yet Muhammad drew on his reserves of inner strength and integrity to establish himself as a reliable caravan worker. He was entrusted with storing the possessions of other merchants and was given the nickname of al-Amin, "the Trustworthy." At the age of twenty-five, after successfully managing the caravans of a wealthy female merchant named Khadijah, he accepted her offer of marriage even though she was fifteen years his senior.

When Muhammad was about forty himself, he began to receive revelations from the angel Gabriel in a cave where he went to meditate. These transmissions from Allah—Arabic for "the God"—eventually formed the Quran, Islam's sacred scripture. Yet as Muhammad relayed the revelations first to a close circle of family and friends and then to others in the cities of Mecca and Medina, he began to draw fierce resistance from fellow Arabs. Many opposed these new teachings, which forbade the worship of idols and threatened the role of the Kaaba, an ancient Meccan place of worship that was also a great source of commerce in that part of the Arabian peninsula (modern-day Saudi Arabia). The local clans also scorned the social reforms included in the Quran, which mandated caring for widows and orphans, and greater rights for women, who at the time were treated largely as chattel. At one point Muhammad was forced to seek refuge from threats against his life in the mountain fortress of Abu Talib, where he became a virtual prisoner. A lengthy military campaign and pitched battles followed, but Muhammad prevailed, initiating a long era of spiritual and material growth for the very tribe that had so fiercely rejected him at first. His message has since spread to include about one-sixth of the universal tribe.

Once each of these spiritual leaders became conscious of his purpose, it reshaped his life entirely. Abram, for instance, was a fairly prosperous herdsman in the nomadic tradition of the Semites before he was awakened by the voice of God. Moses too was apparently content tending the flock of his father-in-law, Jethro, before the same voice woke him up. Jesus toiled as a carpenter until the heavens spoke to him at the age of thirty. The Buddha was twenty-nine and a child of privilege when the inner call sounded; Muhammad was prosperous and forty. These men did not grow up knowing that they had a divine destiny; they had to learn their Contracts.

The Great Missions

Even after Abraham, Jesus, and Muhammad were given their specific missions to fulfill, they still often challenged their agreements and the heavens. They struggled to accomplish tasks at the direction of the Divine, but they were not told the reasons why they had to do what they had been commanded. Given how uncertain they were even *with* direct intervention and guidance, you need to accept that only through acting to uncover your Contract will it be revealed to you.

Because the masters' biographies are filled with stories of miracles, apparitions, profound interactions with the Divine, or near-superhuman accomplishments of self-discipline, love, and will, and not of the details of their daily lives, we do not know how they sustained their faith in between divine communications. It is possible that, during the ordinary days and weeks of their lives, they questioned even more relentlessly and insistently whether they were doing exactly what was expected of them. They may even have questioned their own identity. Jesus once asked Peter, "Whom do men say that I am?" It seems less likely that he asked this because he was curious about whether his divinity was being duly recognized than because he sought further validation that he was on the right path.

Our own process of learning our Sacred Contract is unlikely to parallel the experience of these extraordinary leaders, of course. We are not likely to have profound mystical experiences or direct contact with the Divine. Yet we can still learn to recognize the basic outline of the unfolding of our Contract through the masters' stories.

The First Sacred Contract

The story of Abraham is one of the most renowned of all the sacred scriptures, recounting the beginning of the nation of Israel and the Jewish people, destined to become one of the most mystical and enduring cultures on earth. The founding of Israel emerged out of a vision in which the God called Yahweh communicated to an ordinary mortal named Abram that he was to found a nation and father a people. Yahweh gave a specific command that was to represent the bond between Abraham, his descendants, and God forevermore: the Covenant of Circumcision. The precedent for this covenant had been created when Yahweh made the covenant with Noah, but we have few details about the implementation of that covenant. The new covenant—an agreement by God to do something for Abram and his offspring if they adhered to its terms and indicated their fealty to Yahweh—is the first officially declared Sacred Contract of which we have a detailed account. The biblical narrative follows the gradual revelation of Abraham's Contract and notes his response at each step of the way. Abraham's relationship to Yahweh is central to our understanding of the nature of our Sacred Contracts. Here is the opening of the story of Abraham as it occurs in the Hebrew Bible:

> *Yahweh said to Abram, "Leave your country, your family, and your father's house, for the land I will show you. I will make you a great nation; I will bless you and make your name so famous that it will be used as a blessing."*
> *I will bless those who bless you;*
> *I will curse those who slight you.*
> *All the tribes of the earth*
> *Shall bless themselves by you.*
> *So Abram went as Yahweh told him, and Lot went with him. Abram was seventy-five years old when he left Haran. Abram took his wife Sarai, his nephew Lot, all the possessions they had amassed and the people they had acquired in Haran. They set off for the land of Canaan, and arrived there.*
> *Abram passed through the land as far as Shechem's holy place, the Oak of Moreh. At that time the Canaanites were in the land. Yahweh appeared to Abram and said, "It is to your descendants that I will give this land."*
> *So Abram built there an altar for Yahweh who had appeared to him. From there he moved on to the mountainous district east of Bethel, where he pitched his tent, with Bethel to the west and Ai to the east. There he built an altar to Yahweh and invoked the name of Yahweh. Then Abram made his way stage by stage to the Negeb.*
> (GEN. 12:1–9)

We sometimes overlook how out of character with the life of Abram was the Lord's command. According to the scripture, prior to this divine encounter Abram was not occupied with founding nations. We can fairly surmise that he was a man in a leadership role, because his preparation for the journey included gathering together "all the possessions [his family] had amassed and the people they had acquired in Haran." But it would be a stretch to say that an individual of Abram's modest leadership stature would have felt he was cut out for creating a nation or fathering a vast tribe.

No sooner had Abram settled in Canaan than he was forced to move his people to Egypt to escape a famine. He feared the Egyptians and devised a plan in which he essentially offered his attractive wife to Pharaoh in exchange for his safety. He told Sarai to identify herself as his sister so that the Egyptians would treat him well and spare his life out of regard for her, or for the right to court her and probably, although it's never overtly stated, bed her. Once Pharaoh took Sarai into his palace, Abram was rewarded with "flocks, oxen, donkeys, men and women slaves, she-donkeys and camels." Yahweh inflicted severe plagues on Pharaoh and his household because of Abram's wife (although Abram himself was not punished). Pharaoh summoned Abram and said, "What is this you have done to me? Why did you not tell me she was your wife? Now, here is your wife. Take her and go!" To make sure, Pharaoh had his men escort Abram back to the frontier with his wife and possessions.

The story of Abram's sojourn in Egypt gives us our first insight into the character of the man who received the greatest task in the history of Israel, and what we see isn't attractive. He was a self-concerned coward who lied and pimped his wife to save himself and amass wealth. Having agreed to complete a profound undertaking for Yahweh, Abram proved his lack of faith right off by assuming that Yahweh would fail to protect him in the midst of danger, even though they had a Contract that required that Abram live to fulfill it. There is no mention that Abram invoked the grace of Yahweh. Further, in accepting the gifts from Pharaoh, he clearly had no problem receiving wealth under false pretenses, nor any conflict with owning the slaves that Pharaoh also gave him. In fact later, as Abraham, he again gave away Sarai, who had been renamed Sarah by God, to another king, explaining, "There is no fear of God at all in this place, and they will kill me for my wife" (Gen. 20:11). Yet God in this case appeared in the king's dream to tell him that Abraham was actually a prophet and to restore his Sarah to him and to live peacefully with him.

How are these aspects of the life of Abram related to our journey of discovering our own Sacred Contracts some four thousand years later? Let me review Abram's story symbolically rather than literally. To begin, the flaws in Abram's character indicate that he was not a perfect spiritual being or a man of unlimited faith and vision. From the onset of trouble, he turned to acts of deceit as a means of survival, in spite of the fact that he had had a profound encounter with the Divine. The man who held the Contract to found the nation of Israel struggled with his own nature, which included moral weakness, fear, and even greed. Yet it is crucial to recognize that these were character-istics of his ego, not his soul. Underneath Abram's personality was a soul that had been awakened by divine intervention, a soul with vision-ary strength and the potential for spiritual stamina. I suspect that Abram was not aware that he carried within him these deeper qualities, but they surfaced when the time was right and when his faith was strong enough to allow them to thrive.

The key to understanding God's choice of Abraham as a vehicle of divine will is to acknowledge that Abraham's soul was able to rise to what the occasion demanded of him, just as we are asked to do in our own lives. What you may think of as your ordinary attributes are not a fair indication of what spiritually extraordinary attributes lie within you. The obvious is never the whole truth. Often the truth needs to be packed in great illusion to protect it from the carrier of that truth as well as from those who will eventually find their lives changing because of it. Abraham was an ordinary man with the same flaws as other human beings, yet he carried within him a most extraordinary Contract, the consequences of which would result in the birth of Israel and the rise of one of the earth's great spiritual traditions. Abra-ham's story tells us that our own flaws serve only to conceal the valu-able nature of our potential contribution to humanity. For all our egotism and narcissism, we still tend to focus more on our faults than on our capacities and promise. And yet we all hold within us the potential for greatness and the potential to be of great service to others.

In fact, Abraham's is the story of the birth of two great nations, in which lies another lesson of a Sacred Contract. Abram's wife, Sarai, could not have children, a fact that grieved them both, so Sarai told Abram to lie with her slave girl, Hagar. He agreed, and in time Hagar conceived, immediately changing her social status within the household. Notwithstanding her own role in creating this situation, Sarai was infuriated and told Abram that the shift of attention to Hagar was an insult to her. To appease his wife, Abram told Sarai that she could do as she pleased with Hagar, allowing Sarai to treat her so badly that she ran away.

As a slave, Hagar no doubt had little to say in the matter of bearing a child by Abram—she was more than likely forced into submission. She was then further forced to endure cruel treatment from a jealous wife because of a pregnancy that she had not desired. Eventually she ran away, only to encounter an angelic messenger sent by Yahweh, who told her to return to Sarai in spite of her mistreatment.

By forgiving people who mistreat you, you do not absolve them from personal responsibility or condone their actions. We each exercise free will in carrying out our own Contract, and we always have the option to avoid doing evil. Yet in Hagar's case, her endurance of what was perhaps a necessary evil or obstacle led to her ultimate liberation. For the angel also told her that her son was to be called Ishmael, which in Hebrew means "God hears," indicating that Yahweh had heard her cries of distress. When Hagar returned to Abram and Sarai, she was granted divine protection, and God promised both Hagar and Abram that their son would also found a nation. After the birth of his and Sarai's son, Isaac, Abram did send Hagar away, and again God protected her and Ishmael in the desert. According to Muslim tradition, Hagar left the Israelites and traveled down the Arabian peninsula to the Becca Valley with her son Ishmael, who established a line of succession stretching to the Prophet Muhammad. Today the world's Muslims recognize Abraham as the father of their people and Hagar as their matriarch. Their story shows that we may need to endure necessary evils in the service of our Contract.

Two other significant events in the story of Abraham require discussion because they illustrate the acts of faith that are inherent in all Sacred Contracts and that are required by them. The first is the establishment of the covenant between God and Abraham, which reads as follows:

> *When Abram was ninety-nine years old Yahweh appeared to him and said, "I am El Shaddai* [Heb. "the Almighty"]. *Bear yourself blameless in my presence and I will make a covenant between myself and you and increase your numbers greatly." Abram bowed to the ground and God said this to him, "Here now is my covenant with you: you shall become the father of a multitude of nations. You shall no longer be called Abram* [Heb. "exalted father"]; *your name shall be Abraham* ["father of a multitude"], *for I will make you father of a multitude of nations. I will make you most fruitful. I will make you into nations, and your issue shall be kings. I will establish my covenant between myself and you and your descendants after you, generation after generation, a covenant in perpetuity, to be your God and the God of your descendants after you. I will give to you and to your descendants after you the land you are living in, the whole land of Canaan, to own in perpetuity, and I will be your God."*
>
> *God said to Abraham, "You on your part shall maintain my covenant, yourself and your descendants after you, generation after generation. Now this is my covenant which you are to maintain between myself and you, and your descendants after you: all your males must be circumcised."* (GEN. 17:1–11)

This Covenant became the open declaration of the external and spiritual manifestation of Abraham's Contract with the Divine. It is actually the second time God used the word *covenant* with Abraham, but this time he required a sign of loyalty from Abraham and the men in his household. Earlier, after Abram had bemoaned the lack of a son, Yahweh ordered him to sacrifice livestock and then appeared to Abram in a dream reaffirming His promise to make him the father of a great people (Gen. 15:7–21). The orders He now gave to Abraham, however, introduced into his tribe the belief that a divine force watches over us while expecting that we complete tasks it requires of us. The experiences and relationships that fill the calendar of our lives are there by design, all in support of the Sacred Contract established between us and God prior to our births. The Covenant represents an image of an "honorable" divine force that keeps His side of the bargain as long as Abraham and his kin keep theirs.

In this profound interchange between Abraham and Yahweh, an archetypal imprint was introduced into the Western psyche to parallel the imprint conveyed by the Vedas of India and the cult of Mithra in Iran: covenants exist between ourselves and God. The story of Abraham represents our first detailed glance of Divine-to-human intimacy in action, making that quality of union an active desire within the unconscious of every human being. Moreover, the concept of ethical responsibility to others before God, which Israel introduced to the world, was itself an invaluable contribution to the development of human spirituality that was implicitly sealed with this same Covenant.

The final event in the life of Abraham that holds great significance is the birth of his son Isaac, when Abraham was a hundred years old. In the biblical account, when the boy was still quite young, God is said to have "tempted" Abraham and told him, "Take your son, your only son, Isaac, whom you love, and go to the region of Moriah. Sacrifice him there as a burnt offering on one of the mountains I will tell you about." Abraham agreed to the Lord's directive without question. Early the next morning he got up, saddled his donkey, cut enough wood for the burnt offering, and with his son set out for the place God had told him about. When they got there,

> Abraham took the wood for the burnt offering and placed it on his son, Isaac, and he himself carried the fire and the knife. As the two of them went on together, Isaac spoke up and said to his father Abraham, "Father?"
>
> "Yes, my son?" Abraham replied.
>
> "The fire and wood are here," Isaac said, "but where is the lamb for the burnt offering?"
>
> Abraham answered, "God himself will provide the lamb for the burnt offering, my son." And the two of them went on together. When they reached the place God had told him about, Abraham

*built an altar there and arranged the wood on it. He bound his son
Isaac and laid him on the altar, on top of the wood. Then he
reached out his hand and took the knife to slay his son. But the
angel of the Lord called out to him from heaven, "Abraham!
Abraham!"*

"Here I am," he replied.

*"Do not lay a hand on the boy," he said. "Do not do anything to
him. Now I know that you fear God, because you have not with-
held from me your son, your only son."*

*Abraham looked up, and there in a thicket he saw a ram
caught by its horns. He went over and took the ram and sacrificed
it as a burnt offering instead of his son. So Abraham called that
place The Lord Will Provide.* (GEN. 22:6–14)

Although Abraham had already agreed to circumcision as the
Covenant between him and God, Yahweh asked him to perform
another task that would test his faith. So even though we may reach
the point at which we feel that we are finally doing what we are supposed to be doing, our faith will never stop being tested, because gaining insight into our Contract does not mean that we have perfected
faith. Finally, we will be asked again and again to release the parts of
our lives that mean the most to us. Yet at the end of the "ordeal," we
will find that we have not given up anything but have instead been
given much more in return. I am not suggesting that we will actually
be asked to kill our loved ones as a test of our faith; the act of sacrifice
should be understood as symbolic. You cannot come to know the
depths of the purpose of your life, however, if you are not willing to
release those parts of your life that are no longer necessary.

Your Sacred Contract can carry you through the dark times of your
life just as Vasalisa's tiny doll directed her steps through the woods.
Like Vasalisa, you are presented with seemingly arduous tasks but also
with the intuitive means to accomplish them. And like the great spiritual masters, at times you may question the Divine's motives or feel
that you cannot do what is expected of you. That is when you should
recall how the masters struggled with their Contracts and have faith

that you already possess the intuition and inner skills you need to fulfill your own Contract.

Although events often seem to occur haphazardly, your Contract unfolds gradually, each aspect arriving as you are ready for it, giving you many opportunities to respond to the challenges it presents. In the account of Abraham's interaction with God in Genesis 12–22, for example, God either appears or speaks to Abraham no fewer than seven times over a period of several decades. Along the way, Abraham voices his doubts about the promises the Lord has made, and God not only repeats his Covenant but also expands its terms to include the requirement of circumcision and extends it to cover Isaac as well. There are requirements, tests, twists in the plot (Hagar and Ishmael leave, return, and leave again) and unexpected graces (the birth of a son in his and Sarah's extreme old age). Throughout all the unexpected developments and his own doubts, however, Abraham's will does not waver, and he follows the terms of his Contract through to the end.

In time, you will discern a progression in the way your own Contract is revealed to you. However different your life may seem from those of Abraham and the other masters, its unfolding follows a pattern that is similar to theirs. In the next chapter we'll examine how their Contracts revealed themselves and learn to recognize the steps that make up that progression.

CHAPTER 3

The Stages of a
Sacred Contract

A ll growth occurs in stages, and spiritual development is no exception. Yet sometimes we are not even aware that we have passed
from one stage to the next until sometime afterward. One of the leading mystics in the West today, Ram Dass, was born into a wealthy
family and was already pursuing a successful career as a Harvard professor and research psychologist when his life suddenly changed.
While at Harvard in the early 1960s, Richard Alpert, as Ram Dass was
known then, became interested in human consciousness and, together
with Timothy Leary, conducted intensive research with LSD, psilocybin, and other psychedelic drugs in a circle that included Aldous Huxley
and Allen Ginsberg. The psychedelic experiences completely upended
Alpert's rationalistic world and introduced him to realms of consciousness outside anything he had learned about in his studies and
research in psychology.

After Alpert and Leary were dismissed from Harvard because of
the controversial nature of their work, Alpert continued his research
with a private foundation for four more years. Although the mind-
expanding drugs had transformed him, he was also concerned about
the transient nature of his "highs"—no matter how marvelous they
were, he always came down. Like Leary and Ginsberg, Alpert in 1967
decided to travel to India in search of new experiences. A fellow
American seeker whom he met there introduced Alpert to a spiritual
master named Neem Karoli Baba. The holy man instructed him in

yoga and meditation and gave him the spiritual name Baba Ram Dass, or "Servant of God." Alpert had finally found a high that he didn't have to come down from. Returning to the United States as Baba Ram Dass, he lectured widely, wrote several influential books about the spiritual path, including *Be Here Now*, and developed the Prison Ashram Project, designed to help inmates grow spiritually, and later the Living Dying Project, which helped the terminally ill to experience mindfulness, insight, and peace as they died.

"There are three stages to the journey I have been on!" Ram Dass wrote after returning from India. "The first, the social science stage; the second, the psychedelic stage; and the third, the yogi stage." They each contributed to the next, he said, "like the unfolding of a lotus flower." Yet looking back, he realized that "many of the experiences that made little sense to me at the time they occurred were prerequisites for what was to come later."[1]

But the stages of Ram Dass's journey were not finished. Now in his sixties, after he finished writing a new book about conscious aging, his publisher returned the manuscript, feeling it lacked conviction. While he was trying to figure out how to improve it, Ram Dass had a stroke that left him paralyzed yet fully conscious. For the first time in his life, this eloquent teacher and mystic, who had sometimes been accused of arrogance, found himself totally dependent for his survival on the help of close friends and medical personnel. After years of struggling to heal, Ram Dass did continue teaching, and having experienced some of the challenges of aging, he was able to bring profound insights to his book on aging—entitled *Still Here*—which was published to great appreciation.

The stages of Ram Dass's spiritual unfoldment could hardly have been clear to him at the time they were happening. Before he suffered his stroke, he probably had little sense that further growth and life challenges were necessary for him. Each stage made perfect sense— the lotus flower unfolding—but only in retrospect.

Many other mystics, including Teresa of Ávila and John of the Cross, also went through multiple stages of awakening or enlightenment: Saint Teresa likened their progression to walking through the rooms of a mansion, and Saint John, to ascending a mountain. Based on the experiences of these and other mystics from different spiritual traditions, the scholar Evelyn Underhill, in her classic book *Mysticism*, distilled the enlightenment process into five stages. She called them the stages of awakening, purification, illumination, the dark night of the soul, and divine union.[2]

In the unfolding of the Sacred Contracts of the great spiritual masters, we can see a similar progression. These mystical stages represent an archetypal model of progression to "soul clarity," that is, the capacity to recognize that the material contents and relationships of our physical world are here only as props or parts of our service to our Contract. The stages by which the spiritual masters became aware of the nature of their Contracts are the same as the five stages through which we must go. Indeed, the same resistance to what we might label the "divine call" that the prophets felt is evident in our own resistance to the inner voice of intuition. The difference is mainly one of degree.

You may want to pause and reflect for a time here on any promptings or coincidences or intuitions you've had over the years. Write them in your journal or notebook. Note whether they came to you in a dream; through a comment, warning, or compliment from a loved one or stranger; through the lyrics of a song or a feeling you got from music or nature; or through something you experienced or learned through work or a pastime. How did you react to these inklings at first? Did you welcome or ignore them or even suppress them? Did you act on them? What happened afterward? The way you receive intuition or callings or guidance will help you determine the kinds of archetypal forces that are at work in your life and will ultimately help you discern your Sacred Contract.

Abraham's awakening to the nature of his Sacred Contract follows the five stages outlined below. As with anything we learn, the stages generally overlap and continue to unfold throughout our life as we grow or develop a skill or insight. The stages are not a strictly linear progression but rather a continuous process of growth and unfoldment that you may go through a number of times in your life as you encounter new challenges or circumstances.

1. Contact:

A moment of connection occurs
between you and the Divine.

According to the biblical account in Genesis, seven direct encounters occurred between Yahweh and Abraham. In the first encounter, we're told that the Lord spoke to Abram, but in subsequent directives, the Lord "appeared" several times to him, and "the word of the Lord came unto Abram in a vision." Jesus, while being baptized by John in the River Jordan, experienced enlightenment as "heaven was opened, and he saw the Spirit of God descending like a dove and lighting on him" (Matt. 3:16). For the Prophet Muhammad, the connection came while he was meditating in a cave not far from Mecca, and the angel Jibril (the Arabic name for Gabriel) delivered his first revelation from Allah. The Buddha did not believe in a Supreme Being, although he did accept the presence of many lesser gods from the Hindu pantheon. Yet during his enlightenment, as he sat in prolonged meditation under the bodhi tree, he connected with a level of universal knowledge and wisdom that rendered him omniscient.

We will all be introduced to the Divine through ordinary and extraordinary experiences, even if spiritual messengers are not involved. For instance, the divine influence is evident when a cluster of disasters occurs in a remarkably short period of time and reroutes your life. ("Dis-aster" means "from the stars," indicating a long-held belief that bad things happen for reasons known by the heavens.) Or an unforeseen opportunity might present itself. The Divine might also be revealed through dreams, extraordinary "coincidences," a transcendent experience of the natural world, or during prayer or meditation. The hallmark of a divine experience, regardless of what form it takes, is that it gets your attention and leads you to think something out of the ordinary might be happening to you. Divine encounters will be ongoing as opposed to one-time phenomena. That does not mean that disasters will be continuous, but it does mean that once you make a conscious connection with divine energy, that Presence is forever within your awareness and life.

Your encounters may not be as dramatic or clear-cut as Abraham's, but their outcome is generally irreversible. Take a few minutes to examine your life for turning points that represent some departure from the tribal values in which you were raised. Perhaps you encountered an inspirational figure or mentor, either in person or through reading or the arts. Ask yourself how that individual, book, or aesthetic experience entered your life, and draw a line from that point to where you are today. Then add other points along the line where other individuals or experiences helped to reinforce the initial message.

For Ram Dass, the moment of contact occurred on his first trip to India, when he was still known as Richard Alpert. One night during his travels, Ram Dass related in *Be Here Now*, he had a vision of his mother, who had died the year before of a spleen ailment, in which she urged him not to turn back on his search for inner liberation. Not long after that vision, he was standing out under the stars thinking about his mother and felt her presence guiding him. The next day he was taken to meet the man who would become his guru, whom he then called simply Maharaji. The first thing Maharaji asked was whether Alpert would give him the expensive Land Rover that he had driven there and that belonged to a friend of Alpert's—a request he quickly declined.

Sometime later Maharaji took Alpert aside and said to him, "You were out under the stars last night. You were thinking about your mother." Maharaji somehow knew that Alpert's mother had died the previous year. "She got very big in the stomach before she died," the guru said. "Spleen. She died of spleen."

"The first thing that happened," Alpert later wrote of that moment, "was that my mind raced faster and faster to try to get leverage—to get a hold on what he had just done. I went through every super CIA paranoia I've ever had. 'Who is he?' 'Who does he represent?' 'Where's the button he pushes where the file appears?' and 'Why have they brought me here?' None of it would jell. It was just too impossible that this could have happened this way. The guy I was with didn't know all that stuff, and I was a tourist in a car, and the whole thing was just too far out."

He tried to relate the experience to those he had had with psychedelic drugs, but it didn't fit that pattern, and instead his mind continued to speed up. "I felt like what happens when a computer is fed an insoluble problem; the bell rings and the red light goes on and the machine stops. And my mind just gave up. It burned out its circuitry . . . its zeal to have an explanation. I needed something to get closure at the rational level, and there wasn't anything. There just wasn't a place I could hide in my head about this.

"And at the same moment, I felt this extremely violent pain in my chest and a tremendous wrenching feeling, and I started to cry. And I cried and I cried and I cried. And I wasn't happy, and I wasn't sad. It was not that kind of crying. The only thing I could say was that it felt like I was home. Like the journey was over. Like I had finished."

At that point Alpert was willing to offer Maharaji the Land Rover or anything else he wanted, although the guru simply took him on as his disciple for no fee. Through the medium of an Indian holy man, this American academic had made contact with divine power, and his life was irrevocably changed in a way that LSD and psilocybin would never have accomplished.

2. Heeding the Call:
Having been awakened, you apply new wisdom to your life at hand.

Abraham's first step after receiving his directive from God—at seventy-five years of age—was to set out with his wife, family, and possessions and head for the land of Canaan. Awakening to the Divine is meaningful only as a step in the journey of spiritual transformation. It is a big first step, to be sure, but then you must act and take another step, as Abraham showed.

An old Zen saying has it, "Before enlightenment, chop wood and carry water. After enlightenment, chop wood and carry water." Heeding the call of the Divine within does not mean retiring to a life of contemplation in the mountains of Nepal or a cabin in the north woods. As rigorous and demanding as the traditional monastic life can be, with its enforced periods of silence and vows of obedience, it is also a somewhat privileged life in which the responsibilities of raising a family and earning a living are replaced by prayer and study in a controlled environment. Today's mystics are more likely to continue to live in the material world but with an entirely different orientation and set of values—a challenge that can easily be as rigorous as any cloistered life.

Once you feel the stirrings of initial contact with the Divine, look for ways to act on that experience. Ram Dass has said emphatically that genuine spiritual awakening always manifests as a desire to be of service to others. That service can take myriad forms—parenting, teaching, counseling, healing, volunteering, or any form of creative work—as long as its underlying goal is to help others realize their divine potential in some form. As Jesus says in the Gospel of Matthew, "By their fruits will you know them," and in many of his parables he places acts of compassion above religious practices. Your compassionate acts are the physical manifestation of all the inner spiritual work you are doing.

The apostle James, in his letter to fellow Jewish Christians, asks (James 2:14–26), "How does it help, my brothers, when someone who has never done a single good act claims to have faith? Will that faith bring salvation? If one of the brothers or one of the sisters is in need of clothes and has not enough food to live on, and one of you says to them, 'I wish you well; keep yourself warm and eat plenty,' without giving them these bare necessities of life, then what good is that? In the same way faith: if good deeds do not go with it, it is quite dead. . . . It is by my deeds that I will show you my faith." Like Jesus, James was steeped in the Jewish tradition that values compassion so highly. The Hebrew word *mitzvah* refers to any of the hundreds of commandments Jews are traditionally bound to follow, but in customary usage, *mitzvah* means an act of kindness.

3. Renaming:
You assume a new name or role with spiritual significance.

After God established his Covenant with Abram, He gave him the name Abraham—and renamed his wife Sarah—to signify his expanded role as father of a great nation. Although the name had a literal new meaning, its deeper significance lay in Abram's reorientation from a traditional clan patriarch to the sire not only of a new nation but of a new spiritual paradigm. As Thomas Cahill describes it in his book *The Gifts of the Jews*, that paradigm includes the Jewish people's belief in "a unified universe that makes sense," in which each individual has value and significance, as opposed to the impersonal, compassionless ethos of the polytheism of his day. The descendants of Abraham, according to Cahill, gave us even more than that.

> They gave us the Conscience of the West, the belief that
> this God who is One is not the God of outward show but the
> "still, small voice" of conscience, the God of compassion,
> the God who "will be there," the God who cares about each
> of his creatures, especially the human beings he created "in
> his own image," and that he insists we do the same.[3]

In the Roman Catholic tradition, boys and girls at about the age of thirteen take a new "confirmation name" for the ceremony in which they are confirmed in their faith. Like the bar and bas mitzvah of Jewish tradition, this ceremony is an echo of an ancient initiation ritual. A significant number of adults have undergone renaming rituals as well, often as the result of embarking on a consciously spiritual path. Initiates into the various branches of Buddhism, Sufism, yoga, Vedanta, and other mystical traditions too may take or are given names in the ritual language of their respective tradition to indicate their new spiritual identity. When Neem Karoli Baba gave Richard Alpert the spiritual name Ram Dass, it marked Alpert's entry into a life of devotion to the spiritual needs of other people.

Most of us, of course, do not assume an actual name when we embark on our path. And yet you may feel significantly changed and may signal that change in a variety of ways. You may create a home altar or other sacred space where you live; set time aside each day for prayer and meditation; work with a teacher or spiritual director to guide your development; create or join a small community of like-minded souls that meets regularly to advance your spiritual practice; or change your diet or other habits to reflect the new self that you feel emerging within you. In the sense that a name signifies an identity, these changes in spiritual identity are the metaphorical equivalent of renaming.

4. Assignments:
Throughout life you encounter extraordinary opportunities and challenges that require continual transitions and adjustments.

Abraham was a clan leader and a man of some means, yet nothing in his past seemed to indicate that he would father two nations of people as well as two of the great spiritual traditions in history—Judaism and Islam. Abraham's assignments included challenges that were both physical (traveling to a new land) and emotional/intellectual (dealing with Pharaoh and other foreign leaders). In a vividly detailed scene in Genesis 18, he even took it upon himself to argue with the Lord that the lives of the righteous in Sodom and Gomorrah should be spared, though he himself was but "dust and ashes." The extent to which he accepted and handled all his challenges as a man and soul makes him a worthy model for coming to terms with a Contract.

At crucial points in our lives, we are placed in situations that require of us unaccustomed skill, courage, or wisdom. Such moments are indications that our Sacred Contract is in play, but how we respond to these moments is up to us. We grow primarily through our challenges, especially those life-changing moments when we begin to recognize aspects of our nature that make us different from the family and culture in which we have been raised. Swimming against the current—which may begin as adolescent rebelliousness but later provides valuable opportunities for artistic, political, or spiritual expression—becomes part of our energy vocabulary.

Examine your own life, and look for unusual challenges that presented themselves *and* that seemed to go against the grain, more or less forcing you to make changes that you might not otherwise have made. Often we are unhappy with how well we respond to such challenges and opportunities, but total competence, success, or victory isn't always necessary, as long as you make *some* response. The old truism "Whatever doesn't kill you makes you stronger" may well apply.

Don't be overly harsh in your self-assessment, but look for unexpected results. By his own account, Christopher Reeve wanted to die after a riding accident left him a quadriplegic, and he asked his wife to pull the plug on his respirator. But in time he came to the point where he chose not only to live but to show other people how to live. He chose to embody the truth that your value as a human soul does not decline just because your body is seriously impaired. He accepted what was necessary to reach his highest potential. It's quite possible that he would not have been able to do that if he had not been injured, although his track record before the accident already shows an orientation to higher goals. Still, the sight of Superman in a wheelchair is an image of such archetypal power that that alone has doubtless caused many people to rethink their own lives.

5. Surrender:
You are given ongoing tests that ask the question Which world will you choose to follow, that of the Divine or that of the earth?

Abraham's son Isaac meant everything to him, yet when God told Abraham to sacrifice the boy, he set out to do what was asked. Although the command was the most difficult order of his life and clearly seemed to go against his best interests, Abraham chose to follow the voice of the Divine.

Abraham's response is indicative of the faith you need to have that your Contract will never ask more of you than you are able to give. You will never finish the process of choice and surrender until you have surrendered all to the will of the Divine. Just when you feel you've reached your limits, you are pushed further. Perhaps your career or a relationship seems to decline faster, for instance, the harder you try to revive it. Then maybe you decide to let God take over your life's direction, come what may, and it takes off, but in an unexpected direction. Or perhaps you feel an inner urging to try a more creative line of work that is financially risky but could repay you with a deeper sense of fulfillment. Should you follow your intuition? Perhaps you feel drawn to include more spiritual activity in your daily life, even as your rational mind is saying that you should be putting in more time at work, earning more money, laying away a retirement nest egg. This is where you need to combine intuition and intellect and use a symbolic perspective of your internal and external urgings, so that you can discern the voice of the Divine within. We'll talk more about how to develop your symbolic sight in later chapters.

All five stages of your Contract overlap and interweave throughout the arc of your life, and this is especially true of the stage of Surrender. Abraham surrendered to God's will when he followed His voice and left home at an advanced age. He continued to surrender as the voice of the Divine within led him through Egypt into Canaan, when he had to lead an army to rescue his brother Lot from captivity and invading forces, and when his rational mind told him that it was impossible for him at one hundred and Sarah at ninety to have a child. The order to sacrifice his son was perhaps his greatest act of surrender, in response to his toughest challenge.

As we continue to examine how these five stages unfolded in the lives of the great spiritual leaders Jesus, Muhammad, and the Buddha, please look for ways in which the stages apply to your own life. Don't focus only on the extraordinary details of their careers but also on their symbolic meaning and underlying truths. For one extraordinary paradox lies at the heart of each of their histories: although they were uncertain of their Sacred Contract at key points along the way and sometimes questioned or even asked to be released from it, they nonetheless surrendered to divine will at each of those points.

Jesus' Contract

The entire life of Jesus can be interpreted as an unfolding of his Sacred Contract and his continual surrender to it. But I'll limit the discussion to four of the most significant events of his life: his baptism and enlightenment; his forty-day fast in the desert; his experience in the garden of Gethsemane; and the crucifixion.

The Synoptic Gospels all record the baptism of Jesus by John the Baptist. The Gospel of Mark itself begins with an account of this seminal event: "And at once, as he was coming up out of the water, he saw the heavens torn apart and the Spirit, like a dove, descending on him." This, the oldest of the four Gospel traditions, gives the clearest description of a classic enlightenment experience. Luke gives a similar description but places the "opening" just after his baptism, while Jesus was at prayer. A voice is heard saying, "You are my Son, the Beloved, my favor rests on you."

This ritual marks the initiation of Jesus, an act of public revelation of archetypal proportions representing that Jesus had attained a degree of enlightenment that earned him direct contact with the Divine. It was the first stage of his Sacred Contract, initiating contact between Jesus and the Divine, whom he called *Father* (or *Abba*, a word that translates more accurately as "Daddy"). The act of baptism is also an archetypal ritual suggesting the full acceptance of the life one has been given to live. In Jesus' case, the baptism shows the mediation of another spiritual master, in the person of John helping Jesus attain enlightenment. After his baptism, Jesus was recognized as a master and was called that throughout the rest of his life. His soul had been anointed and its power awakened.

Immediately following his initiation, Jesus went into the desert for a forty-day fast to deepen the insights and level of commitment following enlightenment. Yet there he met the devil, who tempted Jesus to sell his spiritual birthright for three different, escalating levels of ego aggrandizement. The devil waited until Jesus was at his physically weakest point from lack of food, then suggested that he use his advanced spiritual powers to satisfy his hunger and material desires. Jesus, of course, refused all "worldly goods," a profound act and response to his first major spiritual challenge.

Each one of us will encounter such challenges in the form of "temptations" again and again, and we should not expect them to appear only once in our lives. Every time we enter a new sphere of power, which can include obtaining more money, earning more university degrees, or, as with Jesus, attaining a higher level of spiritual insight, we are given a "test" to see how we will manage the influx of yet another level of earthly power into our lives. Power as such is not a negative energy, but the question is always how we will use that energy. Having emerged victorious from his war against the delusions of the ego, Jesus began his public ministry, introducing a new spiritual paradigm every bit as important as that initiated by Abraham almost two thousand years earlier.

We can't fully appreciate Jesus' new paradigm without an understanding of the geographic and historical world into which he was born, a world characterized by declining economic stability and increasing psychological stress brought on by the Roman occupation of Judea. Taxation and debt were forcing Jews who had held their land for many generations to give it up to meet their tax burdens. As one recent study of political and economic realities at the time of Jesus put it:

> Villagers who may previously have felt a responsibility to
> help their neighbors in times of shortage were no longer
> under legal obligation to do so, especially since they were
> themselves now debtors, hard-pressed to provide their own
> children with food to eat. Local feuds which could have
> been easily resolved in normal times now often erupted into
> insults, fistfights, and family feuds. Land or goods taken as
> loan collateral—that should have been returned to its origi-
> nal owners by the law of the sabbatical year—now became
> the big-city creditors' permanent property. The simple fact
> was that the people of Israel were badly divided.[4]

The assignments Jesus carried out were shaped in part by a need to help the people of that time and place, heal their psychological anxiety and social anguish, and return them to the practice of love and compassion at the root of the Jewish tradition. Because of the extreme political instability, in fulfilling his Contract Jesus would ultimately be led to his death. Yet Jesus accepted all these factors and made the poor and outcast the primary audience for his teachings and healings.

The Synoptic Gospels tell the same version of the third significant event in the life of Jesus. Following the Last Supper Jesus left with his disciples for the garden of Gethsemane to pray, telling them, "I am sorrowful to the point of death," and asking them to stay with him while he prayed privately to the Father. In his agonized prayer, Jesus asked the Father to "remove this cup from me; but not my will but yours be done." In the account in Luke, an angel appeared to Jesus, "coming from heaven to give him strength. In his anguish he prayed even more earnestly, and his sweat fell to the ground like great drops of blood" (Luke 22:39–44).

This passage is the jewel in the crown of our connection to divine power and earning soul clarity. Jesus openly stated in his prayers that he did not want to do what was being requested of him. In my terminology, he was asking for a way out of that part of his Contract that he had to endure "by necessity." Jesus received help and comfort in the form of an angel, but nonetheless he was not released from completing his life's calling. He surrendered his will to the Divine, uttering a phrase that has since become the central Christian mantra: "Thy will be done." Without asking why, having lived a life of love and service, having now to suffer a gruesome death, Jesus accepted his lot. His prayer was a declaration of supreme trust in the wisdom of the Divine, consciously giving up the authority to direct the dynamics of his life.

In a fascinating footnote to Luke 22:43–44 in the New Jerusalem Bible, long renowned for its scholarly accuracy, the editors state that some translations have omitted the verses referring to an anguish so great that Jesus' sweat resembled drops of blood. The reason indicated was primarily "concern to avoid a humiliation of Jesus that seemed too human." The idea that Jesus could suffer the same kind of anguish as the rest of us at the presentiment of intense physical and psychological suffering was apparently too embarrassing for some New Testament translators to acknowledge. Yet the fact that Jesus suffered in that way and still was able to release his will to the "necessity" of his Contract makes the passage all the more remarkable.

Jesus' agony in the garden was not his final act of surrender, however; it was followed closely by the crucifixion. Luke's description is intriguing because he makes mention of Jesus saying, "Father, forgive them, for they know not what they do." This statement, which the other canonical gospel authors do not repeat, is central to Christianity and to learning how we should reply when "acts of necessity" occur in our life that were agreed to prior to our birth.

In Jesus we encounter a real human being who found it necessary to undergo a harsh and seemingly unjust death. Yet from that scenario he created a model of forgiveness that now stands as an inspiration for all whose suffering is undeserved. Jesus as a man found it necessary to seek assistance to awaken to his Contract and prepare to live it. He went through the ritual of baptism as a way of expressing his gratitude for his Contract, even though he may have sensed how it would end on earth. And he lived out the divine reality that each one of us will be tested numerous times during our lives and always at a new choice point that defines our power.

During his last days, Jesus modeled the archetypal ritual of surrendering all that we are to the Divine. He showed that we are here to serve divine wisdom, as opposed to divine wisdom serving us. And so when we are in those desperately painful experiences that we must pass through because of the agreements we have made before our earthly lives began, the practice of forgiveness, illogical though it may seem to our minds, is the only practice that finally soothes our soul.

It's unlikely that most of us will ever be asked to make the kinds of sacrifices required of Jesus, yet many people have experienced life-transforming moments of contact with the Divine that have led them to alter how they think and live. Among the most striking of such encounters are near-death experiences (NDEs), which have been reported in greatly increased numbers in recent years. Partly because of improvements in medical technology, it seems, many more people today are being revived after having been clinically dead for a time. They frequently describe entering a tunnel of light and being greeted by relatives and their angelic guides. Most of the people I've met who have had such experiences report being told that the time is not right and that they must return because they have work left to accomplish.

While Sheri was in her mid-twenties, she was involved in a car accident that left her seriously injured and unconscious. She felt herself being lifted out of her body and saw a tunnel of light coming toward her. Within the tunnel she recognized her father walking next to an angel. "I've come to tell you," her father said, "that I regret I never supported your dreams in life. Follow them now."

Sheri explained to me that at the age of eighteen, she had become involved with an Asian-American man named Yoshi, whom she loved dearly. Her father strenuously opposed this relationship, however, and pressured her into breaking it off. Sheri realized that her family would never accept Yoshi, and she was too young to strike out on her own. Even after her father died, Sheri's memory of the bitterness her relationship had caused prevented her from trying to reestablish it.

Now, as she embraced her father while out of her body, all of the rage that Sheri had felt toward him was healed. When she was brought back to life after the accident, she became enraptured at just being alive. "I feel so guided now," she said, "so close to Heaven. I feel that everything I do and say is of the greatest importance. And I take the responsibility of knowing that truth very seriously. The love and gratitude that I now feel toward my father has made me appreciate that everything in life has a purpose—even the most painful parts."

After her reconciliation with her father, Sheri felt moved to look up the man she had been in love with years before. It took her some time to find Yoshi, and when she finally did, he still resented the fact that she had let her father talk her out of seeing him. But after several months they did begin to see each other again and eventually rekindled their old romance.

Not every out-of-body experience yields such dramatic results. A sixty-five-year-old woman named Marilyn, for example, told me of an NDE during which the Divine made direct contact with her. She was revived following a heart attack that had left her clinically dead for several minutes. "While I was out of my body," she said, "I was embraced by the most loving being. Suddenly my life meant more to me than it ever had before, because I felt as if the whole universe somehow knew my name. I was filled with a sense of awe, and by the time I regained consciousness, I felt that I had been allowed to live for spiritual reasons and spiritual service. Now I thank God every day for 'attacking my heart.'"

Marilyn's external life didn't change in any obvious way. But her whole internal attitude toward her life underwent a remarkable transformation. She realized that everything was exactly the way it ought to be. Her anxiety about approaching the end of life melted away, and she no longer feared death as she once had.

Muhammad's Contract

The West is far more familiar with Jesus and Christianity than with the story of Muhammad and the founding of Islam. For reasons having largely to do with conflicting political agendas and fourteen

centuries of animosity between Muslims, Christians, and Jews, we also
have a distorted impression of the teachings of Islam. The fact is that
Islamic teachings are based on the same moral and ethical principles
that lie at the heart of both Judaism and Christianity. Allah, the Muslim name for God, is identical with the God of the Hebrew Bible and
the New Testament; in the Quran, Allah refers to his previous interactions with many key figures from Jewish and Christian tradition.
Allah's revelations in the Quran itself were made to Muhammad
through the same Angel Gabriel who announced to Mary that she was
to be the mother of Jesus. And so Muhammad is revered by Muslims
as the last in a series of great prophets that included Adam, Noah,
Abraham, Isaac, Moses, John the Baptist, and Jesus, providing a sense
of continuity among these three great monotheistic traditions.

Muslims can be as sensitive about interpretations of the life of
Muhammad as Christians are about Jesus, yet widely accepted
accounts of the Prophet's life make no secret of the fact that Muhammad was far from certain about his own mission until well past midlife.
Muhammad spent much of his youth working the Arabian caravans as
far north as Syria, talking along the way with the hermits, monks, and
gnostic Jewish practitioners who lived in desert caves and remote
communities. Illiterate but gifted with a retentive memory, he
absorbed much of the Jewish and Christian scriptures from the monks
and eremites he met in the desert. After Muhammad married Khadijah at age twenty-five, they produced four daughters and two sons,
both of whom died in infancy. For the next fifteen years, Muhammad
managed Khadijah's estate and lived an apparently normal, if prosperous, Arab life.

By all accounts, Muhammad was upright and moral before he
began his mission to the world, but he had not distinguished himself
spiritually in any obvious way. At most Muhammad might have been
considered a *hanif*, one of the desert-dwelling contemplatives who
worshiped exclusively the One Creator God, whose name *Allah* in
Arabic means "The God." It was not unusual for a few men of
Muhammad's desert clan to retreat from society for a time as he did
for solitary meditation and prayer. But at about age forty, Muhammad
began to have what he called "true visions" in his sleep, "like the
breaking of the light of dawn," and he was drawn to the solitude of a

cave in Mount Hira, near Mecca. There an angel appeared to him in human form and commanded, "Recite!"

Perhaps thinking that the angel was asking him to read something, Muhammad replied, "I am not a reciter." But the angel embraced him and repeated the command three times until Muhammad recited as instructed. Fleeing the cave in awe, Muhammad heard a voice telling him, "You are the messenger of Allah, and I am Gabriel."

Like Abraham and Jesus, Muhammad had to be awakened and prepared in this first stage of awareness so that he could live out the full magnitude of his Sacred Contract. The early deaths of his parents had directed him inward, and once he made that connection to his soul, the transcendent level of his Sacred Contract could begin to unveil itself. Muhammad then spent more time in the cave of Hira in worship and meditation, preparing for his mission.

According to his earliest biographers, the Prophet was initially terrified by his visions and actually feared that he might have become possessed by one of the *jinn*, or local spirits. For that reason he fled the cave of Mount Hira. When he reached his home, weary and frightened, according to one recent biography of Muhammad, he asked his wife to cover him in a blanket.

> After his awe had somewhat abated, his wife Khadijah asked him about the reason of his great anxiety and fear. She then assured him by saying, "Allah (The One God) will not let you down, because you are kind to relatives, you speak only the truth, you help the poor, the orphan and the needy, and you are an honest man."
>
> Khadijah then consulted with her cousin Waraqa, who was an old, saintly man possessing knowledge of previous revelations and scriptures. Waraqa confirmed to her that the visitor was none other than the Angel Gabriel.[5]

Clearly Muhammad did not grasp the full magnitude of his Sacred Contract until the moment was right and he had attained the necessary strength of soul. Like Abraham and Jesus, he did not know what would be asked of him, and after the initial revelation he needed constant encouragement, from both human and divine sources. "The reassurances of Khadijah and Waraqa were followed by a reassurance from Heaven in the form of a second Revelation," writes the prominent Muslim scholar Martin Lings.

> The manner of its coming is not recorded, but when asked how Revelations came to him, the Prophet mentioned two ways: "Sometimes it cometh unto me like the reverberations of a bell, and that is the hardest upon me; the reverberations abate when I am aware of their message. And sometimes the Angel taketh the form of a man and speaketh unto me, and I am aware of what he saith."[6]

But these first disconcerting messages from the angel were followed by a period of silence, Lings relates, "until the prophet began to fear that he had incurred in some way the displeasure of Heaven, though Khadijah continually told him that this was not possible. Then at last the silence was broken and there came a further reassurance, and with it the first command directly related to his mission."

That command is recorded in the Quran, in the *sura* (chapter) known as "Daylight" (93), where Allah speaks directly to Muhammad:

> *By the light of day, and by the dark of night, your Lord*
> *has not abandoned you, nor does He ever forget.*
> *The hereafter holds a richer prize for you than this present*
> *life. You shall be gratified with what your Lord will*
> *give you.*
> *Did he not find you an orphan and give you a home?*
> *Did he not find you astray and guide you?*
> *Did he not find you poor and make you rich?*
> *Therefore do not wrong the orphan, nor reprimand the beggar.*
> *But proclaim the goodness of your Lord.*

It was as though God had to remind Muhammad at each step of the way, just as the Lord reminded and aided Abraham, that he was not alone in all this. This blending of moral, psychological, and material comfort and support was a form of charism with which the Divine infused Muhammad to help him fulfill his Contract. Such instances of spiritual nurturing are not uncommon among more recent mystics as well. The nineteenth-century Indian sage Sri Ramakrishna often went into prolonged periods of *samadhi,* or ecstatic union with the Divine, during which he was in such bliss that he was oblivious to everything taking place around him. Although he died from a painful form of cancer, his spiritual life was filled with intense periods of divine communion.

Hilda Charlton, a modern mystic and teacher who had worked as a dancer and choreographer, went to India on a dance tour in the 1940s and stayed there for fifteen years, studying with masters, including Sathya Sai Baba. Charlton had been working intently on a spiritual practice to develop love and compassion for others. Yet she felt no results until she sat down in the woods one day and asked herself what was the use of continuing. "I closed my eyes and took a breath, and wham!" she wrote in her autobiography. "My heart center in the middle of my chest seemed to open up and love poured in like a torrential stream." The spontaneous opening she experienced was a form of comfort and support from the Divine that reinforced her determination to continue her long search for more immediate knowledge of God.[7]

When Muhammad began conveying his divinely revealed message to the larger community, he faced great resistance. In Arab society at that time, women, orphans, the disabled, and poor were treated with scant compassion. The social reforms that Muhammad was called to institute angered some fellow Arabs who did not want to change the social order that benefited them at the expense of the less fortunate. They attempted to lead an assault, yet Muhammad prevailed. He improved life for Arab women by prohibiting female infanticide and the prostitution of slave women, and by establishing the rights of women to inherit a half-share. He did what he could to shift the balance of power in marriage by proclaiming that couples have reciprocal duties and rights, and that women should be educated. He made it part of Muslim law that the followers of Allah must donate a fixed portion of their income to the support of orphans, beggars, and anyone in financial straits. Muhammad's followers have not always maintained his reforms or abided by his teachings, just as followers of other great mystical leaders, including Jesus, have not. After the founders died, the entrenched customs of male dominance endemic to the honor-and-shame-based cultures of the Middle East and Asia often reasserted themselves in short order.

Muhammad's Contract contained many challenging assignments, as he moved from being a successful merchant to raising an army to fight off his enemies. Yet what is most instructive is Muhammad's ongoing alertness to messages and inspiration from the Divine, which he continued to receive up until the end of his life. In his last years he conveyed revelations regarding the nature of the afterlife, the role of Jesus as a great prophet, and our ongoing struggle with the self. After returning to Medina from successful battles in Mecca and Hunayn, for instance, Muhammad exclaimed, "We have returned from the Lesser Holy War to the Greater Holy War." When a follower asked what he meant by the latter, Muhammad replied, "The war against the soul." His biographer Martin Lings explains this statement:

> The soul of fallen man is divided against itself. Of its lowest aspects, the Quran says: *Verily the soul commandeth unto evil.* The better part of it, that is the conscience, is named *the ever-upbraiding soul*; and it is this which wages the Greater Holy War, with the help of the Spirit, against the lower soul.[8]

Muhammad could have been talking about the struggle to see things from a higher symbolic or archetypal perspective too, rather than from the physical level. Even as he neared death, he strove to refine his understanding of God's revelations and of what it means to surrender to divine will. Indeed, the Arabic word *Islam* means "surrender," and *Muslim*, "one who surrenders." Yet for all his willingness to surrender to the Divine, nowhere do we get the sense that Muhammad knew what his Contract held for him from the beginning, or that he could have continued his mission without periodic guidance all along the way.

The Buddha's Contract

According to Buddhist historians, the man known as Siddhartha Gautama was born in the sixth century before the Christian era, in the foothills of the Himalayas, in what is now Nepal. His father, Suddho-dana, was the *raja*, or king, of the Sakya clan of that region and a member of the warrior caste. After the royal astrologer pronounced that his son would become either a great warrior king or a great spiritual leader, depending on how he reacted to "four signs," Suddhodana had a wall built around his estate to protect Siddhartha from having to view the harsh realities of old age, illness, and death.

One day in his late twenties, Gautama managed to get out of the walled environment of the palace and roamed the streets of his town to see how the people were living. It was then that he encountered the "four signs" that the astrologer had predicted would change his life: the sight of a decrepit old man, a sick man, a corpse, and a monk. Seeing the first three, he realized that he also was subject to old age, disease, and death. But he noticed that the monk, amid that disintegration of life, looked serene. At that point Gautama renounced all attachment to the physical world, stating that "worldly happiness is transitory." How could he enjoy his life if he knew that someday he would get old and sick and then die?

Soon afterward, at the age of twenty-nine, Gautama said a silent good-bye to his young wife and infant son and left home and went looking for a spiritual teacher. He is said to have worked with two primary teachers of different forms of meditation that were practiced at that time in India. Gautama mastered both forms and quickly ascended to the position of teacher himself, but ultimately he found that the techniques did not produce the state of complete freedom from desire that he sought. He then undertook yogic practices as well as *pranayama* (breath control) and severe austerities with a group of five disciples. Determined to attain enlightenment by practicing self-mortification, Gautama abstained from food almost entirely, eventually becoming frail and weak. Finally he reached the conclusion that extremes of self-denial would eventually end in death and a resumption of the endless wheel of *samsara*—birth, death, and rebirth. Recalling a state of blissful tranquillity and freedom from all desires that he had once experienced as a child sitting under a tree and watching his father plow, he went and sat under a large tree that became known as the bodhi (or bo) tree, the tree of enlightenment. Aware that he needed to recover his strength, he accepted a bowl of rice and

yogurt from a village woman named Sujata, who happened to be fulfilling an offering vow she had made in gratitude for the birth of her
child.

Siddhartha remained underneath the tree from early morning to
sunset, maintaining a fierce resolve to find an answer to human suffering. He would rather perish than get up from his seat until he received
full illumination. Plunging himself into deep meditation, by nightfall
he had entered into a superconscious state of illumination that is said
to have lasted forty-nine days. Gautama became fully enlightened and
at last discovered the state of being for which he had been searching.
This state was accompanied by the insights that became the center of
his teachings.

The Buddha didn't believe in a supreme being along the lines of
Yahweh, Allah, or Brahma, the godhead of Hindu belief, but he did
accept the presence of many lesser deities, such as the creator god
Brahma. These deities lived in a blissful realm that lacked only one
thing—the ability to become enlightened. And yet, although he would
not have acknowledged making contact with the Divine, the Buddha
did establish contact with a universal level of wisdom and insight that
transcends ordinary human awareness and qualifies as the first stage of
a Sacred Contract.

According to legend, during the lengthy meditation and enlightenment process, Gautama, now the Buddha (Sanskrit for "the Awakened One"), was tempted by Mara ("Death," the Evil One), in various
guises. Mara was afraid that the Buddha now had the insight to escape
Death's realm and so tried to frighten and intimidate him by unleash-
ing an army of fearful demons. But the Buddha was supported by the
grace of merit he had accumulated in his past lives and was not frightened off. Buddhist scholars Richard H. Robinson and Willard L.
Johnson pick up the story:

Then Mara, having failed with intimidation and compulsion, turned to temptation. He sent his three daughters,
Discontent, Delight, and Desire, to seduce the future Buddha, who remained as impervious to lust as he had to fear. As
the sun set, Mara and his hosts gave up and withdrew.

This temptation episode is quite a late addition [to Buddhist texts] and entirely mythical. The myth, though, is a suitable expression of an experience common to most contemplatives. The seeker eventually is committed to an integral attempt, overcomes doubt and inertia, and sets to work. This conjures up the demons of fear from the unconscious. All the habit-hardened dispositions protest against their coming destruction. But good habits sustain the seeker's resolve. The waves of fear pass, and doubts arise about whether the candidate is really equal to the challenge. If the seeker possesses genuine self-confidence, the doubts are vanquished. The last peril is of course the rosiest and the deadliest. Perfect love may cast out fear, but it all too easily changes into personal pleasure.[9]

According to tradition, the Buddha had seen all his rebirths on the Wheel of Existences, going back to the animal kingdom, including a past life as a stag who gave his life to save the herd. He had realized the tragedy of identifying with the ego as separate from everyone and everything else. Seeing ourselves as separate from the "outside" world gives rise to passionate craving, hatred, and ignorance. These forms of attachment are the principal causes of suffering.

Tradition has it that even after his enlightenment, the Buddha was tempted further by Mara to keep this liberating insight to himself and continue to realize the bliss of nirvana, casting off his body and forgoing return to the physical world. The gods were so disturbed by this prospect that they sent Brahma, the Hindu deity of creation, to convince the Buddha to go and teach what he had learned. The Buddha heeded the call to wander the land, begging food and shelter with his band of itinerant monks and teaching in the vernacular to men and women of all castes—a radical approach at odds with the social mindset and caste laws of his day. He was thirty-five when he achieved enlightenment and assumed the name Buddha, and he spent the next forty-five years teaching the insights he had learned in deep stillness under the bodhi tree. Like Moses, who wandered in the desert with the Israelites for forty years before he died and his people were allowed to enter the Promised Land, the Buddha taught his vision, settled disputes among his followers, and wandered the forests of northern India.

The challenges and opportunities that the Buddha faced during his six years of preparation and even during his great enlightenment experience itself were not the last he was to deal with. Throughout the rest of his life, he carried out numerous assignments regarding his teaching and the orders of monks and nuns he founded. According to Buddhist legend, his life ended when he visited a smith and accepted some tainted food rather than offend his host.

As in the lives of Abraham, Jesus, and Muhammad, Gautama the Buddha had to enter into the fullness of his Sacred Contract over time, first by being mentored and then by undergoing "tests" that challenged the strength of his soul over the force of his ego. His decision to forgo both extreme asceticism and self-indulgence for a more moderate existence—which he called the Middle Way—was the key to his finally achieving enlightenment. No effort by itself can induce the process of soul clarity. We may choose to engage in the discipline, but the Divine chooses when we will be given sight.

The Buddha's convention-breaking approach to teaching the spiritual path lives on in a number of modern teachers who have applied the principles he discovered 2,500 years ago to the vastly different challenges of modern life. The lives of renowned American Buddhist teachers such as Pema Chödrön, Charlotte Joko Beck, and Bernie Glassman continue to prove that the Contracts of even the most accomplished spiritual masters are not always apparent to them from the beginning. Glassman, for example, was born in Brooklyn, New York, to marginally observant Jewish parents and was only mildly interested in religion growing up. His real passion was for mathematics and engineering, which led to a career in the aerospace industry, working at McDonnell-Douglas on weather and communications satellites and a project to develop "interplanetary handbooks"—charts showing the optimum times to launch flights to Mars and the outer planets. But he gradually became fascinated with Zen Buddhism and developed his practice over time, until it became more important to him than his aerospace work. After years of study with the great Japanese master Maezumi Roshi, Glassman was ordained a Zen priest and in 1980 founded the Zen Center New York.

Almost from the beginning, his Zen practices were controversial. He created a bakery business in a run-down area of Yonkers that became so successful that the Center was able to purchase a $600,000 mansion with the profits. But Glassman also had an innate concern for issues of social justice, instilled in him by his socialist relatives. After a time he sold the mansion with its elegant *zendo,* or meditation hall, and used the money to start a program to create housing for the homeless in the area, while moving the *zendo* to the top floor of the bakery—right next to a noisy all-night bar frequented by prostitutes and drug dealers.

Glassman later established an interfaith center and living quarters for people with HIV/AIDS, founded a Zen Peacemaker Order dedicated to the cause of world peace, and led Zen retreats in the death camps of Auschwitz and Buchenwald. But at the height of his success, even with these unconventional projects, Glassman left the Zen Center and headed west with his wife, also a Zen monk, to set up a new center in Santa Fe. Just a short time after arriving there, Glassman's wife suffered a stroke and died. Glassman took to the road once more, continuing to seek a path that best fit his unique gifts.[10]

Their Unified Message of Ongoing Guidance

Abraham, Jesus, Muhammad, and the Buddha shared an awakening process that is an archetypal journey. The progression they experienced as they moved into their enlightenment corresponds to the stages through which each one of us will pass at one time or another, for it appears that this is the way the journey is written. Even the small fragments of their histories presented here suggest quintessentially human profiles rather than lives that needed no spiritual instruction, introspection, prayer, or self-discipline. And we can find similar profiles in the lives of more recent mystics such as Hilda Charlton and Bernie Glassman. By comparing our own doubts, questions, fears, and reluctance with theirs, we can see that the archetypal road map created by their spiritual awakenings is already at work within us. We may not yet have progressed as far as they, but we are on the same path; they do not exist in some stratosphere impossibly high above us, beyond our reach.

Each of these spiritual masters had a moment in which his soul was called forth and the deeper significance of his life was revealed to him. Each in his own way required guidance and education, and each was brought to a series of "surrender points," tested to see if his faith had become stronger than his need for earthly power. Upon completing these stages of spiritual awakening, they all maintained a profound spiritual practice while teaching those around them. Even after his enlightenment, for instance, the Buddha is said to have continued to meditate daily. Jesus and Muhammad also prayed up until the end of their lives, and Abraham ever performed the rituals of his nascent religious tradition.

Our pathway, like theirs, has assignments and tests, each one part of a spiritual learning process that is meant to help us move through our illusions about the relative merit of external power and inner power. We need never feel either that we have too far to travel or that we have already arrived and can stop practicing the everyday virtues of compassion and mindfulness.

There is one final and most important lesson to be gleaned from observing these lives. Along the way, each spiritual master was contracted to meet not only his most faithful disciples but also those who would bring out his shadows and fears—the "petty tyrants" I mentioned earlier. Each had to experience resistance and betrayal. This is especially true in the case of Jesus, who was betrayed by one of his closest disciples, and Muhammad, who had to wage war against elements of Arabic society that wanted to stop Islam before it spread its radical social reforms. And there is evidence that even the Buddha, who lived a relatively tranquil life of itinerant preaching, had a blind spot regarding the role of women in the spiritual order he sought to establish. He felt that women's sexuality represented a threat to the celibacy and serenity of his monks, and that even if women devoted themselves to the same austere life, they would soon abandon it. So he initially resisted the idea of allowing women to form monastic orders. But his foster mother, Prajapati, who had cared for the Buddha when his own mother died shortly after giving birth, and Ananda, one of his closest disciples, argued the point with him, exposing the Buddha's shadow in this area, and they finally convinced him to accept women as nuns.

The great religious leaders had to find their Sacred Contracts in order to overcome their own limitations, fears, and shadows. You and I may never become fully realized beings, at least in this lifetime, but all we actually need to do is strive to realize our fullest divine potential. That may not be the same potential as that of the masters we've been studying; it may be less, or even more. But it's *our* potential, and that's all that is expected of us.

The lives of these four great spiritual masters provide a road map for charting the stages of your own spiritual transformation. In Chapter 6 we will look at another kind of map, one that charts the structure and flow of energy within your body and spirit through the centers of psychospiritual energy known as the chakras. In Chapter 7 we will work with yet another map in the form of a cosmic wheel that helps you chart the significance of your personal team of archetypes. Together these maps will allow you to interpret the meaning of your Contract and see your life in an entirely new way. But before we go any further, we'll first need to explore the nature of archetypes and their role in your life.

CHAPTER 4

Speaking Archetypes: Your Four Principal Energy Companions

or intimate companions

Archetypes are your energy guides to your highest potential—the fulfillment of the five stages of your Sacred Contract. You have four constant archetypes at work in your life: the Child, Victim, Prostitute, and Saboteur. Now we'll work with these four universal archetypes.

The Child is among the most powerful patterns in our psyches because we are born into it. It is our first state of consciousness. Before Freud, the influence of childhood experiences on psychological and emotional well-being was rarely investigated. In the late twentieth century, that attitude not only changed, it became extreme and even self-indulgent, in my opinion. Most Western societies now attribute adult behavior and motivations to the quality of an individual's childhood. Much blame for aberrant, immoral, or sociopathic actions is off-loaded onto childhood resentments, sadness, and neglect. Judging from the people who have come to see me professionally, validating many people's views of their early experiences can provide a passageway to healing, but it has also often led people to become stuck in their early wounds.

The Child actually has many aspects, including the Wounded or Orphan Child, to which many people relate, and the Magical or Innocent Child, among others. Engagement with the Magical Child is rare, but it is pure delight to be in the company of someone who radiates that archetype. Sir George Trevelyan, who has been called the "father of the New Age movement" in England, was such a person. Educated in the Old World tradition at Cambridge, George was the quintessential Victorian gentleman—eccentric, deep-voiced, and captivatingly dramatic. Although his father had expected him to follow family tradition and pursue a career in academics, George was consumed early on by an interest in spirituality and alternative healing. His entire life was a mythic journey in which he explored the nature of human consciousness. He consciously lived in two realms, the physical and the spiritual. He spoke about having conversations with nature spirits and wind sprites, garden spirits and angels, making this type of interrealm dialogue seem exactly what it should be—natural. Although I tend to be skeptical of people making such claims, I believed Sir George because of his matter-of-fact attitude, selflessness, and innocence—he never demanded that others acknowledge what he described as his world.

I met Sir George on New Year's Eve 1982 at the Findhorn Community in Scotland, when he was in his early seventies. Thereafter he and I presented several workshops together during the 1980s in different parts of England, and each one was an adventure into his alternate reality. One time he took me to the place that is believed to be the mythical home of Camelot and Avalon, and he spoke about the Knights of the Round Table as if he knew them on a first-name basis—and by this time in our relationship, I would have believed he did. The most memorable scene in which George's Magical Child stepped into action took place in 1986 at a workshop we did in a classic English manor house. As we were lecturing to a group of people, George suddenly stopped speaking and focused his attention on the back of the room. I hesitated for a moment and then, knowing that I might be opening us all for a real surprise, asked him, "What are you looking at?"

"Why," he replied, "the god Pan has just decided to join us." Immediately everyone turned to the back of the room, but all they saw was the wall, not the mythic Greek god of the forest, half man, half goat, with cloven hooves and two horns on his head. "So what does he want?" I asked George.

"He simply wants to join in on the fun."

"Well, tell him he's welcome to stay with us as long as he likes," I said. George laughed with delight and went back to teaching. I, on the other hand, kept staring at the back of the room, hoping that I could catch even a glimpse of this god who had decided to honor us with his presence. I didn't see a thing, yet as I watched George inspire the group while reading them his favorite poetry, I realized that I had made my own spiritual work too serious. Although the intense demands of my own spirit repeatedly affirm that I am in touch with another dimension, George showed me that the process of working with our spirits should be magical. He helped many others open to their own personal gods and energy companions, allowing magic back into their lives, through his knightly, enchanting views and teachings.

That evening over dinner I asked George how it was that he could see Pan and the spirits of the nature kingdom. "Oh, that's easy," he said. "I look through the imagination of my inner Child. All children can see into that world when they are very young. The door between worlds closes as you get older and begin to believe that there is no such thing." For George, this archetype and its imaginative world had become a companion.

In the Beginning

Sir George was an extraordinary character, but his experience is not unique. Others throughout history have been aware of the living presence of archetypes and been comfortable discussing them and discoursing with them. In ancient Greece Plato asserted the existence of archetypal Ideas or Forms as the centerpiece of his philosophical view of the world. As the intellectual historian Richard Tarnas points out, "Platonic Forms are not conceptual abstractions that the human mind creates by generalizing from a class of particulars. Rather, they possess a quality of being, a degree of reality that is superior to that of the concrete world. Platonic archetypes form the world and also stand beyond it. They manifest themselves within time and yet are timeless. They constitute the veiled essence of things."[1] According to Tarnas, Plato often saw the gods and goddesses of Greek tradition as symbols of universal patterns of emotion. In his *Symposium*, for instance, Plato envisioned Eros, the Greek god of love, as "a complex and multidimensional archetype which at the physical level expresses itself in the sexual instinct, but at higher levels impels the philosopher's passion for intellectual beauty and wisdom, and culminates in the mystical vision of the eternal, the ultimate source of all beauty."[2]

As we have seen, the great Swiss psychologist Carl Jung was the first to define and explore extensively the nature and role of universal archetypes in human consciousness.[3] By their very nature, Jung explained, archetypes have their origins in the dawn of human history. "The psyche is not of today," he wrote, "its ancestry goes back many millions of years. Individual consciousness is only the flower and the fruit of a season, sprung from the perennial rhizome beneath the earth."[4] Jung tied archetypes inextricably to his concept of the collective unconscious, which is distinct from the individual unconscious. The collective unconscious is the inherited experience of the entire human race. Your consciousness is affected by this greater unconscious, and yours also makes a contribution to the collective. Echoing Plato, Jung defined archetypes as "definite forms in the psyche that seem to be present always and everywhere."

Jung's best-known disciple, Joseph Campbell, wrote that "since archetypes or norms of myth are common to the human species, they are inherently expressive . . . of common human needs, instincts, and potentials."[5] When Jung propounded his theory of archetypes, he had been steeping himself in the mythology and folklore of the world, from the Egyptians, Babylonians, and Greeks to the Gnostics and American Indians.

> Just as some kind of analytical technique is needed to understand a dream, so a knowledge of mythology is needed in order to grasp the meaning of a content deriving from the deeper levels of the psyche. . . . The collective unconscious—so far as we can say anything about it at all— appears to consist of mythological motifs or primordial images, for which reason the myths of all nations are its real exponents. In fact, the whole of mythology could be taken as a sort of projection of the collective unconscious.[6]

Volumes have since been written about archetypes. Clarissa Pinkola Estés, Jean Shinoda Bolen, Robert Bly, and many other authors have made immense contributions to this vast subject. Drawing on an apparently limitless supply of myths and folktales from disparate cultures around the globe, these writers have identified hundreds of archetypal patterns that have a significant effect on our daily lives and relationships. Their work implies that although archetypes are patterns of influence that are both ancient and universal, they become quite personalized when they are a part of an individual's own psyche. Since your Sacred Contract is embodied in a support system of twelve archetypes, perhaps the most advantageous way to think of them is as intimate companions.

Actually the nature of your archetypes is both intimate and impersonal. Viewed through the heart, they are personal enough to be called companions. Viewed with the mind, they are impersonal, symbolic patterns that serve in the energetic organization of your spiritual evolution. As I say in my workshops, a personal experience filtered through an impersonal or symbolic attitude creates a vastly different psychic chemistry from taking everything personally. Just as your archetypes have a dual nature, you too have the constant challenge of holding within yourself a personal heart and a symbolic mind.

Don't misinterpret this statement to mean that all relationships and life experiences will be simple and painless if you just treat your interactions impersonally and impassively. That, of course, is nonsense. What we need to do is make conscious choices and take responsibility for ourselves, including our thoughts and attitudes. Working with your archetypal patterns is the best way I know to become conscious of yourself, the effects of your actions, and the need for choosing wisely every day.

The Four Archetypes of Survival:
Child, Victim, Prostitute, Saboteur

Current attitudes hold that our characters and personalities are formed during childhood through a combination of nature and nurture. Indeed, during the first two decades of life we make our first promises to ourselves to provide for and protect ourselves. Many people have told me that as adolescents they promised themselves they would never be physically abused or humiliated again. Children make vows to themselves that they will become scientists, artists, or mothers or simply find a way to become wealthy. These commitments are part of our path in the physical world. All are influenced by the four primary archetypes.

During the first years of our lives, we come to realize that the quality of our physical lives depends on our sense of personal power, on our ability to survive. Long before we become emotionally and spiritually empowered, we must engage our personal power in the material world. We also begin to understand that we must deal with moral issues or suffer the consequences. In engaging with the physical world and the moral choices that present themselves, we develop self-esteem. This is the beginning of spiritual maturity.

The four primary archetypes—the Child, Victim, Prostitute, and Saboteur—symbolize our major life challenges and how we choose to survive. Together they represent the issues, fears, and vulnerabilities that cause us to negotiate away the power of our spirits within the physical world. They also can come to represent spiritual strengths for dealing with real-life and spiritual issues. These four archetypes are like the four legs of a table on which our Sacred Contract rests. The table legs represent our relationship to the ground beneath our feet and to the universal energy that supports our life. They might be straight or curved or embellished with carvings and images, depending on how these four archetypes work within our psyches during the course of our lives. But they need to be stable to support the weight of the tabletop—our life and mission.

All four archetypes influence how we relate to material power, how we respond to authority, and how we make choices. These archetypal energies are neutral, and I must reinforce that point here because of the connotations of their names. Although it can be difficult to see how the Victim, Prostitute, and Saboteur can provide us with powerful and supportive imagery, they do and you will. You'll come to see how even the most common variant of the Child archetype, the Wounded Child, can help you deal with your life today.

These four archetypes are the intimate companions of your intuition. They make you conscious of your vulnerabilities, your fear of being victimized. They allow you to see how you sabotage your creative opportunities or abort your dreams, and in the future they will become your allies in fulfilling opportunities and dreams. Your archetypes will become your guardians and will preserve your integrity, refusing to allow you to negotiate it away under any circumstance. Your archetypes can help you transcend the shadow belief that "everyone has a price" and allow you to see that you are not for sale. They will allow you to become completely self-reliant; through them you will come to see options where others see excuses.

The richest reward in working with these survival archetypes, however, reveals itself in the manner in which your Contract unfolds. While it is a given that you have Contracts to meet certain people, it is not determined ahead of time what kind of interaction you will have with each of them. That is up to you and, of course, to them. You can choose how you interact, but the more conscious you are about the patterns that influence your behavior, the more likely it is that your choices—and the lessons you get from them—will be positive. If your choices are formed only by your unconscious, however, and you are unaware of the archetypal energies influencing you, you will more likely act out of insecurity and defensiveness. By remaining aware of the archetypal energies, you stay conscious of both your divinity and your potential *and* the everyday world. Through your archetypes, you will find your own Middle Way, the path of your Sacred Contract.

The Child: Guardian of Innocence

The Child archetype is our beginning point. We most easily identify with the Child, especially after several decades of popular books and workshops on the inner Child. This archetype establishes our perceptions of life, safety, nurturing, loyalty, and family. Its many aspects include the Wounded Child, the Abandoned or Orphan Child, the Dependent Child, the Innocent Child, the Nature Child, and the Divine Child. These energies may emerge in response to different situations in which we find ourselves, yet the core issue of all the Child archetypes is dependency and responsibility: when to take responsibility, when to have a healthy dependency, when to stand up to the group, and when to embrace communal life. The stages of growing up, from coming to the age of reason at about seven, to entering adolescence at around thirteen, to reaching the official age of adulthood at twenty-one, represent plateaus of spiritual and physical maturation. When we are completely dependent, from birth to age seven, we develop the first skills for taking care of ourselves, our bodies, and our possessions. At age seven, we begin learning what it means to be responsible not just for our belongings but for our actions and deeds as well. Through ages seven to thirteen we develop further emotionally, as we are introduced to larger issues of morality, ethics, loyalty, and the rules of relationships.

During adolescence we become self-aware, self-conscious, and self-centered. We become aware of—if not consumed with—the power of our mind, the pull of our heart, and the passion of our body. During these wild years images of all that you could be or all that you fear you will never become also step to the fore. During your late teens and early twenties, you discover your vulnerabilities as an adult along with your strengths and talents. You make substantial choices about your life, and even though you will doubtless change your mind many times, or circumstances will reroute you, this is the beginning of your real contact with the world of physical responsibility separate from your tribe. Finally, the power of the spirit emerges around the age of twenty-one, as you begin to see beyond the physical aspect of life to find symbolic meaning in your actions, from political activism and social idealism to love and spiritual exploration. Around age twenty-eight you naturally transition into the next cycle of your life as an interconnected, responsible adult.

The process that I have just described is, of course, how we ideally mature. Because of the complex challenges of everyday life, however, this spiritual maturation varies for most people. From an archetypal point of view, when these cycles are not followed in some way, adults will find it difficult if not impossible to be responsible for themselves in the physical world and to create successful relationships. Your inner Child will exhibit aspects of the Wounded or Orphan Child and will reflect that, somewhere along the line, you did not receive the nurturing necessary for you to become responsible and independent. And so you may well spend the early years of adulthood trying to heal and compensate for these deficiencies.

Confronting the Child archetype within you awakens a new relationship with life, a fresh beginning. Regardless of which aspect of the Child you relate to most intimately, this archetypal pattern brings you into contact with the untapped resources connected to creative thought. This is the core of the Innocent Child—the sensation that anything and everything is possible.

As the guardian of your innocence, the Child helps heal, repair, and put a stop to the inner-directed abuse of the Wounded Child. If you are consumed with the Wounded, Neglected, Abandoned, or Orphan Child's psyche, you need to identify—or initiate—a new relationship or creative enterprise that makes you appreciate your life. Ask your Child what it needs in order to heal or feel nurtured or cared for. The Child often inspires you to act outside restrictive boundaries or to explore an adventure without the burdensome weights of the adult mind. Indulge some of these inspirations as a means of making contact with your inner Child. Don't become overattached to the wound, however; don't overindulge the Child so that it becomes an inner brat. But give it the support it needs to grow up.

Ollie's Story: Boy, Interrupted

When children are forced to take on more responsibility than they should have to at an early age, their spiritual development is disrupted. An adult who feels that he never had a childhood can feel resentful or bitter either toward his parents or about life in general. We suffer deeply when we are deprived of those precious years when we are meant to live in our imagination, between the realms of fantasy and reality. Native American tribes such as the Hopi believe that it takes a spirit seven years to incarnate fully into physical form. During that time the child is watched over and cared for by his guardian spirits, who then turn the primary care of the child's imagination over to the parents. Fairy tales, folk stories, and traditional lore about Santa Claus, the Easter Bunny, and the Tooth Fairy are meant to preserve children's sense of wonder. Without a connection to the fantastic, magical realm, hopes and dreams are hard to envision.

At age six Ollie arrived home from first grade to discover that his mother had left for good. Even Ollie's father was shocked, because his wife had not given any indication that she was miserable enough to take flight. Suddenly Ollie was charged with helping take care of his four-year-old twin sisters. Instead of being allowed to play with his friends after school, Ollie had to color or play games with his sisters as a stand-in for a baby-sitter. As the years went by, his responsibilities around the home increased. By age ten he was preparing meals, cleaning house, and doing the laundry.

"My father did the best he could given the circumstances," Ollie said. "He came home straight from work and tried to spend as much time with us as he could. But he was tired and had his own share of caretaking to do. Sometimes he would give me the old 'you have to be the man of the house' routine and then apologize that things could not be different. But I hated every minute of it. I couldn't play baseball in the summer or sports during the school year, because I was never sure if I could make practice or the game. I don't even remember now what it felt like to be a child."

Ollie's childhood had a profound effect on both his professional and personal life. His job as a computer software vendor included occasional travel. "About a year into this job," he said, "I started to add an extra day here and there on my trips without letting my boss know. I felt that I deserved it, because I was putting so much time into my work. I didn't realize it then, but I was doing this to get back to my childhood. I wanted to 'go out and play,' and this is the way I did it."

In time Ollie's "extra day" habit was discovered, and he was fired. He had married at age twenty-two and now, at twenty-eight, he was unemployed and his wife had to support the household. "I told her that finding another job would not be a problem, since everything in this world is connected to computers. I started looking for a job a few days after I left the old one, but I couldn't find one that seemed right for me. The weeks of being unemployed turned into months, and my wife was getting increasingly frustrated with me. I think she was picking up the fact that I did not want to go back to work. I liked being supported and taken care of. I told her I was trying my best, but I wasn't really trying at all."

Ollie's wife eventually presented him with an ultimatum: either find a job or move out. "It was one of those ultimatums that no matter which end I chose, I would have to find a job," he said. Ollie did go back to work, again selling computers, but whatever ambition he had at his previous job was now replaced by resentment. "I was angry going to work, being at work, and coming home from work. I had no place to run anymore, and finally I had a breakdown."

Ollie entered therapy and with the help of his counselor began to excavate his inner Child. "I discovered so much about myself. I knew that I had regrets about my early years, but I never imagined how consumed I was by my feelings of abandonment. I realized that my psyche ordered my life around my feeling that I had been abandoned by my mother and forced to take her place. And the irony was that, as an adult, I was now abandoning my responsibilities just as my mother had. I wanted to experience now what should have been a part of my life then. I now wonder if my mom had a missing childhood as well and left us to find that part of herself. When I think of her in that way, I feel compassion for her, because I doubt that she could ever understand the real source of her pain. My Abandoned Child was so active in my psyche that it ordered everything in my life."

The Victim: Guardian of Self-Esteem

Being a Victim is a common fear. The Victim archetype may manifest the first time you don't get what you want or need; are abused by a parent, playmate, sibling, or teacher; or are accused of or punished for something you didn't do. You may suppress your outrage at the injustice if the victimizer is bigger and more powerful than you. But at a certain point you discover a perverse advantage to being the Victim. You may be afraid to stand up for yourself, or you may enjoy getting sympathy. The core issue of the Victim is whether it's worth giving up your own sense of empowerment to avoid taking responsibility for your independence.

Many people in my workshops have described their Victim as their most vulnerable aspect. "I felt that I was set up to be a victim," said Tim, "because I was taught never to fight back, but to avoid conflict. Avoiding conflict is certainly the wiser path, but only when you know you can stand up for yourself if you need to. Otherwise you are running away, and I have always felt that I was running away from something or someone. One time when I was shopping, the salesperson gave me the wrong change. I had given her a fifty-dollar bill, but she handed me change for a twenty. Yet I stood there saying nothing. I told myself that I didn't want to embarrass her, so I walked out of the store. As soon as I made it to the street, I almost exploded in anger at myself. Once again I had allowed myself to be victimized. I saw it happen, and I just stood by and allowed myself to get ripped off. And to make this situation worse, even when I told myself to go back in there and get the right change, I managed to talk myself out of it by saying they would never believe my story of the invisible fifty-dollar bill."

Eventually Tim realized that he had to confront this Victim energy, because the quality of his life depended on it. "I knew that as long as I could not or did not protect myself, I would always feel like a victim of something or other. And even if I were not being victimized, there would come a time when I would no longer be able to tell the difference. I made a commitment to myself to act in behalf of my own well-being no matter how uncomfortable it made those around me.

"I soon learned that every action one takes after making a choice to protect oneself is a major action. One time when I was at work, a guy asked me if I would run his errands for him. I had always said yes to him in the past, but this time I said no. Both of us stood looking at each other; I had shocked him as much as I'd surprised myself. I told him that I was not responsible for seeing that his work got done. A few weeks later I noticed him as he was walking toward me down the hall. He got a smirk on his face and commented, 'Don't worry, I'm not going to ask you to do my job.' The moment he said that, all I could feel was respect for myself, and I knew from that point on that I could protect myself, not only because I could respond honestly, but also because I knew I could live with the consequences of my honesty."

The Victim archetype had come full circle within Tim's psyche, from being a symbol of weakness to being a reminder of his own strength. When he thinks of the Victim now, he does not think in powerless terms but measures what he will or will not do so that he never again feels taken advantage of. As Tim puts it, "The Victim archetype is the guardian of my personal boundaries. Before, what I recognized as personal boundaries were more like self-inflicted prison walls. It's amazing how your world changes when you feel that you can take care of yourself."

The lessons associated with the Victim archetype demand that you evaluate your relationship to power, particularly in your interactions with people with whom you have control issues and need to construct personal boundaries.

The primary objective of the Victim archetype is to develop self-esteem and personal power. When you are in a situation in which you feel threatened or you suspect that you lack the appropriate social, professional, or personal power, take notice of that reaction physically, emotionally, and mentally. That is the intuitive voice of your inner Victim. To help direct your responses to all of your experiences and relationships, say "I am committed to my own empowerment. What choice can I make here that will serve my own empowerment?" Name the problem or threat you need to overcome and the power that you need to possess in order to do so. Keep your eye on the truth that everything and everyone in your life is there by Contract to assist in your spiritual maturation.

You have Contracts with people who are directly connected to the Victim archetype. Their primary role is to help you develop your self-esteem through acts of honesty, integrity, courage, endurance, and self-respect. Those people whose Contracts are linked to empowering your Victim will play, or have played, the leading roles in awakening in you an awareness of the value of these spiritual qualities and how essential they are to your well-being.

The Prostitute: Guardian of Faith

The act of prostitution is generally associated with selling one's body for money, but to my mind that is perhaps the least significant example of the Prostitute archetype. The Prostitute thrives most bountifully in subtle ways and in ordinary, everyday circumstances. It comes into play most clearly when our survival is threatened. Its core issue is how much you are willing to sell of yourself—your morals, your integrity, your intellect, your word, your body, or your soul—for the sake of physical security. The Prostitute archetype also dramatically embodies and tests the power of faith. If you have faith, no one can buy you. You know that you can take care of yourself and also that the Divine is looking out for you. Without faith, however, you will eventually meet the price you cannot turn down.

The majority of Prostitutes that I have met and continue to meet are men and women who are either in bad marriages or in miserable jobs. Their inability to move out of their toxic environments is totally tied to economics. Women have told me that they do not want to be middle-aged and single, or lose their social status, or have to support themselves, and so they stay in unhappy marriages. Men tell me this too, but not nearly as often, and both men and women say that they remain in jobs that make them miserable or sick, violate their ethics, or make them feel bad about themselves for the sake of financial security.

Many people tell me how unhappy they are and that they are waiting for just the right moment in their lives to make the "big break" and follow their dreams. Most often, these are the people who ask again and again, "But what *exactly* is my Contract? If I only knew, I could get on with it." These people are actually hoping that I can direct them on a path that will guarantee them money and peace of mind. They want to hear that their Contract will give them all the time in the world, all the money they need while doing only what they want, a cabin retreat in the woods, and last but not least a soulmate. They also never want to age. (The energies and expectations of Prostitute, Child, and Victim *all* have to be addressed!)

All power, whether from lottery winnings or spiritual visions, will draw to you some outside opponent who will try to buy, use, or contaminate you. When Jesus was met by Satan as he prayed and fasted in the desert, Satan offered to give him the entire physical world in exchange for the power Jesus now had within him. Likewise, every time you take one step on your path of personal empowerment, you will meet someone who will want to buy a piece of your soul to render you less powerful and themselves more powerful.

A shadow characteristic of the human psyche in general is that we want to find the shortcuts in life, including shortcuts to our own empowerment. If we spot someone whose power appears as if it could be bought or shared, we will be attracted to it. A perfect example is the game of "name wealth" ("I am a friend of a friend of Mr. or Ms. Famous"). The diluted energy that comes down this path of who's who is, for many, valuable enough for them to remain in a relationship long past the time the friendship has grown cold—another expression of the Prostitute archetype.

Confronting the Prostitute within you transforms this archetype into your guardian. It will watch over your relationship to faith. Think

of the Prostitute as the ally who puts you on alert every time you contemplate shifting your faith from the Divine to the physical. Anytime
you are in a crisis of faith, try to become mindful of your thoughts and
fears. Name exactly what you are afraid of, especially those fears that
try to talk you into compromising yourself in any way. The Prostitute
appears when you begin to believe that you could order your life if you
just had the money to control the world around you—and to buy just
a bit of everyone in it. It appears when you stay in a relationship that is
not good for you just because you don't want to be alone. It appears
when you're asked to do something unethical or illegal "for the good
of the company." People who are meant to bring out the Prostitute in
you represent your most painful relationships. Because Prostitute
interactions make us confront our fears of survival, they are often terrifying and humiliating.

A woman named Belinda told me that once she became conscious
of the fact that she had a Prostitute archetype, she saw it everywhere.
"I am one of those millions of people who thought of a prostitute as
someone selling sex. Never did I think that I could apply that title to
myself. But I'm noticing that even when asked an opinion at lunch
about anything from someone's new shoes to a different office policy, I
run it by my 'What's this gonna cost me?' screen. If I think an opinion
is going to cost me in terms of popularity or office politics, I pass. I
often say things that earn me points, even when I don't believe a word
of them. After I told one executive that I thought his ideas were brilliant, I was consumed by an overwhelming urge to wash my mouth
out with soap. But he has the kind of power that can make things happen in my life. I guess what I'm saying here is that I am still a practicing Prostitute, but I've come a distance because at least I'm honest
about it. I fully admit that I don't have enough faith to put my
integrity before my mortgage and my spiritual direction before my
promotions in the physical world."

Although I've been talking about figurative, symbolic prostitution, I have also met working prostitutes in my seminars. Ronnie had
developed AIDS as a result of his work as a prostitute, and during a
private conversation with me and his brother he described all the healing methods he was using to bring about a change in his condition—
except for one thing. He was unable to stop working in the sex

industry. "This is the world I know, and I have no idea how I would support myself if I stopped going to the bars," he said. "I realize that this is not helping me heal, but I don't think I have a choice."

I asked Ronnie if he informed his clients that he had the illness, and after first saying that he did, he finally admitted that he didn't always. "If the word got out, and it would," he said, "I would not be able to work." Asked why he started in this profession in the first place, Ronnie replied, "I wanted to get into acting and nothing opened up, so I had to do something. And sex is no big deal to me. Hell, I was sleeping around anyway, so why not get paid for it? Besides, it was instant money and I was on my own time."

Sadly, Ronnie's brother was also a prostitute who had AIDS. Together they felt that they needed to save a lot of money to provide the type of care they needed to heal this illness, or at least delay its progress. But as I listened to them, I realized that they were actually describing the kind of care they would need as they were dying. I got the impression that their Prostitute archetypes were like Siamese twins, and that the collective force of their energies, combined with the loyalty they felt for each other, demanded that they both quit the street, because it was impossible for one to go it alone. Both Ronnie and his brother passed away in the autumn of 1991.

The Prostitute archetype can act as a guardian that awakens you to situations in which you must decide to "take up your bed and walk." Once you get away from a circumstance that costs you too much—money, energy, dignity, or time—lasting transformation is possible. June worked as a high-powered executive secretary for the president of a major multinational corporation. She was extremely good at her job and had a vibrant, gracious personality, which her boss, Dorian, learned to use to his advantage. A few months into the job, Dorian invited her to join a group of executives at a cocktail party celebrating their new client. He noticed how well she mingled and how quickly she could put people at ease. June was asked to attend more and more social events and was asked to explain to valued employees or clients why the company needed to make certain decisions. She became, in her language, "a secret weapon that got launched in whatever direction was necessary for the company to get what it wanted."

One day another secretary approached June and asked her what it was like to attend all those social functions. "I told her it was nice," June told me, "but then she asked me if I was expected to do anything at these functions. 'Like what?' I asked her. She gave me that 'you know what I mean' look, and in that instant I realized that I was being used by these men for their financial gain. That was the first and last time I would ever be made to feel like a prostitute."

The next day June "exploded" into her boss's office and resigned. "And I didn't just resign," she said. "I let him know what a pimp he was, and I kept the door open so that everyone in the office could hear what I had to say to this guy."

Nonetheless June was grateful for her experience at this firm. "I learned how easily I could be used," she said. "What I had thought was being supportive and social had totally different implications. My boss had an agenda that I didn't see. Now I think very carefully about what I agree to do for someone, and I remind myself that I can say no as well as yes."

⚹ The Saboteur: Guardian of Choice

Like the Prostitute and the Victim, the Saboteur archetype is a neutral energy within you that usually makes itself known through disruption. It can sabotage your efforts to be happy and successful if you are not aware of the patterns of thought and behavior that it raises in you. It can cause you to resist opportunities. The Saboteur is the mirror that reflects your fears of taking responsibility for yourself and for what you create.

The Saboteur archetype may be the one most intimately connected to your ability to survive in the physical world. Fears of being without the basic needs in life—from food to home to a social and personal network—often provide this archetype with the power to haunt you. You can silence the Saboteur with acts of courage and by following your intuition. It serves you brilliantly as a gut instinct that directs you to take action based on hunches rather than on rational thought. To learn to experience that voice, you must respond to it. Only through response can you manifest the courage to expand your creative environment. Start with small choices, which may be life-transforming acts of will disguised as harmless impulses.

The core issue for the Saboteur is fear of inviting change into — your life, change that requires responding in a positive way to opportunities to shape and deepen your spirit. Yet it is impossible to stop the process of change. Deep in your tissue, you know that having power and using it necessitates change. And although many people want to have it all, they don't want to *be* all. All choices you make *do not* have the same potential to transform the environment of your life. The decision to meet a group of friends for dinner, as a rule, does not change your life as dramatically as the decision to get married, start a business, or move to Europe. The choice to respond to an inner voice that directs you to pursue your spiritual life is obviously one that can rearrange your familiar world.

"I am a great one to sabotage my self-esteem," Erin said. "Instead of saying thank you to someone who pays me a compliment, I deflect the kind words being offered. I am forever discounting my talents. But this self-sabotage is the worst in my partnership. I have a wonderful partner, and when he tells me that he loves me or that he thinks I'm lovely, I tell him he's crazy. That's about as close as you can come to behavior that is directly trying to sabotage a relationship. He has challenged me on several occasions, asking me why I don't believe him when he tells me how he feels. I told him that I feel I am giving him a break, kind of like telling him he doesn't have to do any acting to make me feel good. It's a lethal pattern that came right out of my shadow Saboteur.

"Now I am practicing to be conscious of when I'm shortchanging myself, and I compliment myself all the time. It sounds like a game, but I'm not playing at all. I feel that the Saboteur is now my chess partner, sitting right across the table from me. Every move I make, I look across that table to study the response. I am determined not to stand in the way of all that my life can be with my partner. Our life together is part of my highest potential, which means having the experience of wife and mother with someone I truly adore."

Living in the Shadow

Although our archetypal patterns are essentially neutral, they do have both light and shadow aspects. The word *shadow* itself suggests a dark, secretive, possibly malevolent countenance that looms in the background of our nature, ready to do harm to others as well as to ourselves. A much more appropriate understanding of the shadow aspects of our archetypes, however, is that they represent the part of our being that is least familiar to our conscious mind. "Whether the shadow becomes our friend or enemy depends largely upon ourselves," wrote Marie-Louise von Franz, Jung's closest colleague and confidante. "The shadow is not necessarily always an opponent. In fact, [it] is exactly like any human being with whom one has to get along, sometimes by giving in, sometimes by resisting, sometimes by giving love—whatever the situation requires. The shadow becomes hostile only when [it] is ignored or misunderstood."[7]

The Queen is among my own personal family of archetypes, for example, and it serves me quite well when I'm teaching a workshop. I have to be certain that everything I need so that I can work at my peak is ready when I need it, from my travel accommodations to the white board I write on, even a cup of tea with honey to soothe my throat from all the talking. My Queen makes darn sure everything is just as it's supposed to be—or heads will roll. But at other times, when I least expect it, my shadow Queen can make an appearance and start demanding things in an inappropriate way. Often I'm not aware of my Queen's agenda until after she's come and gone; it remains "in the shadow" until I take a good look at whatever damage it may have done.

I'll never forget the time I blew up at a couple of airline ticket agents because my flight had been delayed and I felt they weren't being straight with us passengers. As I stormed off in disgust, a young couple who had been waiting in line behind me caught my eye and came over. I thought they were going to thank me for speaking out, but instead the man said, "We just wanted to tell you how much we love your workshops."

"Yes," the woman said, "we have all your books and tapes."

I wanted to tell them that they'd just seen a textbook example of the shadow Queen in action, but I was too humiliated to say anything. I just thanked them and kept on walking. It was about what I'd deserved for attacking a couple of airline employees who were probably just doing their jobs.

The shadow aspects of our archetypes are fed by our paradoxical relationship to power. We are as intimidated by being empowered as we are by being disempowered. That disempowerment is a threat to our well-being is easy to understand, at least at the surface level. But why should we also fear becoming empowered? That, in essence, is the paradox that feeds the shadow. The shadow can be seen as unexplored power. It expresses itself through behavior that often sabotages our express wishes and image of ourselves. These complex aspects of our personalities filter into our behavior by outwitting our conscious minds, after which they often assume a dominant role. We frequently don't know why we do the things we do, or why we have to cope with inexplicable fears. This leads to painful conflict when we feel one way and act another, separating mind and heart.

Living with mind and heart divided is like having two battle encampments within, each one fighting for authority over our power of choice. When isolated from each other, the heart and mind are each handicapped; the mind tends to become hyperrational, and the heart, overly emotional. This imbalance of forces fragments our power. And like a nation in which opposing forces are constantly at war with each other, when our nature is fragmented, it is vulnerable to being dominated by fear. As Jesus said, "If a kingdom is divided against itself, it cannot stand" (Mark 3:24).

Even when we know we are acting fearfully, we sometimes choose to be willfully ignorant about it. If I don't know why I am acting in a negative fashion, then it is easier to excuse my behavior or blame someone else. But if I *am* aware both emotionally and intellectually that I am harming another being, I not only have to hold myself accountable, I must also admit that I consciously chose to be negative. I can no longer hide behind the state of confusion created by the split between heart and mind.

As long as your mind and heart lack a channel of clear communication, you will be confused about what to do with your life. Inevitably, as soon as you make contact with your life's passion—which can mean finding your vocation, your life partner, or even your sexual identity—you are going to experience a kind of spiritual suffering until you act on that passion. That suffering is actually a form of divine motivation, urging you to pursue a more authentic life.

Awareness of a greater truth adds time pressure to your psyche and spirit, because the more you know, the faster you need to respond to that truth. I call this *spiritual accountability*. If you realize that negative judgments, including judging yourself, cause harm, then you must reevaluate your behavior as soon as you realize that you are being judgmental. You also need to recognize when you are justifying yourself and your actions. Judging others and creating excuses while knowing better are only two of the spiritual challenges that will arise as you work with your survival archetypes. The more aware you are of the demands of managing your consciousness, the fewer hiding places will be available in your psyche and soul for the shadow play of the Child, Victim, Prostitute, and Saboteur. This relationship between awareness and responsibility also applies to your health. Once you become aware of how toxic anger or guilt is to your body and spirit, the consequences of these energy poisons become more pronounced than if you did not know better—if for no other reason than that you now know their biological effects. This is negative visualization in action.

The Shadow and Your Divine Potential

Jesus said to his disciples, about his miraculous healing abilities, "All this shall you do and more, if you have faith." The Buddha's enlightenment not only allowed him to view his past lives going back aeons but to become omniscient as well. Yet he also told his followers that with diligence they too could achieve enlightenment, and he urged them to "be lamps unto yourselves." These enlightened beings saw our highest potential as virtually unlimited. They were not necessarily referring to learning how to walk on water or effect miraculous cures, however, but to the fact that we can become as trusting of the Divine as they. The Buddha, for example, insisted that his followers discover who they would be if they called their spirits back from attaching to the illusions of the external world. And Jesus said, "Unto you it is given to know the mystery of the kingdom of God. . . . Do you bring in a lamp to put it under a bushel or a bed? Instead, don't you put it on its stand? For whatever is hidden is meant to be disclosed, and whatever is concealed is meant to be brought out into the open" (Mark 4:11, 21–22).

To engage in the journey that takes us from living outside of ourselves to processing the world inside ourselves means bringing light to our shadow. Your shadow aspects are primarily rooted in fear patterns that have more control over your behavior than does your conscious mind. This limits your ability to make choices in which you are aware of your motivations.

Your shadow self includes emotional and psychological patterns that come from repressed feelings that you do not wish to deal with consciously for fear of the consequences. For example, rather than face the fact that your partner is in some kind of trouble or your child is using drugs, you may repress those strong, accurate instincts— possibly with disastrous results. And you may become short-tempered, angry, and depressed without realizing why.

Your shadow also contains the secret reasons why you would sabotage the opportunities that come your way. People often tell me they have a fear of success. When I ask them to explain where that fear came from, many draw a blank. They have no idea why they have that fear, they just do. Having an unknown force controlling so much of the creative expression of our lives is a shadow. Eventually we have to confront each of our shadow aspects. This exploration into our shadows is so complex that it may be one reason why Eastern philosophy maintains that we need many lifetimes to achieve liberation.

Your highest potential, then, is that part of you that is not limited in its expression by the fears of the physical world and the business of living. It is what you actualize when you are willing to confront your shadow, openly acknowledge the reality of its presence within you, and then take steps to deal with it. To rely on your inner resources and to follow your inner guidance before all else is to express your highest potential at all times. It shows you who you would be if you could live constantly within the knowledge that genuine power exists inside the self and never outside of it.

Confronting your shadow requires that you strike out on your own. That isn't to say that you can't receive help from friends, therapists, and wise counselors, but you will have to make choices that exclude the collective needs of your family, tribe, or group, and separate yourself from them. If you do decide to follow an inner call and its unavoidable psychic ritual of separation, you have to withdraw your spirit from the magnetic field created by the collective power of your group's will so that you can organize your own energy, much as a mystic or seer might withdraw to hear divine promptings—like Jesus going into the desert or Muhammad to the cave of Mount Hira. This process of birthing your own power requires that you put yourself first, even though this may appear to the outside world to be "selfish."

During your separation you will have to face the most narcissistic aspects of your ego, such as the shadow Child, who is concerned only with its own well-being and will try to scare you back into the fold. Your shadow Victim, meanwhile, revels in its victimhood and will entice you to feel sorry for yourself for ever leaving. The shadow Prostitute will urge you to sell out your integrity and your vision of true independence at the first opportunity. And the shadow Saboteur will play to your suspicions that you just aren't good enough to accomplish anything on your own. You will have to strengthen your soul identity until it is strong enough to eclipse all these fears. You are birthing your power of individual choice, increasing your potential for insight and for opportunities serving your highest potential. In dealing with the shadows, you ready yourself to accept full responsibility for the management of your spirit and the consequences of your choices.

gloria and
the rooms in the castle

Shadow Contracts

Just as your archetypes are neither good nor bad, so too your Sacred Contract is essentially a neutral force. One person's Contract is not more important to the universe than another's. Every Contract is essentially the same in that it covers what each individual needs to learn in his lifetime. For that reason we are put in places and in roles that best serve our Contracts, whether that means we are born into royalty or poverty or somewhere in between. Whether you find yourself in a life filled with challenges such as serious illness, injury, or war, or whether your life is relatively free of trauma, you will have agree-

not "do"

ments to keep and a Contract to fulfill. As the Tibetan Buddhist teacher Sogyal Rinpoche likes to say, "There is poor people's suffering and rich people's suffering. Don't envy others, because you can't know the extent of their suffering just by looking at externals." Whatever your material lot in life, any external difficulties are vehicles for you to work on your internal challenges. On some levels it's obviously much easier to be rich than poor, but even the prosperous cannot sidestep their inner challenges—or their Appointment in Samarra.

In this regard people often ask me if a Contract can include an agreement to commit murder, rape, or other heinous crimes. Could Hitler, Stalin, Mao, or Pol Pot have had Contracts to murder millions of people? Questions about such enormous villainy are difficult to answer, but no, these criminals did not have a divine order to kill. It may be that some people have agreed to a life in which they encounter dark forces and have to choose how to deal with them. As each of us is growing individually, we are also all evolving collectively. Each of us has a dark side, along with our own grace and light. The extent to which we can acknowledge the former while maximizing the latter may determine how we choose to fulfill the terms of our Contract. When the shadow side takes over even one person, the consequences are tragically felt by many.

Even psychiatrists and brain scientists cannot offer a conclusive response to the question of whether individual people are born to murder. Social psychologist Stanley Milgram's groundbreaking book, *Obedience to Authority*, demonstrated that "often it is not so much the kind of person a man is as the kind of situation in which he finds himself that determines how he will act."[8] Milgram developed the controversial "obedience experiments," conducted at Yale University in 1961 and 1962, in which subjects were told by scientific authority figures to administer electric shocks to another person if he answered a question incorrectly, no matter how that person reacted. Milgram had expected that American subjects would not follow orders that seemed to hurt another person, especially if the person being shocked were screaming in obvious pain.

Yet he found, surprisingly, that 65 percent of his subjects, ordinary residents of New Haven, were willing to give apparently harmful electric shocks—up to 450 volts—to a protesting and seemingly suffering victim. Of course, the "shock machine" was a sham, and the subjects were not really hurting the other people, who merely pretended to be in pain and even begged for mercy as stronger and stronger shocks were supposedly administered. Sadly, though, Milgram reported, "With numbing regularity good people were seen to knuckle under to the demands of authority and perform actions that were callous and severe." In the aftermath of World War II, when people had assumed that Germans were more influenced by orders than other cultures, the "obedience experiments" were a cultural shock for Americans, who prided themselves on being nonconformist. As Milgram said, "It may be that we are puppets—puppets controlled by the strings of society. But at least we are puppets with perception, with awareness. And perhaps our awareness is the first step to our liberation."

What is in one is in the whole: murder and torture occur because humanity as a group does not yet sufficiently value life in all its expressions. Perhaps that lack of a sacred vision leads to the incarnating of bleak and brutal experiences. We all share a potential for becoming either the instigator or the victim of harm, whether physical or emotional. What we do to heal the victim—and the aggressor—within ourselves is the universal contribution we can each make toward healing the whole. And if we are ever to achieve our highest potential, we need to be, at the very least, "puppets with awareness."

People who committed heinous crimes, including mass murder, did have other options to learn what they needed to learn. They had the choice to act appropriately and morally, just as we all do, but they exercised their free will, chose wrongly, and heaped untold suffering on others. Ultimately, I believe, they themselves do suffer, whether in this life or the next or both. Perhaps these individuals have agreed to act as reflections of the darkest shadows of human nature. Although God has not "assigned" them to commit great evils, they may have been presented with a choice to act, and evil is one outcome of their choice.

It is a basic spiritual impulse to try to find meaning even in tragedy, which awakens our need for greater action, justice, and protection of human rights. Uncivilized behavior, murder, and tyranny strengthen our belief in civility, civilization, and democracy. Undisguised bigotry and hatred wake us to the need to practice love, compassion, and tolerance. It may seem facile to say that the Crusades, the Inquisition, slavery, the Holocaust, Stalin's purges, or the killing fields of the Khmer Rouge were meant to be learning experiences for the rest of us—especially when atrocities continue today under the guise of "ethnic cleansing" or "the will of God." But I would argue that our awareness of the potential for escalating evil has led us globally to condemn and curb attempts at mass murder. Nonetheless, looking at the forces of fundamentalism, civil war, and corporate greed around the world, we may have even harder lessons to learn.

Confronting the Shadow

Learning to confront—and ultimately manage—your shadow, no matter how daunting it may appear, is an essential step on your road to spiritual maturity. Lucy's life is one illustration of how your world can change once you decide that you and not your shadow will create your future. Lucy spent years trying to please everyone but herself, which is hardly a rare dilemma. "I had read a book a few years ago about a woman who decided one day just to pack up a few belongings and take to the road without a map or a personal agenda," Lucy told me. "She was just going to take her life one day at a time. I was filled with envy when I read that. Her story made me feel like a prisoner, and from that moment on, I was miserable. It wasn't my job, it wasn't my family. It was me and my belief that everyone's happiness depended on my being in their lives. I encouraged their dependency, and at the same time I resented every one of them."

Lucy realized that she was determined to control every person under her care because by keeping them dependent on her, she would not have to face her own weaknesses. She could tell herself that her family members were the Children or Victims and she was in charge of the tribe. The anger that would erupt in her when their problems got to be too much was her inner self attempting to communicate to her that she was using her power to prevent people from taking charge of their own lives. Her fear of not being needed caused her to fear their independence, and yet their lack of independence caused her to resent their weaknesses.

Many people fear their own empowerment and unconsciously encourage their shadow to thrive. This happens in particular when conscious empowerment represents change, which can be terrifying. Change signals loss of control and entry into the unknown. But even beyond fear of change, empowerment represents isolation, which people will do anything to avoid. Perhaps this is the very core of our paradoxical view of empowerment. Our image of awakening to and fulfilling our divine potential evokes the idea of an individual who is whole and complete, separated from lesser mortals, isolated and alone.

Culturally, we have yet to envision a realistic, appealing model of the spiritually empowered human being—someone who is simultaneously vulnerable, capable of sensual love, and worthy of a mate. We believe that enlightened people don't have the same needs or vulnerabilities that we do, or the same shadows. We also believe that enlightened people don't age, don't suffer or mourn. I have seen the archetype of the whole, perfected Human at work countless times in people. "You would think that someone with her occupation would be above such emotions," people say when a spiritual role model is shown to have feet of clay. Or "You should see the way he lives. He's anything but celibate."

We do not want to be whole if it means being alone. And we do not want enlightenment if it requires living as an ascetic. So deep within our unconscious, we feed the energy of the Saboteur, that part of ourselves that maintains our shadow pattern and fuels our fragmentation. We fear our own empowerment because it represents changes in our lives that would remove us from the warmth of those who love us for being vulnerable. And we fear being empowered because then we can no longer claim that we are not responsible for our actions.

Although we want to be around a person who is enlightened or consciously working on becoming enlightened, we deeply fear the high price our own enlightenment will make us pay. Assuming personal responsibility for the quality not only of our actions but also of our attitudes is a lifetime discipline. We cannot rest in the harbor of blame, so we unconsciously, and sometimes consciously, encourage our own weaknesses and hold on to our fears. As long as becoming enlightened represents isolation for us, we will shun our own empowerment. We fear to realize our highest potential, and this inevitably affects our creative, financial, and career potential.

"After you introduced me to this idea," a man named Maury told me, "I started to look at each person in my life as representing some power in me that I needed to realize. This perspective was naturally far more useful when it came to dealing with those individuals with whom I knew I had a power struggle. But still I became observant of exactly what made me feel powerless in certain relationships, and I would then study that feeling in me. I thought about how I would change were I to fill in that part of me with self-esteem, for instance. In each case, I could see immediately that my life would change dramatically with each choice I made to respond consciously to every interaction I had.

"In one case I was with a friend who was celebrating his new membership to a very exclusive country club. I don't have the income required to belong to that place, and my first response was envy. I resented his being able to afford the type of life he has. But then I separated from him and turned the mirror on me. I confronted the fact that he represented a kind of power that I had not developed. And the more I thought about it, the more I realized that my resentment went beyond just that description. I had to admit that I resented the fact that he had the discipline to go the extra mile to mature that power in him. Whereas I was more inclined to look for reasons to knock off early from work, he saw everything as an opportunity, and did all he could with his job. My resentment had nothing to do with money; it had to do with the manner in which he managed his potential.

"Once I admitted to that little insight, I knew that from that point on I would have to take full responsibility for making lesser choices regarding my own opportunities in life, because he and I were being handed the same chances. The only thing that was different between us was our response to those opportunities. Now I force myself to go that extra mile, but it's not easy. Every time I hang in there, I hear a voice telling me to find an excuse to take the easy road. Some part of me obviously does not want to grow up, and it's that part of me that waits until Friday afternoon at three o'clock to declare that the weekend has begun, just as I did when I was a kid. The symbol of the three o'clock school bell told me how deeply the child in me wants life to be a vacation. But I am understanding myself better each step of the way. I am recognizing my Saboteur and my Dependent Child and other patterns that indicate that some part of me simply does not want to manage an empowered life. I also have to admit that I derive great inspiration from my country club friend, because I now see him as representing my potential instead of the life I cannot have. He's simply a few opportunities ahead of me."

to address envy.

Maury chose to respond to his feelings of envy about his country club friend by recognizing that they were the consequence of his own power deficits. He separated his shadow responses from his feelings of friendship. He realized that he resented the power his friend had to maximize his potential and appreciate all the opportunities life had to offer. And he was finally able to unearth his deepest resentment, which was that his friend could handle rapid changes in life, whereas he needed to have things move slowly because he was so afraid of losing control. His friend had faith in the unknown, but for Maury it was fraught with danger.

Because Maury could analyze his shadow responses through his archetypal patterns, he was able to realize that his Saboteur and Child within were in fact extending him an invitation to realize his potential. On yet another level Maury decided to work through an issue with his friend with whom he had a Contract to support his own empowerment.

Return of the Orphan

We could probably reduce all our struggles with empowerment, such as those of Lucy and Maury, to our need to transform the abandoned, wounded, or dependent aspect of our Child archetype to one that is healthy and self-sufficient. Because fairy tales and children's stories are such a rich source of insight into the innate courage and power that is contained within our archetypes, I find the clearest depiction of this transformation in the modern fable *The Wonderful Wizard of Oz*. In this well-known story, Dorothy has to seek out aspects of herself that she didn't know she had, including courage and intelligence well beyond those of the young orphan who left her Auntie Em back in Kansas. Seen as an archetypal adventure, *The Wonderful Wizard of Oz* presents the challenges of survival that we all face on our own Yellow Brick Roads.

In the book by L. Frank Baum, originally published in 1900, and the 1939 MGM movie starring Judy Garland, Dorothy is, like so many heroes of fairy tales and folk stories, literally the Orphan Child. Because she does not fit into the conventional tribe, her consciousness is her own to develop from the beginning. As the story opens, a cyclone is approaching, representing the chaos that is the classic precursor to transformation. As the cyclone looms menacingly, Dorothy runs to the storm cellar, trying to return to the tribe before the chaos, but they don't hear her and, in effect, won't allow it.

Dorothy runs back into the house with her beloved dog, Toto, whom she is holding on her bed as the cyclone lifts the house into the air. She bangs her head on the headboard, losing consciousness. In symbolic, archetypal terms, a house represents the whole of the self, from the subconscious in the basement to the superego in the attic. The whole of Dorothy's life is lifted off in the chaos and begins to spin, to be symbolically reconstituted. Having to undertake the Hero's Journey, she has awakened her charism, the special grace that will see her through her ordeal of growth.

Dorothy's journey takes her to Oz, where the house crashes down and she says famously to Toto, "I have a feeling we're not in Kansas anymore." She begins to sense that she has been separated from her familiar environment; that what is going on is happening only to her, not to the tribe; and that she has to find within herself the strength and courage to endure what is coming. For the first time she sees little Munchkins, who represent fragments of herself. Like any hero adventurer or spiritual seeker starting on a journey of self-discovery, Dorothy asks questions: "Where am I?" and "How do I get home?" The Munchkins tell her that she has to go to Oz—in essence, to go on a journey to an unknown destination.

Dorothy's guardian for the journey is Toto, the Latin word for "everything." Toto is an extension of Dorothy; he is her intuition, like Vasalisa's doll, and an archetypal image of a guardian. In shamanic terms, we would say that Toto is her power animal. Toto is also Dorothy's reminder that "everything" she needs is always with her, if she'll just stay aware of what's going on. All spiritual traditions emphasize the need to keep your attention in the present time. As long as you remain present, everything you need is present with you. As soon as you project yourself back through the rest of your life, you begin to manifest a sense of vulnerability and insecurity characterized by fear of failure. Projection is the act of taking your present moment and stretching it across a lifetime, an impossible formula that will always leave you powerless.

Then Dorothy meets the Munchkin leader, who represents the unified self emerging to give her direction. Even as you feel lost and ask "Where am I?" a part of your interior self immediately arises to give an answer. In Dorothy's case, the answer is to go to Oz. As she undertakes her Hero's Journey, the four archetypes of survival—Child, Victim, Prostitute, and Saboteur—enter the playing field. Dorothy's Orphan Child has been leading to this point, her basic theme being, "I'm a child. I've lost my way. I've got to get home." But the forces around her say, "You're on your own, kid, and it's time for you to grow up."

At this point in the film (although not in the original book), the two witches arrive on the scene, representing shadow and light. The Wicked Witch of the East says, "I want your dog, Toto," meaning that she wants to deprive Dorothy of her guardian. When the Wicked Witch goes after Toto in anger, Dorothy becomes frightened, and her Victim emerges. Glinda, the Good Witch of the North, holds off the Wicked Witch and gives Dorothy the famous ruby slippers. Those shoes represent another charism or grace that will see Dorothy through her journey to Oz. (The book, which calls them silver shoes, makes it clear that Dorothy never takes them off. She is so comfortable with them that she even sleeps in them, making it hard for the Witch to get them away from her.) When the Wicked Witch says, "I want those ruby slippers!" she is waking up Dorothy's Prostitute. What the Witch is actually saying to Dorothy is, "At any given time, you can get off that difficult road if you will sell those shoes. That's the bargain." Every time you are given a new charism, or clearer sense of self, the Prostitute will test you to see if you're willing to sell your new spiritual power for material gain of some sort. It's as though you've won the lottery and somebody calls you up and asks if you'd like to invest in some swampland in Florida. That's also where the Saboteur comes in. Are you going to sabotage your personal growth for a little comfort, or will your inner Saboteur alert you to danger in time to keep you on the Yellow Brick Road?

The next person Dorothy meets is the Scarecrow, who complains that he doesn't have a brain. Her interaction with the Scarecrow represents a dialogue with her own intelligence, in which for the first time she has to assess her intellectual reality. As an extension of her inner self, the Scarecrow will also have to go to Oz to get a brain, and so they set off together. Down the road they meet the Tin Woodman who has rusted into immobility and who, once lubricated, complains that he needs a heart. In symbolic terms, Dorothy also needs to awaken the sense of love and compassion that lies within.

Both the Scarecrow and the Tin Woodman were dormant until Dorothy awakened them, and herself, to the need to go on the Hero's Journey to gain what they were essentially lacking. Along the way they meet the Cowardly Lion, who is immobilized by fear. The Lion lacks courage, which is a function of self-esteem and is related to will and choice.

On their journey to Oz, Dorothy encounters many difficulties and detours, each of which arouses the Victim archetype in her. She can act like a Victim and give in, or she can call on her companions and guides for help, which she does on several occasions. The most dangerous obstacle is the field of poppies, which causes her to fall into a deep sleep, along with the Lion and Toto. Certain realities are too much for us to handle on a conscious level, and so we must process them in an unconscious state, say, in dreams or deep sleep. When Jesus took his twelve Apostles to the garden of Gethsemane and asked them to stay awake and watch with him, for example, they couldn't do it. It's as though the force field of anguish that he was giving off was too much for them to bear and they fell into unconsciousness. You may notice yourself that if you're reading a book or attending a lecture that deals with spiritually or psychologically heavy material, you may fall asleep (perhaps aided by a boring lecturer). A similar phenomenon also occurs during healing services, when certain people "go down under the power," meaning that they lapse into momentary unconsciousness so that healing can take place on a deeper level. Some old wounds that are being healed may be too traumatic to be addressed consciously. Dorothy's transition from childhood to adulthood, from Orphan Child to Hero, is going to require not only grace but also a healing of her past, which is accomplished in part in the unconscious state.

Dorothy and her companions eventually arrive at Oz and go before the Wizard. As any good spiritual master would do, he immediately puts them to the test, saying that he won't help them unless they bring back the broom of the Wicked Witch. The paradox here is that you will always have a test to invoke grace, and you need grace to pass the test. You can't just suddenly become courageous; you have to act out courage to know you have courage.

When they go to the Wicked Witch's dark castle to get the broom, Dorothy is captured, just as, during our own spiritual development, even if we get past our desires, we always get captured in some way by our fears and feel isolated and abandoned. The prison in the dark castle is reminiscent of the dark forest through which Dorothy passed on her way to Oz in search of integration. The dark forest is a time-honored image of the dangers of the search for self. In Dante's *Divine Comedy*, another allegorical account of a spiritual journey from the lower regions through Purgatory to Paradise, the hero went through the "dark wood of error." When stuck in a dark wood or prison, we need to look to the Saboteur, who reminds us that we must keep the faith and not give in to our fears.

But at each stage of her journey, Dorothy is able to call on the Lion, the Tin Woodman, and the Scarecrow to rescue her. In effect, she is calling on her own courage, will, and heart, which she is in the process of unifying. As her three companions are trying to rescue Dorothy, the Witch shows up and sets fire to the Scarecrow, beginning her attack on the intellectual level, as often happens when we try to follow a spiritual path. (The mind says, "This is ridiculous. People couldn't possibly get enlightened by sitting on a cushion and closing their eyes.") But Dorothy picks up a bucket of water, representing her unconscious, and throws it on the Witch, thereby making herself self-conscious. As the water hits the Witch, she chides Dorothy for doing the one thing that could free her of the Witch's power, and then she melts away. As soon as Dorothy calls on her unconscious, the whole world that had once scared her dissolves, and she sees only safety.

Dorothy and her companions return to Oz feeling totally successful. They bring the broom to the Wizard, only to be told that it's not enough. Toto the guardian will not accept their rejection and says in effect, "This is wrong. You have to see that it's fraudulent. I'm going to show you." The guardian goes over and pulls the curtain hiding the role-playing Wizard, showing Dorothy that she does not need to rely on a shadow Guru to do her spiritual work for her. In fact, if you project your own needs and fantasies onto a guru, you may end up getting burned.

Exposed, the Wizard is forced to make good on his promises and help Dorothy find her way home from Oz. Although Oz represents the achievement of spiritual power and independence, it's essentially meaningless unless she can bring back home what she has learned and apply it to her everyday life. Spiritual insight is not an end in itself, but a means to transform our life on earth from mere survival and dominance into compassion and service to others. Dorothy is now confronted with yet another test, this one regarding false power. Even though the Wizard has been less than forthcoming on his promises, Dorothy is planning to accept his guidance and accompany him in his hot air balloon (note the ironic choice of vehicle), but Toto—following his nature by pursuing a squirrel—jumps out of the basket as if to say, "Let's get out of here."

Dorothy has the good sense not to want to be separated from her guardian and runs out after Toto, allowing the Wizard to leave without her. Having made one good choice, Dorothy is rewarded by the appearance of her other guardian, Glinda, the Good Witch of the North. Glinda reminds Dorothy that she has had the power to return home all along, only she didn't know it. The ruby slippers, which have not left her feet since she first put them on, are all she needs. Her words are reminiscent of the Buddhist teaching that we are already perfect buddhas, we just don't realize it, and so we act like unenlightened children. If we truly knew we possessed Buddha nature, or Christ consciousness, or God-realization, we would be home free. Dorothy clicks her heels together as instructed and chants the mantra her angel guardian gives her: "There's no place like home. There's no place like home."

In L. Frank Baum's original text, the exchange is even clearer than in the film version:

"Your Silver Shoes will carry you over the desert," replied Glinda. "If you had known their power you could have gone back to your Aunt Em the very first day you came to this country."

"But then I should not have had my wonderful brains!" cried the Scarecrow. "I might have passed my whole life in the farmer's cornfield."

"And I should not have had my lovely heart," said the Tin Woodman. "I might have stood and rusted in the forest till the end of the world."

"And I should have lived a coward forever," declared the Lion, "and no beast in all the forest would have had a good word to say to me."

"This is all true," said Dorothy, "and I am glad I was of use to these good friends. But now that each of them has had what he most desired, and each is happy in having a kingdom to rule besides, I think I should like to go back to Kansas."

"The Silver Shoes," said the Good Witch, "have wonderful powers. And one of the most curious things about them is that they can carry you to any place in the world in three steps, and each step will be made in the wink of an eye. All you have to do is to knock the heels together three times and command the shoes to carry you wherever you wish to go."9

Dorothy has completed her Hero's Journey, come to terms with her four survival archetypes, and with courage consolidated her mind, heart, and will. Her most challenging adversary, the Wicked Witch, has proved to be the one who did the most to expand her soul. And so Dorothy wakes up safe in her bed, right back in Kansas with the same foster parents with whom she had been so disenchanted at the beginning of the story. Only now she embraces them wholeheartedly.

Dorothy appears to be in the same physical reality but is not; she is fully transformed. She emerges not as the frightened little Orphan Child but as an intelligent, fully awakened heart-consciousness in the same body. She has returned whole from chaos and her journey.

Our work has essentially the same goal. By learning to recognize the archetypal patterns at work within your psyche—which I will teach you in Chapter 5—you can begin to view your life symbolically, rather than taking every interaction personally and viewing it on only the physical plane.

Like the Lion, you need courage to look at the Victim archetype within you and learn to make it into your ally. You need the heart that the Tin Woodman sought so that you can love yourself when you see the Prostitute at work in your psyche, and to turn it to your advantage. And the intellect that the Scarecrow prized so highly can work with your Saboteur to recognize the warning signs that you are about to do yourself in. When you tie those together, you can, like Dorothy, use your will to transform the Child within—whether Abandoned, Wounded, or Dependent—into an empowered being capable of directing your own life with passion and skill. For then you have the elements of the soul, the eternal self, and you are on your way to discovering your spiritual identity.

CHAPTER 5

Identifying Your
Archetypal Patterns

The physical workaday world you live in is an archetypal theater. The substance of myths and ancient tales is constantly manifesting in the power plays, personality clashes, and competitive psychic forces that abound even within a few hundred square feet of seemingly ordinary office space. If you think of your interpersonal relationships only in terms of conflicting egos or competition, you will overlook the spiritual significance of these everyday interactions. When you rely only on the perspectives of your first three chakras, chances are that you will act inappropriately, jump to conclusions, second-guess others, take everything personally, and even misinterpret casual kindness for romantic affection.

You have twelve primary archetypal companions. Four of them are survival archetypes—the Child, Victim, Prostitute, and Saboteur—which everyone has. You also have eight others, personal archetypes that you will learn to identify in this chapter. They might include ancient figures—such as the Goddess, Warrior, King, and Slave—or contemporary ones, such as the Networker, Environmentalist, and Political Protester, which are actually variations on ancient themes (Messenger, Steward, and Rebel, respectively).

The Networker, for example, became a modern-day archetype once people began to associate certain behavioral characteristics with that name. Yet it has mythic origins stemming from the ancient Greek god Hermes (on whom the more familiar Roman god Mercury was based). The patron of heralds and a bringer of good fortune, Hermes also served as messenger of the gods and was reputedly the only being able to find his way to the underworld and back again. With his winged sandals and magical herald's staff, known as the caduceus, Hermes/Mercury spawned a number of descendants through the ages, each reflecting the social structures and needs of an age's civilization. Among various primal tribes, certain figures took charge of communication through "talking drums," smoke signals, and long-distance runners, marathoners, who delivered messages from tribe to tribe. As the demand for communication through letters and other documents grew, the figure of the Messenger emerged.

Telegraph and telephone operators, the postman, and the journalist shaped the face of Mercury for still later generations. Now we have radio and television networks and those who network via the Internet. All of these media represent Mercury's ability to don the wardrobe of the day for the sake of delivering "the message." And so, although the term *networker* may conjure up people who maintain extensive e-mail lists for spreading political and social warnings, it is linked inextricably to the messenger of the gods.

Later in this chapter a series of questions will help you determine the eight patterns that have the greatest influence in your life. Identifying your archetypal patterns is basically an enjoyable process because you examine the experiences and relationships of your life from new and often extraordinary perspectives. As a rule—or a clue—the archetypes that will guide your Sacred Contract have a direct influence on your physical relationships with people.

Identifying your archetypes can also be somewhat challenging, since you may need to reevaluate your life as you view your relationships and experiences symbolically. For instance, you may come to recognize that you are involved in a relationship not as a Lover but as a Rescuer. This realization can help you understand why your romantic bonds tend to fray easily, since mixing Rescuer with romantic energy produces co-dependency. It can also be liberating, because it enables you to reenvision your entire relationship history. Instead of believing that he has failed at one relationship after another, the Rescuer begins to get a symbolic understanding of why he is drawn to people who need help rather than to people who can take care of themselves. He understands his feelings of rejection as behavior that is inherent in the pattern, an inevitable consequence of conflicting agendas rather than as a personal rejection. This shift in perspective, from the personal to the symbolic, offers the opportunity to heal the wounds of personal history and to rescript an entirely new future.

For instance, a man named Kert knew that he tended to be unfairly critical and judgmental of other people, yet he nonetheless wore his opinions openly on his face. Then one day an acquaintance confronted him and told him that his scornful attitude only caused people to feel the same way toward him. "I was deeply humbled," Kert said, "when this guy told me that his circle of friends, my targets, so to speak, would be delighted to have me as a friend, with the condition that I be open to finding something to appreciate in each one of them. I didn't know what to say, and I actually started to cry. The guy walked away, and I was washed over with intense feelings of humiliation and self-loathing. I was judging myself with the ugly harshness that I had always applied to others, and now I knew how that felt. I didn't think I would ever be able to forgive myself, or even approach this group of people who were now saying, 'We would like to like you.'

"I had to see the lesson in this event for me. I had to find a higher purpose, because I sure wasn't finding any comfort on the ground level. I decided to use my symbolic sight. I came to see that, from an archetypal point of view, my Child energy was an Orphan, and the other people were a "family" apart from me. I was jealous of their bond and their love and support for each other. I resented the fun they had together and how they could tease each other, nickname each other, and create a history together. Now they were adopting me, and it was up to me to sign the adoption papers. So I did. I got together with them one evening for dinner, and that was the beginning of my finally having a family of friends."

Learning to read the language of symbols has a positive effect on your self-image and energy. You do not have to wait for a crisis to see things symbolically and accurately. You can start wherever you are. You can gain as much spiritual insight from examining the archetypal patterns that influence the enjoyable parts of your life as you do when you look at those that are operating during troubled times. Every aspect of your life is worth understanding from a symbolic perspective, including why you have a good relationship with a particular person or why you are involved in an especially rewarding line of work. When you start working with your archetypal patterns and interpreting their role in your life, do not exclude looking into all that makes you glad you're alive. I am forever reminding people that their spiritual life should not be only about trying to figure out why bad things have happened to them and finding the right prayers to get out of their dark nights. The emphasis in too many people's lives has more to do with healing than with enjoying life. A delightful woman once remarked to me, "I have a Muse archetype. I adore inspiring people, like I'm landing where Heaven wants me for a moment, so that I can whisper a positive word or thought into someone's mind about believing in their own talent. I've read the mythology on the nine Muses, the daughters of Zeus, and I believe that somehow I am a 'descendant' of those archetypes."

Nonetheless, people are far more motivated to begin an inner journey as a result of a crisis in love or work than when all is right with their world. Whatever your motivation, the first step is to get to know your own archetypes.

Where to Begin

Remember that archetypes are all essentially "neutral" patterns of the psyche, neither positive nor negative. Even those to which you initially have negative associations, such as the Prostitute or Victim, have strengths that are psychologically helpful. Keeping that in mind, you can begin to reflect on the archetypes in your immediate personal family of twelve. Perhaps you've already become aware of some as you've been reading this book. If not, you can begin reading through the list of archetypes in the Appendix, marking off or writing down in your journal the names that resonate most powerfully with you. Even though this is a rational process, please remain open to intuitive feelings, hunches, and impressions as you proceed. You may find it helpful to make your selections at a time when you will be relatively free from distraction and to clear your mind through meditation, prayer, or deep breathing before you proceed.

You will initially find that you identify with more than eight archetypes. This is natural and part of the process of determining which
energies are most closely related to your own. We can relate to almost
every archetype because our psyches and spirits are connected to the
great collective of all the archetypal patterns. During my seminars
when I ask the audience how many can relate to being a Rescuer, a Servant, or a Martyr, among others, most hands go up. Many people resonate to this trilogy because our culture has replaced its emphasis on
the virtues of the rugged individual with an obsession about victimization. These three archetypes are patterns of disempowerment, but
don't confuse occasional feelings of martyrdom or a few incidents of
rescuing people who were in emotional or financial crisis with an
archetype. We have all helped people, and we have all had "martyr
attacks." Keep your attention on identifying archetypal patterns that
are consistent rather than occasional forces in your life. Choose at least
eight "primary" archetypes about which you feel very strongly, but also
include a few "secondary" ones to which you feel a connection.

Choosing your archetypes demands that you stretch your imagination and draw on your capacity to assess yourself honestly. Your
conscious mind may completely overlook an archetype that is one of
the most forceful in your life because it doesn't want to admit its influence or doesn't recognize one of its variations. A man in one of my
workshops, for instance, strongly radiated the energy of the Lover
archetype. He had not chosen that archetype as one of his intimate
eight, however, because he thought of the Lover as an exclusively
romantic or sexual energy. Quiet, passive, and shy to the point of
being withdrawn, he worked as a poet. For him, the object of his love
was life itself. In his verses he saw only beauty in the world. Although
he lived alone (Hermit), it wasn't because he was antisocial or angry at
the world. He wanted his life to be simple and wanted to live reflec-
tively (Mystic). The Lover in him was a spiritual force, and his writing
expressed the heightened love described in the poetry of Rumi and the
Song of Solomon.

I urge you to think about archetypes from both their literal perspective and their symbolic, hidden, absurd, and even frightening
potentials. Look at the energies of your life as a poet would. First,
work with your intellectual conception of an archetype and stretch

your associations as far as you can. Then step into the second-column perceptions, into your internal crucible, to test if you have the right mix. If you can ask someone you trust for feedback on your choices, you can also get some fascinating feedback and insights.

Be aware that you may be drawn to certain archetypes because you like their connotations or physical appearance. You may find it attractive to think of yourself as a Mystic, Midas, Healer, King, Goddess, or Visionary, but liking the sound of an archetype is not the same as having a spiritual bond with it. To help you determine the authenticity of a bond, you need to be honest with yourself as you answer the questions I've prepared for you. You need to assess the quality and depth of a possible archetypal bond as thoroughly as possible. If, for example, you are drawn to the Healer archetype, pause for a moment and ask yourself why. Be aware that working in the field of health services or complementary healing does not automatically make you part of the Healer archetype; the Servant might be more appropriate, or even the Rescuer. You will need to respond affirmatively to the questions regarding this archetype's role in your life before you can conclude that the Healer is one of your companions. The Appendix can help you clarify archetypal characteristics.

If you already know your eight primary and three secondary archetypal companions, note them in your journal. If you need some help, refer to the Appendix for ideas.

Interview with an Archetype

After you have singled out your eight archetypes, I'm going to ask you to interview them one at a time using the questions I provide. I think this will help you become more familiar with how the archetype affects you and will make you comfortable with your choices. You may find that you want to interview only one or two, or you may not want to interview any at all at this point. But even if you want to skip this interview process, you will benefit from reading through the rest of this chapter.

To begin your interview, imagine that the archetype you have chosen is seated opposite you as if it were an actual person or being.

Although the questions are phrased in the third person, don't be afraid to address the archetype in the second person. The first question I suggest you ask yourself, for instance, is "Why did I choose this archetype?" If you are comfortable doing so, ask the archetype directly, "Why did I choose you?" Let the archetype answer in its own voice and, if appropriate, respond in your voice. Record the questions and answers in your journal for future reference. The second question reads, "In what way do I feel this archetype serves my Contracts with other people?" You may ask the archetype, "How do you serve my Contracts with other people?" When you have a natural rapport with an archetype, a kind of intuitive dialogue slowly opens up. Insights and connections emerge in this process of self-revelation that will feel right and true. If you feel as if your rational mind has constructed the information, you may be on the wrong track or talking with the wrong archetype. If the image is unresponsive and you are unable to get a feeling of resonance with the archetype, this particular pattern may not be a good candidate for your intimate support group of twelve. Your aim is to find a feeling or gut instinct that confirms that you have an energy link to this pattern, a connection to your chakras rather than your brain.

The process of establishing a genuine bond with an archetype can also be enhanced by reading into the myths, religious traditions, fairy tales, legends, and other classical literature or movies in which they appear. The Appendix suggests many of these. People frequently discover in these archetypal adventures the identical challenge or wonderment that they are experiencing in their own lives, thinly veiled by metaphorical or fantastical trappings. Men who are having difficulty leaving home and getting on with their adulthood, admitting that some part of them does not want to grow up and assume personal responsibility, for example, often recognize that they are contemporary versions of Peter Pan, or the Flying Boy that John Lee wrote about. These literary figures represent the Eternal Boy, the *Puer Eternis* aspect of the Child.

Among the most popular archetypes for women is the Queen, a choice that has intriguing overtones. A woman tends to choose the Queen because she wants to see herself as the one giving orders in her environment, whether workplace or home; she needs to be in charge without question. (Two modern examples of Queens who fit this profile are Leona Helmsley and Evita Perón.) The extent of her rulership generally includes her mate, and women often express this characteristic of domination over their partners in a snide or sarcastic tone of voice. "Oh, yeah," one may say, "he definitely knows I'm a Queen." Rarely do women project or describe themselves as benevolent, happy, or playful Queens, which in itself is a fascinating social statement. When they comment about their Queen qualities, their demeanor often becomes aggressive, as defending against the possibility of male domination. Their Queens are usually domineering archetypes who demand full control of those in their court—especially the men.

The vast majority of classic fairy tales (which, incidentally, are rarely about fairies) have been written by men, and in these stories Queens are portrayed negatively. Take, for example, the Queen in Snow White, who orders a man to murder a beautiful maiden on her behalf. One might deduce from this that Queens are threats to male power, and that the male authors of most of these tales present them in a negative light out of fear. Yet almost all of the "Queens" in my workshop audiences, while admitting that they had not realized it, acknowledge on reflection that their attraction to the Queen *is* based on their desire to control those in their working environment, especially the men. When they describe their Queens, they use words such as *direct, forceful,* and *commanding* but rarely, if ever, *kind* and *benevolent,* like the Queen who ruled the Land of the Giants in *Gulliver's Travels.* The Queen archetype has also come into prominence within the gay community, and her energy is expressing itself just as authentically within that culture.

If you feel that you are a Queen, ask yourself what characteristics you associate with that archetype, and which of them you yourself have. Reflect on whether you have a lifelong pattern of coping with anger, particularly toward your mate or male authority figures in general, by trying to dominate them. If you associate control and domination with this archetype only because of a fear of being "conquered," ask yourself why. As with each archetype, give serious thought to how and why it has a direct bearing on what you consider to be your Contracts with others in which your Queen is the dominant archetypal force.

Letters to Your Archetype

Try this exercise if you find it more appealing than interviewing your archetype. Write a letter to your archetype, explaining how you discovered it and why you think it in particular is in your life, and tell it about the situations in which it reared its head or stepped to the front of the stage. Talk to it in the second person, as in, "Here's where I believe I see you (my Victim) working in my thoughts and actions: I see you in my need for people's approval. I see you in my belief that people are rejecting me if I don't get the attention I feel I need. I see you in my belief that others have more opportunities than I do. Now that I know you're there, how can I make you into a friend or ally or at least a benign force? I see you every time I hear myself say, 'Why is this happening to me?' or feel myself becoming angry when I think other people are preventing me from doing what I want. What does your negative or critical or destructive side need in order to stop getting me into trouble or bothering me and to become positive or supportive—or even powerfully positive? What will it take from me to change my thoughts and actions to make you more important or to subdue your influence? What do you need? What is it that you're teaching me?"

Take as long as ten minutes to a half hour to write your letter. After you've written as much as you feel is necessary to elicit a response from your archetype, sit for a couple of minutes and let yourself think about what you've written. It might be good to take a break and stretch, get yourself a glass of water or a cup of tea, and even change your seat. Because now you're going to enter into the persona and mind of the archetype and write yourself a response. Have the archetype write you back, addressing the questions that you and it feel responses for.

The first archetype I want you to interview and write to is your Child, because it is the easiest for many. As an option with this archetype only, you can use the technique of writing the questions with your dominant hand and answering them with your opposite hand. For instance, if you're right-handed, I want your Child to answer you with its left hand; if you're left-handed, your Child will answer you with its right. This technique will help you gain access to your intuitive, unconscious mind, because it requires you to focus without distraction to maneuver your opposite hand. Yes, this will take longer, just as it took you a while to learn to write and drag thoughts from your mind to the paper when you were just learning. But it will give you a physical and emotional connection to your Child. And it may cut right to the chase, since your Child will not want to write for a long time and will give you frank, succinct answers.

Once you have the letters and responses, I want you to take another short break, stretch, and then find a neutral seat to reread the letters and listen to the voices. Do you see any places where you can begin to meet the archetype's needs and work with its (your) needs and energy? For example, what changes would you immediately implement in your life as a result of dialoguing with this archetype? Are you more easily able to recognize the voice of this archetype when you hear it speaking to you? Do you see any reasons why you would *not* cooperate with the suggestions that your Child archetype has made?

Warrior on Demand

As you think through the many archetypes, try to remember times when you rose to an occasion or acted against "type"—became someone you almost didn't recognize. For instance, Rita is normally quiet and reserved. When her son was beaten by three boys on the school playground, however, she took on the persona of the Warrior as she exploded into his school to confront the principal and other administrators. Rita proclaimed that if anything like that ever happened again, she would wage a "battle"—the Warrior word she used—in the local courts and take on the school authorities who failed to protect her son. That got the administrators' attention, and they addressed the issue appropriately.

Once Rita felt that her son was in safe territory, she could afford to release the intensity with which she had drawn on the psychic field of the Warrior archetype. She told me that when the air cleared from this incident, she nearly collapsed with exhaustion. Part of that exhaustion resulted from a sudden break with an unconscious source of power that had been generating energy for her during that crisis via the Warrior archetype.

When an archetypal pattern steps into the foreground of our life dramas, most people describe a dramatic shift in their energy field. This explanation felt on target to Rita, who quickly noticed other places in her life where the Warrior made an appearance whenever she needed it most, and she concluded that the Warrior was one of her twelve archetypes.

A major directive that helps you determine your archetypes is "Describe in detail my unfinished business with someone." Many people give a brief answer the first time around, or even state that they have absolutely no unfinished business with anyone. That response often indicates so large a reservoir of unresolved conflict or guilt that they cannot bear to go near the memories. Instead, allow the questions gradually to open up your memory bank and draw to the surface bits and pieces of your past, which could be as minuscule as a conversation with a stranger or as traumatic as sexual molestation. These memories may not present themselves on first recall, since most of us do not often visit the murky waters beneath the surface of our history.

The list of questions is long, but your psyche is vast. It never rests, but you cannot rush these associations through your unconscious and conclude that you have discovered all there is to know by answering them. You may want to go back through this list more than once for each archetype too. Each time you conduct an interview with an archetype, you awaken more memories and new associations. You are collecting fragments of your life almost as an archaeologist gathers the shards of ancient pottery. Later these fragments will organize themselves because they "know" where they belong.

Throughout my own life, for instance, I have met fragments of my Rebel in many places and within the electricity of several relationships. Being a Rebel is a part of my Contract, a path through which I have come to know God. I have rebelled against the politics of my religious upbringing, although I decided to rebel with the aid of "masters" by entering a graduate program in theology. I reflect the Rebel in my writing, in my teachings, and in my research.

The Rebel archetype has provided me with my greatest personal, academic, and spiritual challenges. I can feel it emerge in my psyche under certain circumstances, sometimes positive and sometimes not. But whenever I feel that force coming forward, I am alerted that something of spiritual significance for me is about to occur. This archetype is a part of the reason why standing up to convention has never been difficult for me, but rather an attractive investment of my time and energy.

I am also aware that my rebellious nature sometimes hits the extreme and that I can lose sight of the issues I am confronting. Yet the Rebel is me, and it affords me an appreciation for this trait in other Rebels I have met along the way. One summer night not long ago, for instance, I came across a group of fifteen-year-old Rebels in the parking lot of a White Hen Pantry near my home in Chicago. These semi-tough kids were making their independence known with their tattoos and piercings—their version of communicating with swords rather than pens. The leader was easily recognizable because he had more of both insignias than anyone else in the group. He obviously was also the Warlord, because when I spoke to them as a group, all eyes looked to him. I asked these young Rebels if they would explain to me why they chose to pierce their bodies.

Like James Dean in the classic film *Rebel Without a Cause*, the group leader had to respond to me sarcastically and with an appropriate display of street gang disrespect by stating that they pierced their bodies "because of the yellow duck I have in my bathroom." His dismissive answer was a test of whether I would respect them. When I simply nodded my head in acknowledgment, I was accepted into their field. I asked them if they were aware that piercing was an ancient spiritual practice common to many civilizations. I told them that piercing rituals were ways of honoring one's inner power and recognizing that a young man had come into a stage of maturity in which he was capable of taking charge of a part of his tribe, thus commanding respect. I explained further that all this had to do with the power that comes from understanding spirituality.

"We don't believe in religion," the leader said.

"I didn't say religion," I replied. "I said spirituality—the journey of the power of your spirit."

His defensive demeanor suddenly melted. "We don't know anything about spirituality. Can you teach us?" he asked. I was momentarily stunned by their response and display of emotional vulnerability, and I told them that they would first have to ask their parents for permission for me to teach them. If it was acceptable to their parents, we could begin. Unfortunately I never met them again, and so that opportunity never came to pass, but I hope that these Rebels will seek out more information on their archetypal passage into adulthood. I remember them and their profound spiritual impact on my own soul, along with the way my own Rebel archetype gave way to the Teacher in that exchange.

Asking the Questions

You are certainly free to respond to the questions quickly and off the top of your head if you wish. But you can also decide to spend time with this process of self-examination and wrestle with your angels and archetypes. Every memory or association that occurs to you through this process of self-examination has value to it, even if you cannot appreciate its significance immediately. So use your journal. Remember that you're reclaiming your spirit in these fragments and constructing a hologram of your Sacred Contract.

You will be happy to know that you are already more fluent in "speaking archetypes" than you ever imagined. Indeed, you probably have been speaking archetypes your entire life. "I am such a Fool," one woman says. "My mother has always run the Martyr routine on me. 'You know how much I gave up for you?' That type of thing." Another relates, "It's not that I think of myself as a Hero, but others do. I think of myself more as a Rescuer." You have been in contact with archetypal imagery all your life and are probably pretty good at recognizing their patterns in other people. Indeed, the archetypes you most frequently see in others most likely have some role in your own life.

Begin asking the questions about (or to) the eight "primary" archetypes you have chosen. After you have eliminated some of them based on your responses to the questions, move on to interview the three "secondary" archetypes you chose, until you have eight that you feel comfortable with. You may be surprised to find that some of the archetypes you were least certain about end up carrying the most weight.

The following questions are arranged in groups. Answer them by recording any present-day and past experiences and relationships that seem connected to the archetype. Include the good memories along with the bad. Let the process of questioning and answering stir things up inside you. Welcome the energy of your psyche that comes with this process. You cannot ask penetrating questions and assume that your psyche will remain forever silent. Be as specific as possible in your answers. Give your prominent memories, and note any details that come to mind. Since everyone has a Child archetype, you might interview your Child first to see which aspect presents itself: the Divine Child, the Orphan or Abandoned Child, the Eternal Child, the Magical Child, or the Dependent Child. You'll want to interview your Victim, Prostitute, and Saboteur too. Even though you won't need to determine that they are among your family of twelve, you can still gain a great deal of insight into how they manifest in your life by answering these questions. And because you know that these four are definitely part of your intimate team, you may find it somewhat easier to begin with them.

Historical Questions

- Why did you choose this archetype? / "Why did I choose you?"
- Were you aware of having this archetypal pattern prior to reading this material? / "Where have we met before?"
- How do you see the shadow of this archetype within you? / "How does your shadow self influence me?"
- If this archetype is one that you were led to choose even though you would have preferred not to, list what does not appeal to you about it. / "What do I least like about you?"
- What opportunities in your life do you associate with this archetypal pattern? / "Which opportunities in my life are connected to your energy?"

Personal Questions

- List all the people who you feel have a connection to this archetypal pattern, and give the ways they have assisted or are assisting you. Include ways that you have also assisted them. / "Who are you most connected to in my life? How has this connection contributed to our spiritual development?"

- In what way do you feel this archetype serves your Contracts with people? / "How do you help me fulfill my Contracts with people?"
- With whom do you have power plays that you could connect with this archetype? / "Who in my life do I associate with your power?"
- How does this archetype factor into the unfinished business in your life, such as people you haven't forgiven, or an aspect of your past that you can't let go of? / "Who are you connected with from my past that I still have unfinished business with? In what way can your influence help bring closure to each of these relationships?"

List any myths, fairy tales, legends, folklore, or spiritual stories that you associate with this archetype that have meaning for you. Then identify any parallel features between those stories and your own life, such as feeling like Cinderella or Peter Pan. Then ask yourself (or your archetype) the following:

Energy and Intuitive Questions

- Are you aware when you are engaging in the energy field of this archetype? / "How do I know when your energy is influencing my thoughts or actions?" (Record your immediate impressions as having an authentic connection.)
- Have you ever been aware of dreams in which this archetype has been present? / "How do you present your energy to me through the dream state?"
- In what way does having a conscious awareness of this archetype in your psyche empower you? / "In what ways does your influence enhance my sense of personal power?"
- Does this archetype in any way disempower you? / "Do you have a negative influence on my self-esteem or on my behavior or attitudes?"
- Describe what you consider to be the wisdom that this archetype carries for you. / "What have I learned lately that comes directly from you?"

- Can you recall any instances in your life (preferably at least three) in which you have received some form of intuitive guidance that you could associate with this archetype and its role in your Contract? / "When and where in my life have you communicated with me most directly?" (Record your first impressions.)
- What fears or challenges do you have that you associate with this archetype? List a minimum of five. / "What do you make me afraid of?"
- What strengths or positive qualities do you have that you associate with this archetype? List a minimum of five. / "What positive characteristics do I have that you enhance and help me with?"
- Have you ever imagined yourself to be any of the archetypes you have chosen, such as a Warrior, King, Slave, Femme Fatale, or Princess?

Apply the perceptions you have gleaned from answering the preceding questions to your memories. Then one at a time work with your memory of the people or the event in these scenes within the context of a Contract that you had made for the purpose of spiritual empowerment.

Spiritual Questions

- How has and does this archetype influence your spirituality? / "What is your central contribution to my spiritual development?"
- What have you come to know about yourself through this archetype, both positively and in terms of your shadow? / "What are the most important personal lessons that you have taught me?"
- How would your life be different in the present by acting on spiritual insights from this archetype? / "What immediate guidance can you give me in this present moment?"
- Describe—even briefly—how this archetype factors into your Contract. / "How do you help me work with my agreements and Contract?"

- Are there any patterns in your life that you would change because of insights regarding your connection with this archetype, such as healing a relationship, or because you can now approach those parts of your past as aspects of your Contract? / "What is the most immediate personal change connected to your influence that I can make that would best empower me at this point in my life?"
- Can you make those choices? If so, when? And if not, why not? / "How do you cause me to block personal change?"
- What changes in your life do you fear the most? / "What do I fear most about your influence?"
- Add any further notes.

You need to perform this kind of inner excavation with each archetypal pattern. You may find that you need to do it more than once, since working with one archetype inevitably wakes up a memory or two, or many, inspiring you to return to an archetype that you had already "interviewed," comparing notes and connecting fragments. This process becomes more intriguing the deeper you go.

As you review the above series of questions and test statements, weed out archetypes that you have selected until you arrive at eight that you feel certain about.

When you write your list of archetypes in your journal, don't just give their names. Use a brief sentence or two to describe the primary reason why you chose each one. You'll have plenty of supporting reasons and a whole history of people and events that led up to and confirmed your selection. But you should be able to state the principal reason succinctly. This will help you when you begin to work with your archetypes to interpret your Contract and seek guidance on a variety of issues.

One Student's Choices

Brian's story shows one way of selecting archetypes. I hope it gives you a sense of what the selection process feels like.

Brian had an immediate connection to the Author, the Hermit, the Scholar, and the Scribe, among others. The Author was an obvious choice for him because of his academic background and his occupation as a writer. Upon meeting Brian, for instance, what is almost immediately evident is that he relies on the mental plane for his work.

Brian also related strongly to the Hermit archetype, recognizing that his emotional well-being and creativity were dependent on his being able to have solitary time. Here again much of his physical life has been designed consistently around the demands of his Hermit. What made the Hermit an intimate archetype for him was that it is a constant characteristic, rather than one that comes into play every now and again. A good rule in general when considering your archetypes is that they must represent characteristics that are continually at work in several areas of your life.

The Scholar was also a good fit for Brian because, as an author of nonfiction books, much of his work requires assiduous solitary research, something he quite enjoys doing. Brian eventually determined that the Scribe was less significant to him than the Author and Scholar archetypes, because scribes traditionally did not create books—they copied manuscripts. After taking time to think through the differences that characterize these two archetypes, he ruled out the Scribe. You will need to give the same kind of attention to your choices, because so many archetypes will initially seem to have an intimate connection with you. Upon careful scrutiny, however, you will be able to identify the fine lines of distinction that completely reshape your archetypal wheel.

Brian added the Judge to his initial group for two reasons. Like his father, he has a strong critical streak, which in its negative aspect manifests as constant criticism of those around him for what are often minor flaws or lapses. But in its constructive aspect, the Judge serves him well in his profession. He began his writing career as a critic, and his critical eye has allowed him to supplement his writing income with occasional editorial jobs. The significant aspect of this choice was that Brian chose the Judge based on his recognition of its shadow qualities in him. He was able to admit to himself that he has a highly judgmental nature and that this aspect of himself contributes a great deal to the growth challenges that he has to confront in his spiritual and personal lives.

Although it seemed counterintuitive at first, Brian also chose both the Monk and the Hedonist as key archetypes. He spends a lot of time exploring and practicing spiritual paths, but he also loves good food and wine. He admitted to being puzzled at the apparent contradiction himself, but on reflection he recalled that in the Middle Ages the Christian monks planted and cultivated many of the first vineyards of Europe, and so the connection may be paradoxical but neither incongruous nor unprecedented. The Monk represents, for example, a spiritual lifestyle of discipline and self-reflection that is essential to how Brian supports his inner life. Spiritual knowledge and his tools for inner growth provide the nurturing that his Monk and Hermit require for balance. And these balanced aspects of his psyche in turn serve to maintain the work of his Author. Together these archetypes form a team, which is their nature.

Brian also recognized the Teacher in himself, not simply because he occasionally gives writing courses but because in his own work he is also seeking to teach his readers. From another perspective, he is always welcoming new teachers into his life as part of his work. The old job-offer cliché of "learn while you earn" never seemed more appropriate.

Brian's most interesting choice was his twelfth archetype, the Rebel. Because of his problematical relationship with his father, a strict disciplinarian, Brian developed a tendency to go against established authority, not only in the political arena (where he was active in the civil rights and antiwar movements of the 1960s) but also in his work. Moreover, his Rebel aspect is precisely what so richly supports his Author and his Monk, because he seeks to challenge conventional thought and forge new paths of insight and spiritual interpretation for others. In his early years his Rebel emerged through its angry and defensive aspects and led him into prolonged experimentation with drugs and an alternative lifestyle. But as he quelled his anger, his Rebel became more of a support to his life, assisting his psyche in seeing and contributing to life as it could be, as opposed to destroying what is.

After he selected his eight individual archetypes, Brian began to see that his Contract had to do in large measure with helping other people with their own writing on many different but interconnected levels. For years he had believed that he was intended to be a writer and produce significant works on his own. Over time, however, he came to appreciate the various roles he played not only as an original author but also as an editor, collaborator, teacher, and facilitator, even helping other authors or would-be authors find the appropriate agent or publisher for their own works, all of which deal in some form with the evolution of spiritual awareness. This last insight required a certain degree of humility. Writers, like most artists, need a large degree of healthy egotism just to survive in a competitive and often unfriendly marketplace. As a creative person, you have to believe in yourself even when your work is rejected or receives harsh criticism. But Brian also needed to let go of his attachment to having all his projects advance his own name or professional reputation in some linear way. Once he was able to do that, he realized that the richness and diversity of his vocation was not a sign of having failed at being a "great author" but actually represented a Contract of far more significant, if less grandiose, proportions.

In an insight that surprised him, Brian realized that the religious artists of the Middle Ages often worked in relative anonymity to produce great art, literature, and music. Individual aggrandizement was considered less important than contributing to the growth of knowledge, wisdom, and spiritual power in the larger world. Although such an attitude may seem impractical, if not actually counterproductive, in today's world, in the end Brian found that it suited his nature—and his archetypal support group—extremely well.

The fact that you do not have a primary connection to a particular archetypal pattern does not preclude your being able to enjoy the world associated with that archetype. You don't have to have the Artist or Musician in your support group to love and enjoy art and music. But attempting to align yourself to an archetype that is not one of your twelve companions can sometimes cause psychological and emotional trauma because incidents of personal rejection result, all due to trying to be what you are not meant to be. Two classmates of mine from college were both in the music department. One was a natural Musician, and the other was merely a music major. During their final performance of senior year, the Musician closed her eyes when she played, and we could all see the spirit of the music being expressed through her. By contrast, the music major played with her eyes open, conscious of every note. Although her performance was technically correct, it lacked the feeling and confidence so evident in the Musician. When you are acting outside of the guiding field of your twelve companions, you lack the magnetic force field to pull together the opportunities or relationships that you desire.

This same imbalance occurs when you attempt to initiate agreements with certain people, or succeed at a particular occupation, but lack the archetypal template. As I listen to people describe the difficult times they are having professionally, I realize that many of them are pursuing a life they were not meant to live. And all the workshops in the world, all the education they can attain, cannot bring about the success they are seeking. Either you have good investment instincts or you don't: on-target stock market sense comes from the gut of someone who has an archetype associated with financial risk taking, such as the Gambler or Midas. And while those two archetypes by no means guarantee financial success, they certainly generate more financial opportunities than other archetypes.

How do you know if you are simply not trying hard enough to realize your skills or Contract? Perhaps the time just isn't right for your tree to bear fruit, even though you might indeed be standing under the right one. Perhaps you are working the wrong aspect of the Musician archetype, for instance. Maybe you are meant to work in the production side of the industry or as a musicians' agent instead of actually being a performer. How do you know that you are not just bailing out when you should be hanging in there?

It's an easy answer, and a hard one. All clarity about the self is dependent on your self-esteem—your knowledge of yourself. A strong sense of self can sense when it is going in the right direction and when it is knocking on the wrong door. When you know yourself, you know exactly when you are not being true to yourself. Your gut instincts alone provide you with all the guidance you need. Your intuition will help you find your archetypes and your path in life.

When deciding on which archetypes belong in your support group, trust those instincts above all else. You'll need to practice your critical powers of discrimination, of course, weighing factors in favor of or against including a particular archetype. But in the end you should listen to your inner voice. All else being equal, the deciding factor between two archetypes that stack up about the same in logical terms will be the one that your gut tells you plays a key role in your life.

CHAPTER 6

The Chakras: Your
Spiritual Backbone

I f one is not oneself a sage or a saint," Aldous Huxley once wrote,
"the best thing one can do, in the field of metaphysics, is to study
the works of those who were, and who, because they had modified
their merely human mode of being were capable of a more than
merely human kind and amount of knowledge."[1] That is why we study
the writings of the great mystics of the world's religions, and the lives
of the masters who founded those religions. The masters and mystics
have tapped into the underground stream of spiritual knowledge that
flows beneath the bedrock of all the great traditions, uniting them and
washing away their surface differences. Through these spiritual
guides, we gain access to the collective wisdom that feeds the human
spirit, filtering into our psyches, souls, and biology. In a symbolic
sense, the teachings of the mystics, based on their own immediate
experience of the Divine, form our spiritual backbone, radiating out
into every aspect of our lives.

But there is another kind of spiritual backbone that is related to
the wisdom of the masters and the five stages of a Sacred Contract.
The system of energy centers known as the chakras defines and supports our spiritual life much the way the spinal column—along which
they are traditionally located—supports our physical body. Like the
stages of a Contract, they too follow a progression that reflects our
spiritual development from childhood through maturity. But in a
more literal sense, the chakras are also connected to the everyday

functions of our bodies and minds. They regulate everything from our survival instincts, sex drive, and self-esteem to our emotions, intellect, will, and spiritual aspirations. A knowledge of how they function and how they help *you* to function is essential to a complete understanding of your Sacred Contract.

Our Energy Anatomy

When I first began doing intuitive readings, the data that I received did not come to me in any specific order. I would sense an emotional pattern and then the physical problem that had arisen from it, but the energy information was not organized. Over time my readings became more structured and unfolded in layers: first I would sense an emotion or trauma, then a physical illness or disease. At a certain point the order switched, and I saw the physical content and problems first, followed by the emotional and psychological issues, and finally insights into the spiritual issues. I did not realize that these layers of information followed the natural alignment of the chakras until I wrote *The Creation of Health* in 1988. Indeed, these seven centers are like an energy spinal cord through which the life force, or *prana*, flows into our physical body. Each one represents a different configuration of physical, emotional, and psychological concerns. Eastern religions have determined the spiritual meaning of the chakras in a way that matches perfectly to the psychological and physical information that I gleaned from my readings. To me, the chakras are our energy anatomical system.

In Sanskrit, the language of the ancient Indian seers who first identified these energy centers, the word *chakra* (pronounced CHUK-ruh) means "wheel" or "circle." (The English words *cycle* and *cyclone* are derived from the same root.) Chakras are traditionally pictured as lotus blossoms, with varying numbers of petals, each inhabited by the energy affiliated with a sacred deity, with a characteristic color, sacred syllable, and animal symbol attached to it. The ancient seers and yogis experienced the energy of the chakras as constantly spinning. I find their function somewhat analogous to that of the hard drive of a modern computer—a powerful disk, constantly in motion, that provides vast amounts of information while also helping to run other major programs of the computer itself. The chakras concentrate and transform the enormous psychophysical energy that is stored in different parts of your body into spiritual energy and distribute it throughout your entire system.

According to the spiritual systems of the East, the chakras ascend in a line from the first, or root, chakra at the base of the spine through the seventh chakra, just above the crown of the head. Between them, in ascending order, the other five chakras correspond to the genitals and lower intestine; solar plexus and navel; heart; throat; and pineal gland or "third eye." (See Figure 1.) Although each of the chakras corresponds to a different part of the body, they are not material and actually reside within subtle energy sheaths that surround the body, where physical and psychic energies interpenetrate each other. These invisible but highly potent sheaths, or levels of psychic energy, are sometimes called the mental, emotional, etheric, and astral bodies, and they extend well beyond the physical dimensions of our frame.

During my years of doing health readings, I could sense only the seven energy centers of the chakras. When I began to get impressions of archetypal patterns, however, I sensed an additional center that I consider to be the eighth chakra, where our archetypal energies reside. While the seven lower chakras are largely personal in nature, relaying information that reflects the physical, emotional, psychological, and spiritual details of our life, the eighth chakra is transpersonal. Connecting to the infinite source of all archetypal energies, it also maintains a connection to every individual body and soul.

To get a sense of the activity of this chakra, imagine a three-dimensional infinity sign whose one arm encompasses and spins through your body and energy sheaths as the other extends out into the universe. Unlike the seven chakras that are directly involved in your physical anatomy, your eighth chakra is like a Möbius strip that runs between the personal unconscious and the collective unconscious, linking the literal and symbolic dimensions, your personal life and the impersonal universe. This Möbius strip represents a continual current of cosmic intelligence that feeds into your psyche.

FIGURE 1: THE CHAKRAS

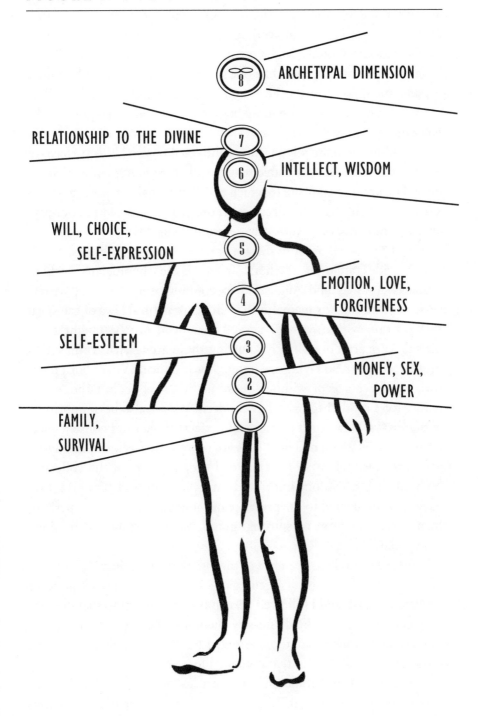

Because the eighth chakra contains your archetypal patterns, it is also the home of your Sacred Contract. In physical terms the eighth chakra is located about an arm's length above the crown of the head. In the esoteric Golden Light meditation, Taoist adepts visualize an "energy body" that appears like one's own body but made of luminous crystal, standing atop the head and an arm's length in height. The crown of the head of your energy body, then, would correspond to the location of your eighth chakra.

In addition to archetypes, the eighth chakra also holds patterns of experience and soul knowledge that are inherent in human consciousness. The archetypal plane to which the eighth chakra connects acts as a magnetic field that organizes life on this planet as well as in our psyche. Its influences are variously referred to as "Mother Nature" or "Gaia," the natural order of things, or even the laws of physics.

A wide range of teachers, from classic theologians such as Thomas Aquinas and Augustine to contemporary spiritual writers such as Matthew Fox maintain that there are natural laws of the spirit that operate within each of us and that need not be taught to us directly. We are born already knowing these archetypal truths—that murder, stealing, and lying are wrong, for instance. We are born territorial, and we accept without question that it is against the law of nature for a mother to harm her children. We are also born imprinted with universal laws such as cause and effect, choice and consequence, or magnetic attraction. These laws are represented as much in physics as in the spiritual laws of karma, and they are part of the collective body of divine wisdom imprinted into the eighth chakra. We may have to be awakened to the presence of these truths within us, perhaps by a parent, mentor, or spiritual guide, but we are bound by them nonetheless.

After I sensed the presence of the eighth chakra, the structure and nature of my readings changed again. Now the archetypal patterns came to me first, and I followed their subtle currents into that individual's personal energy field and saw them stir the psyche, then move into the conscious mind, the emotional body, and finally enter into a physical manifestation in that person's life.

The Child archetype and its patterns of vulnerability, for example, to which we can all relate, takes on a more personal identity as it connects to each individual psyche. This was true of Jessie, a young woman I met in a workshop. Her inner Child first manifested as a deep-seated fear of living alone, although she was not consciously aware of the reason. She grew up in a comfortable home in a safe neighborhood and had never been harmed or threatened there, so an atmosphere of both emotional and physical security had surrounded her all of her life.

Yet Jessie's inner Child held enormous authority over her emotional and psychological well-being. Once she understood that we all have a Child archetype at work in our lives, she was able to identify hers in action: specifically, fears of being kidnapped would overwhelm her when she was home alone at night. As a result, she kept lights on all night long and had a sophisticated alarm system installed. As soon as Jessie got into bed, she felt as she had when, as a little girl, she had waited for her parents to come home. "Even with a baby-sitter," she felt safe only once they were "back where they belonged."

Jessie found it easy to relate her personal fears and behaviors to the aspect of the Child archetype known as the Abandoned Child. Some of the characteristics that are inherent in the Abandoned Child are feeling as though your emotional needs do not matter to your parents, and seeing the entire world as a place you will never be able to handle alone. The universal archetype of the Abandoned Child was directly connected to aspects of Jessie's personal life. This initial insight marked the beginning of a process of self-discovery through which Jessie could approach her fears through her Abandoned Child, which gave her some distance and detachment as she investigated her relationship with her parents. Asking herself questions such as, What is the symbolic purpose behind these fears? How can you change these fears into strengths? and Are there other areas in your life or other relationships in which the Child projects its authority? helped her sort out her emotions.

Jessie realized that she had not been born with these fears but had developed them as a teenager. They became more intense the older she got, because getting older represented independence and living alone. In fact, her parents had encouraged her throughout her childhood to think of finding a place of her own as soon as she was out of high school, because they felt it was important that she learn how to take care of herself. They also wanted Jessie to become strong enough on her own so that she would not make decisions about her life based on fear. They didn't want her, for example, to get married out of a desire for protection rather than for love.

Although Jessie realized intellectually that her parents had wanted her to move out not to get rid of her but to help her learn to be effective on her own, she was still upset with them. Yet Jessie was able to begin working with that insight, beginning with her eighth chakra and threading it through her seventh chakra, then her sixth, all the way down to the first chakra. With each chakra, she investigated her fear of the dark within the meaning and context of the characteristics of that energy center. When she visualized her fourth, or heart, chakra, for instance, where the emotions reside, she saw that she was really quite angry at her parents. As she came to realize the wisdom of her parents' decision for her, she resolved the anger and, with it, her fear. For Jessie, this process opened a door of personal transformation. The Abandoned Child emerged from its shadow and became a source of strength, reminding her that she need no longer fear the unpredictability of the outside world and the onset of adulthood.

You too can apply the chakras to each archetype to help you uncover further indications of your Contract. If you feel that you touch on an issue that needs deeper work, I encourage you to seek the help of a therapist or a spiritual director.

The Chakra System

Each chakra contains information that is essential to your ability to interpret the symbolic meaning of your life experiences. Each also is the center of a power source that you are meant to acquire, such as wisdom in the sixth chakra or self-respect in the third chakra. At the level of personality, these power sources are reflected in strengths, such as intellectual skills for the sixth chakra or self-discipline and courage for the third. Deficits in your chakra energy, caused by trauma, show up in your personality as weaknesses in your life, as challenges that force you to try to heal your wounds and history.

In my previous books I worked with the chakras from the ground up, from one through seven. In the first part of this chapter we're going to work with the chakras from the eighth down. This is because we're focusing on your archetypal energies, which reside in the eighth chakra. We're going to track each one through its spiritual significance (seventh chakra) and its projections in your psyche (sixth chakra), to see how it influences your choices (fifth chakra) and activates an emotional response that emanates from your heart (fourth chakra). A dramatic shift occurs when this current of life-force enters your three lower chakras, which correspond to your self-esteem, sexuality, power, and survival, and finds expression in your physical life. There your perceptions become instinctual rather than rational and emotional, more reactive and not particularly concerned with spiritual growth.

By observing how the native intelligence of your chakras interacts with the influential patterns of your archetypes, you gain insights into your Contract, into how the Divine reveals Its partnership with you. Also, you see how energy data connect to the physical aspects of your life. Your archetypal energies determine your life patterns, which is another way of saying that your biography becomes your biology.

Although we say that each chakra "contains" certain knowledge or "regulates" particular activities, it might be more appropriate to say that the chakras resonate energetically with various aspects of your life. The survival "stuff" of your physical life, such as a car or a house, for instance, resonates to dense reality. While such items are important to your physical comfort, they are not essential to your spiritual development. They resonate with your first chakra, which is your anchor to the physical environment. With each ascending chakra, your individuality emerges, along with the specifics of your life that reflect your own spiritual path and your many Contracts. Each chakra is a doorway to another energy reality, a means of perception that helps you see your archetypal journey through life more clearly.

The chakras resonate with ever less refined spiritual energies as you work your way down the spinal column. For example, the emotional connections you have to other people, which resonate with your fourth chakra, have a far greater effect on your personal development than the kind of car you choose to drive. Each chakra also represents a degree of spiritual awareness and personal power that you need to manage consciously. For instance, it takes a great deal more thought and presence of mind to make the best and healthiest emotional choice for yourself than it does to select the best car. For much the same reason, although you are always working with the energies of all your chakras, you confront the issues and areas of your life regulated by your chakras in ascending order as your life progresses chronologically. Later in this chapter, I'll take you through an exercise in which you'll work with your chakras in the more conventional progression from the bottom up. But right now, let's examine their relative strengths from the top down.

The Eighth Chakra

Lesson:
Integrate the Self
Power:
Symbolic Sight
Strengths:
Detachment, staying in the present moment, unconditional trust, ability to recognize illusions, acceptance of intuitive guidance
Shadow: Every archetype has both positive and shadow manifestations. (For the shadow aspect of specific archetypes, see the Appendix.)

The eighth chakra, or "transpersonal point," marks the realm where, looking up, the individual soul merges with the greater universe. Looking down, it marks the point at which the soul manifests into matter, into your individual energy body. Your twelve archetypal companions (whom you identified in Chapter 5) are the symbolic "residents" of the eighth chakra. They guide your Sacred Contract. Your bond with your twelve is considerably more intense than it is with the countless other archetypes that make up the collective unconscious, although some of them may influence you from time to time also, particularly during periods of social upheaval, wars, and natural disasters. You can, of course, relate to many archetypal patterns, even if they are not part of your immediate archetypal family. For example, I am not physically a mother to a biological child and the Mother archetype is not among my twelve, yet I can empathize with what it means to mother someone. By contrast, the Hermit archetype is such a strong influence on me that I constantly have to satisfy that aspect of my psyche, from the seventh chakra on down to the first, where it influenced even the kind of home I live in. When I chose my home, I had to feel that it was more a "hermitage" than a house, because I need to withdraw from the world in order to create.

Achieving an impersonal archetypal overview of your personal life empowers you to deal with your day-to-day life. When you can recognize the pattern of a particular archetype at work in your life, you hone in on emotions or tendencies that need your attention. In identifying yourself as having a Wounded Child archetype, for instance, you are acknowledging that you have been hurt. Then you can examine your spirit for first-chakra energy leaks—for instance, Did the hurt come from a family member? If so, can you practice a first-chakra strength, detach from the hurt or grief, find whatever wisdom has come out of that injury, and see how it has become part of your Contract? Like all of us, you had to learn forgiveness, so this wound or loss was your route to learning that spiritual lesson. Learning to deal with necessary losses is part of everyone's Contract. Although we feel physical and emotional pain, our spiritual purpose is to become aware of the reasons for such events—or to create meaning out of them. So a physical wound needs to be transformed into a spiritual passageway, converting the actual experience into its symbolic purpose.

Once you learn to see your archetypes at work in your physical experiences, you can more easily understand your emotional and psychological responses—and find their symbolic meaning. If you're having a dispute with a family member over how to care for an aging parent, for instance, you can analyze whether the dispute is an issue of the first chakra (tribal loyalty), the second chakra (money and power), or perhaps the fourth chakra (placing love and compassion above loyalty and money). That knowledge will help you decide on the most appropriate course of action. If you are in a relationship that seems more hurtful and confusing than enjoyable and empowering, you will need to determine whether the core problem involves a sexual power play (second chakra), a chronic lack of self-esteem (third chakra), the inability to express your needs (fifth chakra), or a struggle to free your spirit (seventh chakra).

Your chakras tell you, in essence, how you manage your power. By looking at a difficult situation or event, past or current, through each of your chakras, you can determine where the problems lie and how to address them. One man I know named Mark has chosen to divorce his wife despite great opposition from both their families, who worry about the couple's children and whose religious beliefs oppose divorce. Mark is following through with the divorce because he feels he needs it to be healthy and fulfilled. He and his wife married very young and have grown in opposite directions, no longer sharing much of anything except a cold civility. From Mark's perspective, he also has to prevent his family from making his choices for him. He is able to use the positive energy of his first chakra, which regulates family matters, and his understanding of his Victim archetype to withstand the resentment and guilt with which his "tribal elders" are trying to burden him. He sees the potential to be victimized in this situation, but he also sees that his relatives are acting out of their own first-chakra need to hold the family together at all costs.

"I've made a full assessment of what I will face by moving forward with my choices," Mark says. "I know that no one will support me, and I'm prepared to live with the consequences, because I cannot see living an empty and bitter life. I've made arrangements to take care of my kids and my ex-wife. I will not abandon my financial responsibilities as a father, and I also hope that I can teach my children through my example that it is important to make certain choices in life even when they are difficult. Many of the things we have to do will hurt other people, not because we want to hurt them but because life puts us into circumstances in which hurt just cannot be avoided. I will try to teach them all I can from this, and I am prepared for them to reject me, but I hope that rejection will not last forever. Still, I am grateful that I have what it takes to stand on my own two feet in this lifetime."

Our archetypal patterns are only part of the vast stores of soul knowledge inherent in our eighth chakra. The eighth chakra calls you to find God. It draws you into seeking your higher potential. It helps you see your life as a spiritual journey disguised as a physical experience. Your passion to live a meaningful life, your need to make peace with your conscience—these yearnings are all expressions of the soul speaking through your intuition, through your chakras of body and mind. Following their promptings, you will fulfill your Sacred Contract.

The Seventh Chakra

Lesson:

Live in the Present Moment

Power:

Inner Divinity

Strengths:

Faith in the Divine as well as in inner guidance, insight into healing, devotion

Shadow:

The need to know why things happen as they do, which causes you to live in the past

Using your imagination, picture your archetypes descending into your seventh chakra, which is located just above the crown of your head. This is the area of the psychophysical body where divine energy—*prana, ch'i,* or the life-force of the universe—enters your physical energy system. This is the initial point at which each archetypal pattern becomes personalized into your life. The universal Child archetype, for instance, takes on the characteristics of your own inner Child. At the seventh chakra the Child may announce itself in the form of inspiration or imagination, the ability to see things afresh, without preconceptions. Our seventh-chakra childlike inspirations, musings, or dreams coax us to make those "dreams come true." (In your lower chakras the Child patterns can be identified within physical expressions from childlike glee to petulance.) On the material plane the seventh chakra will evaluate the spiritual implications of an event or relationship, advising you whether it serves your highest potential.

The seventh chakra's energy resonates with the imagination, with the greatest potential of the human spirit and the physical body. When athletes first aimed to run a four-minute mile, or aerospace engineers imagined that they could put a man on the moon, their idea of what was possible was a seventh-chakra image. Every greater vision manifests as a personal goal when it descends into the sixth chakra, where visionary energy allies with that of the rational mind.

In the Indian system the seventh chakra is known as the "thousand-petaled lotus," an indication of the tremendous potential energy it holds. The locale of our spiritual aspiration and development, this energy center's power becomes available to us through meditation. The ancients described mystical experience as a sudden expansion of the energy of the seventh chakra flooding into the psyche and soul, elevating one's entire being to a level of consciousness that is fully transcendent of the physical world. Over a century ago the Canadian psychologist R. M. Bucke labeled this experience "cosmic consciousness." He believed that humanity was on the path to evolutionary change from self-consciousness to cosmic or spiritual consciousness, and he felt that this change would parallel the prehistoric shift from animal awareness to self-consciousness that marked the emergence of Homo sapiens. Bucke based his theory on his experience of a moment of illumination in 1872, as well as on the records of mystical experiences of extraordinary individuals including the Buddha, Jesus, Saint Paul, Plotinus, Muhammad, Dante, Saint John of the Cross, William Blake, Walt Whitman, Balzac, Spinoza, and Sri Ramakrishna. His evidence suggested to him that human spiritual evolution was accelerating.

While the third chakra is your seat of self-esteem and gut intuition, your seventh energy center can inspire you to see beyond the limited range of the separate self and into transpersonal or cosmic vision. In an epiphany or awakening, the priorities of your inner perceptions are reordered to perceive the presence of the Divine within your life. Einstein's discoveries of universal laws relied on the energy of his seventh chakra. Visionaries who foresaw great possibilities for humankind, such as Martin Luther King, Jr., Gandhi, and Abraham Lincoln, also work through the energy of this center.

The Sixth Chakra

Lesson:
Seek Only the Truth
Power:
Wisdom
Strengths:
Intellectual skills, evaluation of insights, receiving inspiration, generating wisdom from experience
Shadow:
Defining the truth in self-serving ways

This chakra resonates with the pineal gland, which is located behind and between your eyes and so is often called the third eye. The center of wisdom in the body, its power affects the intellect and your ability to articulate vision and inspiration. While we may be able to envision endless dreams and possibilities, we still need an instrument that is skilled at focusing attention and applying imagination. A focused mind and disciplined imagination are two of the strengths associated with the sixth chakra. Once you have the seed of an idea, your sixth chakra helps give it shape. You run the idea through your intelligence to see if you can work with it. You evaluate the idea intellectually and decide whether you want to "manage" the birth of this idea into its physical form. On the physical level your sixth chakra mobilizes your intellect and attitudes to deal with any situation and communicate your ideas to those involved.

This is also the energy center that empowers our attitudes, beliefs, memories, and the overall character of our rational mind. Whether we are fair- and open-minded or judgmental and limited in our capacity to consider new ideas is a manifestation of how we direct the power of this chakra. When we speak of creating our own reality, we are referring to the sixth-chakra laboratory in which that process occurs.

When Thomas Edison needed to solve a problem with one of his inventions, he would engage in what we would call today active dreaming. He would sit in a rocking chair with the question in mind, rocking slowly and rhythmically while holding a small ball in each hand. When one of the balls dropped out of his hand, signaling that he had begun to doze, the sound of it hitting the floor would awaken him. Edison would then recall what he had been visualizing or dreaming about at that moment, and more often than not it was a potential solution to his problem, or at least a step in the right direction. He was gaining access to his unconscious, allowing his Inventor archetype free rein to interact with his sixth chakra. Once the solution had presented itself to him, he would weigh its implications and see how best to employ this latest bit of inspiration.

Sir Isaac Newton, besides being a great scientific philosopher, was also deeply involved in alchemy and theology. Although he is now considered the embodiment of the rational mind, he relied greatly on the imaginative power of his sixth chakra. Newton felt that his imagination gained prominence as the sun went down, and that his intellect tended to take over as the sun came up. He would work until one or two in the morning, then go to sleep for a few hours, allowing his imagination to go to work. When he awoke, he would invoke his intellect to give shape to the ideas and fantasies that had been spawned while he slept.

A man named Hank feels that his Musician archetype best projects the power of his sixth chakra, because he creates music that "reflects my own reality." Although Hank has yet to make a name for himself, he believes that his psyche and soul are in complete harmony with the Musician in him. "I felt directed to write music since high school," he says. "My world is constructed around this part of myself. Most of my mental energy is directed toward feeding the power of this archetype within me, and because this connection is so strong, it does not occur to me that I will fail."

The use of visualization and positive thinking to maintain or restore physical health is an example of directing the power of the sixth chakra. The sixth chakra imagines a body that is free of illness and then pushes this energetic vision into the fifth, fourth, and remaining chakras to utilize their power as a united system to rebuild the physical form. The blueprint for the overall healing, however, begins in the mind. The energy of the sixth chakra connects with all the other power centers in the body.

The Fifth Chakra

Lesson:
Surrender Personal Will to Divine Will
Power:
Choice
Strengths:
Faith, self-knowledge, personal authority, ability to keep your word
Shadow:
An obsessive need to control relationships and events

Corresponding to the throat and thyroid gland, the fifth chakra is your center of will, your ability to express your needs and desires, and your power of choice. The force behind acts of creation, choice creates consequence. The fifth chakra also is the center of the energy of honor. It resonates when you "give your word" to someone. When you make a commitment, you agree to use the power of your will to hold within you a part of another person's spirit, to be psychologically supportive. "Giving your word," or making a social vow of marriage or a religious vow is a ritual of personal revelation. When a person breaks his word, that action reverberates for years within the psyche of the betrayed. It cuts to the soul.

Fifth-chakra vows are promises of the body, mind, heart, and spirit merged into one. Acts of soul retrieval, or confession, are also fifth-chakra rituals in which the individual consciously calls back fragments of her spirit that have been out on "negative missions," such as telling a lie. The need to participate in such rituals for the health of one's spirit is recognized in some form by most spiritual traditions. The ritual of last rites as performed in the Roman Catholic Church acknowledges that the whole of one's spirit must be called back into the self prior to death so that the whole of one's being can move on to the afterlife.

The inherent soul knowledge of the fifth chakra communicates to us that we must develop the strength to make choices that reflect who we are. We suffer deeply when our fifth chakra is controlled by someone else through social customs, restrictions, or tyranny, or by thought-forms, superstitions, and emotional weight such as guilt. When that happens, we find ourselves living a life that serves the needs of others to the detriment of our own, and we must learn how to liberate our voice and spirit. Archetypes of the Slave or Servant hold the potential for liberation for those who must birth their own will, the spiritual equivalent of buying your freedom from servitude.

You develop a powerful personal will by making choices that draw on both the desires of the heart and the wisdom of the mind. In a physical setting, for example, your fifth chakra spontaneously organizes the manner in which you will communicate with others within that setting, helping you choose whether to be defensive and circumspect or direct and open. Developing the strength to manage the power of will is perhaps the most difficult stage in the process of spiritual maturation. In all of life's interactions we must make choices, and choices direct our spirit into action. All Contracts draw us into at least one act of will. When Malcolm X went to Mecca in 1964 to make the *hajj*, the pilgrimage required of every Muslim at least once, he was the chief disciple of Nation of Islam leader Elijah Muhammad, who preached hatred toward the white race based on what he claimed were Muslim teachings. During the *hajj* Malcolm met and mingled with Muslims from India, China, Indonesia, and North Africa, including many whites. His heart was deeply moved by the love and unified spiritual purpose he experienced from his fellow Muslims. "I could see from this," he wrote home, "that perhaps if white Americans could accept the Oneness of God, then perhaps, too, they could accept *in reality* the Oneness of man—and cease to measure, and hinder, and harm others in terms of their 'differences' in color."[2]

Filled with this insight that had both moved his heart and stirred his mind, Malcolm returned to America and broke with Elijah Muhammad, bringing many other African-Americans with him into an orthodox Islam that preaches tolerance to people of all races and religions. Malcolm X could only have made this powerful choice, which had enormous consequences for the future of race relations in this country, by joining together the desires of his heart with the wisdom of his mind.

The power of choice and self-expression can be viewed from another perspective in the life of a woman named Lee, who believed she had a powerful Crone or Wise Woman archetype. An enthusiastic feminist, she joined Goddess circles and wrote about social justice issues. Even though she saw that cultural improvements had been made in women's status, Lee was admittedly angry at men and could not establish a satisfying relationship. A longtime member of a feminist community of friends and activists, Lee "really got into the role of being the wise Crone," she said. "I wanted to be seen as someone who could dole out soul advice for the women in my group. In the process I gradually started to give orders instead of insights. I didn't realize it at first, but I was trying to exert my influence over the choices the women were making about what do to with their lives. I felt that my experiences should be honored by everyone in the group."

Conflicts eventually arose within Lee's community of women as some began to challenge her counsel, with which she had great difficulty coping. "What began as a loving and supportive group of women ended up being a source of great trauma for all involved. Eventually the group disbanded, and I was left feeling completely rejected and misunderstood. A year went by before I was able to discuss this situation with a friend, who pointed out that in my enthusiasm to be the central voice of this group, I had negated the value of everyone else's contribution. In the language of power, I eclipsed their will because I wanted their admiration."

Lee was misusing the energy of her fifth chakra in the way she related to her Crone archetype. Once she recognized her energy power plays within the group, she knew she had some serious work to do on herself. "I thought that I had grown beyond the need to control others, that the Crone in me was wiser than that. Obviously as soon as you think you've mastered yourself, you meet the people who are meant to show you how far you have yet to go."

The Fourth Chakra

Lesson:
Love Is Divine Power
Power:
Love and Compassion
Strengths:
Forgiveness, dedication, inspiration, hope, trust, the ability to heal
Shadow:
Jealousy, anger, resentment, and the inability to forgive

The fourth chakra is the heart center of the body. As the keeper of wisdom and the power of forgiveness and release, this chakra rules the process of transformation. The heart center regulates all issues related to emotions, from love, compassion, generosity, and empathy to hatred, jealousy, and malice. The heart chakra also governs the spiritual challenges of forgiveness of others and of oneself. The power of this energy center animates the life that surrounds you, lending all activities and exchanges personal texture and significance. And although each of your chakras serves the whole of your energy field, the fourth is the most vital of all, because love, passion, envy, generosity, compassion, and all the emotions connected to your fears and other strengths reside here. Where your heart is, there is your power. Without this energy nothing in your life can manifest or flourish, from your romantic relationships to your artistic creativity.

Your fourth chakra perceptions also automatically assess your emotional response to a physical setting or relationship. Do you feel love or anger toward someone in your vicinity? Does someone appeal to you emotionally? You may not even be consciously aware of the chakra's assessments, but it passes them on energetically to your fifth chakra to determine how you will communicate your responses to those around you.

The fourth chakra also regulates emotional inspiration of the kind that can inspire great creativity, such as songs and love poetry. Emily Dickinson's fourth chakra was so dominant that she was able to write brilliantly perceptive poetry even without having extensive contact with other people. The energy of her fourth chakra enabled her to feel not only conventional love—for her family and for the married man with whom she may have been in love—but also the mystical love affair of the natural world that is reflected in her poetry. Indeed, poetry was the language with which Dickinson prayed to the Divine. So too was the great love poetry of Rumi, the thirteenth-century Sufi mystic whose poems address God with the detailed, sensuous lyricism of a lover singing to his beloved.

In eighteenth-century Bengal the Hindu mystic Ramprasad Sen composed a series of love poems to the Divine Mother as manifested in the goddess Kali. Like Rumi, Ramprasad used the metaphor of intoxication with wine to describe losing himself in the Divine. "The explosion of awakened language which authentic poets experience after . . . creative birth can transform their individual being entirely, because the substance of humanity is infused with language," writes the modern-day Sufi sheikh Lex Hixon about Ramprasad. "If the poetry is strong enough, the surrounding cultural body feels its impact and is transmuted, as dough is kneaded, rises through the potency of yeast, is baked, and becomes a new reality."[3] Hixon may well be talking about the power of the fourth chakra to transform the human soul.

A woman I met named Nadine also had a Poet archetype, and it absolutely enchanted the lives of countless people. Nadine had written poetry "since forever," and her love of poetic expression was reflected in her entire persona. Her softness of manner and the way she interacted with others made it seem as if she were floating through them. When people learned that she was a poet, they generally said something like, "Oh, I can see that in you" or "That figures." She was the gentle, inwardly beautiful aspect of this archetype incarnate. Nadine wanted to write poetry that made people feel warmth in their hearts. "More than pondering the great philosophical questions of life," she said, "I want to make people feel good without having to have a reason. I just don't see why being happy should be such hard work."

The Third Chakra

Lesson:
Honor Yourself
Power:
Self-Respect
Strengths:
Self-esteem, self-discipline, ambition, courage, generosity, ethics, instincts, intuition
Shadow:
Abdicating personal power of choice out of a need for approval; narcissistic behavior

Continuing down the spinal column, the next chakra corresponds to the solar plexus, located between the navel and the sternum. This is the power center of your self-esteem, personality, and ego.

All of your interactions with people begin via your third chakra. I once overheard someone say that the greatest curse of the human experience is low self-esteem, and I could not agree more. The insecurities that arise from a lack of self-esteem generate an almost disabling degree of vulnerability. You are unable to "hold your center" or withstand criticism; you have trouble expressing your opinions and needs and drawing your boundaries of self-protection; you don't trust your intuition. Without self-esteem we lack the courage to carve our place in the world and may end up being controlled by other people.

Your third chakra is, in effect, your loudest voice, and it is also your intuitive guide—hence the term *gut instinct.* According to your third chakra's initial impression, your other chakras either shut down, send warning signals, or open up to welcome the person into your energy field. For although your five senses provide your mind with the lay of the external land, the sensory system of the third chakra conveys the "feeling" of the land, from sensing what could be hiding behind the bushes to feeling an atmosphere pregnant with potential and opportunities.

The third chakra is also the place where you define your sense of integrity and your personal code of honor. The fifth chakra regulates the choices you make in expressing and living up to your honor code, but the third is the center where that code is first formed. The more fully your third-chakra values are developed throughout your life, the more positively they will be expressed by your fifth-chakra choices. This energy center resonates with your integrity, personal pride, and dignity, which are the positive aspects of the ego. Shame, loss of face, and a lack of personal identity are the power crises of this chakra. An honor code is essential for you to maintain a healthy spirit and body. Compromising your values or lacking a spiritual backbone puts you at physical and spiritual risk.

On the material plane your third chakra lets you know "where you stand" in a given situation. Its energy directs you to the location in any physical setting that is most advantageous to your sense of self-esteem, how you will project yourself to other people. In a social gathering, for instance, this chakra's energy might direct you to stand against a wall, sit in a chair in the corner, or position yourself in the middle of the room and move from one group of people to another. At a business meeting the third chakra is continuously sending you messages about where best to sit and where to address your attention.

A woman named Georgia's third-chakra energy was dominated by the archetype of the Martyr, which caused her to feel that she always had to work harder and struggle more than the rest of her family to get by. Her sister had married a successful man, and both her brothers seemed to be living free from any responsibilities. Georgia, on the other hand, did not like her job or the place where she lived. She wanted to move but was afraid to strike out on her own in another town. By the time I met her, she had more or less given up hope of ever being happy. When she agreed that she had a Martyr archetype, she at first interpreted it to mean that she was born to suffer, which is not necessarily the case. I explained to her that she had a choice about how the influence of that archetypal pattern could work in her psyche and life. If she decided not to examine the meaning of her Martyr experiences, she could give the archetype the power to create more "martyrdom" experiences for her. She could also choose, however, to examine her motivation for controlling others through her Martyr behavior and begin to challenge this destructive pattern in her personality.

It took some doing to persuade Georgia to open up, but once she did, we discussed some historical figures who had Martyr archetypes yet represented great power, such as Jesus and Gandhi, along with a few people from her personal life. She recognized that they all had inspired others to find courage in their fears and to believe that their lives could be better. This insight made Georgia consider finally facing her fear of moving and changing her life. "I can see where I have Contracts with my brothers and sister to examine the Martyr in me," she said, "and that they are doing me a favor by bringing that about. And I can see that I am consumed with self-pity and have felt for a long time that my life has nothing to offer me. They are very positive people—and that's another trait of theirs that I have always resented." Georgia ultimately chose to use her Martyr as a symbol of death of self and rebirth to a new life, one of its most empowering aspects.

The Second Chakra

Lesson:

Honor One Another

Power:

Creativity

Strengths:

Survival instincts, including "fight or flight," resilience, perseverance, ability to create and take risks, sexuality and sensuality, financial acumen

Shadow:

Disempowering or using others for your own advantage

This chakra is centered in the sexual organs and lower back region. While the power inherent in the first chakra is part of a tribal family, or group energy, the energy in the second focuses on your individual ability to manage the power of sexuality, money, influence or control over other people, competition, and self-defense. Chakras located near each other overlap somewhat in their focus, and these powerful second-chakra energies are all clearly related to survival, also a first-chakra and third-chakra concern. Our ability to make and handle money, our sexual orientation and attitudes around sex, and our relative level of personal power and ability to use it are all governed by agreements we have made regarding the second chakra.

On the level of physical perception, your second chakra automatically evaluates any situation according to how it affects your survival: Are you physically safe? Are there any financial implications? Is your power in this situation threatened by someone bigger, stronger, richer, sexier? A part of you instinctively assesses each moment of your life for its potential threat to your survival. Even if you enter a room full of loving friends and family, for example, your brain and body still scan the room and the energy around you for any impending physical dangers or negative attitudes. You also automatically scan for any threat to people you love. How often have you felt, on running into a friend or family member or thinking of someone, that you "knew" something was wrong, even though you could not identify it?

Through this energy center you are attached to your addictions, regardless of whether they are drugs, work, or other habits. Having to be first in line or needing to have the last word in a discussion or debate with someone is a form of addiction as surely as alcoholism or overeating. Addiction is the act of giving away your power to a substance that in turn controls you, a type of second-chakra tug-of-war. This is the "fight or flight" chakra that is another manifestation of your survival instinct. It is also the center of your body that thrives on creativity and your need to give birth, either literally or figuratively, to creative projects. But if birth is associated with this chakra, so is literal and figurative abortion. When creative projects or activities in which you are involved cannot be completed, their premature death represents an energy abortion. Given this perspective, men as well as women should recognize that they have abortions. Many of the men I have read who were coping with prostate cancer had their creative projects "aborted" in midstream.

The act of rape and the energy of vengeance are also products of the second chakra. In this sense, rape is a violation not only of one's physical body but also of one's emotional, psychological, and creative life. Many people carry the scars of rape in their psyches, but because they have no association with rape as an energy crime, they are completely unaware of the source of their trauma, much less how to heal it.

You may have many Contracts with people that will come to light consciously when you evaluate your energy bond with them through issues related to this chakra. Because all second-chakra issues are somehow concerned with physical survival, this chakra reflects some of our deepest vulnerabilities.

Arleen, who has a strong Rescuer archetype, got involved with a man by "rescuing" him emotionally when he was going through a particularly lonely period of adjustment in his life. He had just moved into town and had not yet gotten his feet on the ground. Arleen approached the man, whose name was Jacob, while he was shopping alone and struck up a friendship, offering to help him get to know his way around town. Her private agenda, however, was that she hoped this offer would lead to a romantic relationship. Arleen was forming an energy attachment to Jacob through her second chakra, because she had a sexual attraction to him and had the intention to control the direction the relationship was taking. Yet the archetypal pattern that her energy was forming was that of the Rescuer rather than the Lover. Her need to have a partner, combined with her fears that this would never come to pass, animated the "personality" of her Rescuer archetype. Whenever she thought of Jacob, her Rescuer automatically turned on the same thoughts in her head, which then became the fantasy within which this relationship existed in Arleen's mind.

Although Arleen and Jacob began to see each other on almost a daily basis, the friendship never seemed to move into a romantic affair, which frustrated Arleen. One day as they were seated in a restaurant, a friend of Arleen's named Jane came over to the table, and Arleen introduced her to Jacob. Later that week Jane ran into Jacob without

Arleen, and the two of them started to date. His attraction to Jane, unlike his attraction to Arleen, was romantic. When Arleen found out about their relationship, she felt betrayed and rejected and struggled with a burning desire to publicly embarrass the couple. She envisioned herself destroying Jane's car and told herself repeatedly that Jane would eventually disappoint Jacob and that he would return to her.

Arleen's negative attachment to both of these people created an energy hemorrhage through her second chakra, because all of the issues that she was dealing with were second-chakra ones, such as her intense feelings of envy, vengeance, and fear of being alone. In order to break her energy connection to both of these people, and to her relationship fantasy, Arleen had first to approach this life experience from a symbolic perspective. She had to interpret the meaning of the events from the position that she had a Contract with each of these individuals for reasons that served her spiritual development.

Even when we get an insight that sheds a spiritual light on a painful situation, we may have trouble coming to grips with old feelings of hurt, anger, and rejection. To free yourself of enmeshment in anger or old wounds, you have to climb the ladder back up through the chakras until you can view a painful experience symbolically and objectively. Healing can sometimes take practice, and this inner work of viewing your history symbolically is rarely completed overnight. Besides considering the possibility that she had this painful experience because she needed to encounter her Rescuer archetype, Arleen also had to be willing to learn, forgive, and move on.

The First Chakra

Lesson:
All Is One
Power:
Groundedness
Strengths:
Family identity, bonding, and loyalty
Shadow:
Excluding others, prejudice, illusions of superiority

The first chakra corresponds to the area where the body makes contact with the earth when seated in the classic posture of meditation. It grounds us in physical life: in the physical arena, every experience, every encounter we have automatically engages our first chakra, which assesses our immediate environment for the basic details of size, shape, people, and all other factors that relate to physical characteristics. The first chakra also grounds us to the groups that support our life. Our relationship with power begins with learning how it works within our family and other social groups or tribal connections, including friends, gangs, religious affiliations, and social class. Other forms of group power connections include genetic inheritance, ethnic heritage, and national identity, as well as group beliefs, values, attitudes, and superstitions.

An enormous supply of your energy is invested in potent beliefs common to thousands or millions of other people. Many people have been told that a certain illness runs in their family, for example, and that they have a natural propensity toward that disease. As a result of having this notion reinforced in their psyche, they invest their energy in that thought, giving it power and authority over them. I have worked with many people who, in the process of healing a serious illness, try every form of alternative medicine, including visualization and positive thinking. Yet when I ask whether they believe that they can heal the illness, a high percentage admit to hoping they can while at the same time expressing their doubts, because modern medical research maintains that no cure has been found. So although their mind is focused on maintaining a positive attitude, their energy, or power—which is the only investment that matters—is connected to the findings and beliefs of the medical community. Their attachment to the power of that group thought-form inevitably dominates, because hope without power is no match for fear with power.

Your chakras, like your archetypes and Contracts, are essentially neutral, providing you with either strength or vulnerability depending on how you make use of their energy. Your first chakra, for instance, connects you to family loyalties, traditions, rituals, social laws, and the many positive elements of society that give you a sense of identity. I believe that we agree to be born to parents whose genetic traits and family lineage provide precisely the assets and liabilities that will help us most in learning and contributing what we need to in this life. Our parents' financial situation, level of intellect, psychological and emotional predispositions, and geographic location are all part of the equation that yields the sum of our own life. There are no "accidents of birth," as the phrase goes; everything is provided for your particular journey, including the social, ethnic, and religious value systems of your family, which form the foundation of your consciousness and the lens through which you will first encounter life.

The Three-Column Model: A User's Guide

Although the chakras appear to progress in a logical fashion from bottom to top, a shift in energies occurs between the third and fourth chakras. This change is so clearly defined that I consider the seven traditional chakras actually to be two distinct perceptual systems within the human psyche and body. To illustrate this configuration, I divide the chakras into two columns. The first, or left-hand, column contains chakras one, two, and three; the second column, chakras four through seven.

The two teams of chakras function on very different levels of consciousness. The first-column chakras are aligned to physical power and the physical plane of life, to the experiences that concern our survival. They are fed information by our five senses. How much power we give to money, sexuality, authority, fame, control, social position, and other manifestations of our physical world is regulated by these three energy centers. The second-column chakras are aligned to the internal forces of our minds, hearts, and spirits. I refer to this column as a person's *internal laboratory*, because these chakras resonate with the energy dimension of life.

A symbolic line of separation exists between our sensory experiences and our internal lives. We are often unaware, for example, that our response to external objects is the result of emotional and psychological projections that come from a repository of personal experiences. We view physical reality through an elaborate set of internal filters that prevent us from seeing things as they really are. In studying how emotional stress and trauma leave their marks on our personal biology, I have learned that healing requires a merger of these two

FIGURE 2: THE THREE-COLUMN MODEL

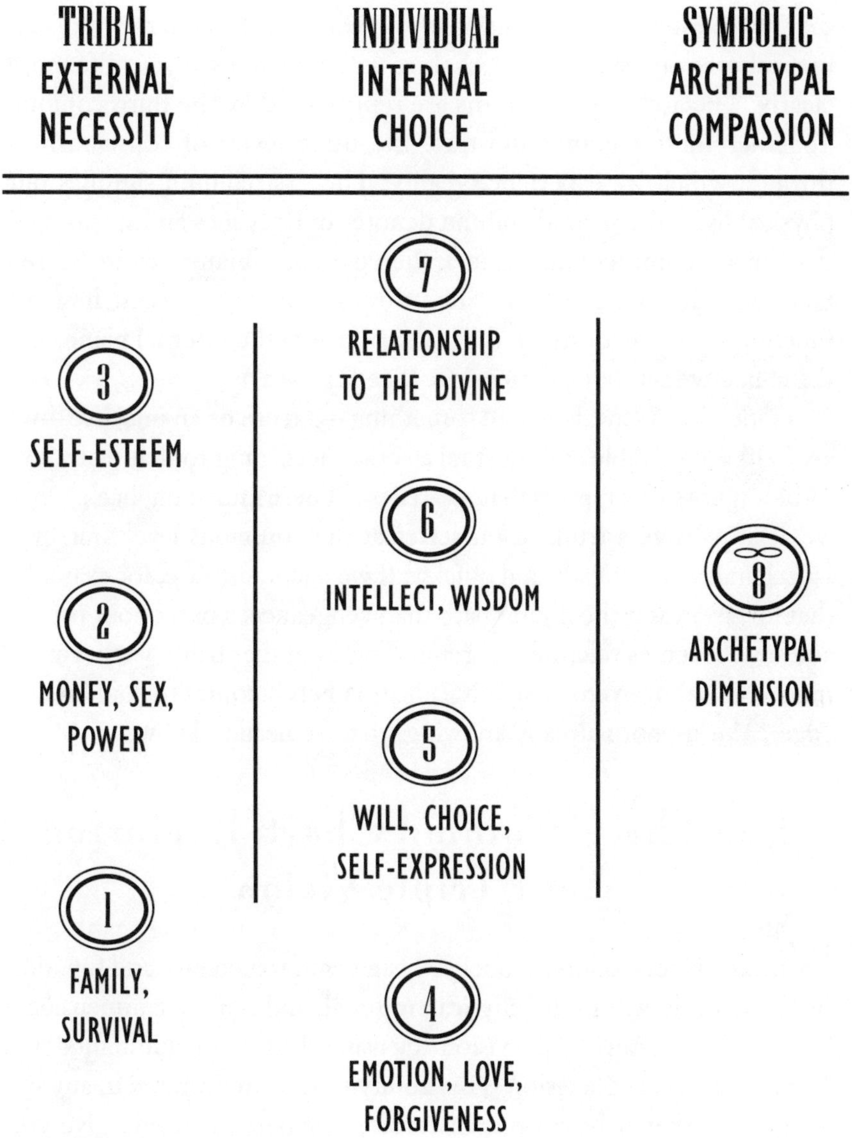

TRIBAL
EXTERNAL
NECESSITY
INDIVIDUAL
INTERNAL
CHOICE
SYMBOLIC
ARCHETYPAL
COMPASSION
7
RELATIONSHIP
TO THE DIVINE
3
SELF-ESTEEM
6
INTELLECT, WISDOM
8
ARCHETYPAL
DIMENSION
2
MONEY, SEX,
POWER
5
WILL, CHOICE,
SELF-EXPRESSION
1
FAMILY,
SURVIVAL
4
EMOTION, LOVE,
FORGIVENESS

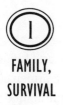

polarities of the psyche. Your internal world has to find a way to build a bridge to your external world so that you can see through to the truth that connects your intentions with what you actually do.

Archetypes are the most effective bridge between these worlds that I have found. Identifying them and working through the information inherent in each of your chakras will help you see your life more clearly. The archetypal patterns are represented by the third column. Together these columns illustrate the three levels of consciousness through which we experience reality. The first column signifies our physical lives; the second column denotes our psyches and spirits; and the third column contains the archetypal coordinates of our Sacred Contract, the eighth chakra. The three columns represent how we function simultaneously on the physical plane, the internal plane, and the collective symbolic dimension. (See Figure 2.)

Once we are awakened to something—a truth or an injustice—we are held accountable and must take action according to that truth. We cannot ignore or suppress that awareness. There's no going back. Once we acknowledge a truth to ourselves at the conscious level, our lives will change dramatically and quickly. If we become aware, for example, that forgiveness is the higher path than vengeance, a part of our psyche and soul becomes relentless in reminding us of that truth whenever we must choose forgiveness or vengeance. When it comes to soul knowledge, "We are born already knowing what we need to know."

The Three-Column Chart: Exploring Your Triple Vision

With the three-column model you can begin to perceive and function simultaneously within the physical, internal, and symbolic dimensions. You can develop this "triple vision" by using the three-column model.

In essence, triple vision is the ability to remain centered in any situation, whether it be joyous, disturbing, or neutral. It will give you poise and perspective. When you can translate any physical experience into archetypal coordinates, you are able to understand your emotional responses to that situation. For instance, I once became involved in a heated exchange at a workshop with a woman named May, because she felt that I was not "honoring her wounded childhood." Immediately I recognized that, from an archetypal perspective, I was speaking with a Child, although May was at least forty years old. Based on that archetypal impression, I modified both my tone of voice and my vocabulary. I knew that "reasoning" with May would not accomplish anything, because children cannot be reasoned with when they are angry and in need of emotional support. I remained present and sympathetic while she cried about the abuse she had experienced. Once she had vented those painful feelings, however, she relaxed, and we were able to proceed in a more adult fashion, looking for something positive that could be salvaged from her memories.

Often when I interact with someone in the audience for more than a few minutes, other people become restless and irritated, even though I use all interactions with individuals in a way that serves the entire group. The anger that sweeps through the audience in those moments is rooted in childlike feelings of neglect. I am not attending to them, and so they become resentful. Several times I have asked my audience if the reason they get irritated when I am speaking to one person is that they feel "Mommy likes her better." And even as they laugh at this question, they inevitably acknowledge that it is exactly how they were feeling.

The three-column model gives you a way to consolidate your many perceptions into a high-power prism that reveals the symbolic interconnection of your experiences. This is, actually, the intent of a spiritual practice—to see through the seeming disorder of everyday life, past your illusions, and into the underlying divine order.

The lens of the three windows helps you ignite *spiritual alchemy*, the process through which we convert physical perceptions from their "leaden" manifestation into their highest expression, the spiritual or "golden" level.

Take a look at the center column in Figure 3, which represents your inner self, your internal laboratory. Here you take the raw experience of a relationship or job and "melt" it down. You add the catalyst of choice—the desire to raise the experience to a higher level and see its underlying purpose as part of your Contract. This molten combination of perception and will determines how you direct this informed energy alloy into a final physical conscientious action or symbolic insight—spiritual gold.

FIGURE 3: THE THREE-COLUMN CHART

1 *Chakras 1–3*	2 *Chakras 4–7*	3 *Chakra 8*
Basic survival	Higher perceptions	Symbolic sight
Irrational group mind	Rational self	Divine logic
External	Internal	Archetypal
Literal view	Emotional view	Archetypal view
Lead	Alchemical lab	Gold
Ego	Self	Soul
Job	Career	Vocation
Matter	Energy	Divine light
Necessity	Choice	Compassion
Social chaos	Personal confusion	Divine order
Sight	Sensation	Perception
Control of others	Self-control	Surrender
Time and "weight"	Timeless "wait"	Simultaneity
Five-sensory sight	Multisensory sight	Holographic sight
Coming toward me	Coming from me	Coming through me
Past	Future	Now
Local	Nonlocal	Fully present

This chart is just a small sampling of how things appear different depending on your level of perception. The first column lists how the world is ordered according to your first three chakras. The second column presents the fluid perceptions of chakras four through seven, and the third column represents the realm of symbols, imagery, and your spiritual nature. What looks to be an "ordinary" relationship in your physical world might well be highly significant when seen from an archetypal perspective.

We are all under divine observation. Our motivations are under the looking glass, even more than our choices or actions themselves. With the three dimensions of perception, you can consciously work with your choices as a spiritual art form, aiming to transform them into gold. The consequences of your actions will exceed this lifetime.

To start working with your own perceptions in order to turn them into gold, draw a three-column model like the one on page 191 in your journal, and list all eight chakras. Then proceed to the following exercise.

Exercise: Walking Through the Columns

Working with your chakras can help you work with your archetypes. So if you want to bring awareness to your chakras using the three-column model, here's an exercise that can help you. If you want to skip ahead to work more directly with your archetypes, however, you can proceed to the next chapter.

In this exercise you'll focus on one of the four survival archetypes, because its role in your life is more than likely obvious. Everyone can identify a situation or event that is linked to the Child, Victim, Saboteur, or Prostitute. You may choose the Saboteur, for example, because you feel that you have blown an opportunity to follow a dream. Perhaps you decided without even giving the dream a chance that the financial risk was too great.

Your intention in doing this exercise is to understand yourself and the motivations behind the choices you make. You are looking for insights about what has disempowered you in the past, as well as what has empowered you. You are going to identify your weaknesses along with your strengths, talents, and spiritual qualities. It is as important for you to know where you need to do more inner work as it is to know where you have made spiritual progress.

Choose one situation or event in which you can see an obvious connection to one of your four survival archetypes: Child, Victim, Prostitute, or Saboteur. Then choose a person who played a central role in the situation you chose to examine, someone with whom you can imagine having a Contract. If you chose a situation related to the Prostitute, for example, then the person might be someone who suggested a business activity that could compromise your ethics, or your partner in an unhappy relationship in which you remain for reasons other than love.

In examining your own situation or relationship in the light of the archetype you chose, look for ways to use the archetype's positive energies to gain insight into the problem. Beginning with the first chakra, list the information or answer the questions as instructed for each chakra. Remember that you are evaluating the patterns of only the one archetype and situation that you chose for this exercise. (You can refer to the earlier section in this chapter called "The Chakra System" for more information about each chakra.)

Reviewing the **first chakra**, look for ways in which the archetype you've chosen relates to the situation you are exploring through issues of family loyalty, tribal or group identity, superstitions that control you, social values, and attitudes based on class and ethnicity. For example, your family might project onto you their expectations of what occupation you should pursue, based on traditional jobs within their own ethnic group or traditions. Tribal values may also dictate who your family feels is an appropriate life partner for you.

- Why do I have unfinished business with this situation? (List all the reasons that come to you.)
- What positive first-chakra strengths served me or continue to serve me as I deal with this memory? (List everything that comes to you. For example, the power of your first chakra is groundedness, and its related strengths include physical stability and loyalty. Their shadow side would be exclusion, vengeance, dependency, pity for being victimized, and disloyalty.)
- What family-related issues can I connect to this archetype? Do interactions with my family tend to reduce me to, for example, a Dependent Child or a Victim?

Review the **second chakra** now, and describe your survival issues as well as your decision-making process. Include your strengths in these chakra evaluations. The second-chakra power is creativity, and its strengths include your ability to give birth to new ideas and projects, the stamina to survive physically and financially, and resilience. (Refer to "The Chakra System" for details.) Remember that you are working to identify the manner in which you perceive reality within a single archetypal pattern. When you are working with the pattern of the Prostitute, for example, you will evaluate whether you see events or circumstances only in terms of financial benefit to you, and whether you are willing to sell some part of yourself to survive or get ahead. Yet reminding yourself that all archetypal patterns are neutral, be aware that your Prostitute pattern can also give you the insight to recognize that you need to move forward or else you will be selling out your visions and your spirit.

In the event that you feel that you have sold out in some way, consider the fears that you associate with the second chakra, because these are the fears that your unconscious will project onto a situation or opportunity. If you fear the loss of financial capital, for instance, then anytime a person presents you with an opportunity to invest in a dream, the lens of that fear will automatically cover your eyes, and all you will see is failure, excluding any possibility of success. The point is always to keep your attention on identifying the way you see the world through this archetype. Then ask yourself how you can work through the fears and limitations that prevent you from living up to your potential life.

- What positive second-chakra strengths do I have, and how have they served me in this situation or relationship? What are their shadow sides?
- What control issues do I have? Are they connected specifically to the Prostitute? (For example, do you control people with money, or are you controlled by money?)
- Have I ever felt that I "sold out" my integrity or my opinions for the sake of physical security?
- Would I be somewhere else today doing something else, if I weren't afraid of not surviving in the physical world?

Moving to the **third chakra**, describe how you felt about yourself in the situation or relationship with which you began this exercise. Comments such as "It (or he) just didn't feel right to me" or "I have this feeling that something is wrong" are direct communications from your third chakra. They should not be considered just musings or thoughts. Because the third chakra is your center of self-esteem, your psyche assesses your sense of personal power, self-respect, and integrity through this energy center. Using these strengths as references, evaluate the circumstance or relationship you have chosen.

- Did the person or people involved make me feel dis-empowered?
- Did I want their permission and approval before I would even risk following my dream, or did I fear their rejection?
- Have I ever harmed another person's self-esteem because of issues related to money, sex, or power?
- Have I ever empowered a person over those same issues?

Your **fourth chakra** evaluates your feelings about the situation you are examining, automatically analyzing the potential of a circumstance or relationship to either nurture you or to hurt you emotionally. This energy center always corresponds to issues of self-love, meaning how well you care for your own needs and about your own well-being. In relating to others, you draw on your strengths of compassion and forgiveness. From the angle of business and career, your fourth chakra evaluates whether you want to "put your heart" into opportunities or suggestions. Ask yourself:

- How do I feel about this situation or this person?
- Am I harming myself?
- Am I compromising my emotional well-being by doing or agreeing to something that doesn't feel right to me?
- Am I bitter because of something I did or said?
- Do I have to forgive myself for having given in to my Prostitute (or other) archetype? For example, have I "sold out" or caused another to compromise his or her integrity?

Move your attention into your **fifth chakra**, whose energy helps you formulate how you intend to communicate externally within a situation or relationship. You choose your words and determine your tone of voice based on how you want to manage your power, drawing on strengths such as self-knowledge, personal authority, and decision-making ability. In evaluating the event or relationship from the past that you have chosen, assess your present emotional state by asking yourself:

- How do I want to represent myself in this situation?
- Am I holding on to any unfinished business?
- If so, what is it?
- Am I prepared to do what it takes to release it?
- Do I feel that someone forced my choices?

- Did I have any choice at all?
- What would I choose to do or say differently now?

Your **sixth chakra** organizes your external reality according to your intellectual knowledge, your beliefs and attitudes, and how you perceive the same forces in other people. Your strengths include your ability to evaluate conscious and unconscious insights and to glean wisdom from them and from a wide range of experiences. Ask yourself:

- What excuses did I create for myself that gave me permission to act as I did?
- Do I allow the perceptions of others to open my mind or to help me review my actions?
- Do I frequently make up reasons that allow me to act against my own best options?
- What fears do I allow to control my mind regarding my Prostitute (or any other) archetype?
- What attitudes are causing me harm concerning issues of money, sex, and power?
- How do I use my strengths when faced with circumstances that hold the potential of causing me to negotiate my inner power?
- What have I learned through my experiences with my Prostitute (or other) archetype?

Your perceptions in any situation flow through your first to sixth chakras immediately and constantly. Your attention then moves to your **seventh chakra**, although not always at once. Questions from the seventh chakra that you should examine relate to how you have constructed your memories, attitudes, and responses to a situation or relationship. This center requires a bit more work, in that we create our own realities and organize our memories to support the choices we have already made. It is not an easy matter to detach from yourself and assess your own behavior and private agendas objectively. Yet by doing so you enhance your sense of spiritual empowerment. Your personal challenge is to get *impersonal* about yourself so that you can evaluate your choices from the higher position of how you manage the distribution of your spirit into physical matter. As if looking at your life from a balcony, you want to be able to follow your energy circuits, or the "lines" of your spirit, to all the places, people, memories, attitudes, ambitions, fears, and unfinished business that you have animated through a spirit-connection. You want to be able to evaluate how much your spirit-connections are costing you in terms of your power. And you want to do this objectively, as if you were evaluating the technical management of a robot or computer. Ask yourself:

- What symbolic meaning can I draw from this experience or relationship?
- Which details of the experience or relationship remain a mystery to me?
- What potential for empowerment could come from an experience such as this?
- Is there any area in my life at this present moment that seems to hold the same challenges as this experience?
- If so, can I see different choices that are possible?
- What issues related to this experience or relationship do I have yet to resolve, and why is the resolution of them so difficult?
- What would I have to do to retrieve my spirit?

Moving to your **eighth chakra**, your aim is to understand how the given situation or relationship is part of your Sacred Contract. If you recognize that you have a Contract with your father, for instance, then rather than interacting with him as the Angry Child, you can detach from your anger and appreciate that he is in your life for a positive reason. What you experience together is intended to teach you something—now examine your relationship to see what you are supposed to learn.

- How would an archetypal understanding of my situation inspire me to change my behavior toward someone?
- What steps can I take, using an archetypal insight, to resolve my unfinished business in this situation?

When you use the three-column model to identify and interpret the bits and pieces of the self that surface throughout each situation and relationship, a path of integration will reveal itself. You discover how you are influenced by other people and your own history in ways of which you were previously unaware. To assess what you have learned, now ask yourself the following questions:

- What have I learned about my relationship to my Prostitute (or other) archetype? Have I learned to identify circumstances that bring out in me the patterns that this archetype influences? Am I more inclined to negotiate my ethics or values in business, for example, when I fear for my financial security? Have I allowed fear to block intuitive guidance that would challenge my deep-seated insecurities?

- How can I see this archetype as serving me in a positive way through the rest of my life? (Once you become aware of how a particular archetypal pattern is influencing your actions, you can learn to cooperate with its power. For example, the Saboteur usually surfaces at moments of opportunity, because that is when you are most likely to undermine yourself. The positive aspect of the archetype intuitively urges you to examine your actions and motivations at these moments for any sign of self-sabotage. Learning to seek out that guidance rather than blocking it, and honoring it once you receive it, can help you avoid undermining yourself in the future.)

- What issues do I have yet to resolve that are attached to the patterns of this archetype? (If, for example, you determined through this exercise that you have unfinished business with your mother because you feel she didn't fully nurture you—a first-chakra concern—you can evaluate how separating from your family has helped you to develop an independent spirit. Perhaps one result of this lack of nurturing has been that you are less susceptible to tribal attitudes that might have stifled your individual development.)

The implications of all the information you have gathered during this exercise will allow you to see yourself in an entirely different way. To hone your symbolic sight, you may need to explore more than one of your survival archetypes through the chakra exercise. But this exercise is a valuable first step in identifying your Sacred Contract.

CHAPTER 7

Reinventing the Wheel

According to legend, Egil Skallagrimmson, one of Iceland's early settlers, was well versed in the art of writing and interpreting runes—the magical ancient word-symbols common to Germanic and Scandinavian legend "that can calm the sea, extinguish flames, and blunt the edge of an enemy's sword." The eight-hundred-year-old *Egil's Saga* describes events that happened some 250 years earlier. In one episode, Egil visits a farm where he finds that the farmer's daughter is sick and has been wasting away for quite some time. Egil asks whether anyone has tried to heal the young woman, and he is told that the farmer's son has carved some runes, "but ever since it has been far worse for her than before." Egil finds those runes on a piece of whale-bone in the woman's bed. He scrapes the bone clean and burns both it and the shavings. Then he carves new runes, laying them under her pillow. She quickly becomes well. Egil then pronounces the moral of the story in poetic language: "No leech should unleash runes save rightly he can read them."[1]

Runes, casting lots, divination, the *I Ching*, Tarot cards, numerology, the Enneagram, and the different astrology traditions of Western, Vedic, Tibetan, and Chinese cultures are among the many practices that people have long used to gain access to the unconscious mind and harness the valuable intuition locked within. Working with your archetypes and chakras is also a way of consciously channeling divine energy and your own intuition. Yet skill, knowledge, and the willingness to become a clear vessel of transmission are essential elements in gaining that access. The quality of the guidance that you receive from any of these methods also depends on the intention and attitude with which you approach the tool.

People seek guidance from intuitive methods for reasons ranging from curiosity and entertainment to desperation and the yearning for divine connection. Most people seek guidance to try to gain or maintain control over their personal life, loved ones, health, and property. They want direction and instructions to act on, and they usually hope to be told the safest path to follow. They want guidance that gives them material security more than they want spiritual guidance.

No matter what their motivation, however, few individuals can open themselves unconditionally to such direction. Our expectations about what we will hear or what we *want* to hear limits our openness to insight. For instance, say you are divinely intended to move on from your current occupation, but in asking for guidance you really are seeking to hear only ways to remain where you are. So any information that you do receive you will interpret from a biased perspective.

When you interpret intuitive information, whether it be images and gut feelings or messages from your archetypes, it's important that you cultivate a detached or symbolic point of view. That means, as we have seen, that you need to look at the events and relationships of your life through the third (archetypal) column rather than the first (physical) column. In other words, you want to see the events as part of your Contract—which you agreed to enter into—rather than as arbitrary limitations or purposeless encounters. You want to look at your archetypes with this same symbolic sight. Many people interact with their archetypes to try to find out why others have hurt them, when they should be looking to see how their archetypes have given hurt to others. I want you to do this, though! How have *your* shadow archetypes played out in your relationships? Who from your present or past is in therapy getting over you, just as you've been getting over someone else? For guidance to help you, you have to look at yourself as honestly as possible. That is what personal growth is all about: honesty about yourself and others, about your path, about your strengths and weaknesses. Working with guidance is not just a method of peering into the psyches of the people in your life to get a fix on them—that would be spiritual voyeurism. Rather, it is a method of learning about yourself and your relationships in this lifetime.

All tools and methods of guidance are essentially the same: they are like radio receivers, and *you* are the receiver and operator of the radio. Still, you need to know how to prepare yourself as the receiver, so that the signals come through clearly. For example, any radio needs an adequate source of electricity—a battery or plug—and it must be tuned and adjusted. Because *you* are the source of the energy on which your intuitive radio relies for activation, your attitude is key to the clarity and quality of the guidance you receive. When people throw the *I Ching* as a game, for example, the answers that it provides tend to be limited in meaning, largely because the users' lightness of attitude limits their perception. Superstition also blocks clear reception, because whether you realize it or not, your underlying fear influences the way you interpret the information.

When you approach intuitive methods with respect, you become open to hearing from your interior channels. The accuracy of the guidance you receive will be in direct proportion to the sincerity of your attitude. Before you begin to work with your archetypes, take some deep breaths to clear your mind of any expectations. If you are trying to influence the guidance, you will not get honest feedback. If anyone helping you read yourself wants to influence you or has an expectation of what you want to hear, you will not get honest feed-back. You should have no attachment to the guidance you're seeking either for yourself or for someone else.

Most people initially search for guidance about their physical lives, about their careers, love lives, or investments, that they can use immediately. But the more valuable form of guidance is symbolic or archetypal, although it may take you longer to interpret. Just as dreams have many layers of meaning, so often does intuitive information. Guidance taken at the literal level will enhance your life only minimally. For example, the airplane dreams that I shared with you at the beginning of this book would hold much less significance for me had I interpreted them only in terms of how they applied to my physical life. I could have interpreted them as reflecting my everyday issues and worries about traveling, but when I saw the airplane as a symbol, their true significance—their helpfulness, consolation, and inspiration—was revealed.

The Twelve

After I surrendered to the way the archetypes rearranged my way of conducting intuitive readings, I began to perceive many more of them. In addition to the four survival patterns, among the most frequent ones that presented themselves to me were the Rescuer, Servant, Princess, Knight, Queen, King, Wounded Healer, Mystic, and Shape-shifter. As I tried to organize what their energy signified for my students and for others, I remembered an exercise that my dearest college professor and mentor had taught. To convey to a class on spirituality the great power of detachment in perceiving reality, she had us imagine that we were each sitting in the center of a clock. Each of the twelve hours of the clock represented a totally different reality. One hour represented the spiritual teachings of Buddhism; another, the principles of the Hindu traditions; the others, Judaism, Christianity, Islam, Taoism, Confucianism, Shinto, Wicca, Zoroastrianism, shamanism, and atheism. This image shows that there is no such thing as one reality, that truth presents itself in many forms. Detachment from preconceptions or sitting in the center, she was saying, is the only way to begin to perceive life clearly.

The clock also represents a complete cycle of life. Day and night both have twelve hours, and twelve months complete a year. Twelve signs of the zodiac surround our planet, twelve apostles were sent out by Jesus on their missions, and twelve tribes of Israel made up the biblical Jewish nation, arguably the foundation of the entire Western spiritual tradition. The mystical implications of this number twelve suggest that it too is an archetypal pattern. The clock, when divided into twelve sections, also resembles a wheel, one of the most ancient representations of spirit, fate, fortune, and the cycles of life.

I decided to use this wheel as a pattern and filled in each of the hours, which I renamed houses, with archetypes. I listed one archetype within each section and imagined that I was once again standing in the middle of a circle, this time surrounded by my archetypal family. The strong visual image that I got was of a united cosmic support system. As I looked at my drawing, I also realized that I had also unconsciously duplicated the ancient design of the astrological wheel and had even numbered the twelve houses of the signs of the zodiac. It immediately struck me that this cosmic template was the perfect form for making the archetypes more tangible. (See Figure 4.)

Carl Jung believed that our ancestors "projected" archetypal patterns into myth and folklore in the same way that they shaped

FIGURE 4: THE TWELVE HOUSES OF THE ARCHETYPAL WHEEL

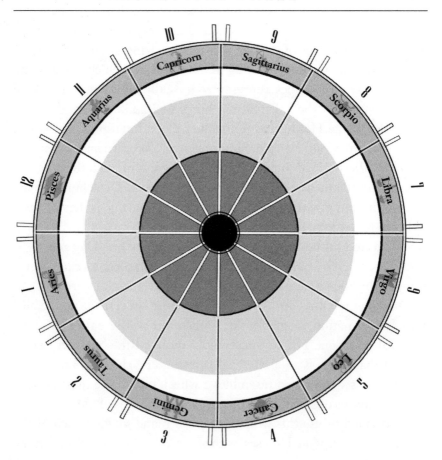

arrangements of stars into human and animal figures and gave them names and personalities:

> We can see this most clearly if we look at the heavenly con-
> stellations, in which original chaotic forms were organized
> through the projection of images. This explains the influ-
> ence of the stars as asserted by astrologers. These influences
> are nothing but unconscious, introspective perceptions of
> the activity of the collective unconscious. Just as the con-
> stellations were projected into the heavens, similar figures
> were projected into legends and fairy tales or upon historical
> persons.[2]

This explained the link I had intuitively felt between archetypes and the zodiac. Perhaps I was catching a glimpse of the collective unconscious as I saw the twelve houses of the zodiac overlaid on my Archetypal Wheel! The overlapping design of these wheels might have been just a nice "coincidence," but the more I worked with the confluence between the twelve archetypes and the twelve houses of the zodiac, the more firmly I became convinced that they could shed light on our Contracts and get us to see ourselves in new ways.

The Archetypal Wheel is an intuitive method that makes symbolic information accessible to you. Your archetypes become even more significant when you see them at work in the houses that signify twelve different aspects of your life. The Wheel helps you decode the behind-the-scenes patterns of your life. It shows you your experiences and relationships as spiritual dramas, filled with opportunities for personal transformation.

Your moods and emotions influence how your archetypal patterns arrange themselves in your Wheel. The manner in which the runes or bones fall in a reading, for example, reflects your energy emotional state as well as the energy atmosphere at that moment. Full moons and other phases, for instance, are well known to affect emotions, as do planetary aspects, sunspots, or the influence of electrical storms. Methods of intuitive guidance are particularly in tune with cosmic energies, because all energies are interconnected.

Like an astrological chart, the purpose of the Archetypal Wheel is to expand your understanding of yourself. Specifically, the Wheel is a medium through which your archetypal patterns can best communicate their role in unfolding your Sacred Contract. Your archetypes are like magnets, drawing together the essential elements required for an experience to manifest, including the people with whom you have Contracts and the points at which you are to make important choices. Each of the houses is also aligned with the energies of one or more chakras, where their areas of influence overlap. This confluence of energies should help you get a deeper picture of the nature of your archetypal houses.

The first house of the astrological chart, for example, represents the ego and the personality. The archetype that falls into that house represents the dominant unconscious pattern of influence of your ego and personality. Because it is the house that grounds you in the world and rules your sense of who you are, it is aligned with the energies of both the first and the third chakras. When I am teaching the Wheel in a workshop, I ask people to intuit which archetype a particular member of the group has on his or her house of ego. Many are able to identify the exact archetype while others will usually describe characteristics that are associated with that archetype. Men who have the archetype of the Knight on their first house, for instance, frequently project an aura glittering with chivalry, romance, and charm. They may also seem protective of others, especially women, and courtly or even formal in their manner of dress or speech. Sometimes this archetype is obvious, sometimes subtle.

One time I gave a workshop in my hometown, Chicago, that was being taped by a network television crew as part of a feature on my work. As I was speaking about the Knight archetype, I commented that a Knight would be more inclined to send his maiden a red rose than lilies or tulips. I then turned to a young man seated in the front row and said, "Now, take this man. He strongly projects the Knight archetype to me. He is obviously romantic in nature." As soon as I finished that sentence, he pulled a red rose out from behind his back and handed it to me as a gift. It shocked even me, not to mention the TV crew. The interviewer turned to his cameraman and asked, "You did get that on tape, didn't you?" The archetype that rules our first house projects the initial impression people have on meeting us, and believe me when I tell you that knowing what your archetypal mask is can be a great social advantage.

According to astrological teachings, each of the twelve houses in a natal chart (a chart showing the precise position of the planets at the moment of your birth) represents a different focus of your life. The twelve houses of the Wheel provide a format through which you can evaluate how your archetypes operate in your daily life, both literally and symbolically. The eighth house, for instance, labeled "Other People's Resources" in Figure 5, relates to other people's money and how you use it, and to inheritances and legal matters. Your inheritance can refer not only to your financial legacy but also to your DNA and ancestral biological memory, as well as to your inherited tribal attitudes and beliefs going back a generation or a millennium.

Even though you can interpret your archetypes and their houses literally, you want to stretch their meaning into the symbolic. If you stop at the literal meaning of a word, you may get frustrated, because you cannot always "literally" see a connection between an archetypal pattern and the meaning of the house into which it falls. You want to see the literal meaning of what is taking place in front of your eyes. For instance, emotional, psychological, and genetic inheritances are just as real, if not more so, than money and property, so when considering your inheritances, please consider physical, attitudinal, and emotional characteristics you share with your family as well. When you are trying to interpret the meaning of any archetypal pattern within its house, consider all sides of the image and the information it holds. By doing so, you will create a fuller portrait of all the patterns and purpose of your life. Remember, your archetypes are your guides to discerning your Contracts and achieving your divine potential.

All of your archetypal patterns are certainly present in the concerns of each of the twelve houses, for they interact as one hologram-like system within the psyche. Nonetheless, one pattern takes the lead regarding the theme of each house. In Chapter 8, I will show you how to locate your twelve archetypes into their appropriate houses and create your personal Wheel. But first let's go through the meanings of the houses themselves. (See Figure 5.)

FIGURE 5: THE ARCHETYPAL WHEEL

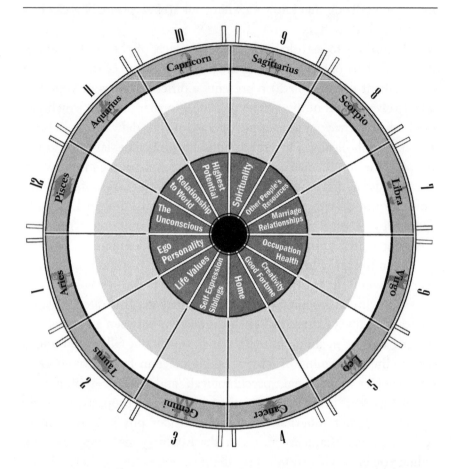

Making Your Houses Your Home

FIRST HOUSE:
EGO AND PERSONALITY
(First and third chakras)

In an astrological chart the twelve houses correspond to the twelve signs of the zodiac and to the four cosmic energies: earth, air, fire, and water. The houses of the Archetypal Wheel share some of these same characteristics. The first house of the Archetypal Wheel, for example, corresponds to the astrological sign of Aries, the first house of the zodiac. Beginning on the first day of spring, it represents new beginnings. And since Aries is also a fire sign, this house has the climate of passion that animates birth, including the birth of the self and the constant rebirthing we undergo as we mature. And so the archetype takes up energy in your persona.

A woman named Charlotte, for example, identified the Shape-shifter as one of her twelve archetypes, and it landed on her first house. So the Shape-shifter is a dominant characteristic in her persona. Charlotte strongly related to fairy tales such as "The Ugly Duckling" and "The Princess and the Frog," in which the fearful, unattractive aspect of the main character is instantly transformed to beauty and empowerment. The Shape-shifter has long been known to shamans of the American Indian and other native traditions as having the ability to change its appearance for a variety of reasons. Among other things, it can maneuver among different levels of consciousness, between dream and waking states, and among the astral, mental, and etheric planes. Its energy is apparent in Charlotte's struggle to hold on to her beliefs and opinions. She changes the "shape" of her opinions—just as fire goes where the wind blows it—to such an extent that people find it difficult to get to know her. Charlotte seems unreliable, scattered, and disloyal. She is forever attracting people who assume she is a certain way—which indeed she is at that moment—only to discover that she is not really who she seems. One of Charlotte's challenges, as she readily admits, is to develop and maintain a strong sense of self so that she does not change her shape to suit the person she is with or to say what she thinks someone else wants to hear. Numerous interpersonal Contracts are pushing her to do this.

Your identity, self-esteem, and awareness of your ego lay the groundwork for your life. How you conduct yourself with others, and whether you have the strength to make your way without needing to ask for another's permission, depends on how well you succeed at the many challenges that awaken your need to take charge of who you are.

SECOND HOUSE:
LIFE VALUES
(Second chakra)
The second house of the Archetypal Wheel corresponds to Taurus, an earth sign that rules your relationship to the land in its broadest sense.

It represents what you most value and hold dear. In energy terms the second house represents the next stage in the formation of the self: "Now that I'm here, what's mine? What do I want out of life? What power is essential to my interacting with physical life?" This house represents your appreciation for the physical nature of life—the objects of this earth that appeal to your ego and spirit, and what you need most to feel grounded in the world. This house most reflects which objects or energy you associate with earthly power: money, status, ownership, art, the capacity to control others, sensuality, beauty. These are the most seductive means through which the spirit becomes attached to physical form. The archetype that resides within this house, therefore, is the one that is most aligned with your relationship to physical power and its icons.

Glen had the Midas archetype in his second house: he converted all of his entrepreneurial ideas into physical gold. He had the proverbial touch, but like Midas, he also struggled with how the power of money challenged the power of his spirit. Just as Midas killed his daughter when he inadvertently changed her to metal, Glen's emotional life was cold and barren. For years he was unaware of anything except money. In his relationships with others—with whom, he now recognizes, he has Contracts—the question often became whether he valued his finances more than he valued them. One of the central lessons he must learn is how to interact with other people without needing to control or dominate them, and to interact with the things of the world without being controlled *by* them.

The challenge of this house is to see beyond the physical form of our attachments to objects, money, status, power, and all the other manifestations of the physical world, to your spiritual values. People often suffer great anguish because they believe that to be happy, they must possess a particular person, place, or thing. And yet the ability to love unconditionally is antithetical to attachment.

THIRD HOUSE:
SELF-EXPRESSION AND SIBLINGS
(Third and fifth chakras)
Once you establish your values, you move into self-expression: how you present what you are and what you hold dear to the world. The

third house, aligned with Gemini, an air sign that rules communication, represents your capacity to express yourself as an individual, as well as your siblings. The symbolic link of siblings with communication represents the natural process of specialization, of first discovering your voice among your fellow "children." Siblings, therefore, should be interpreted not only as your biological family members but also as those who aid your growth. Because the energy of your third house involves both your sense of self-esteem and your self-expression, it resonates with the third and fifth chakras. It contains the lessons inherent in learning about the causes and effects of your choices—how you wield your own power. It reveals how you direct your energy into the world, how you put it into motion, and how you engage with the laws of magnetic attraction and cause and effect. You want to become conscious of how you use your personal energy and power so that you become aware of the consequences of your thoughts and deeds. Becoming conscious means awakening to your own power and learning to direct it responsibly.

The archetype in residence in your third house influences how you weigh your decisions. Choices that are consciously negative or damaging, especially those aimed at deliberately harming other people, represent the challenging or shadow aspect of the third house.

A man named John in a workshop had the Servant archetype in his third house. This situation brought him endless delight, because he believed that his role in life was to be of service to others. John brought this commitment into everything he did and into all of his relationships. The idea of being of service had inspired him as early as he could recall. When the time came for him to choose a profession, he went on a retreat to pray for guidance. In his prayer he said that what he did in life was of no concern to him and that he would do whatever Heaven directed him to, because he had faith that the Divine would place him where he could best be of service.

This demonstration of faith in the unknown would not be possible for most people, but John also had the Wanderer archetype as a companion. Residing in his ninth house (spirituality), the Wanderer led John to relocate to a different part of the country every two to three years, working at odd jobs. For John, this path of service gave him a feeling of freedom that he loved and also allowed him to meet people from all over. Because he clung to no special place, he felt free to be fully himself and to give unconditionally. He also felt abundantly satisfied with the simplest pleasures, most of which came from spending time with people who needed someone to talk to or any other help that he could offer. I have never met another person like John, and for a moment I was tempted to ask him if his first name might be Saint. He certainly radiated a quality of grace that inspired others to see the great power in service.

The challenge of the third house is to become conscious of your motivations. Every thought, word, action, and deed is an expression of your power, and ultimately only two genuine motivations stir the psyche: the empowerment or disempowerment of the self and others.

FOURTH HOUSE:
HOME
(First and fourth chakras)

The fourth house corresponds to Cancer, the first of the three water signs of the zodiac chart. Water is the element associated with our emotional natures, so the archetype that resides within your fourth house has the strongest influence on the foundation of your emotional nature. Your self-expression, be it as an individual or through creation, needs to be grounded, to have a home. The fourth house is connected both with the home you came from and with your present home. The word or image *home* clearly has many meanings, and in the dream state it is often associated with the true residence of the heart, or your deepest passion in life. The theme of home that rules this house includes your connections to both your biological and your extended families. The archetype that resides in this house is the one that has the leading influence on the emotional energies associated with all that represents home to you. Because the fourth house relates both to your family roots and to your emotional life, it corresponds to the energies of your first and fourth chakras.

The challenging aspects of the fourth house can include toxic memories and emotions, the consequences of which can be depression and melancholy. When I am working with a person who has unfinished business from painful childhood experiences, which is very common, I refer to the archetype in that person's fourth house as my main source of insight for beginning a dialogue. A woman named Lydia, for example, was coping with the memory of a drug-addicted mother who often left home for months at a time. When Lydia's mother was home, she would manage to stay clean for anywhere from a week to three months, but inevitably she turned again to drugs. Lydia told me several stories about how her mother returned from a bender only to make off with any item in the house that she could sell for drug money. One time her mother returned to their home while Lydia was in class at her local college, gathered up all of Lydia's personal belongings that might be of value, and sold or bartered them for drugs. After that Lydia did not agree to see her mother for seven years.

When I met Lydia, she was twenty-eight and had yet to reconcile with her mother. Lydia radiated the energy of someone who could shower the Child within people with abundant compassion. Yet she had a capacity to feel the hurt in others and was constantly motivated to help them. It helped her greatly to note that her Mother archetype resided in her fourth house. One way to interpret this alignment was to suggest that mothering others—including her own mother—would be central to her life's journey.

Lydia's husband, whom she married at age twenty-six, lavished love on her and felt that she was his ideal mate. "I love this woman beyond anyone," he told me. "The moment I saw her, I knew that she would be my wife and the perfect mother to our children. And that is exactly what she is, the perfect wife and the perfect mother."

The challenge of the fourth house is to complete the unfinished business of our childhood years and to establish healthy homes for ourselves as adults. You have a choice between handing down to your children and loved ones your family wounds and patterns of negativity, and passing on to them optimism and love of life. Healing your personal history, so that you do not pass on your own wounds, is therefore essential to creating a healthy home for yourself and your family.

FIFTH HOUSE:

CREATIVITY AND GOOD FORTUNE

(Sixth chakra)

The sequence of fire, earth, water, and air is repeated twice in the zodiac/Archetypal Wheel. Leo, the second fire sign, is aligned with the fifth house, which rules creative expression, sexuality, children, and good fortune. This is also the house of love and spontaneity, of abundance and opportunity. The archetype that resides in this house is the one that represents the strengths that you should most rely on to make things happen. After grounding yourself with a home base, you instinctively move on to exploring the power of creativity and the creation of life. Because the fifth house rules creativity, it corresponds to the sixth chakra, which regulates intelligence and imagination.

The shadow aspect of the fifth house manifests as the expression of creative or sexual fire out of control, as in the misuse of sexual power or creativity for selfish or manipulative ends. One can use creative talent for unethical or illegal activities, or for sexual seduction and manipulation. I remember a man named Will who had the most outrageously wonderful personality. He was the incarnation of charisma, and everyone adored his company. Will made people feel that anything was possible, and he could see the light in even the darkest situation. The archetype in residence in Will's fifth house was the Child. And he was exactly that, almost a fairy-tale figure who inspired people to see the good in life.

Whenever events caused Will to slip outside the sweet atmosphere of his childlike innocence, he would imagine himself as a child again. He also would become an imaginary father to his child memory and could comfort this child by walking him through the years of his life. Will the parent would point out to Will the child how frightened he had been at age six about something, and how by age eight it had worked out all right. He summed up his imaginative ability by saying, "When I slip, I return to my inner place by reminding myself of all the many ways everything worked out without my having to do a thing. Someone is watching over me, because I sure can't organize all the things in my life. That's a message I love to share with others no matter where I am. And as someone who runs a fairly large corporation, I can tell you that this attitude is in short supply."

The need to create is an essential aspect of consciousness and spirit. But to define and determine our creative ability by our professional accomplishments, even artistic ones, is an illusion. Will embodied the energy of creativity in its highest expression because he channeled that electricity to jump-start the spirit of everyone he met. He also represents another profile of creativity: the creative nature of the self that does not have to "do" something outside of itself in order to be recognized and validated.

SIXTH HOUSE:
OCCUPATION AND HEALTH
(Second chakra)

The sixth house corresponds to your second earth sign, which is Virgo, and rules your occupation and health. The earth energy of Virgo differs from that of Taurus in that its focus is on grounding you as a person to the main work of your life rather than on the physical cycles of nature of the second house. The focus of this house on occupation is survival-oriented, and the archetype that resides here influences how you seek out paths of security. When you are in the midst of a business transaction, for example, your sixth-house archetypal pattern will play a very prominent role in the way you interpret business-related conversations and opportunities. The challenge of the sixth house is to balance work and health. An archetype might indicate unhealthy or destructive habits that do not serve your physical well-being. Or it might indicate how you negotiate your ethics and morals for the sake of financial and job security. Because this house is involved with money and values, it most closely corresponds to the second chakra.

A woman named Cathie chose the Detective archetype as one of her twelve patterns, and it ended up in her sixth house. Cathie said that she had chosen the Detective because she had a natural talent for solving mysteries. Unfortunately she directed this talent into a shadow aspect, spying. She even admitted to having an attraction to voyeurism, although she labeled it merely a fascination. Whenever Cathie felt insecure—which was frequently, either by choice or weakness—she would use that feeling as an excuse to rifle through the files and personal belongings of her co-workers in search of memos or other communications. She claimed she was looking for evidence of plans to undermine her position in the office. I asked Cathie if any of her efforts ever paid off by proving her case. "Well, no," she said, "but so much the better. It's very comforting to learn that you are secure at work."

When I asked Cathie how long she had had this need to play Detective, she said that from her earliest memories she recalled feeling compelled to sneak around to find out as much as she could about everyone, from parents and friends to colleagues. She admitted that she had once been fired after being caught going through someone's desk. Cathie was so convinced that people were spying on her that she felt she had to spy on them for her own protection. I recommended that Cathie consult a therapist, and although she said she would, I could tell that her sense of safety resided in her feeling that she could discover others' secrets.

Cathie's story illustrates how we unconsciously influence the health of those around us. Her paranoia was felt by her co-workers and subtly influenced their own well-being. Ask yourself on a regular basis, "How does my behavior influence the health of those around me?" This question is a natural bridge to the seventh house, in which your health, including the healthy or unhealthy views you hold about life and other people, becomes part of what you bring into all your partnerships.

SEVENTH HOUSE:
MARRIAGE AND RELATIONSHIPS
(Second and fourth chakras)

The seventh house includes marriage as well as other forms of partnership, such as close friendships and business relationships. This house is aligned with the astrological sign of Libra, the second air sign. Unlike Gemini, which rules communication in general, Libra represents the more intimate kinds of communication between individuals. The central quality associated with Libra is balance, symbolized by a woman carrying a scale. This house is also prime territory for acts of betrayal, which so often reveal the shadow aspects of relationships. Because the seventh house rules both business partnerships and marriage, it corresponds to the energies of the second and fourth chakras, which regulate money, values, and matters of the heart.

By our very biology we are designed for physical, emotional, and psychological partnerships. Our relationships with one another are prime areas in which to glimpse our Contracts. We can also see them through our archetypal partnerships: Parent/Child, Mentor/Student, Servant/Master.

During the normal course of every day, as we go about our business, extraordinary dialogues take place between our souls. If I were to see you in a workshop, for instance, my Teacher archetype would engage with your Storyteller as you recounted how archetypes work in your life. Although the Storyteller isn't one of my intimate archetypes, your story will add to my life as a Teacher. Your Storyteller, in turn, can profit from exposure to my Teacher, because I may be able to help you see a greater meaning, wisdom, or spiritual truth in your story. People who have embodied both these archetypes at the highest level include Jesus, the Buddha, Homer, and the many anonymous sages whose wisdom stories make up the *Bhagavad Gita*, the *Upanishads*, and Sufi, Taoist, Hasidic, and African teaching stories.

Partnerships can also play out in more mundane situations. Some time ago I was invited to the home of some friends who were hosting a dinner party for fourteen of their "favorite" people, although most of the guests knew only the couple who were giving the party. As I was meeting the other guests, a man named Bruce introduced himself in a loud, obnoxious manner, doing everything he could to draw everyone's attention to himself. I couldn't get away from him fast enough, but he followed me in a persistent attempt to make me find his humor amusing. Then he unexpectedly became very composed. "You know," he said, "I like clowning around with these guys. I started playing the clown with them years ago, and now they kind of expect me to be the life of the party."

The moment Bruce referred to himself as the Clown, I wanted to get to know the man underneath the makeup. We talked about the common associations people have with the Clown archetype, and then I asked him if he related to the perception that many Clowns hide feelings of loneliness behind their masks, or need their costume to communicate feelings they would otherwise have to keep private. Bruce said that he was definitely a different person when he was clowning around, and that he often felt he was actually communicating affectionate feelings or criticisms that he could never otherwise express. As he regaled me with some of his adventures, he set up an atmosphere of play in the room, making the other guests more comfortable with each other. In a sense he was forming a comedic partnership with every other person in the room.

"Do you ever resent the fact that people expect you to be the party Clown?" I asked Bruce.

"I would definitely resent people, including myself, if I felt that I was always expected only to entertain everyone when we got together," Bruce said, "but I am actually pretty well-rounded. The Clown is the part of me that allows me to meet friends. If all I did was goof off, no one would take me seriously. I believe in the power of being optimistic, and so when I am in a bad place, nothing works better than humor. And I'm the same with myself as I am with everyone else, which is a good thing because I can see how tempting it is to show to the world only the side of your persona that does the most for you."

Besides being an enjoyable dinner companion, Bruce made me take a good look at how certain assumptions were clouding my own perceptions about particular archetypal patterns. For one thing, I realized that I never liked the kids in school who were "class clowns." Their behavior drove me crazy, and somewhere around the fourth grade I decided that clowning around was something that people did to hide their failures. Bruce woke up all those memories and helped me clean out a drawer in my psyche, finding—and I hope fixing—an attitude I hadn't realized I had. Bruce's Clown provided me with some Libra energy, or balance, for my Teacher.

We invest great energy in enjoying, maintaining, or recovering from our relationships, and in the process we learn more about our motivations. One of the healthiest gifts we can give ourselves is to constantly monitor our reasons for being critical and controlling. The challenge is to allow others to be themselves regardless of our fear or insecurity. Maintain your core relationship to yourself and live according to the truth that the greatest gift you can give another is a fully healthy self—your own.

EIGHTH HOUSE:

OTHER PEOPLE'S RESOURCES

(Second and sixth chakras)

This house corresponds to Scorpio, the second water sign, and water, as already noted, is the element most connected to your emotional nature. Scorpio is also the ruler of secrets and secret activities as well as the passionate energies associated with erotic sex. (The most closely guarded secrets usually have to do with either sex or money or both.) Unlike the second house, which deals with personal ownership, the eighth house rules your use of money in the public arena. The theme of inheritance in this house relates to your financial and legal concerns, your DNA, and your ancestral biological memory. Legal and financial matters involve both your intellect and your sense of values, and so this house is influenced by the energies of the second and sixth chakras.

Eighth-house issues bring out our darkest shadows because, as Benjamin Franklin once noted, the true test of a person's character comes through in matters of family inheritance. This house takes our involvement with power outside of our personal lives, marking a passageway into the more public arena of external power.

You want to understand the emotional nature of this house, because money, sexuality, and secret knowledge are seductions that can block your pursuit of your divine potential. Dealing with these energies can be extremely challenging. It is difficult to remain emotionally centered and empowered where financial and sexual matters are concerned. Money, sex, and power represent authority and security, so when these areas of life are threatened—or we perceive them to be—we become extremely fearful and can act irrationally. Expressions of the shadow of this house present themselves in the arena of legal and financial misconduct, including, among other things, misappropriation of business funds and family conflicts over matters of inheritance. In this house we can also discover the magnificent force of our strength and courage during our most vulnerable experiences in life.

Many of the Contracts you have with other people come together because of money, sex, and power, and this house too carries the potential for betrayal and misunderstanding. Yet bonds of loyalty and love are also inherited qualities, and this house and archetype may be a great source of strength to you. The following example of a relationship between two people is what I describe as a classic eighth-house Contract.

Alfred had an extremely dark nature. He was jealous, greedy, and manipulative—to me he represented the Spell-caster archetype. He actually admitted to being addicted to money, sex, and power, because he felt that he was on the road to recovery. Yet even though he was aware of his shadow, it obviously still ruled his mind and spirit. He seemed to be using his recovery to cast himself as someone who did not mean to use others but was simply not in control of his power. He clearly manipulated others so that he could feel superior.

Within two days of meeting Alfred, I met a woman named Susan who had been involved with him and who confirmed that he was a master manipulator who had slowly chipped away at her self-esteem, a subtle form of spell-casting. By making her feel inadequate and continually correcting her both in public and private, Alfred slowly drained her self-respect, so that she eventually believed she was as weak as he insisted she was. One day, however, Susan had a moment of insight and snapped out of the hold Alfred had on her. In that brief instant she saw that she'd been made a Slave to an evil Wizard and that she was not who he said she was. She broke the spell she was under so thoroughly that she realized that she no longer had any emotional ties to him whatsoever. Susan freed herself psychically and emotionally and even felt gratitude for having been forced to liberate herself.

In Susan's mind she had a Contract with Alfred that led her into her own strength. Both of them had ultimately benefited from their dysfunctional relationship—which is unusual, however. Susan went on to healthier relationships, as we're all meant to do whenever we find ourselves in unhealthy ones. And Alfred actually did further work to control his addictions and his craving to control others, although he admitted that he did not truly want to become the person he knew he should become, because his addictions served him so well. Alfred's true challenge was that he liked his shadow. Intellectually he could admit that it was causing negative consequences, but he had also convinced himself (cast a spell on himself) that made him emotionally immune to the hurt he did to others.

The archetype matched to your eighth house is the one that is your guide into your fears, challenges, and strengths in dealing with money, inheritance, and sexuality. Keep in mind that what lies beneath your fears cannot always be fully understood within the confines of one house. The archetypes and the houses with which they are partnered are points of entry into your chart. Each entry point provides you with a different specific perspective, but to view your overall Contract, you ultimately need to draw on the whole chart. If you had a crisis about how important money is to you or about your resistance to having a full life, you would look at the second house, because those are issues of personal values. (You should also refer to the house where your Saboteur is located to see if a thematic connection exists there.) But if you are investigating a business or financial relationship, you would begin the process of interpretation with your eighth-house archetype. Then study that same relationship with another archetype and house, proceeding through the Wheel one by one. This is like putting a wide-angle lens on your psyche and soul.

NINTH HOUSE:

SPIRITUALITY

(Seventh chakra)

The ninth house, which corresponds to Sagittarius, the third fire sign, rules spirituality, religion, travel, and wisdom. The energy of Sagittarius is associated with boldness and independence, qualities that enhance the quests you are drawn to pursue. The element of Sagittarius fire fuels inspiration, devotion, and the passion to realize an intimate relationship with the Divine. While the fire sign Leo that rules the fifth house is strongly linked to dramatic personality characteristics and theatrics, Sagittarius fire lifts a person's spirit into transcendent pathways in keeping with the symbolism of the centaur directing his arrow into the cosmos. Shadow aspects inherent in this house relate to the challenge of managing your spiritual ego, often characterized by the archetype known as the Messianic complex.

The ninth and tenth houses sit on top of the chart and represent the guiding forces that help us to remember, however unconsciously, that life is a spiritual journey and that our role is to act continually on our highest potential. For that reason both houses are strongly influenced by the energy of the seventh chakra, which regulates our relationship to the Divine. The spiritual awakening referred to as a "dark night of the soul" resonates powerfully with the energetic profile of the ninth house. Our contemporary culture has largely shifted from the group practice of religion to the deeply intimate search for an individual spiritual path. While this is a positive movement in our evolution, many people today are attempting to live by the more exacting inner standards once reserved for monastics but without the privileged environment that once allowed monastics to focus solely on their spiritual practices.

The shadow side of this migration of formerly cloistered spiritual practices into the mainstream is the potential for spiritual crisis or even madness. Going deep into the self to attempt to make contact with the Divine traditionally requires the guidance of someone spiritually equipped to hold your hand through the points of passage into the soul—namely, a spiritual director, a guru, an abbot, or a mother superior. During the process of spiritual introspection, you may descend into profound stages of loneliness and emptiness, detach from emotions and everyday senses, and even, ironically, develop a feeling of meaninglessness.

Yet many people now find themselves in a detached emotional state of mind, while struggling at the same time to maintain life on the outside, going to work and paying the mortgage. Frequently the burden of living in two such opposing dimensions can virtually disable people with depression. But how do you distinguish between conventional psychological or clinical depression and spiritual crisis, whose symptoms can seem similar?

To begin with, all depression arises out of feelings of disempowerment. The balance of power in your life shifts, and you feel that you are no longer calling the shots. Clinical depression generally arises from external or physical events. It may have its roots in a chemical imbalance or a traumatic life change—anything from a divorce or the loss of a loved one to being diagnosed with a serious illness. Such depression often results in an inability to function effectively and needs to be treated by an appropriate mental health professional.

By contrast, spiritual depression is more likely to be triggered by an absorption in metaphysical issues than by material concerns. You may feel that you have reached a dead end, that you've been abandoned by God or have no hope of ever experiencing divine union. Spiritual crises can sometimes be caused by a traumatic change such as a serious illness or a divorce—*if* it leads you to question the meaning and value of your life rather than focus entirely on your material misfortune.

Clearly, the distinction between a clinical depression and a spiritual crisis can sometimes be a fine line. Another way of recognizing it is to observe the way you respond to a crisis. If you react by asking yourself how you will ever find someone to replace your divorced spouse or lost loved one, how you can get out of a job that's killing you, or how you can find enough money to live, more than likely your depression is primarily psychological. If you respond specifically to the feeling of having been rendered powerless by being consumed with anger, resentment, or blame directed toward others, you are most likely not spiritually depressed. (When in doubt, of course, you should always consult your physician or a mental health professional.) If, however, you are asking yourself questions about the meaning of life or about why God seems so distant from you, then most likely you're in a spiritual crisis, and you may need to seek out a spiritual director rather than a psychotherapist.

If you determine that your depression is largely spiritual, one solution may be to surrender all your worldly fears and concerns to the Divine—to "let go and let God," as the saying goes. You can make a simple declaration to the Divine that your own attempts to direct your spiritual life have come up empty, and that you need divine assistance. Surrendering to divine guidance is different from giving up all your worldly goods as you would do if you were to take the traditional vow of poverty. Yet realizing that you live under the protective field of a Sacred Contract, which provides you with all that your life requires for the evolution of your spirit, can allow you to end the struggle between your personal will and that of the Divine. The act of surrender is a statement that says, "I allow the Divine to make my investments according to a wisdom greater than my own."

Marissa's life illustrates precisely this kind of experience. An intellectual professional who had the archetype of the Scholar on her ninth house, Marissa was able to examine any idea as closely as if it were a microbe on a glass slide. She was well-read in virtually every academic field from history to botany, and she was blessed with a keen memory. Marissa pursued God in the same manner in which she researched any subject, with the intention of conquering it. Whether she read mysticism or history, her ultimate intention was to find a path to God as a reward for her studiousness and dedication. To fulfill her Sacred Contract and divine potential, her Scholar would have to lead the way. Had she had her Victim archetype in the ninth house, for example, then her journey into the Divine might have been begun through experiences that left her feeling disempowered, vulnerable, and in need of spiritual strength. If the Child were in that house, she might have related to God as a protective, parental figure, which in some cases can be a helpful way of seeing the Divine.

Marissa eventually hit the wall beyond which intellect cannot go. The mind cannot pin down the power of the spirit, which answers to divine, not human, logic and laws. When asked about historical perspectives of God, she was fluent, but when asked about the experience of the Divine, she was baffled. Eventually her bafflement shifted to frustration and then to depression as she realized that her brainpower alone was not enough to produce the states of ecstasy about which she had read so much.

Marissa decided to go on a retreat—to pound at the chapel door, so to speak. In effect, she was allowed to enter the monastery, but she did not meet God, as she had hoped.

When I met Marissa at a workshop, she was confused, weary, and almost despairing. Drawing up Marissa's chart, the first house I looked at for a clue into her spirit was her ninth. When I found the Scholar there, I began to understand her problem. "No wonder your spirit is half insane," I said. "It's fasting, given the mental diet you've been feeding it." We spoke about the spiritual significance of the Scholar and its role in pulling her deeper and deeper into the rational mind, only to show her again and again that her soul is not rational.

The soul's field of study is the nature of God, which does not yield to logical examination. Marissa had reached a "choice point." She had to humble her Scholar and immediately cease reading about the Divine. Her books would not give her the answers she was looking for.

Marissa had no idea what I was talking about, which was another good sign; already her mind was shutting off. I suggested that she allow herself to enter her madness, to feel the frustration, and to wait for the time when meeting God on the road to reason no longer mattered. "When you can reach that point, God will be there," I told her, which was the identical instruction I had been given years before by a nun and mentor whom I love dearly.

A little over a year later I received a letter from Marissa telling me that she had followed my instructions. "I have learned during these past many months that I am not the disciplined person I thought I was," she wrote. "I am controlling and terrified of being controlled by others. I wanted my experiences to follow my rules. When I would meet people, I introduced myself mind first. I wanted to overwhelm them with my brilliance and that way dominate every group. I decided somewhere during these past months never to do that again. When I'm with people now, I listen instead of talk. I genuinely want to get to know them, and I share with them my feelings as well as my thoughts. I feel that I am becoming softer inside, and in this softness I have made ready a place for God. Already I am more content. I am keeping a diary on the conversations I have, and my Scholar is learning to study the many ways people appreciate being alive. In short, I'm doing okay."

I love Marissa's story because she fought surrender with all the power she had, and lost—and then won. She did not have to give up her profession, move her home, or become poor and celibate. She simply had to reevaluate the control the Scholar had over the manner in which she related to life and to God.

TENTH HOUSE:
HIGHEST POTENTIAL
(Fifth and seventh chakras)
The tenth house is ruled by Capricorn, the third earth sign of the astrological chart. The energy of this house works on your highest

potential. It pushes you to be all that you can in your physical world and your spiritual life. What is the highest potential of your compassionate self or your generosity? What is your highest potential when it comes to empowering another? What is the highest potential you can strive for with your talent? Your highest potential is what your Sacred Contract is prompting you to recognize and realize. Because this requires that you make choices regarding your spiritual destiny, the house corresponds to the energies of both the fifth and the seventh chakras.

The archetype that resides in this house is your entryway into deciphering the choices open to you and the quality of your motivations. The shadow side of your highest potential is self-sabotage or doubt or lack of faith. Fear of failure, as well as fear of success and responsibility, characterizes the challenges inherent in this house. These are basically fears of your own powers and empowerment and the changes they require you to make in your life. You will need to face whether you would deliberately block your highest potential from emerging, and why. You will also be challenged to retain humility as you become more empowered.

Pursuing your highest potential is the most difficult marathon. With each upgrade, whether personal or professional, something or someone will arise to test the depth and solidity of your inner growth. On the earthly plane this encounter might present itself as a confrontation between you and another person who doesn't want you to change. Or you may find yourself in a relationship with someone of whom you become jealous, which will test your own potential to support another's talent and gifts. Or you may be given an opportunity to pursue a goal of inner transformation, only to discover that such opportunities always require that you leave a part of your life behind, that you make a necessary sacrifice. Some people find sacrifice and change too high a price to pay and do not pursue or fulfill their potential.

The archetype in your tenth house is the indicator of how your unconscious organizes your thoughts when you are faced with choices that can lead you into fulfilling your potential. Remember that although all of your archetypal companions provide influence in every aspect of your life, the archetype that resides in this house represents the symbolic language that you want to use to begin deciphering all that your highest potential holds.

Foley's life holds an extraordinary Contract. Foley has an identical twin brother named Dennis, and like many twins they were inseparable until they reached their college years. Dennis had assumed that they would both go into business management. Foley, however, fearing his brother's objections, had kept hidden from Dennis his own desire to study botany and move to Costa Rica for a few years. Soon after they began college, Dennis became aware that Foley had a different future in mind and became withdrawn. He felt completely betrayed and said that Foley should have kept him informed all along about his growing interest in a different future. Dennis viewed Foley's decision to move to Central America as abandonment.

Although Foley anticipated that Dennis would be upset, he was surprised by the severity of his brother's reaction. Dennis changed schools in their sophomore year. In time the pressure exerted on Foley by his parents and his broken relationship with his brother compelled him to forsake his ambition.

I met Foley about three years after he sacrificed his dream. By then he had completed a degree in accounting. He was working as a waiter and hoping to continue studies in computer science, but his heart wasn't in anything he was doing. Until Foley admitted that he had compromised his dreams, he would never feel fulfilled.

At first glance Foley's problem may appear to be a third-house concern over siblings and communication, but Foley's *primary* issue was that he was negotiating his own calling in life, a tenth-house issue: he was not following his inner voice to pursue his highest potential. Dennis may have been the immediate reason, but the core issue was Foley's own anguish over losing his highest potential. In many situations, as in Foley's, different concerns may overlap. You may need to peel away several levels of issues and several houses before you get to the central one.

Foley had the Hero archetype in his tenth house. When I asked him why he had chosen the Hero as one of his twelve archetypes, he said that he associated endurance, dedication, and loyalty with the

Hero. He had consciously worked on developing these qualities all of his life, particularly in regard to helping and looking out for his twin. He added, however, that he always felt that he would be directed on a mission that would require he separate from his twin. "I knew it since I was a kid," he confided, "because I have been aware for a long time that I was carrying my brother's psyche on my shoulders. I was always trying to make sure he was happy and safe. I was the one always working out his problems and helping him to make the grade. And I knew that I would have to part with him if only to give that same level of attention to myself. I wanted to know what it felt like to put me first and who I would be if I were totally free to make any choice I wanted to without having to check in with my other half."

I asked Foley to describe the difference between how he saw his Hero in the business arena and how he saw the Hero as a botanist striving to maintain the health of endangered nature life. The phrasing of the question alone almost crushed him. "There's just no comparison," he said. "I'll never contribute to life by adding numbers as much as I would working in the field." We discussed what prevented him from returning to his original course. By now his twin should have been able to take care of himself, and I asked him to name three compromises that his brother had made in *his* life to insure that Foley would be happier. He couldn't offer even one.

When I asked Foley to describe the health of his Hero archetype, he said that he felt that the Hero had become a weak and defeated force in his spirit and that it embarrassed him to remember that he had walked away from his own inner guidance. "I don't believe I have any courage left, and maybe I never had any in the first place. If I did, I think I would have gone ahead and moved to Central America."

Foley was living in the shadow of his Hero, and his way out was to pull himself out of his own misery by finally deciding that his life meant enough to him to go ahead and live it. Adjusting his physical life to suit the demands of that commitment would be his initiatory Hero's Journey, and it would give him a sample of his highest potential. The next test—choosing to break free of his tribe and to pursue one of the tasks of his spirit—would represent the next stage of the Hero's Journey.

After visualizing this break to freedom, Foley felt renewed. His breathing changed, and his energy temporarily shed its depression. He began to glimpse that his brother and parents were not the real reason why he had failed to take hold of his highest potential. Foley had the Hermit archetype in his third house, siblings and communication, expressing his need to separate from the strong family psyche that held so much influence over him. Unlike his brother or other family members, Foley needed his own space to express his life, expression being a third-house characteristic. With or without his brother's clinging to him, he would have had to seek an independent path. As in all Contracts, his family was actually a gift for him. Many families serve out their roles as obstacles, then become powerful supporters. Foley's was the embodiment of a collective challenge that would refine his inner Hero, forcing it to be determined and independent.

One of the manifestations of the shadow aspect of the third house is in the way we communicate, not just with others but with ourselves, our psyches, our spirit and intuition, and with the very essence of our life. When Foley did not follow the voice and yearning of his own spirit and did not communicate his desires to his brother and family, he betrayed his inner voice and alienated his spirit. Now he would have to call on his Hero to recapture his soul.

ELEVENTH HOUSE:
RELATIONSHIP TO THE WORLD
(Fourth and sixth chakras)

The eleventh house corresponds to Aquarius, the third air sign, and it rules your relationship to the external world and your ideas about the outer sphere. Your viewpoint about life in general is connected to the energy of this house. Those sentiments reflect how you see your sense of power operating within the social or global environment. People who are drawn to paths of service that have global consequences, such as environmental causes or international peace work, have strong connections to the energy of this house. Optimism or pessimism about the future of humanity is an extension of the spiritual energy of the eleventh house. The eleventh house rules how you relate your creativity to humanity and engages the energies of your fourth and sixth chakras, which regulate your heart and mind.

The presidential race between George W. Bush and Al Gore was an archetypal eleventh-house tug-of-war. The difficulties in deciding who had won the election focused national attention on the power that individuals do have to change the whole future of humanity. As a result, Americans seriously evaluated the importance of single votes as never before.

People who are empowered by an attitude that says anything is possible live in an energy field of pure eleventh-house potential. They are frequently larger than life, precisely because they do think in global terms. For them, eleventh-house perceptions flood into their first thoughts of the day and are the last to leave their minds as they retire at the end of the day. People like Martin Luther King, Jr., and Mahatma Gandhi, who created new awareness in the mind and soul of all humanity, embody the influence of the eleventh house. As they peered through the lens of their eleventh house into the global village, they saw the possibilities for positive change against impossible odds.

Not all people need to start or participate in a cause to contribute positive energy to the planet. I meet countless people who energize powerful attitudes about life such as "All people are basically good" and who help those in need. These people nurture the entire human soul. As Jesus said, "Whatever you did for one of the least of these brothers of mine, you did for me" (Matt. 25:40). Developing the capacity to see the whole of life as beautiful, and to see people as essentially loving beings, is like participating in a spiritual environmental movement. We have no way of measuring the power of a single thought, yet we know that attitudes and beliefs have universal consequences.

Spiritual masters, popular leaders, scientific geniuses, and great artists who are dedicated to serving humanity all illustrate what good can be generated by dedicating your spirit to incarnating a single perception. For instance, Copernicus reordered humanity's understanding of planetary movements by disputing the notion that the earth was the center of the solar system. That one thought dismantled the scientific paradigm of his time: one day the earth appeared flat, and the next day it was round; a single perception reshaped the collective view of the globe.

You too may be the channel through which an entirely new understanding of reality will manifest. Review your life and your relationships. Look for changes that you have inspired in others who then went on to move mountains in their own lives. Most of the mountains we deal with are not necessarily enormous global movements but everyday challenges or invisible forces, like attitudes. Generations benefit from even one parent deciding to become a more active father to his children or to stop hating people who are different from him. When John Lennon effectively retired from public life to care for his infant son Sean, for instance, the concept of the "househusband" was essentially unheard of. Lennon took considerable abuse for supposedly trading in his guitar for an apron, and yet his example formed a model that millions of men have since embraced, much to the delight of their wives or partners—and children. Maintaining that single thought-form, nurturing it with loving attention and an ever-deepening appreciation for what it means to live in an interconnected universe, transmits spiritual electricity to the collective system.

Great spiritual masters have continually directed their students to become aware of the power of their own spirits. In an effort to enlighten their students about their inner potential, such leaders echo the words of the Buddhist patriarch Bodhidharma: "I am but a finger pointing to the moon. Don't look at me; look at the moon." When Jesus said of his miraculous healings, "All this and more can you do if you have faith," his message was clear: each person can become a force for the transformation of the whole of humanity if only we recognize and live according to the true nature of the Divinity within. The external world is but a manifestation of the authority of our internal life.

In the Chicago suburb of Des Plaines, Illinois, is a Carmelite monastery. For only one afternoon many years ago, the Carmelite nuns permitted a group of people to visit a very limited portion of the interior space of their cloister. I was among that group, and I can vividly recall their stark dining room, their private cells with bare white walls, and the long corridor that led to rooms we would never enter. As soon as we were all seated in the reception area, the abbess spoke to us about the spiritual significance of the nuns' commitment. Living under a vow of silence and in a continual state of prayer on behalf of all people, these women believed that all their prayers resulted in outpourings of grace from the Divine upon the humanity they almost never saw. A few nuns were permitted to speak with the visitors that afternoon, and I asked one why she believed that the prayers of a group of seventeen women could possibly affect the world community. "I can tell by your question," she said, "that you have yet to truly need the power of a single prayer."

Years later in Paris I had the opportunity to have dinner with the Tibetan Buddhist teacher Sogyal Rinpoche. Among the many stories he shared with me was the story of his master's death. "When it was time for my master to die, he called together his students and his astrologers," Rinpoche said. "He announced that he was now preparing to leave and asked his astrologers to cast a chart with the intention of locating the perfect time for him to withdraw his spirit from the earth. He wanted to leave as silently as he could so as not to cause disruption." Sogyal Rinpoche also explained that the power of one enlightened spirit is strongly involved in holding in balance the positive and negative energies in life.

The archetype that resides within your eleventh house is symbolic of how you view the power of your spirit in relation to the whole of life. The Victim archetype on that house, which I have often seen, can suggest that you find the world an intimidating place, where everyone has more authority over your life than you do. On the other hand, I've also seen the Victim in this position in the charts of people who are on fire with courage and optimism. For them the Victim becomes a symbol of the negative energy they refuse to give in to, pushing themselves to the limits to help themselves and others avoid ever being victimized.

Archetypes in the eleventh house cause us to evaluate how we see our place in this world and how we measure our sense of power. My graduate teacher of Christology told me that the more aware you are of the power of your spirit, the less you have to travel physically, because you can send your thoughts and prayers to do the work for you. It may be difficult to apprehend that, even while hanging out in your own home, your thoughts are influencing the whole of life, but that truth is something we are all under Contract to learn.

The shadow side of the power of one mind can be seen in people such as Adolf Hitler, Joseph Stalin, Charles Manson, and Jim Jones. The characteristics of the shadow side of the eleventh house feed on an ego that makes one believe that the entire globe can be transformed according to the dictates of one's desires. The psyches of people in whom this shadow is active are like spiderwebs. They lure and entrap the multitudes who are in search of someone to give them a vision of what life could be like if they, the powerless, had authority over others. As history tells us, such negative eleventh-house perceptions inevitably implode, taking their supporters with them.

TWELFTH HOUSE:
THE UNCONSCIOUS
(Sixth and seventh chakras)

The twelfth house corresponds to the third water sign, Pisces, which is the sign of intuition, of gut instinct. This is Persephone's house, the underworld ruled by Pluto, or what I would call the major channel into deeper guidance. The twelfth house rules the unconscious mind as well as our innermost fears. The energetic nature of this house pushes our underground images into our mind through every available portal: dreams, conversations, synchronistic encounters, any means that provide an opportunity to see a fragment of our Contract in action. Uncovering your unconscious requires your intellect, intuition, and spiritual aspirations, and so this house resonates with the energies of the sixth and seventh chakras.

Your intuitive abilities are part of the energy of this house. Refer to the meaning of the first house, and review the circular journey of the Archetypal Wheel; note that the other houses relate to rational and emotional aspects of your nature. Forming your identity and choosing your values are largely products of the physical world. Finding a union with another person and evaluating whether you want to continue to carry your tribe's symbolic DNA in your system is very much an emotional and psychological issue. Completion of this circle, however, leads you to your intuitive voice.

Intuition is our primal sense. Long before we are introduced to rational thinking, we sense life. As babies, we absorb the energy climate of the world we live in, including the emotions of our parents and the atmosphere of our home. As we grow older, the rational abilities of the mind develop, and the intuitive experiences that many children describe, such as seeing angels, are dismissed as imagination. These psychic forces then go underground, although usually they do not go completely silent. I am convinced that the polarity between our rational and intuitive selves creates an inner atmosphere that sets the stage for intense suffering and depression. To sense energy information but then repress that information for lack of rational support is to court madness.

Learning to speak archetypes and see symbolically awakens and uses your intuition. The archetypal pattern that resides in your twelfth house is your guide into your underground. Although your fears may seem multitudinous, each one is ultimately just a different version of the fear of change, which is by far the most powerful obstacle to the ultimate irrational act of spiritual surrender. Your twelfth-house experiences carry the theme of surrender, as in the scene from *It's a Wonderful Life* in which George Bailey (played by Jimmy Stewart), contemplating suicide on a bridge over an icy river, finally reaches his breaking point and cries out to God for help.

A few years ago I met a woman named Chris who was herself at a breaking point. Her husband had been arrested for extortion, and the authorities had taken all of their possessions in an effort to recover the money he had stolen. Their lives went from the fairy-tale couple with two children living in a charming home to a destitute family living off the charity of family members. Chris had the stamina and strength of a Soldier, the archetype in her twelfth house. She had chosen the Soldier not just because it helped her cope with her problems but also because she had always been the one to fight the battles for the family's emotional survival. Her father was a military officer who condemned any form of emotional openness, and her brothers were alcoholics. Because her mother was not capable of coping with so much dysfunction, Chris had become a lightning rod from her earliest days for all the tension in the house. On a more mundane level, Chris chose the Soldier because it represented strength, dedication, loyalty, and honor, qualities that she felt were among the highest that one could aspire to.

At the time I met Chris, she was in crisis. Without self-pity she nonetheless had reached the point at which she was questioning why she had to endure so much, while those around her could live in abusive ways. "I was on the brink of a nervous breakdown," she told me. "I had no one I could talk to, and no idea of where to go or what to do next. My entire life had changed in one afternoon"—the afternoon of her husband's arrest.

To gather symbolic information that could help Chris decide how to proceed, I directed her to think in the language of the Soldier. "I always did think of my childhood as boot camp," she joked. Then I asked her to describe everything in her life that was involved with her present crisis as if she were a soldier. To begin with, she responded, "I was always taking orders from my dad. When I wanted to do something for myself, I had to sneak past enemy lines to get out on my own. This pattern did not change after I got married. Obviously I married in the pattern of my family, except that my father is an honest man.

"All the while my husband was breaking the law, I knew something was wrong. His moods were changing, and he was becoming more and more withdrawn and secretive, but he kept insisting that he was just tired from the stress at work. I didn't listen to my gut instinct, which is a Soldier's best weapon. While he was living in this secret world, I could feel myself bracing for a war, an invisible emotional battle that would tear our marriage apart. I just couldn't find the enemy. I knew he wasn't cheating on me with another woman, but I never dreamed that he was stealing."

Chris's husband was eventually caught because he left a paper trail at his office and his superiors followed it. I asked Chris to separate from this trauma and think like a soldier who had just been asked the question "What are your worst fears?" She said that her strongest fear was having her life spin out of control. "That is precisely why I married someone who I thought had what it took to keep order in our lives. At the same time I resented the fact that I was surrounded by so much male authority. I also resented that I was allowing myself to be ordered around. I wasn't blind to that fact. I simply liked the feeling that I was being looked after, as I was when my family was living on an army base. But now that's changed, and my life has been shattered as if a bomb hit it. I have to take care of myself, because I feel that I need to leave my marriage and get on with my life."

Breaking-point experiences are classic to the twelfth house, and Chris's marriage reflected that kind of drama. Obviously her Contract with her husband did not include that he become a thief. That was a choice he had made, but he also had the option to make positive choices.

"If a soldier were to ask you for advice," I said to Chris, "what would you say in this situation?"

Chris said that she would order the soldier to draw a map that led to a destination, even though she knew nothing about the destination. She had to prepare her equipment and brace herself for a rough journey, though sometimes these treks turn out to be much easier than expected. The nights are long, she said, because that's when she feels most vulnerable. "But I hold on to the thought that I am under Contracts instead of orders these days and that the military is responsible to protect and provide for its soldiers. I know that's true because I grew up in that world and never saw it fail one soldier. I'll be fine."

Chris felt a growing sense of self-reliance as she released her need to be under someone else's "command." She got on with her life, and every time she felt lost in the jungle, as she put it, she referred to her Soldier archetype and all the symbolic force that it held for her. By substituting the word *Contracts* for *orders*, she signified that her commanding officer was Divine.

The shadow side of the twelfth house can feel very much like a gothic chamber of horrors precisely because it is so closely linked to the numerous fragments of our psyche. Many of our addictions and compulsions are rooted in our deepest fears of being abandoned, which thrive in the shadow of this house.

Now that you have familiarized yourself with the nature and role of each of the twelve houses that make up the Archetypal Wheel, it's time to create your own personal Wheel. By following the intuitive process outlined in the next chapter, you will place each of your twelve archetypes into a different house of the Wheel. This, your personal Archetypal Wheel, will become the single most important road map to working with your archetypes and understanding your Sacred Contract.

CHAPTER 8

Creating Your
Chart of Origin

Your Archetypal Wheel shows you your soul's relationship to power. In this chapter you will learn how to place each of your twelve archetypes into its house of service within the Wheel. Each archetype touches the others through the center fulcrum of the Wheel, so even though each house is "ruled" by a particular archetype, it is nevertheless also influenced by all of the other archetypal energies in your chart.

If your Child archetype, for instance, falls into the ninth house (spirituality), it signifies that understanding the nature of your Child will help you explore your spirituality. A woman named Meg had a ninth-house Child archetype and realized that she held a very strong parent-child image of her relationship to God; she expected God to reward her when she was good, punish her when she misbehaved, take care of her needs, and receive little in return, just as her parents had. As a result of her expectations, Meg realized, she "practiced a very immature spirituality," a passive view of God. This insight led Meg to understand why she felt abandoned or thought that she had done something wrong whenever she did not get what she wanted. At the same time the Child represented an image of trust and safety in God. "I pray to an image of God the Father," Meg said. "I do not relate to the concept of the Divine, which for me is impersonal, cold, and distant. I need the father figure. I feel safe and loved within this image in a way that the concept of the Divine doesn't provide. This is the positive side of my Child-like spirituality. My Child also reminds me that, like a child, I often do not hold myself accountable spiritually, and addressing this absence of spiritual maturity has now become a focus of my inner life." Meg used this archetypal image to help her reshape her spiritual life. Each of her challenges required that she learn to accept Divine guidance rather than demand that all of her needs be met like a spoiled child.

As an intuitive instrument, the Archetypal Wheel takes you beyond rational and logical perceptions. It also serves as a creative vessel in which you have access to images and inspiration and can mix them to get extraordinary insights. Out of this spiritual crucible can emerge a refined, more durable vision of your life's purpose. In working with the Wheel, I often picture King Arthur with his twelve Knights of the Round Table. Each archetype rules a portion of the kingdom under the guidance of the king—your intuition. Arthur converses with each one, learning the intimate details of each knight's estate, what is beautiful about that part of the country, and any potential troubles or challenges. To maintain his kingdom—to create a Camelot—he must consolidate the power of all twelve knights, forming one united, harmonious circle. Loss, separation, and revolt in any one estate would threaten the health of the whole realm.

As you read your own Wheel, you may see how each of your knights interconnects with the others. Memories of one part of your life link to a conversation you are having today that is somehow connected to a book you read two years ago, and to a creative venture inspired by a business associate who made an offhand comment this morning.

In my workshops people share stories of their lives in which they recall how one experience led to another, forming a finely linked chain that connects them to the whole of their lives. One remarkable man named Jim told a story that epitomizes that process. "I had an accident when I was eleven that left me partially paralyzed," he said. "After my accident I was afraid of everything, and I believed that I would never have a normal life. Then one day I decided that rather than focus on my fears, the time had come for me to learn to accept that all things happen for a reason. Everyone needs to learn that truth in some measure, but for me it amounted to releasing my attempt to control my life.

Especially after my accident I believed that as long as I demanded order, I could minimize any more unexplainable, undeserved traumas. Now I look at everyone as energetically connected to everyone else and of course to me. I look for the one thing that each person brings into my life that contributes to my empowerment. Regardless of whether a relationship is positive or difficult, my attention focuses on holding the thought that invisible purpose leads to divine empowerment."

Even though you may not always see how the people and events in your life are linked to each other and to you, your Wheel provides a map on which you can plot the points of interaction between them. This helps you to "connect the dots" and form a clearer picture of what is happening.

Casting Your Wheel

The Wheel you are about to cast will serve as the basic chart of your life, and so it is meant to be cast only once. In Chapter 10 you will learn to use the same technique to seek guidance on specific questions and issues that are confronting you. But this first Archetypal Wheel is akin to your natal chart in astrology. Just as you cannot have more than one moment of birth, so you cannot make more than one first Archetypal Wheel. This is your beginning point, which I sometimes call your Contract Wheel or Chart of Origin, and as you continue to return to your Wheel for interpretations of additional areas of your life, you must use the same Wheel. You are not to reshuffle and cast a new Wheel each time you work, with the intention of understanding the "whole" of your Contract. This is the only Wheel that presents you with an overview of all of the connecting cycles and archetypal patterns of your Sacred Contract.

The actual task of casting your Archetypal Wheel is rather simple. Clear your mind of expectations and desires, and focus on your intention to be open to whatever guidance you receive. Take several deep breaths to clear your mind. Your archetypes will be guided into their appropriate houses by the energy of simultaneity, coincidence, spiritual order, divine paradox, and destiny. As explained in Chapter 7, this psychic electricity creates a kind of magnetic organizational process, as it does for runes, Tarot, the *I Ching*, astrology, and other tools that communicate with your intuition and unconscious. Like them, your Wheel is a means to an end, an organizational system that supplies a form through which the patterns of your psyche and soul can reveal themselves to you.

When you release your intention for casting your Chart of Origin, it is natural to wonder, "Exactly whom am I addressing?" There will come a moment when you will wonder if God or just your subconscious is on the receiving end of your intentions and your questions. It's risky for me to say absolutely that you are addressing God, the Divine, or whatever name you use for the guiding force of the universe, as if you were saying a prayer and waiting for the answer. Some people might prefer to say that all answers come from within anyway. If you feel more comfortable visualizing the process that way, then go with it. I happen to believe that the Divine dwells within us as well as around us, whether we call it God, Atman, Buddha Nature, our Higher Self, or just the still small voice. We are heard when we ask for guidance, and that's all that matters.

So when you come to the point of questioning who or what is at the other end of your request for guidance, and you definitely will, search for the highest perspective you can reach. Look at how your life would feel if you were liberated from fear and private agendas. Investigate your life as if you believed that failure is impossible. Act as if your intentions were prayers and that they were being released into the ears of the Divine. After all, what harm can that do? Or to put this another way, are you ever separated from your own sacred Self? Hardly.

In clearing your mind prior to casting your Wheel, use this meditation as a centering device:

Close your eyes and breathe deeply into your abdomen,
allowing your stomach to expand as you breathe in and contract as you exhale. See yourself as a hollow reed or membrane, expanding and contracting. Continue in slow, deep breaths, repeating, "I have no desires. I have no thoughts.
I am empty of all disturbances. I am empty of all my needs.
I am open to receive."

Be receptive. When you are seeking interior guidance, you are requesting insights that could potentially change the present course of your life. Even though your conscious mind is making the request, your unconscious may block the answers if they are not what you want to hear. Long ago I learned that people come to my workshops on developing intuition more to learn how to block their guidance than to get in touch with it. Their intuitive receptivity is so strong that they suffer miserably from the stress of "intuitive repression." More often than not these people are hoping that they will tap into an ability to see what the future will bring so that they can avoid risk, uncertainty, and unpleasantness. They want intuition to tell them what will happen tomorrow so that they can take the risk factor out of their decisions. That will never happen, and that is not the nature of intuition.

Receiving intuitive information or guidance is effortless. What is difficult is removing your fears about what your intuition is telling you. Should you discover that you are unable to be.truly open to any and all guidance that can come through this tool, that realization in itself speaks deeply about the intensity of your fears, all of which you can identify through working with your archetypal patterns. Holding an open mind will allow your archetypal patterns to assume their most natural positions in your chart. You are embarking on an experience to learn more about your life. Treat yourself and the voice of your psyche with respect, because it is a living force that yearns for channels through which it can communicate.

The Directions

I recommend that you do this work alone or only with people you trust. Set up an atmosphere that has as little distraction as possible, and choose a time when you will not be disturbed, so that you can stay focused. Concentrate on casting this Wheel because it will be the basis for future readings. Remember, you can cast this Wheel only once. Don't cast your Wheel while watching TV or a movie. *You're* the only movie you want to be watching when working with this tool.

There are four steps to casting your Archetypal Wheel. Although an empty drawing of the Wheel has been provided for you to fill in, you may want to trace or copy it into your journal, so that you can reuse the empty wheel for other readings later on. (See Figure 5 on page 210.)

Step 1: Simple Preparation

You will need twenty-four palm-size pieces of paper, about two inches by three inches. On each of twelve of those slips of paper, write the name of one of your twelve archetypes. Refer to your journal if you need to remember which ones you chose. On each of the other twelve slips write one number between one and twelve. Keep the slips with archetypes and numbers in two different stacks, facedown.

Step 2: Intuitive Focus

Use this meditation to begin the next step:

Center yourself as you would if you were doing a visualization for healing or spiritual guidance. Breathe in and out deeply three times, and empty your mind. Direct your attention fully into your body. Focus on your first chakra. Visualize closing the shutters of that chakra so that its energy is fully contained in your body. Feel the silence that results and the relief as you close down any contact with first-chakra concerns, such as family affairs. Bring all your energy connections back into your root chakra and hold them there. You are no longer in contact with outside matters, so for a moment rest in the tranquillity of being contained in one place.

Now close the shutters through each of the rest of your chakras. Move to your second chakra, in the genital area, and let go of any thoughts or emotions concerning money, sex, and power. Consolidate your energy in the second chakra, and just enjoy the pleasurable sensation of having no agenda. Next close the shutters of your third chakra, corresponding to the solar plexus. Release all thoughts or feelings about your self-esteem, how others view you, and how you see yourself. You are entering a state in which you are viewing yourself without preconceptions. Think of the Zen koan, or riddle, "What was my original face, before I was born?"

Now move your attention to the fourth, or heart, chakra, the center of your emotions. Let go of any emotions that may hinder or obscure the process of casting your chart. Draw your energy into your heart center, and hold it there, free of any emotional charge. Then focus on your throat chakra, the center of will and choice. You can release all concerns about making conscious choices, secure in the knowledge that your intuition, the Divine within, will be selecting your archetypes for you. Enjoy the feeling of safety and intimate connection with your inner self. Raising your attention to the sixth chakra, focus on the pineal gland, on an imaginary line reaching back from between your eyes to the center of your skull. Let any conscious thoughts drift through your mind without either clinging to them or forcing them to leave. This is the state known as "mirror mind," in which you observe ideas passing like clouds above a mirror. Finally, bring your attention to your seventh chakra, and imagine that the shutters are at the crown of your head and that you are *opening* them as wide as possible. Your seventh chakra is now the only opening in your body, making you fully dependent on the energy of that spiritual portal.

In this state of mind and spirit, shuffle the stack of numbers and place them back on the table facedown. Then shuffle the stack of archetypes, asking the question, "In which houses do these archetypes best serve me?" Your intention attracts energy and creates a magnetic circuit that will direct the archetypes to their appropriate houses as you work with them in Step 3, reflecting the body of your Contract.

Step 3: Intuitive Choice

Picture yourself as a "hollow reed" transmitting energy. Keeping the cards facedown, choose a number card and an archetype. The numbers correspond to the house into which that archetype should go. Write the name of that archetype into the numbered house on your Wheel. If you chose the number four and the Child cards, for example, your Child archetype belongs in the fourth house of your Wheel. Continue this exercise until all twelve houses are filled.

Step 4: The Partnerships of Archetypes and Their Houses

Once you have paired the archetypes with their houses, you have generated a unique energy field. As you look at the completed Wheel and its lineup of your twelve archetypal companions, visualize yourself at the center of this Wheel surrounded by these energy figures. Imagine that you are seeing into the symbolic hologram of your unconscious.

In this step you will animate the ley lines between archetypes, houses, events, relationships, attitudes, memories, fears, triumphs, love, acts of grace—all the details within the orbit of your life. You'll do this by answering a number of questions that appear in the next section. This process of animation is like laying the electrical wiring in a house, putting in sockets and circuit breakers. After you have laid enough psychic wires, "the lights go on," and you will begin to see clearly into all parts of your life, some of which you have forgotten, some of which have been dark or mysterious.

To start exploring the meaning of each archetype-to-house partnership, list any immediate associations and thoughts that occur to you. You may feel some resistance to some of the partnerships, but please don't suppress any thoughts that come to you. You are learning a new language and a multidimensional method of perceiving your life, and it may feel awkward at first. For instance, say you matched the Saboteur to your seventh house. You might write: "My Saboteur archetype is in the house of marriage and relationships. This means that the fears that cause me to engage in self-sabotage generally have more to do with my relationships than with my professional life. I don't tend to sabotage myself in business dealings, because I have a strong sense of self-esteem in that realm. Yet my fear of rejection leads me to react badly to commitment in my relationships."

As you practice symbolic sight, it will become second nature to you. How might you interpret the Victim archetype in the same house of relationships? When dealing with the Victim, you want to think of how its energy reveals itself in the hurdles, potential opportunities, and personal characteristics that occur in all your relationships: your family, spouse, business partner, children, and friends. How can you transform the Victim within in order to have a healthier relationship?

The idea of "relationship" also refers to how you relate to your own self, to nature, and to all life, including animals. Begin with your earliest memories, and look for lifelong patterns. Don't just look at your present relationships. As you trace the Victim—or any other seventh-house archetype—through all your relationships, you need to look for all of the positive as well as challenging contributions that it has made.

Stretch your definitions and associations with archetypal patterns, particularly when they have challenging names like Victim, Prostitute, Saboteur, Servant, or Addict. Otherwise you may overlook the positive symbolic contributions of those archetypes and their ability to help your personal healing and transformation. Remember that the energy of archetypes is neutral and that you can change any negative expressions of these patterns to positive ones.

Joan has the Victim in her eighth house, which relates to other people's money and how we use it, and to inheritances and legal matters. From her earliest recollection, she was taught that money is essential to her ability to protect herself. Her immigrant parents taught her that without money she would be socially powerless and at the mercy of other people. Her parents inspired Joan to get a good education, and she became adept at earning her own living and making profitable financial investments. The Victim archetype in her eighth house represented her fear that she could be taken advantage of, and she channeled that fear constructively into self-protection. Note that Joan's primary motivation in life came from the wisdom she "inherited" from her parents rather than from an outside resource. Although other people undoubtedly inspired her, Joan's core inspiration came not from a teacher or friend but from a source of "inheritance," which is also native to the eighth house.

To Joan, the Victim archetype had far more positive than negative associations. It was an ally that motivated her to become a shrewd, capable businesswoman. It also led her to volunteer to help other women and men learn how to protect themselves from being "victimized" in the financial world. "Helping people to see that they have opportunities in life comes naturally to me," Joan said. "I am available to those who need that kind of advice. They find me. I obviously radiate a kind of 'how-to-rid-yourself-of-the-victim-within' message."

Joan also related her Victim to some of her other archetypes, including her Prostitute, because she felt that had she not learned to take care of herself financially, she would have become dependent on or subject to the demands of others for her survival. Having an "empowered Victim" allowed her to take risks in her life. Joan had also chosen the Rebel archetype as one of her companions. "I am interested in politics and in working in behalf of people to make my city [Detroit] a better place. And the issues that I am drawn to might be considered rebellious by some, such as equal rights for gays and lesbians. But my nature consistently draws me to chip away at social perceptions that make people powerless. That is the thread of my Contracts with others. I meet people who teach me how to do this better, who challenge me because they believe they can't change things and need my help." Joan described her other nine archetypes in relationship to her Victim as waiting in the wings should she need to call on them.

One of the most significant aspects of this story is that Joan's ability to help others was "natural," as if she were born with it, and she did not have to advertise for people to help. When someone has to break down a door to enter a room, whether that room refers symbolically to a social group or to a certain role, it suggests that he's not meant to be there. The question then arises, "How do I know whether a blockade means that the time is not right for something to happen, and that I should still hold on to my dream, or that I'm on the wrong path?" When the path is right for you, some intervention or act of grace will guide you. It may be as banal as someone saying to you, "Hang in there, it'll work out." Or an apparent accident or coincidence may clear the way just when your path seemed blocked. On the other hand, when you are on a path that is *not* yours to walk, no "animated" intervention will occur. That is, a person might say, "Hang in there," but these words will lack the kind of electricity that gives you hope and strength. Remaining on the path will eventually become "energetically expensive," because nothing will empower you.

Your archetypes are generally visible in every stage of your life. Joan, for instance, could see how the Victim had animated her from her childhood, not just at that moment. Even if you see an immediate connection between an archetype and its house, take the time to look back into your history for past experiences that reflect the pattern. Ruben, for instance, had the Samaritan archetype in his tenth house, which rules one's highest potential. "I enjoy doing what I can for others," he said. "But I also know what it feels like to need help, to hope that a Good Samaritan is out there who will come my way. I needed that when I was a teenager. We had some rough times at home, and believe me, it's hard to need, much less take, a handout. Good Samaritans don't want anything in return. The genuine ones give, and you never feel humiliated by needing their help."

Your archetypes are a mirror of your Self. The more you learn about the nature of an archetype, the more you will learn about yourself. If, for example, Ruben were to read the scriptural story of the Good Samaritan, which is one of the prototypes of this archetype in the Western world, he would discover additional dynamics in his dealings with others. The Samaritans were the avowed enemies of the Jews, and so by helping a Jewish man who had been robbed and beaten and left by the roadside, the Good Samaritan did not merely perform an act of charity. He first had to overcome his tribe's preconceptions about whom he should feel compassion toward. It's relatively easy to help people of your own kind, but the Good Samaritan is an incarnation of the admonition to "love thine enemy."

Examining Your Spiritual Real Estate with Pen in Hand

The questions that follow are designed to elicit your reflections on memories of your major experiences. They're meant to cause you to interpret these experiences in symbolic ways, such as how they introduced you to overall life patterns. As with all the exercises in this book, the more detailed you can be, drawing on your successes and failures, the challenges you faced and the ones you ran away from, the better.

Let your feelings and responses emerge from within. As you enter your answers in your journal, you should also record any imagery, dreams, or associations that come to mind, even if they don't seem to make sense. These questions are directed as much to your unconscious as to your conscious mind. The conscious mind often produces instant replies in one word or brief phrases, while the unconscious will give you impressions and images. If some of the questions baffle you the first time around, come back to them later. Often when you stop thinking about a question and trying to force an answer, an answer or image will present itself spontaneously. Please make a note of any answers, no matter when and where they pop into your mind. Answer all the questions for each archetype and house.

- *What are my immediate associations with this archetype and the meaning of its house?*

In almost all cases, when you focus your attention on an archetype and the meaning of its house, you will get a rapid flow of intuitive perceptions even before your conscious mind takes over and jogs your memories. Your intuition provides you with data that is timeless and transcends literal thinking.

A journalist named David was drawn to the Spell-caster archetype because he believed that by researching stories that revealed the corrupt side of society, he "broke the spells" that controlled people's minds. When David cast his Wheel, his Spell-caster archetype landed in the eleventh house, which rules our relationships to the outside world. His first impression was that he was the one who was under a "spell," and he was so revolted by this impression that he gave a fairly theatrical description of why this archetype was in the wrong place—a sure signal that his rational mind had kicked into gear. But as we analyzed that impression from a more detached perspective, David could begin to consider why he was controlled by his opinion that the world is a dark place dominated by ruthlessness and greed, and why he needed to make his readers agree with him. He finally saw that the Spell-caster's voice had led him into a lifelong pattern of wanting to influence the opinions of others. But by writing about only negative actions, attitudes, and beliefs, he was unconsciously giving people permission to act negatively.

Now when David writes, he expresses his thoughts quite differently, because although he still is dedicated to "spell-casting," he is spreading hope for how life could be rather than dread about how life is and will always be.

- *What specific experiences come to mind as I think of the partnership between this archetype and its house?*

One man, on discovering that his Judge archetype had landed in his eleventh house, which rules our relationships to the outside world, had a first impression that he was always judging everyone and everything in the outside world. He had originally chosen the Judge because he had a lifelong regard for the workings of the law, but he also found this archetype active in other areas of his life. "I realize," he said, "that everyone has opinions, but I am obsessive about my judgments. I find something to dislike in everyone, but I am now learning to curb that fault-finding. When I started to work one on one with these archetypes, I saw that I am inclined to find fault with something or someone long before I find anything of value. I wonder now who might have become a dear friend were it not for my judgments, and what I could have experienced had I not judged it ahead of time to be meaningless.

"At the same time I have had to examine the positive aspect of the Judge, and I have learned that dismissing the Judge entirely, and disliking myself for being judgmental, is inappropriate. I need to learn discernment. I need to release my desire to run the world as a courtroom with me presiding over the crowds and delivering sentences to those I consider criminals. It's up to me to keep my center when I am with people whom I would otherwise have condemned.

"Recently, for example, I met a person who had lived in an ashram for a few years. The old me would have immediately labeled that individual a religious fanatic, but in that moment I decided to pursue a conversation about what had motivated him to choose that lifestyle and what he had gained from it. Instead of dismissing him, I learned something from him about spiritual dedication. This is a hard habit to break for me, however. As soon as the conversation was over, I immediately fell into criticizing every word he had spoken. I had to repeat the conversation in my mind, but when I did I focused on why I was afraid of people like him instead of reviewing what I thought was wrong with him. That represented a major change for me."

- *What associations with relationships do I have with this archetype and house?*

Noting that she had the Saboteur archetype in her third house (self-expression and siblings), one woman told me that as the middle child between two older and younger siblings, she was always working to maintain harmony in the family. "I felt that the rivalry that existed with my siblings was always destroying or sabotaging what could have been a great family," she said. "We had every opportunity to be close. We had great parents and great relatives. But one of my brothers and both of my sisters had what I would call lousy chemistry. They were forever turning the household upside down with arguments and all sorts of destructive behavior. One time I actually yelled at them, 'You are ruining this family for no reason,' and had I been aware then of the Saboteur, I would have said that they broke up the family as if they were on a guerrilla mission. So this archetype in that house makes a great deal of sense to me. And now as an adult I use that experience as a personal point of reference in that I no longer see myself as the one responsible for settling confrontational relationships between people. Getting in the middle of negative exchanges between people is an act of self-sabotage, because I end up doing harm to my own relationships with everyone by getting in the crossfire."

- *What issues of power come to mind as I review this archetype and its house?*

You will have to ask yourself this question more than once, because it requires serious excavation of your motives. Power issues have to do with control and its manifestations, as well as with ambition, values, generosity of spirit and self, and so much more. Every part of our lives involves some exchange of power. We either gain or lose power in everything we do, say, or think. Whether we are conscious or unconscious of our behavior (and we are usually more conscious of it than we care to admit), we intend to use power to gain advantages for ourselves.

Geri had the Mother archetype in her second house (life values), and nothing was more important to her than being a mother. Her life was wrapped around caring for her children, and she believed that her role as "the good mother" afforded her the right and power to determine her children's values. Geri's lifelong desire to have a home and family influenced many of the decisions she had made from her earliest years. She knew the kind of man she would date and the degree program—elementary education—that would allow her to have a job that would have the same vacation days as her own children. Her image of what makes a woman a good mother came from her mother and grandmother, who had passed on the importance of imparting high moral and ethical standards to one's children.

But it wasn't enough for Geri just to pass along a strict code of values. She wanted to ensure that her children would never stray far from her authority or outgrow their need for her, because then it would be difficult to maintain her control over them. She communicated messages of dependency to her children by saying things like "Nobody will ever do this for you better than I do," and "Mother knows best." Believing that she was acting in their best interests, she frequently asked her kids how they intended to survive as adults without her to guide them.

Geri's "good mother" image was more in keeping with the Devouring or Smothering Mother, a shadow aspect of the Mother archetype. Not only did Geri "devour" or undermine her children's power, she also undermined her husband's strength by convincing him that she was better suited than he to take charge of the children. These tendencies grew out of control, until a couple of Geri's close friends sat down with her one day and conducted a kind of intervention, telling her that her need to be the center of attention amounted to narcissism and that her attempts to control everyone around her was threatening her relationships with her family and friends. After the intervention Geri examined other relationships that made her need to be seen as invaluable and saw that she had a fear of not being needed and of being left behind. In order to heal her attachment to being needed, she looked at her house of values (second house) and examined the source of her desire to be of greatest value.

As a result of these insights, Geri initiated a personal practice that she called "stepping outside" herself to view her interactions with others. Whenever she noticed that she was slipping into the pattern of craving attention, she immediately turned the camera on herself, examining her fear of being invisible to others. By calling her own attention to this pattern, little by little Geri was able to engage in relationships without the motivation to be seen as significant to everyone she interacted with.

- *What kind of power do I associate with this archetype?*

Be specific in your description of your power associations with each archetype, and make certain that you list both the positive and the negative associations.

Simon had the Prostitute in the sixth house (occupation, health) and recognized that he was "selling his conscience" through his occupation for the sake of his income. The insurance company he worked for was taking financial advantage of its clients, in that it had a policy not to renew contracts with people once they filed even a single claim, yet his fear of not finding another job kept him working there. Simon felt that he was practicing extortion. Because he earned a good paycheck, however, he was afraid to move on. This situation was costing him his self-respect.

But once Simon was able to see that the Prostitute served a positive function, warning him that he could not continue to negotiate away his ethics, he began planning his move away from the company. It took time, but eventually he found a job elsewhere that did not force him to compromise his values.

- *When I combine the archetype with its house, what experiences can I recall that directly relate to learning about my relationship to power? Am I competitive? Have I ever harmed another person because of my actions, power plays, or ambitions? Have I ever helped to empower someone else in any of the areas of this house?*

The seventh house, for example, rules your relationships. Ask yourself if you have deliberately blocked someone else's opportunities or empowerment because it threatened you. Look in your past for experiences that have taught you about the nature of true empowerment. Then see if you can determine which archetypes awakened your desire to pursue your higher potential.

From the Past to the Present

The next set of questions focuses on your present, day-to-day life. They are scripted to prompt insight into your life as a "work in progress." Answer the following questions for each of your twelve archetypes.

- *What lessons and wisdom have I learned from the partnership of this archetype and house?*

The Fool showed up in Mort's house of communications and siblings. Mort thought of the Fool as the carrier of hidden wisdom. The costumed court jesters of medieval Europe were often closest to the seat of power precisely because they seemed harmless and witless. But their external disguise hid their talent for seeing through the games and power plays of those dancing around the king and queen.

Mort had identified with the Fool's nature from the time he was a child. In making a "fool of himself," he freed himself from adult conventions. As an adult, he used the same rebelliousness in his professional research and work as a chemist. "I am liberated enough—or foolish enough," he said, "to pursue research in areas that other scientists have declared useless or professionally risky. I consider them people who do 'research in approval.' I am willing to be thought a fool when I share or communicate my laboratory findings with others because every path of research leads to a discovery, even if the discovery is that the answer you are looking for is not to be found in this way."

Having recognized the value of his Fool to his professional work, Mort was then able to look for its value at an even higher level. "From a totally outlandish spiritual perspective," he said, "I am also Fool enough for God to inspire me to take on what conventional scientists would run away from. And what could be more tempting to the Fool than to find a way to get close to the throne of the gods?"

- *What challenges am I presently confronting within the meaning and context of this house and its archetypal pattern?*

The Hermit showed up in Rod's eleventh house (relationship to the outside world), and this union felt deeply appropriate, because he very much wanted to keep the external world at a distance. But upon seeing this relationship spelled out in the Wheel he had just cast, Rod realized that he needed to evaluate why he viewed the external world as fundamentally hostile. He began to see that this negative attitude and fear had had a profound effect on his relationships, his choice of occupation, and the way he isolated himself. Rod's struggle to heal his isolation consequently inspired him to seek out a path of reconciliation by looking for ways to engage with the world on friendlier terms.

The flip side of a Hermit in the eleventh house is represented by the lives of Henry David Thoreau and Emily Dickinson, among many others who withdrew from the mainstream of society to make contact with the beauty of life and nature. Dickinson, for instance, withdrew from life in her village of Amherst, Massachusetts, not because she believed the world to be hostile but because, as a Hermit, she chose to live in a way that supported the tranquillity of her soul. She felt undisturbed and able to relate to the whole of the world through her pen, leaving poems that speak of her deep love of life, nature, and God.

- *What strengths and talents can I associate with this archetype-house partnership?*

Tom was deeply troubled about his work. Whenever a conflict arose at the office, he was approached to handle it. "I am a peaceful man," he said, "and not one who generates trouble. Yet people look to me for guidance, and the authorities look to me for explanations and to give warnings. I don't understand my position." After Tom drew the Disciple in his third house (self-expression and siblings), he said, "I had a dream a long time ago when I was at my worst point with this situation. In the dream a man came to me and said that I had to absorb such conflict because I was stronger than everyone else and that I could find the learning and the wisdom in conflict. I told this being that I understood, and then the dream ended."

Tom's Disciple preexisted his present occupation. Tom had always relied on spiritual interpretation to explain conflicts, so it was no wonder that people turned to him for help in seeing beyond their conflicts. This technique made him a Disciple, a soothing voice for the spirit. This interpretation made him feel as if he could deal less anxiously with his valued role as mediator.

- *What opportunities have come into my life that I can connect to this archetype and this house?*

In one of my workshops a woman named Julie had the Goddess, specifically Athena, in her seventh house (marriage and relationships). Julie had many of the characteristics of Athena, the wise feminine force who guides Odysseus through *The Odyssey*. Julie is supportive of her husband in his professional life and helps him organize his power by advising him how to "win" the battles he wages with his associates. Julie credits this partnership aspect of their relationship as the foundation of their success, and her husband believes that without her Athena influence and support, he would not be as confident, motivated, or effective. "He's a strong man, but he would not push himself so much," said Julie. "As a team, we combine our creativity, our time, and our determination."

- *What fears or superstitions do I associate with having a direct connection to the characteristics of this archetype and the meaning of this house?*

Jan related to the Wanderer/Free Spirit archetype and relished being able to pick up and go whenever she wanted. She adored being able to stay somewhere for as long as she desired and to hang out with new people wherever she met them. The idea of settling down represented a form of imprisonment. Julie's Wanderer resided in her twelfth house (the unconscious), and in pursuing the question of what inner fears she most associated with this archetype, she said that confinement represented a death sentence. "Physical confinement is only one aspect of confinement, however," she added. "I fear intellectual, emotional, and spiritual confinement just as much. Yet I fear doing any serious spiritual self-examination because I am terrified that I will hear instructions to settle somewhere or to become dedicated to something. It has occurred to me that my travels are my way of running from myself. That's almost a cliché now, but there is some truth to it as far as I'm concerned."

Out of curiosity I asked Julie to offer an interpretation of her Wanderer had it landed in her first house—ego and personality. She said she would be very comfortable with the Wanderer there because it represents who she is and it speaks of having a liberated nature. "I would have preferred that this archetype had landed in my first house," she said, "but it is obvious to me that my interior work has to do with accepting journeys that the Divine directs me to take, as opposed to creating journeys of my own to avoid divine ones."

- *What unfinished business within this house relates to this archetype?*

Frank had the Shape-shifter archetype in his eighth house, which relates to other people's resources and to finances and legal matters. He had chosen the Shape-shifter because he saw himself as someone who had "a million faces," meaning that on the positive side he could be flexible with people and very cooperative, but on the shadow side he was unable to give his word and keep it. He was always changing his opinions to suit his company. When this archetype landed in Frank's house of legal and financial matters, he recognized that this was the realm in which the Shape-shifter was most prevalent and could be most damaging. He acknowledged that he had given his word to people to help them in business and then backed out for various reasons. Even as a child, he was unable to honor his "financial obligations" when he lost bets on baseball games. This archetype in this house held supreme significance for Frank and inspired him to review his entire relationship with power and business and his dealings with people. "I have to admit," he commented, "that this combination of the Shape-shifter is not unlike getting caught with your hand in the financial cookie jar."

- *What health crises do I associate with this archetype and this house? What challenges relate to the emotional and psychological stress points appropriate to this partnership?*

Freddie's Victim fell into the sixth house, occupation and health. Freddie was ambitious, but he was also unsuccessful. "I victimize myself through the way I interpret my conversations with other people," Freddie said. "I often make myself sick, because this is how I express my feeling that I was victimized. That way nothing is expected of me, and I get the kind of support I need from people." When he considered that he was victimizing his opportunities, however, he recognized that nothing would or could change until he made some significant shifts in attitude. Connecting his Victim to his lack of success became a very real source of motivation for Freddie.

- *Are there challenges that I consider inevitable that are related to this archetype's house?*

The Gambler archetype showed up in Arnie's fifth house, which rules good fortune, children, and sexual encounters, among other areas of life, but he initially interpreted this energy from only a sexual point of view. A venture capitalist, Arnie felt excited by risky business investments and gambling on the stock market. He realized that he also gambled a great deal with his relationships, because he often pursued women whom he knew would mean "nothing" to him. When he considered how children fit into this scenario, he stated that he thought having children was the biggest gamble in life and that he was not in any way drawn to the idea of fatherhood. Ultimately Arnie had to confront the fact that for him, all forms of commitment represented a kind of gamble and that he was not willing to take any risks. At a deeper level he also feared gambling spiritually or making a commitment to a spiritual path that might in some way demand he change his life.

After some thought Arnie began to see that the Gambler in his fifth house might indicate that he could, in fact, try his luck at some form of commitment. Perhaps if he were willing to start small, he said, he would eventually be able to work his way up to bigger and bigger gambles and possibly risk a spiritual commitment of some kind.

- *Am I presently facing a "significant choice point" regarding any relationship or situation that I associate with this archetype-house partnership?*

In looking for significant choice points, don't limit yourself only to the grand choices, such as finally deciding that you must sell your

home or divorce your mate. A significant choice point could be deciding to exercise for twenty minutes a day, eat more healthful foods, or
meditate. Such decisions over time can change your body, mind, and
spirit. This exercise can elevate your appreciation for how intimately
you are connected to the heavens. It is also the one that makes you
admit you need to make choices in your everyday, worldly life.

- *What experiences would I consider divine interventions and
  "surrenders" in this house? What were the consequences of those
  interventions?*

This exercise brings your attention into the very heart and soul of
the Self. Martin had the archetype of the Mercenary, which he chose
because some years before, while living a drug-ridden life in South
America, he had actually killed people for hire. One day as he was
preparing to carry out another hit, Martin tripped and banged his
head severely, going into a coma that led to a near-death experience.
As his soul separated from his body, he was greeted by everyone he
had ever murdered. "We've come to tell you not to kill anymore,"
they said as he hovered several feet above his inert body. Not surprisingly Martin did change his life, and he now lives in service to others,
although he still identifies with the Mercenary archetype because he
realizes that he always has the potential to fall back into his old ways—
his "negative highest potential." Like an alcoholic, Martin acknowledges that he is in a continual state of recovery.

Most acts of surrender emerge not from such dramatic circumstances but rather from the endless frustrations of trying and failing to
improve your life, or from coping with a chronic health crisis that is
listed as terminal, or from "letting go" of the need to have the heavens
explain why things happen as they do. This question directs you to
identify and appreciate the Divine as a continual and intimate presence in every experience of your life. I describe this as playing hide-
and-seek with God.

- *What two experiences of "betrayal" do I associate with this house
  and its archetypal pattern (one in which I was betrayed, and one
  in which I betrayed someone)?*

Describe the reasons behind these acts of betrayal and the changes that occurred in your life as a result of being betrayed by and betraying another person. Betrayal experiences are archetypal and signal the need to release emotional and psychological dependencies that no longer serve us.

Acts of betrayal serve a valuable purpose. They shake our faith in human justice and the social code and move us to place our trust in the chaotic justice of the Divine. Our need for total control derives from the fear of change, and when an act of betrayal shatters that need, we may become more open to change. In a sense the floodgates burst, and we are forced to float along with the raging currents or drown. When we ourselves betray someone else or an ideal we once held dear, it pushes us to examine what desperate need could have led us to go against our own best spiritual interests. Recognizing that we have a Contract with the person who has betrayed us, or whom we have betrayed, can help us see the positive potential in such acts.

This question makes you call your spirit back into present time. Incidents of betrayal are among the most difficult to forgive, yet reframing betrayal within an understanding of its archetypal purpose is like being handed a lifeline that can pull you back from the past.

- *How does the challenge of forgiveness relate to the archetype in this house?*

Each house creates crises that require forgiving. In your first house (ego and personality), for example, you will need to forgive people who you feel in some way harmed your sense of self. Beth had the Servant in her first house and said that she was always seen by others as someone to give orders to, as if she had been born to wait on people. People saw her as useful because this was the image that her ego projected. She described herself as the literary character Jane Eyre, because she felt that she was always in servitude to someone, working to earn even a slight amount of affection.

As painful as Beth's associations were with her first house, her ninth house, which rules spirituality, held her Child archetype. Her associations with forgiveness as it related to her spirituality were a source of joy. Beth did not feel that God meant her to suffer and be alone. While praying one day, she felt that God wanted her to need Him (she described God as male), and so He had to give her a path that required her to need Him profoundly. This path came in the form of experiences that made her realize that she was in charge of her own self-esteem. So from the angle of her ninth house, her bond to God was born through having relationships that gave her much to forgive. From her point of view, this was a blessing.

Blessings come in many forms, and many of the most painful times of our lives give birth to our greatest opportunities. A "blessing in disguise" is itself an archetypal pattern. By realizing the value of overcoming her attachment to the negative aspects of her Servant, Beth discovered a profound sense of inner peace and liberation that existed beyond her earliest negative feelings.

This question allows you to examine your struggles with forgiveness within every category of life. You can pinpoint your major challenges. Nicholas had to forgive one of his children for running away from home. He owned up to this while exploring the topic of forgiveness in the fourth house (home), in which he had his Detective archetype. In real life Nicholas *was* a detective, a role that inspired him for the first time when, as a fifth grader, he saw a film on the famous Prohibition agent Eliot Ness and "the Untouchables." But he had allowed his profession into his home life so that his daughter accused him of always checking up on her and never giving her any space. Although he said that he was only trying to protect her from all of the things that could go wrong in life, she ran away at age nineteen. This rebellion enraged Nicholas and his wife, "but I had to admit that I was even angrier over the fact that I couldn't find her, in spite of all I knew about tracking down people."

When Nick's daughter returned after an absence of eleven years, his "wife welcomed her home immediately, as if nothing had happened," he said. "But I couldn't do that. I felt that she was responsible for the worst years of my life as well as my wife's. But I also knew that my detective pride was damaged, and I feared that she would pass some remark about my not being able to find her, which she never did." Nicholas knew that he still needed to forgive her, but this exercise was like a message from above telling him to get on with it.

Having answered all the questions in this chapter as thoroughly as possible, your journal should be filled with pages of information, the raw data of your life. Now we can begin the process of interpreting your Archetypal Wheel, as well as understanding your life's spiritual path as supported by your many individual Contracts.

CHAPTER 9

Interpreting Your Contracts and Your Archetypal Wheel

In Chapter 8, you investigated your reasons for choosing your personal archetypes and began to identify the challenges and problems that you need to address, along with the talents and blessings you ought to appreciate. All of these gifts and challenges reflect aspects of your divine potential. The Wheel and the three-column model are like the left and right hands of your body. Using both systems in tandem provides you with a symbolic perspective on individual experiences and a conscious method of determining your future actions.

In this chapter you'll be interpreting your Archetypal Wheel as a whole, pulling together all the different interpretations. Before I give you the specific steps to follow, however, I want you to see what the process looks like in general terms.

My Wheel

Although I have written and spoken frequently on how my professional life took shape, I have not been as open about my personal life. Because I work with my own archetypes and energies every day, I did not cast my own Archetypal Wheel in careful detail until I had worked with those of many hundreds of people in my workshops. But while writing *Sacred Contracts*, I decided that the time had come to take a good look at my own life's journey. Since you already know something about me and my work, I hope that my interpretations of my Wheel may help you with your own. My archetypes and their respective houses appear in Figure 6.

Like twelve separate strands of thread, my archetypes and houses stretch backward through the years of my life to my earliest childhood memories. Each of these patterns has such a loud voice in my spirit that I can connect with it easily simply by closing my eyes for a moment. I can feel its energy penetrate my thoughts and perceptions. To know and understand yourself and your place in this world, you need to unravel these twelve threads and keep your fingertips on them

FIGURE 6: MY CHART OF ORIGIN

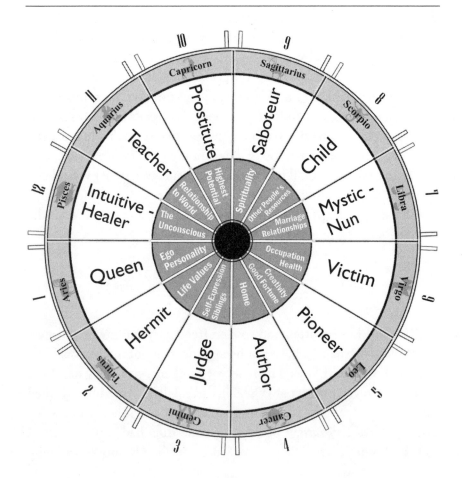

so that you can sense when they vibrate to current events and interactions in which you find yourself. As you follow me through my Wheel, keep track of any associations that spring up in your own mind.

The Teacher resides in my eleventh house, underscoring the primary way I relate to the world, which I see as a classroom. Following the Teacher thread, my own greatest teachers from childhood onward have been my family and a line of superb schoolteachers and professors, most of whom were Roman Catholic nuns. The Nun in my house of relationships reflects how I extend the influence of those teachers through my own spirit to those with whom I engage. Not only did the nuns wake up my love for theology, history, and literature, but along with my parents they also taught me about the domain of angels, saints, and the intimate presence of God. The Nun in me also does most of my book shopping, except that she never heard of the vow of poverty.

The Nun is so prominent in me that while in college I considered entering the convent. Relating to the world through a prayerful life was positively seductive, and many of my friends did enter, drawing me even closer to the community of nuns. Yet in spite of the spiritual atmosphere that such a community could offer me, I felt that it was not a fit, at least not in this lifetime. I needed to be free from the traditional vows so that I could relate to people, symbolically speaking, from outside the convent walls. Yet when I teach and when I do readings on people, I am still under vows to be of service and a vow of silence. If I perceive an illness in someone who has not come to me for a reading, for example, I don't volunteer that information. I maintain my silence unless I am asked specifically about it, either by that person or by a physician. Often when I use my intuition, I first close my eyes and enter the inner chapel of my spirit. I visualize it as the chapel on the campus where I went to college, which was also a convent. It is the crucible of my spirit, the third column of my symbolic sight.

My Nun and my Teacher are two of the three archetypes that have the most presence in my workshops. The classroom is a theater in which I can lead people through their fears and into a passion to live a more liberated and healed life. I have a fire in me that wants to blast people out of their pattern of yearning for a more fully realized life and yet forgoing every opportunity to bring it about. I no longer simply want to help people heal; rather, I want them to fall in love with the life they have been given.

I often give the appearance of being nearly ruthless onstage when I am interacting with certain people, but in those moments I am looking through the personality and into the heart of their passion to transform the ordinariness of their lives into the extraordinary—meaning their greater potential in this lifetime. When I spot someone on that point of breakthrough, my Teacher takes a backseat to the Queen in me. The classroom becomes transformed into my royal court, and I symbolically "decapitate" people who are yearning for liberation from their fears yet are prevented by those very fears from moving forward. My Queen, often appearing aggressive or mocking, puts their fears on the chopping block. If I were a sweet and easy Queen then, as I am after hours, I would allow them to give me teary-eyed excuses full of blame for those who destroyed their potential. Blame gives us permission to remain where we are while pressuring others to tiptoe around our wounds. Blame does not heal and it does not produce change; forgiveness does. Because of that my Queen wants people to confront the way they have cut off their own heads and blocked all communication between their heart and their mind.

As a rule, I don't soften my interactions with individuals in a workshop or reading until I can feel in their energy that they have made a conscious connection to their excuses or self-sabotage, their passions, and at least some of their archetypal patterns. Then I know that they can call back their spirits and get back on their life's course.

My Queen appeared long before I first turned a classroom into a royal court. Ever since my encounters with the nuns in high school and college, I have been inspired by stories of powerful women. Observing these extraordinary women administer the girls' school and college that I attended during the height of the feminist movement contributed to my resolve to become a woman who could take care of herself. Even if it meant that I spent my life unmarried, I would not become dependent on others for my well-being and survival. I owe this inspiration to my father, who encouraged me at every turn to be self-sufficient.

My father, a Marine who fought at Guadalcanal in World War II, was a man of impeccable integrity. He lived the Marine honor code—

Semper fidelis, or "Always faithful"—his entire life, and he taught me how important honor is. Because of him I also have a hobby of reading history, especially military and political history.

The Prostitute in my tenth house (highest potential) reveals the fear of dependency and compromise that my father inculcated in me from earliest childhood. And it reveals the challenge I face of being tempted to negotiate my personal power, to sell my intuitive skills. People have offered me large sums of money in exchange for winning lottery numbers, for instance—as if I'd sell them to anybody if I could actually predict them! This would hardly be using my skills for a higher good, which is another reason I believe I have been led to create a sound professional life as a teacher: I aim to help others find their highest potential as I communicate my own insights. This desire to show the way for others has led me to work with progressive colleges and universities to establish courses in intuitive studies and energy medicine.

My first electric encounter with my own intuitive abilities—which warned me to be careful how I used them—came when I was fifteen. I had just bought a book on palmistry and was flipping through it when my dear friend Maureen insisted that I read the palm of a neighbor of hers named Lucille. Although I had no idea how to read palms (and still don't), I accepted the challenge on a whim. When Lucille sat down with us, I looked dumbly at her palm and heard myself tell her that she had been married twice. A friend of Lucille's who had been observing all this rather skeptically gave a scornful laugh. "You're wrong, kid," she said. "She's been married *three* times."

Suddenly an unfamiliar energy ignited within me, and I could feel heat shoot from the bottom of my spine to the tip of my head. I straightened my spine as if it had just been transmuted into pure steel. My body felt intensely present, although a feeling of impersonal distance from Lucille descended on me. I was aware of no longer being a child and felt as if I had traveled a great distance in the blink of an eye. My voice became strangely steady and out of my mouth came the words, "Yes, but your second marriage was never consummated."

Lucille lunged at me, lifted me up by my clothing, and dragged me to the front door, kicking me out. When I got home and told my mother what had happened, I expected her to be annoyed by what I had said to her neighbor. I also asked her what *consummated* meant, since I really didn't know the word at that time! Instead, Mother laughed so hard that she had to sit down. "Did you really say that?" she asked several times, as she wiped her eyes. After she stopped laughing, she turned serious. "God has given you a very special gift, and you must take care of it," she said. "Someday you'll be shown what to do with it. In the meantime pray for guidance."

The entire incident gradually faded from memory until one night when I was twenty-nine. In a peculiar dream I was visited by a guide who told me, "I've returned. Now it's time for you to go to work." Before a year had passed, I had begun to sense people's health conditions intuitively. Within two years I was giving readings as a medical intuitive. As grateful as people often seemed for the help and guidance I was able to give them, however, I never forgot the look of sudden rage on Lucille's face as she came at me that day. Perhaps she too was an angel sent to warn me to be careful how I used my intuitive gifts.

My Author is in the fourth house, which rules the home, reflecting just how deeply my home is my work space. I have worked from home since I was twenty-nine, and I designed my home around the needs of the Author as well as the Hermit (second house: values). Spending time alone is crucial to my well-being, and when I'm not out teaching, I prefer a quiet life with close friends and family. When I was in third grade, for instance, I announced to my mother that I would become a writer. This was my personal declaration of independence, and from that moment on every decision that had anything to do with school or my professional interests was measured against whether it would enhance or detract from that goal.

I am completely ungrounded in the world of financial energy, legal matters, and inheritance, represented by the eighth house. My need for caretaking and guardians in this realm is signified by the Child in that house. Somehow I've never feared lacking actual resources, even though I feared being dependent. For instance, when the publishing company I was helping to found in 1982, along with two friends, was not yet producing any income, I took a job as a copywriter with a public relations firm. I had absolutely no interest in the work, however, and within a month of starting I was fired. That night, calculating my financial resources, I realized that I had $76 in the bank. My monthly rent was $400 and the fuel bill almost $200. My first thought in assessing this situation was "Okay, this means God will not send me a problem that costs more than $76."

The next day my mother called with some unexpected news. Twelve years before, in an out-of-character venture, she had purchased a few thousand shares of a stock that had been selling for three cents a share. My brothers and I teased her relentlessly about this investment until she refused to discuss it any longer, and we had all long since forgotten about it. Now my mother was calling to tell me that a stockbroker had contacted her "out of the blue" to ask if she remembered buying that penny stock. He then told her that the stock was now worth more than six dollars a share. She told him to sell it immediately and, with my father's blessing, divided the proceeds among all three of us kids. My Child's faith pulled me through that situation in a typical eighth-house way, with the blessings of another person's resources—in this case, a generous and devoted Mother.

My Victim archetype has played a substantial role in my health, since my childhood years, so its presence in my house of occupation and health is appropriate. Early on in my days at school, whenever I was under pressure, I experienced migraines and other maladies. My body has always been almost instantaneously responsive to physical or emotional stress. Having gone through a number of health challenges and years of chronic pain, I know what it is like to wait in the doctor's office to find out whether you have an illness for which there is no cure.

Since I work with the energy of health and illness to try to help others heal their ailments, the Victim also makes sense in this house. Indeed, the Victim in me identifying with the Victim in others inspired my book *Why People Don't Heal*. As I was working on that book, I realized that every time I was preparing to write a book or was about to receive an inspiration, I was visited by some form of health crisis. Before and during work on *Anatomy of the Spirit*, for instance, I suffered from a series of debilitating migraine headaches. After witnessing a woman in one of my workshops engage in what I call *woundology*—trading on the currency of her past traumas—I began asking myself the question that inspired my next book: "Why don't people heal?" The day after I first asked that question, I woke up with the onset of what would become years of chronic pain and occasional depressions. These ailments did not begin to abate until I recognized that I myself had fallen prey to becoming a woundologist—someone who defines herself by the bad things that have happened to her. As the saying goes, we teach what we need to learn. My own body has been a laboratory for my ideas.

The Saboteur in my ninth house, spirituality, has particular meaning for me but perhaps from an unconventional perspective. I have never wanted to be ruled by the religious doctrines and dogmas that I recognized from my earliest years in grade school were not true. I remember vividly the moment when I broke from the Roman Catholic Church. One day in third grade I asked a priest how Jesus had been born. Father replied that Jesus had simply appeared in the lap of Mother Mary. Even without yet having been told the facts of life, I instinctively knew that this was nonsense. Yet my faith and spirituality have always been strong, and I have always had a rich and delicious feeling that angels and saints surround me at every moment. Though I have rebelled against an institution, my Saboteur insures my own safe passage into the spiritual dimension, having blown up the obstacles in my way.

In my workshops and readings my own Saboteur constantly detects the Saboteurs in other people's psyches. As I verbally push their backs against the wall, I do so in service to *their* divine potential. I hold the thought in my mind for them: "Do you really want to look back on your life and see how wonderful it could have been had you not been afraid to live it?" Although, outside of my workplace, I have little concern about how other people live their lives, as soon as I step in front of a classroom, I go on a search-and-destroy mission to find my students' spiritual panic. This is where all real pain comes from—a desperation that we will never accomplish what we were meant to do in life. Deep in the unconscious, our spiritual potential lies in wait for us to release it. Sometimes you will have to blow things out of your own way to get to it.

I would have been surprised if my Intuitive-Healer had shown itself anywhere else but in my twelfth house, where the unconscious and our connection to the collective reside. Despite my early disenchantment with Catholic dogma, I never once questioned that each of us has a guardian angel and that our lives matter to a loving God. As I grew older, I was attracted to the writings of the mystics and spiritual masters, which ultimately led me to do graduate work in theology. This is my golden string (to borrow a phrase from Dom Bede Griffiths), the one that gives me strength and inspiration, hope and delight, and was my lifeline out of the throes of woundology. The Mystic is in partnership with my Pioneer archetype, which is in the house of creativity, luck, and the pleasurable side of life.

As a Pioneer, I rely on my creativity not just to write and teach but to reshape my life moment by moment. I constantly explore the teaching that we create our own reality, whether by examining my own life or encouraging people to change their own. I initially encountered my Pioneer through my desire to do something unique, a feeling that all writers must share. I wanted to live a life unlike that of anybody else, and at age twelve I announced to my mother that I would not have a conventional life of marriage and children. I wanted to explore always beyond the horizon I could see and blaze new trails.

Yet when I think of my life and my twelve archetypes, I feel guided and destined to walk a path that began long ago. My desire to share this vision with others inspired me to lead people into the unconscious spaces behind their eyes so that they too could come to realize that their lives are anything but accidents. With your archetypes' energy, I am sure you can trace the hand of God and destiny weaving in and out of every moment of your life.

Life is meant to be a mystery, and we will never be able to make it a logical adventure. But we can interpret the clues that the hand of God leaves on our path. With any luck, and with the blessings of Heaven, I hope that my Sacred Contract can serve you on your own journey.

If I were sitting with you, teaching you how to gain access to your own unconscious companions, I would symbolically take you by the hand and say, "Follow me, because I know how to find them." I know how they disguise themselves in your psyche and spirit and how they hide themselves in the events of your life. Now that you have identified your archetypes, you too can start spotting their influence at any moment. When I look at someone's face, I look beyond that face and into the cellular memory in my heart that says, "Finally you and I have met again. And now we must find out why." To sense an archetypal thread connecting you to another person is to connect with a soul agreement that has finally manifested in time and space.

Ask yourself what you know about yourself today and what you don't know. What are your mysteries, and what have been your greatest influences, both positive and difficult? Ask yourself, "When did who I am today begin?" Choose the house and archetype that immediately inspires an answer, and jump into your Contract through that door. Random interpretation gives free rein to your memory and imaginings. But others are more comfortable following the numerical order of the chart. Find your comfort zone, and take it from there.

Now here are some steps you can follow in using your Archetypal Wheel to interpret your own Contract.

Finding the Lessons in Your Wheel and Contract

1. As a first step, choose a part of your life that you want to understand more fully: your health, career, relationships, family, or another aspect of your life to which you're drawn. One woman decided to focus on her career and how she had known that it was what she wanted to do as far back as she could recall. Other choices could include your spiritual development, your sexual awakening, the history of your health, or your relationship with a significant figure in your life. Be careful not to ask your Wheel a specific question, such as, "Should I change my current job and pursue the career I dream about?" Do not ask if you should divorce your partner, sell your house, or move to Tuscany. Do not ask your Wheel what somebody else thinks or feels about you. Do not ask for diagnostic information regarding a physical or psychological ailment ("Do I have cancer? Should I see a doctor?"). You will learn how to seek guidance for specific issues and dilemmas in Chapter 10. Keep your questions general so that guidance of any kind can come through to you. For instance, ask, "Why have I been unable to forgive my father (or mother)?" "How can I best heal my negative self-image?" "Give me a clear understanding of why ——— is in my life." Write your question or request for guidance in your journal.

2. Now select one of your twelve archetypes through which to seek initial guidance with your Wheel. One of the twelve will generally capture your attention more than the others as a guide for the area you've chosen to examine. Your intuitive self knows the most appropriate point of beginning. If, however, no particular archetype presents itself intuitively, you can simply begin with the archetype that resides in your first house.

3. Once you've selected an archetype, make note of which house it's in, and look for connections between the archetype and the area of life ruled by that house. Write down your overall sense of the significance of this first archetype-house connection in your journal. Your entry can be as brief as a single sentence or as long as several paragraphs, but try to be as succinct as possible on this first examination.

4. When you feel that you have a clear sense of the significance of that connection, move on to the next archetype that calls for your attention, and repeat the procedure. (If you chose to start with your first-house archetype, then just move to the second house and so on in sequence.) With each archetype review your positive and negative associations with the meaning of that pattern as it applies to the area of your life that you've chosen to examine. For example, if you chose to trace the experiences and relationships that have contributed to your search for God, then note the positive and negative contributions you associate with each archetype in that regard from your earliest recall. The Saboteur archetype in your house of spirituality, for instance, might be reflected in your feelings that God failed to answer your prayers, sabotaging your sense of faith.

5. After gathering memories and associations from all twelve houses and archetypes, study them to see if a single theme holds them together. Sarah noted that her history of spiritual development was built on a cycle of belief and doubt, faith and self-sabotage, until she finally realized that at the core of this struggle was one lesson: God for her was an intellectual concept that did not communicate with her spirit, so her spirit did not connect with others'. She had been unable to establish a spiritual practice or put her faith into action. Sarah's lifetime struggle with God also had a profound effect on how she evaluated her professional opportunities. She turned down offers that did not guarantee her

future security—which was most of them. Because she had limited her career, she had become bitter and had begun to feel that she had no direction in life. Sarah realized that her life's journey required that she learn the meaning of trust and faith, and learn to act as if she had a future. She had to open her heart and find God in others and in the world around her.

After you complete one reading, you can formulate another question with a different aspect of your life in mind. Each time you do a Wheel interpretation, you fill in more lessons that constitute your Sacred Contract. Remember that you are tracing twelve lifelong patterns that serve as the formative threads of your journey of personal empowerment. Combined, these reveal the whole of your Sacred Contract. Each pass you make through the archetypes and houses should supply another piece of the picture.

Since working with your Archetypal Wheel is more art than science, you may want to get a feel for doing it by reading how other people have pulled together their own interpretations. Three examples follow, beginning with the fascinating story of a woman seeking insight into her choice of career and closing with the story of one of the most extraordinary people I've ever encountered.

Maeve's Archetypal Wheel

Maeve is a single mom in her mid-forties, an astronomer who is also a student of astrology. After choosing the archetypes that make up her personal support group of twelve, she cast her Chart of Origin as shown in Figure 7.

Maeve wanted to apply the guidance in her Wheel to the reasons she had chosen her career, so she asked herself, "What experiences and Contracts led me to choose my current profession?" Maeve worked the archetypes and houses with the skill of her Storyteller archetype, which she had chosen because myth and fable form the link between her life as a scientist and her study of the consciousness of the planets. To make her astrological insights more accessible to her sci-

FIGURE 7: MAEVE'S CHART OF ORIGIN

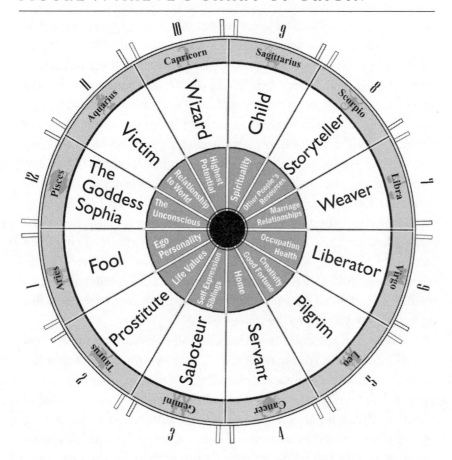

entific colleagues, Maeve often presented them in story form. She chose the Storyteller as the first archetype to examine because of its prominent role in her sense of who she is. "I live in a mythic place," she said. "I've always wanted to live an extraordinary life, and one of my earliest and fondest memories is of telling my parents that one day I would learn how to fly. This desire woke up inside of me when I was around nine years old, and I dreamed of traveling into space. So when my Storyteller archetype landed in my eighth house, other people's resources, that made immediate sense to me. I have always utilized others' research in science. I also believe that this archetype is responsible for my having an open mind. I always invite people to tell me if anything incredible ever happened to them, always looking for extraordinary life stories."

During the last year of grade school, Maeve's class went on a field trip to a planetarium, and that's when she realized that becoming an astronomer was what she had to do with her life. When she was selecting her family of archetypes, she chose the Wizard because "that is the part of me that relates to my occupation—I feel like a Wizard when I study the skies." Because she was seeking insight into her choice of career, she decided to explore that archetype next. Noting that her Wizard had landed in her tenth house (highest potential), she saw something significant about the interplay between her choice of career and her inner nature. "This union validated what I believe to be my profession," she said, "which is to investigate the 'psyche' of the planets within the world of the scientist. Planets are live beings, not just inert balls circling the sun. They communicate their essence into our psyches, and speak to our spirits. Because I believe this so deeply, I became a student of astrology. Combining these two sciences is like finding the mystic key to the universe."

Maeve also acknowledged that she had encountered the shadow side of her Wizard, that part of her "that sometimes hopes that the research of a hard-core scientist will fail, which is equivalent to proving that hard science does not have all the answers. I am not fond of admitting this, but I am also not ashamed of it. It is how I feel, and the greater shame would be to deny it." Her statement illustrates a crucial aspect of learning to interpret your Contract through the placement of your archetypes. Your willingness to confront those aspects of your character that are most hidden and with which you are least comfortable will ultimately help you gain a more complete picture of the dynamics of your Contract.

The Saboteur in her third house represented Maeve's passion to communicate since she was young, but it also represented a warning. "Telling people that I believe that the entire universe is a communicating entity could derail my career and undermine my reputation as a professional. I confronted that fear when I was in school, and deep in my being I know that I will always have to risk how the outside world would respond to me. That led me to develop self-esteem early. It also helped me see how other people sabotage their imaginations because they simply cannot consider that life might be more than what they see before their eyes."

Maeve's Prostitute was in her second house (life values). When first starting out as an astronomer, before she developed her interest in astrology, her goal was to be successful in her specialization, the study of asteroids. But once she started to study astrology, she was infused with a passion that "pure academics never provided," yet she found her colleagues predictably critical. She realized that she would have to manage her enthusiasm for what she calls "the field of alternative astronomy" or risk her financial security. "My values were finally on the line," she said. "Do I sell out, or do I continue to follow my spirit's understanding of the universe?" Maeve chose consciously to balance how much of her ideas she could convey to the conservative world of traditional science.

Her Prostitute gave Maeve a new perspective on her first house, where her ego-self is ruled by the Fool. She saw the Fool as representing someone who is protected in her search for truth, because a Fool can appear to be harmless. "It may be the strongest power I have," she said, "and knowing that my Fool serves me, I work with it. Because I know that to be true, I consciously tend to have a mainstream wardrobe, but that's one of my Fool's hiding places. People don't expect someone who looks like me to bring up the subject of planetary psychic intelligence." Maeve acknowledged that the open-minded people she meets who do accept her unconventional occupations are usually not among those in power, to whom she needs to appear harmless. She admits, "I adore the thought that I am 'fooling' them."

The Servant in Maeve's fourth house, which rules the home, baffled her initially, because like so many others she associated that archetype with serving other people. As a mother and a professional, she felt the need to inspire in her daughter a similar sense of "how important it is to become self-sufficient," which at first seems just the opposite of being a Servant. Maeve originally selected the Servant archetype because that is how she imagines her relationship to God. "But home represents not only the house where I live but also the inner dwelling where my soul resides. And from that perspective I am a Servant to my soul and responsible for the care of its home."

The Pilgrim in the fifth house (creativity and good fortune) felt like a perfect match for Maeve, because the Pilgrim represents seeking new ground, which is where most of her creative energies go—and she has always felt lucky in such endeavors, whether professional or personal. "Some of my deepest fears also reside in this combination of forces," she added. "The fear that my creativity may run dry, or that my work will add up to nothing, for instance. I also fear that someday I will look back on how I have invested my creative energies and regret that I did not follow more conventional studies. Sometimes I have felt like a semiprofessional because I am now more intrigued with astrology than astronomy, which I consider the back-up science."

Maeve also fears that her luck will run out. "I have been fortunate in this life. I love what I do, I have a great daughter, wonderful friends, and a rich relationship with my spirit. How lucky can you get? But all that can change, and I think about that truth a lot. I wonder what I would be like if the Pilgrim finally ran out of luck."

About four years ago Maeve was diagnosed with chronic depression. She believed it stemmed from her obsession with perfection and a drive that did not allow her to take care of herself as well as she should. Her doctor suggested medication, but Maeve felt that if she used antidepressants, she would not recover. "I made a commitment to heal myself," she said, "or as I now think of it, to 'liberate' myself from this situation—I won't even refer to it as an illness. It's merely a situation I needed to change." With the Liberator in her house of occupation and health, Maeve could see how she had approached healing herself. A classic Liberator such as Simón Bolívar, Gandhi, or Nelson Mandela has enough faith in his struggle to stay with it under difficult circumstances, even when defeat seems imminent. Like those historical figures, Maeve would not allow herself the "luxury" of negative, defeatist thoughts. She liberated herself from the conventional medical assessment of chronic depression and made great inroads in freeing herself from the depression itself.

Working with the archetypes and houses in this way led Maeve to see overarching patterns as well. She said, "I can say that I was born to 'liberate' perceptions about the way people believe the physical world operates and to show them another reality. I know the power that runs through my veins, and I know that I am interested in moving realities, not people. Move a reality, and people have no choice but to go along for the ride."

Since depression can often be a spiritual crisis, we looked to Maeve's ninth house (spirituality), where the Child had fallen, for help with explaining her healing. Maeve felt an immediate conflict, because she did not relate to "the parent-child idea of a relationship with God" that characterizes much conventional religion. "I do not trust the behavior of God completely the way a child trusts a parent. I am still braced for concealed 'land mines' and for discovering that God has led me on a lifetime wild-goose chase." Yet she also recognized that the parent-child image represents dependency, which she feared. "I fear God's power over me," she said, "and yet I marvel, just like a child, at the wonder of the stars and planets and what I feel the Divine gave me as this part of my work. I struggle with the image of the benevolent parent allowing so many of earth's children to suffer and endure human cruelty."

Maeve's "deep spiritual need" for divine order in the universe was constantly at odds with her "deep spiritual fears and confusions," so this and her striving for perfection could have contributed to her depression. She acknowledged that she did indeed feel a child's vulnerability in spiritual matters. By facing this shadow aspect of her emotions, she was able to allay some of her fears, in much the same way that turning on a night-light can help defuse a child's fear of the dark.

Maeve interpreted the Victim in her eleventh house (relationship to the world) as representative of her aspiration to help people avoid becoming victims of ignorance: "It is my hope that the more truth that fills the global unconscious, the easier it will be for people to create better lives for themselves." She also admitted that she faced at least the potential of becoming a Victim herself in relation to the world if her unconventional ideas ultimately made it impossible for her to continue with her chosen profession. The Victim urges us to act appropriately when we are in danger of being victimized.

The goddess Sophia (Wisdom) landing in Maeve's house of the unconscious required little clarification or internal stretching, because Maeve saw herself as a kind of Sophia force in the world: "The question What is wisdom? is one that I ask in almost all situations, and of life in general. I want to live a life where I learn, give, share, and grow." For as long as she could remember, she held the image in her head of being "a powerful woman. I am motivated by Sophia and credit her 'being' as the reason for my own intellectual passions."

When Maeve cast her chart, she wanted to examine the conflict she felt between her motivation to be a scientist and her fascination with the apparently "unscientific" exploration of the consciousness of the planets. Much as she wanted to succeed in the academic world, this split often caused her to act belligerently toward her colleagues, whom she felt were closed-minded and threatened by her unconventional theories. This shadow conflict eventually also invaded her relationship to her children. Interpreting her Chart of Origin provided her with a more well-rounded view of how her choice of career fit into her Sacred Contract. If Maeve had stopped here, her life would already have been enriched. But going through her Wheel several more times, addressing different aspects of her life and other relationships, provided her with an even richer understanding of her overall Contract. As in studying a poem to get at its deeper meaning, each time you read through your Wheel you will see new correspondences and connections that you hadn't been aware of. We'll leave Maeve here, though, and move on to someone who received rather different guidance regarding his career.

Byron's Archetypal Wheel

Like Maeve and most people in my workshops, Byron chose to review his profession with his first interpretation of his Wheel. Byron is an actor who has had minor roles in a dozen films, including several well-known features. He began acting in high school, went into summer stock, and then performed small roles in Broadway plays and Hollywood films. Like the stereotypical aspiring actor, Byron also worked as a waiter, anticipating his great break at any moment. His Archetypal Wheel came together in the pattern shown in Figure 8.

After casting his Chart of Origin, Byron said, "Each one of these patterns and the experiences that I can associate with them makes more sense to me now that I view them within the context of an agreed-upon life's journey."

FIGURE 8: BYRON'S CHART OF ORIGIN

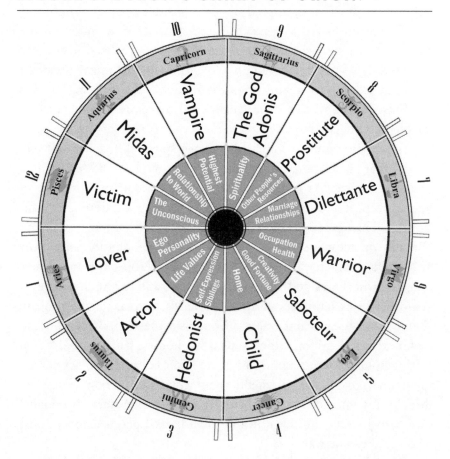

As a child, Byron was molested by a neighbor. Because of that trauma, he was drawn immediately to investigating his Child archetype. That the Child had landed in his fourth house (home) was therefore both startling and spiritually eye-opening for him. Being molested not only formed his memories of childhood and "birthed shame" in him, in his words, but it also became the central emotional force throughout his youth and twenties. It wasn't until his mid-thirties that Byron realized how pervasive the spell of shame had been and that he could do something about it. When he cast his Archetypal Wheel, he began to understand the constructive potential within those events. "Looking at who I am today, both as a person and as an actor," he said, "I realize that the experience of molestation was the 'act of necessity' that prompted all of the positive commitments of my life. The shame I felt as a result of sexual abuse only increased the shame I felt about who I was, especially when I realized in my late teens that I was gay. I believed for a long time that I was gay because I had been sodomized when I was six years old, and that being gay was the consequence of that experience—and therefore another part of my life that I needed to hide."

As Byron came to know his deeper spiritual essence and dismissed that association, he said, he began to understand his life in a greater context: "As a gay man, I maintain a spiritual practice of human respect and dignity as my way of making a difference in this world." This greater vision also led to his becoming an actor. "Because an actor is someone who hides his true identity behind the mask of a character," he said, "I could play roles that genuinely reflected who I was and what I experienced, and the audience never knew that I was acting about myself. This was a great relief for me; in a sense it was theatrical therapy." Given his profession, Byron chose to look next at the Actor, which was in his house of life values. "That pairing holds extreme significance," he said, "because I do act out my values onstage. I make statements about who I am and how I know life through my characters. I'm obviously not a major star—although I sure wish I were—but even in the small parts I play I manage to be who I am in some way."

The Warrior in Byron's house of occupation and health is a perfect counterpart to the Actor because he sees his profession as a means to battle for the equal rights of the gay community. But he also sees his dedication to that cause as a healing one, because he believes that shame was involved in spreading the AIDS epidemic in the gay community. "Despite the fact that I do not particularly look like the classic warrior—I am hardly a large, macho man—my spirit is a warrior's," he told me. "I was frightened as a boy because I couldn't protect myself. Perhaps my Warrior needed to be awakened by my need for it, because I could not rely on anyone to take care of me." Because his father saw him as quiet, nonathletic, and weak, he never gave his son the support he needed, forcing him to rely on himself. Recognizing this for the first time, Byron was able to move toward forgiving his father for what he had long considered to be his merely negative role in Byron's life.

Byron loved having the Hedonist in his third house (self-expression and siblings), because he felt that he communicated the message that we should enjoy the pleasures and riches of life. "I believe that every part of life serves us in some way, and why should we be motivated only by pain? That's ridiculous. At some point I decided that I had enough dwelling on the painful side of the tracks. I changed neighborhoods and began to thrive in a community of artists, good food, fine wine, great theater, literature, travels—everything that made me glad I was alive. God knows I had already experienced enough to make me wish I were dead, and I have to tell you, the pleasure side of life is much better. Once I began to travel in what I call the circles of Oscar Wilde, I began to love who I am."

That's when the Dilettante was awakened in Byron, and that archetype appearing in his house of marriage and relationships reflected his passion for good conversation, good wit, and eccentric people. The Dilettante also influenced and organized his education, as he chose courses in school by thinking, "What would it take to think like Oscar Wilde or Dashiell Hammett or to understand great music?" Now Byron was beginning to understand more fully how the aspects of his personality such as the Hedonist and Dilettante, which could be viewed in a negative sense, actually conspired to help free him of the negative self-image he had been battling since he was six years old.

Byron saw the Prostitute and the Midas as engaged in "a kind of duet." The Prostitute in the house of other people's resources and inheritance represented the obvious way someone in the acting profession can compromise himself for the sake of money. Byron also believed he was written out of his father's will because of his sexual orientation. "He thinks that I sell myself literally and that I'm a prostitute," he said. "I constantly see that the greater financial resources of the entertainment world are distributed to people who provide sexual favors," and while he wanted to create gold for himself, he wouldn't "in the shadow Midas way. I do see the world as my oyster, and I do want to be successful and filthy rich. My Hedonist needs that to be happy. But I want to be a benevolent Midas and use his wealth to help others. From a symbolic point of view, I am working to see the gold in everyone, which is my way of interpreting how my Midas serves the way I view the external world." Seeing his disinheritance symbolically also helped Byron begin to let go of his bitterness over his father's rejection of him.

That the Victim would rule his unconscious (twelfth house) seemed almost axiomatic, given his traumatic childhood experience. After answering the in-depth questions regarding his Wheel, Byron was able to see the positive aspect of the Victim. In feeling so victimized as a result of his youth, he said, he had discovered his inner self. "I don't know if I would have jumped with such desperation into my psyche had I not been victimized as a child. I might have feared so much that I would have continued to be a victim all my life. So I am now grateful that I have this archetype in charge of my unconscious, because I am determined never to feel like a victim again. Every time a new fear attempts to manipulate me without my awareness, the Victim will immediately shoot it into my conscious mind. As a gay man dedicated to helping dissolve victim consciousness, part of my Contract is about working within the collective unconscious and the impact the Victim archetype has on our quality of life."

Byron had a dramatic attraction to the Vampire archetype, partly because the Vampire's need for secrecy paralleled his own need to conceal his homosexuality. The Vampire's power is also largely erotic, and Byron had to confront his need to feed off other people's energy. He was taken aback by finding the Vampire in his house of highest potential, but after giving it a great deal of thought, he decided that, "I could never have come close to pursuing my work if I had allowed the prejudices that the outside world holds against gay people to 'suck' the soul out of me. Thought-forms are vampires as much as people are, and negative thoughts about who you are do suck the spirit and life out of you. For me to reach my highest potential, I had to battle— using my Warrior—every negative thought-form created by lack of self-esteem since I was a child. And believe me, any of them could have done me in. I think that healing the Victim in myself and others is like destroying a psychic vampire."

Seeing the positive potential in the Vampire archetype helped Byron understand the Saboteur in his house of creativity and good fortune. He feared that any good luck in his life would be sabotaged by his sexual identity. "The gay life is not exactly filled with stable relationships," he said. "I was afraid that I wouldn't have a chance for happiness, including romance." The Saboteur made Byron alert to the need to find ways to maximize his chances for love. On yet another level, it called his attention to the danger of sabotaging his romantic happiness by buying into the cliché of the uncommitted lifestyle, and of measuring fulfillment by the number of partners you can acquire.

The contrast or antidote to that kind of life may lie in the very arena with which Byron resonated most strongly: the Lover in his first house, the ego and personality. Because he did want to be seen "as someone who believes that love can be a part of everyone's life," he could also see the pitfalls of mistaking quantity for quality. "That is a part of my overall mission," he said, "to radiate a belief in love in order to inspire people."

Byron picked the Adonis archetype because of his belief that the male body is beautiful, and yet he found it surprising at first that this archetype landed in his house of spirituality—a pairing that once again seemed counterintuitive until he examined it more closely. "I believe that the Adonis in me, my physical form, is a reflection of the God I know deep within me," Byron concluded. "It is no accident that the mythic god Adonis represents my spirituality, because nothing could give me more inspiration or confirmation of my life. The fact that I believed that nothing about my maleness was acceptable for so long makes this union all the more meaningful for me."

Contemplating the complete hologram he had just created, Byron was able to see his Archetypal Wheel as a "perfect and full reflection" of his career. "I can drop relationship after relationship into these houses, along with countless experiences, and see how and why they had to occur. As for being molested, I would have preferred not to have had that experience, but it happened as it happened, and so many of the wonderful parts of my life were created as a result. Knowing that it was part of my Contract and that I was meant to learn from it takes a lot of the sting out of it. But more than that, I believe that I have found the way to accept that experience as a part of the greater theme of my life. I can't tell you how much joy and sense of the rightness of my life as it is this process has given me."

The Story of Mickey Magic

Sometime after I met and cast the Archetypal Wheel for Mickey Magic, the person with whom I'll conclude this chapter, I came across a story that bears a remarkable parallel to his life. Perhaps it's worth mentioning here if only as evidence that an incredible story like Mickey's is neither inconceivable nor unprecedented.

In eleventh- and twelfth-century Tibet, some three hundred years after Buddhism was originally brought to that mountain kingdom by a master teacher and magician from India called Padma Sambhava, the man known as Milarepa was born into a prosperous family. He was apparently destined for a comfortable and conventional life, but when he was seven years old, his father became gravely ill. Realizing that he would not recover, the patriarch gathered his family for a last meeting. After getting his relatives to promise that they would take care of his estate until Milarepa and his sister came of age, he died. An evil aunt and uncle nonetheless took the money and land entrusted to them and used it for themselves, forcing Milarepa, his sister, and his mother to work as servants. Their relatives treated them badly and often beat them.

At his mother's urging Milarepa mastered black magic, studying with a lama skilled in the art of mantra and learning to cast spells that gave him the power to send hailstorms. He then used this power to direct a storm at the house where the evil aunt and uncle were holding a large family gathering. The house collapsed, and thirty-five people were killed; the hailstorm also descended on the village and destroyed the harvest. Milarepa's mother was delighted with his magical feats, but Milarepa himself was torn by pangs of conscience at having caused so much death and destruction. Fearing that the only result of his action would be rebirth in a realm of Hell for him and his mother, he determined to counteract his negative acts by becoming a buddha. Milarepa spent long years in an excruciating course of study and practice with the great Tibetan Buddhist master Marpa. With the same determination and skill that had made him a master of black magic, Milarepa went on to become the greatest yogi in the history of Tibet.

In recognition of Milarepa's reversal of fortune, Marpa gave him a new name: the Gentleman of Great Magic.

The parallels between this legend, which is accepted as gospel truth by millions of Buddhists around the world, and Mickey's life will become clear. I first met Mickey at a workshop in Mexico, where he had been imprisoned some twenty years earlier on drug-smuggling charges. He had since turned his life around and become a successful professional magician. In addition to the Prostitute, Victim, Saboteur, and Wounded Child, Mickey's archetypal companions include the Magician, Rebel, Thief (Robin Hood), Knight, Storyteller, Actor, Hermit, and Healer. After working with him for some time, I found it difficult to separate the combined forces of Mickey's archetypes because they work so closely as a team. Mickey first met almost every one of his archetypal patterns in its shadow presentation, only to have the spiritual aspects of all of them appear to him in a single epiphany while he was being beaten in prison. Rather than examine each archetype/house pairing separately as I have done with Maeve and Byron, I'll just tell Mickey's story. His archetypes are shown in Figure 9.

As a child growing up in Chicago, Mickey had been constantly abused by his father, who beat him regularly until he bled. Mickey interpreted the presence of his Wounded Child archetype in the tenth house as indicating that, given the severe and emotionally toxic environment of his youth, his psyche was almost completely formed by wounds. That this archetype represented his highest potential was an almost perfect spiritual alignment, because Mickey is now dedicated to helping "wounded children" with his magic, teaching them above all else that hope and self-esteem are two of the highest forms of divine magic ever provided by the heavens.

To survive his brutal childhood, Mickey left home after his family moved to the West Coast, and by age nineteen he had become deeply enmeshed in the drug culture of Santa Cruz. When Mickey speaks about his life from this point onward, he uses two primary voices: the Thief and the Magician/Trickster. Mickey's Thief archetype landed in the first house representing his persona, and given that he had carved out his identity as both a drug dealer and a Magician at an early age, the Thief as the archetype representing his ego could not be more

FIGURE 9: MICKEY MAGIC'S CHART
OF ORIGIN

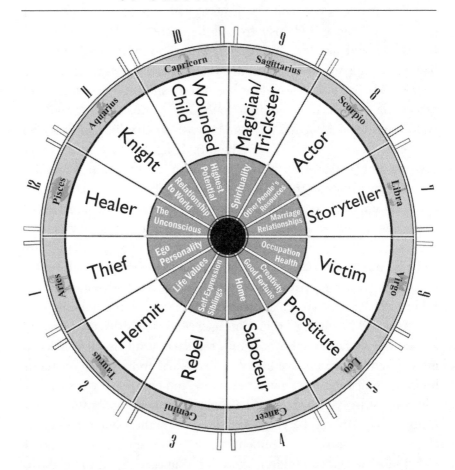

accurate. As for the Magician/Trickster, which landed in his house of spirituality, Mickey developed his remarkable talent and immediately used its shadow aspect for tricks that served his drug-trafficking occupation. Eventually, however, the Magician in him became his strongest spiritual guide, inspiring his own transformation and leading to his dedication to working with magic to entertain children as well as to inspire hope in children who need healing.

His parents drank and smoked, but Mickey instead became a habitual user of marijuana and occasionally of cocaine. "I didn't want to be addicts like them," he joked. "I needed to find an addiction of my own." As he was working his way into the drug culture, he met a locally famous magician and clown named Hocus Pocus (Carl Hansen), who had his own TV program on a local station. Mickey first heard the distinctive Danish-accented voice of Hocus Pocus as he was doing impromptu magic tricks for kids on the street. Mickey figured out the sleights-of-hand, practiced them in front of a mirror until he got them right, and then approached Hocus Pocus to show him what he had figured out. The magician was impressed by Mickey's skill and enthusiasm—and by his tact in not revealing his knowledge in public—and took him on as an apprentice magician for the next five years.

At the same time he was learning to be a professional magician, Mickey was also apprenticing as a drug smuggler and thief. Beginning as a "stateside" dealer working mainly to support his own daily habit, he graduated to working on the Mexican side so that he would be able to oversee the planting and harvesting of the prime marijuana crop. In this endeavor Mickey's shadow Magician archetype became his greatest ally along with his Prostitute, aligned to his fifth house. One aspect of life that is ruled by the fifth house is creativity, not to mention luck. For Mickey and his occupation, both were essential. In the small mountain villages of Oaxaca where the best marijuana crops were grown, none of the locals had ever seen a magician, and they took his mystifying feats for the work of a *brujo*, as the local shaman or wizard was known. Mickey's sleight-of-hand amazed both the children and the adults in the community, and in return they helped him and his drug crew form a network to acquire the best drugs and learn the best routes for moving them out of the country. He sold his talent, a common manifestation of the Prostitute archetype.

The ironic part of Mickey's Magician life was that the locals, who assumed that he was an American shaman, believed that he also had the ability to heal. "Suddenly these people were bringing their sick family members to me," he said. "I didn't know what to do, but I couldn't afford to make these people angry by turning them away. My partners told me to do what those TV evangelists do—just lay your hands on them. So I did, and then these people started healing! I couldn't figure it out, but I just kept doing it. I think it was some sort of rehearsal for what I'm doing now." Mickey's Healer archetype rests in his twelfth house, which rules the unconscious. The last gift Mickey would ever have identified during this time in his life was a healing ability, since he knew he was a user of people as well as substances. Yet underneath his rebellious drug-culture psyche was a spirit in the process of maturation. In spite of the choices he made, his shadow Magician, Wounded Child, Victim, and all of the rest of his companions remained on the course of his mission.

In his late twenties Mickey was busted for drug-running and put into a Mexican prison. During the three years he was incarcerated, he turned to prayer for comfort and began practicing yoga. In this setting Mickey encountered the Hermit within him, the archetype that rules his second house, life values. Having spent much of his time alone during his years of incarceration, he now comments, "I was never alone before, and at first it bothered me. But then I got used to it, and because I was alone, I had time to think. I prayed a lot, and I know this is going to sound weird, but I became a vegetarian. In Mexican prisons people buy their food. It's not like here." The food served by the state was so poor that Mickey threw in with some vegetarian inmates who grew their own produce in the prison yards. "I decided to change my diet," he said. "My values about everything changed while I was in prison."

When Mickey described these three years, I could not help but think of Saint John of the Cross, who wrote some of his most exquisite sacred poetry during his incarceration by Church officials in a prison in Toledo, Spain. Mickey was in a spiritual sanctuary, symbolically speaking, and in keeping with the true power of such places (regardless of their location—prison or paradise), he entered into a process of spiritual transformation. Eventually his spiritual life would become what he valued the most.

In prison the local guards were intrigued with his magical abilities and would make him perform tricks on demand, sometimes waking him up in the middle of the night with the butt end of a rifle. "*Brujo! Truco!*" they called, demanding the wizard perform a trick. Mickey's natural Trickster nature inspired him to make an arrangement with a fellow inmate to assist him in performing a bizarre bit of legerdemain that he hoped would scare the superstitious guards for good. It was 1971, and this particular inmate, who was clearly ahead of his time, had his penis pierced through the foreskin with a safety pin. The next time the guards demanded Mickey do some magic for them, he alerted his companion, then showed the guards a safety pin, which he put in his hand and made disappear. At that moment, cued by a signal from Mickey, his accomplice began to scream wildly at the other end of the large common cell where they were housed. When the guards rushed over to see what was the matter, the man pulled down his pants to reveal the safety pin penetrating his penis. "They ran like hell when they saw that," Mickey said. And they never bothered him again.

But the guards were the least of Mickey's problems. As one of only fourteen American prisoners, he had to fight for survival among the 3,500 other inmates, most of whom belonged to gangs. "They were always after us, trying to get us in fights or something," he said. "I mean, they hated us guys. It's easy to feel like a victim, because I was a victim." Not surprisingly, Mickey's Victim archetype in his sixth house completely manifested in his occupation, because it was precisely his occupation that had put him into prison. During his third year in prison a riot broke out that proved to be the largest Mexican prison riot of the time. "I saw people being killed all around me," Mickey said. "I saw people being beaten to death and burned alive." After the weeklong riot was quelled, Mickey and the Americans were transferred to another prison, where they planned an escape that included a promise that, if caught, they would tell the guards that everyone else had gone to rendezvous in Puerto Vallarta.

The escape was scheduled for Cinco de Mayo, the celebration of a nineteenth-century Mexican military victory that falls on the fifth of May. Mickey was the last to leave on the escape route—and the first to get caught. He was taken to a room in the prison, where he was beaten. Any guards who allowed prisoners to escape would be forced to serve out their remaining sentences, which may have motivated Mickey's interrogators all the more to beat the truth out of him. As Mickey put it, "If they didn't find these guys, it would be their asses on the line." They forced him to sit naked in a chair, where he was beaten until several of his ribs were broken and one rib protruded from his skin. They hit him with cattle whips and burned him with cattle prods. After holding out long enough to make his confession credible, Mickey told them that the escapees had headed for Puerto Vallarta, as agreed. The guards dispatched a troop of their own men to capture them.

"I was left sitting in that chair, when all of a sudden," said Mickey, "I was filled with a burst of compassion for these guards. I could relate to the fear I saw in their faces. It reminded me of my childhood and my fear of my father. Up till then I hated the Mexican people. I had met some nice individuals, but I despised them as a nation. Yet suddenly all I felt for them was love and compassion. I forgave each one of those guards while I was sitting totally naked and bleeding half to death in that Mexican prison."

Meanwhile, however, another American was caught, and under interrogation he told the officials the actual meeting place of all of the escapees. The guards now knew that Mickey had lied, and they were furious at having sent a large number of men on a wild-goose chase. "This time I could feel a red-hot aura coming into the room before the door even opened." Up to this point they still had not hit him in the face, but now they started to pistol-whip him. They filled a bucket full of water and put his feet in it so that they could run an electric wire through it and send an excruciating shock through his entire system. After three attempts Mickey could no longer fight back, and he passed out. In that instant Mickey had a near-death experience. "I went through a tunnel and into this beautiful light," he said. "I was greeted by an angel, but he didn't look like an angel—he didn't have any wings or anything. He hugged me and said it was good to see me again. Then I heard cheering in the tunnel, and I realized that somehow other souls who could not get there by themselves were able to come with me into this light. Next I was walking along a river, and other people were walking on the other side. The river was very deep, but I could see the bottom, and the sky was absolutely beautiful. All of the flowers and the grass were illuminated. Everything glowed. Then one woman came up to me and touched my cheek. Although she looked my age, I realized that she was my grandmother. I passed a man who looked at me with a warm smile, and I knew that he was my brother who had died at birth."

Finding himself in a building with high ceilings, Mickey realized that the spectral figure walking with him was the same being who had come to him when he was in the hospital for a year at age six. "The doctors thought I was going to die then," he recalled, "but this guy was always in the room with me, and he would come over and put his hand on my heart and head, comforting me. He told me that every-thing was going to be all right. Now he was telling me that I had to go back because I had not yet completed my mission."

Mickey didn't want to go back and explained that the guards were only going to kill him anyway. But the angel told Mickey that he had "protection" and would make it through. "The next thing I remem-ber, I was in my body lying in a pool of blood," he said. "The two guards were arguing over who had killed me, because neither of them wanted to be blamed for this. My first thought was that we looked like the Three Stooges, which made me start laughing. That let them know I was alive. They dragged me into a cell and threw me against a concrete wall, which knocked me out. Next thing I knew, my face was being washed off by the other American they had caught, who asked me why I was covered with so much blood. As I started to describe how they had beaten the hell out of me, I suddenly realized that all the bruises were gone, even the fractured rib that had been coming out of my gut. I didn't have a wound left."

When the American prisoner heard this, he advised Mickey never to tell anyone about the experience, because they would think he was crazy. "I was in such a suggestible state that I did effectively conceal what had happened for many years, letting it manifest only in my dreams."

"The Saboteur was still strong in me, though," Mickey acknowl-edged. "Even after leaving prison, I kept smoking dope and using cocaine, because I wanted to get as far away from my thoughts as I could." Yet at the same time the Saboteur began to manifest in positive ways, leading him to read the kinds of books that would eventually open up other spiritual passageways for him—books on mysticism, nutrition, and healing. He also began to take care of himself physically, using the highest-quality vitamins available and starting a regimen of physical exercise. Even now, in his early fifties, Mickey Rollerblades seven miles a day, follows a rigorous diet, and looks remarkably fit for someone whose body has taken so much abuse.

After being released from the Mexican prison and returning to Santa Cruz in 1977, Mickey did not immediately listen to the inner warnings of the Saboteur. By 1984, however, he had stopped dealing drugs and had begun to get his life back on track, meeting a woman, starting a new relationship, and fathering a child. Then he received a call from a former friend and drug customer who begged Mickey to get him some pot to help him through a health crisis. Although Mickey felt something was wrong about the whole deal, he went along with it to help his friend. What he didn't know was that his friend had been busted by narcotics agents and had offered to set up Mickey and another person in exchange for more lenient treatment for himself. The bust jeopardized not only Mickey's new marriage and impending family but also his work and his newly established position in the community. "When this guy called me," Mickey said, "I heard my intuition screaming not to do this, but I just didn't listen."

In keeping with many spiritual tests about power, just as Mickey began his emergence into his new sense of inner power (which manifests in many ways, including intuition), the former "power" force came to call as if it were a divine examination. *Which power will you serve*, he was being asked, *the inner or the external?* As if standing in two worlds and hearing two voices, Mickey confronted the instincts of his Saboteur rising within his psyche to protect him. Ironically, the Magician was betrayed by another person's Trickster.

After unsuccessfully fighting his conviction, Mickey was confined to Soledad prison in California. While serving time there, he befriended the guards and worked toward a college degree. He also became involved in speaking to children who had run afoul of the law, telling them his life story to help them stay straight. "Instead of trying to frighten them, as in the Scared Straight program," Mickey said, "we tried to touch their hearts and show how what they did would affect the people they loved." His Actor and Storyteller archetypes were very effective in reaching the kids emotionally. "By the time I was finished telling my story, the whole audience would be crying. Even the guards, who had heard the story before, told me I would still get them crying." Moved into minimum security, Mickey became part of the Soledad Clowns, organizing classes to teach magic to other inmates. He noted how refreshing it was to use his well-developed acting talent as a way of inspiring other people instead of as a way to manipulate them, his specialty in his drug days. Mickey's Actor archetype ruled his eighth house, representing other people's resources as well as legal matters. "I was great at manipulating other people to get them to do what I wanted. I guess you could say I used everyone's resources to my best advantage. I still manipulate people—I trick them into seeing the best in themselves."

Each archetype has a positive manifestation, and Mickey's Thief underwent a transformation from its shadow aspect. In some ways he was a Robin Hood character who took from the rich and shared with the poor. "Even when I was a dealer," he said, "I would take part of my earnings and drop an envelope full of money through the slot at the Salvation Army, or give money anonymously to somebody in the neighborhood who needed it. I didn't believe in God at that time, but I had some sense that I had to do something to counteract the negative karma arising from my activities." Even today when he is not engaged in any illegal activities and doesn't make nearly as much money, he still donates much of his time to giving magic performances for kids.

The Knight archetype for Mickey landed in his eleventh house, his relationship to the world. His response to this partnership was a fitting summation of the union of all of his archetypal companions: "I'm a Knight to God. My whole thing is to give service to people and make them aware of the greatness of God. I'm not serving a Christian concept of God, but I start every day by thanking God and pledging my service to God for that day.

"When I tell people my story, they sometimes say, 'Boy, you have some karma coming to you.' But I believe now that karma doesn't happen *to* you; it happens *for* you. If you sincerely believe that God loves you, then you're not a victim of anything anymore. It's happening to open up opportunities for us to become more aligned with our higher purpose. I feel so loved that I don't believe God is going to throw anything at me that won't benefit me and help me grow. I feel like a kid waiting for Christmas to open up my gifts. It took a long time to get to that place, let me tell you. My theme song when I was in prison in Mexico was the Rolling Stones' 'You Can't Always Get What You Want.'"

A few years ago Mickey began a club called Magic Pack that entertains and teaches magic tricks to kids who are suffering from life-threatening illnesses. At the time his act was billed as Mickey's Magic. His real name is Mickey Thurmon, but the kids kept calling him

Mickey Magic, and the nickname stuck. "I was so honored to be named by these kids," he said, "that I decided to keep the name and use it professionally." Mickey Magic now divides his time between performing magic for kids, teaching magic, and working as a healer in the Santa Cruz community. He has scaled down his lucrative home-remodeling business to devote more time to magic and kids. Although he now earns less money, he couldn't feel more fulfilled. "I'm rich that way," he said in conclusion. "I'm a wealthy man. I was making a lot more money before, but I'm a hundred million times happier now."

Mickey described his Sacred Contract in these words: "In this lifetime I am here to show people the magic of compassion. I learned this by needing it to survive, and I do everything in my life with this intention in mind."

The Endless Contract

Maeve's, Byron's, and Mickey's stories are just the tip of their Contracts. The more memories you run through the Wheel, the more you strengthen your understanding of how events and relationships fit into your overall Contract.

In the next chapter we will explore casting other Wheels in your life. Once you learn how to apply this tool as a method for guidance, there are no limits to what you are capable of learning.

CHAPTER 10

Using the Wheel for Everyday Guidance

Your Archetypal Wheel is only the first of many that you can cast for guidance in all areas of your life. While your Archetypal Wheel creates a portrait of your life patterns, other Wheels, which I call "working charts," can be cast whenever you have a concern or need intuitive guidance. You can use them to shed light on your relationships, career, and other experiences of your everyday world. The working charts help you practice your symbolic sight and view your life as a continuous process of spiritual growth.

Working charts can also inspire creative thinking when you are beginning a new enterprise. It's profoundly empowering to be in touch with your archetypes when you are dealing with other people. A man named Rick, for instance, cast a chart for guidance in starting his own e-commerce business. In the three most significant pairings in his working chart, Rick's Entrepreneur archetype landed in his sixth house (occupation and health); his Warrior landed in his first house (ego and personality); and his Prostitute fell into his seventh house (marriage and relationships). He interpreted the sixth-house Entrepreneur as a positive sign that it was possible to bring his business idea to fruition. The combination of the Warrior in his first house and the Prostitute in his seventh told him to be mindful of how he approached people when seeking financial backing. Rick realized that in his enthusiasm for this business venture, his excitement or first-house ego energy could come across too forcibly and put off other people. That archetype, combined with the Prostitute in his house of relationships, cautioned him to be mindful of his own motives with people, particularly in terms of any personal compromises he might have to make to get the business started.

The technique for casting a working chart is almost identical to the technique for casting your Archetypal Wheel. You use the same twelve archetypal patterns, and you prepare by clearing your mind. But for your working chart you focus attention and phrase your intention differently. Rick, for example, asked, "How are my archetypes aligned in service to my new business venture?"

Consider this process as similar to the manner in which you pray for guidance. The only real difference is that a grounded, practical, and immediate response comes through working with your chart. Responses to prayer can be immediate too, but they may also unfold in time.

Interpreting the information you receive on a working chart does not require the same amount of time as interpreting your Archetypal Wheel. First of all, you should by now already have a perspective on your lifelong relationship with each archetype. And secondly, you are directing your attention to a specific area of your life. One of the benefits of taking the time to reflect on your answers to the numerous questions involved with your Chart of Origin is that the process familiarizes you with your archetypal patterns and you can interpret your working chart faster and more confidently. Nevertheless, the more time you take to study the symbolic meaning of each chart you cast, the deeper will be your insights and your intuitive rapport with the process.

How Many Is Too Many?

In one sense, there are no limits to how many working charts you can cast, because guidance is always available. At the same time, though, you need to respect the process of receiving guidance so that ultimately you learn to rely on your inner voice. Casting a chart—or the Tarot, *I Ching*, or any other source of guidance—for every minor decision in life will eventually render you incapable of trusting your own instincts. Please also avoid the temptation to cast a working chart repeatedly regarding the same matter. Think through the guidance you have already received from the first chart before casting a second. Allow your insights to make their way through both your conscious and your unconscious mind and to provide you with the feedback on which you make your choices. A working chart is not a means to see the future. The information it offers can help you gain a higher perspective on the meaning of what is taking place in your life.

Many people want the charts to provide them with information on what is going on in the mind or heart of another person. This too is a misuse of the Wheel. Your focus should be on the emotions and thoughts in your own mind and heart, and the quality of your own actions and motivations. One woman asked me to help her interpret a chart that she had cast about her relationship with a man she was dating. She was frustrated that she couldn't get a "fix" on what *he* was thinking about *her* and whether he was serious about their relationship. What he was thinking was not her business—her business was to understand what she was thinking and why she was so insecure and jealous.

Everyone falls prey to the desire to know more about someone else, to find a way to second-guess other people. Keep your attention focused on *your* motivations. Phrase your intentions like an adult. Asking "Why did he do this to me?" is completely inappropriate. The question should be "What is the learning dynamic that has drawn me into this relationship? What is the lesson for me in this relationship?" Your best approach to mastering how to interpret your archetypal patterns is to practice detachment. Get some symbolic distance from the situation, and remain impersonal and open about the information you are seeking. Use the three-column model (on page 194) to help you. The woman who wanted to know about the emotional intentions of the man she was dating had a personal agenda that was dominated by her insecurities and emotional need to discover what he was thinking. I can assure you that you too will confront this same intention in yourself, because being impersonal about your own life feels unnatural at first. Nonetheless, detachment is the most effective way of understanding events and relationships and responding appropriately to them.

A final word of caution: *please do not under any circumstances use this tool to DIAGNOSE either your physical health or anyone else's.* People often ask me how to interpret their archetypes to find out whether they have an illness, what the progression of that illness will be, or whether someone else's illness is terminal. Requests for life-and-death information are outside the purview of this tool. If you have questions concerning your health, consult with qualified medical personnel.

Phrasing Your Intentions

Keep your questions and intentions simple. The following focus, for example, is too complicated: "I am seeking a greater understanding of why my childhood was difficult and why my mother was always critical of me." This is really two questions—one, why your childhood was difficult; two, the lesson inherent in your having a hypercritical mother. Word your questions impersonally, and when possible identify the archetypal pattern with which you are working: for example, "I am seeking insight into the relationship of my Victim archetype to my mother." Your intention should be directed to what you are meant to learn through your Contract with your mother, as opposed to why your mother behaved as she did.

We tend to want to know why things happened to us as they did and ask questions accordingly. We would love the Divine to provide us with logical explanations that condemn the wrongful deeds done to us, while conveniently avoiding any mention of what we have done to others. But life will never be logical, nor will it ever seem wholly fair. Even the many surprise blessings in life defy logic. I know people who met their life partners when they got lost and had to ask someone for directions—and that someone turned out to be the love of their life. Of such an illogical happenstance we could also ask, "What did I do to deserve such a magical experience?" We'll never know that either.

How fairness is worked out within the human experience is not for us to know. Our task is to learn to cope with all that we feel that we do not deserve, good or bad, in ways that empower us, and to pursue as best we can the development of our highest potential in all our endeavors. Remember that your highest potential is not measured by one accomplishment. Everything you do and all your relationships have an inherent potential that seems to reveal itself most clearly when you seek understanding with an appreciative heart. The ultimate goal of all your requests for guidance should be to lead you toward that potential. To stimulate your intuitive intelligence, begin your request with the words *I am open.*

Appropriate Requests

Illness:

I am open to receiving one healing insight about my stress patterns and this illness.

I am open to receiving one healing insight to help me move forward.

Reconciliation:

I am open to recognizing why I block reconciliation with _____.

I am open to guidance as to a positive first step.

Creativity:

I am open to recognizing my best creative contribution to _____ project.

I am open to receiving guidance on how to proceed with my work.

I am open to receiving guidance about why I block my creativity.

Finances:

I am open to receiving guidance about my fears of earning money.

I am open to receiving guidance about my fears of losing money.

I am open to receiving guidance on how to earn money.

Competition:

I am open to receiving guidance about why I feel so competitive with _____.

I am open to receiving guidance on to how to release my negative connection to _____.

I am open to receiving guidance about how to work with _____ for my own empowerment as well as his/hers.

Loneliness:

I am open to guidance about how best to cope in the moment with my emotions.

I am open to guidance about how to appreciate my own life.

Moving:

I am open to guidance about whether this is the right time to move.

Quitting a Job:

I am open to guidance about whether this is the right time to quit my job.

I am open to guidance about my core reason(s) for wanting to quit.

I am open to guidance about my own negative contribution to the disappointment I feel in my work.

Accepting a Job Offer:

I am open to guidance about this job offer.

Relationships:

I am open to receiving the core lesson in this relationship.

I am open to recognizing my deepest fear in this relationship.

I am open to recognizing the gift of this relationship.

I am open to insight into

why I feel so negative toward ____.

why I hold on to feeling hurt in my relationship with ____.

why I feel abandoned by ____.

my tendency toward dishonest words/deeds.

how to work through my difficulty with ____ regarding ____ problem.

why I am losing power in this relationship.

why I withhold my emotional support of this individual.

the reason why I can't forgive ____.

why I need his/her approval.

my challenge with low self-esteem (both in general and in specific relationships/situations).

my struggle with commitment regarding my relationship with (a person, a job, some promise to yourself, or use your own wording).

my ungrounded nature in relationships.

my aggressive nature in relationships.

how to respond to another's aggressive feelings to me.

how to maintain my center of power.

why I do not want to give this person emotional support.

how best to support this person.

my need to control ____ (name one person at a time).

my dependency on ____.

my need to rescue others.

my need to be rescued.

Releasing a Relationship:

I am open to guidance about why I hold on to this relationship.

I am open to guidance about how to release this relationship with gratitude.

Soul Retrieval:

I am open to guidance about how to call back my spirit from (name the relationship or experience).

Spiritual Fears:

I am open to insight into why I fear intimacy with God (or whatever name you use to identify the Divine).

Fear of Surrender:

I am open to insight into why I am unable to surrender my willpower in (identify the circumstance).

Spiritual Guidance:

I am open to any guidance that I should focus on today.

Dreams:

I am open to insight into interpreting a specific dream.

Intuition:

I am open to guidance on interpreting my intuitive hit regarding _____.

Childhood:

I am open to insights into my feelings of (identify your feelings) with (name the person).

Pride:

Why is my pride preventing me from (forgiving, accepting, loving) _____?

Inappropriate Questions

Pregnancy:

Should I have an abortion?

Health:

Do I have (name the illness)?

Should I have this treatment?

Relationship:

Why isn't he/she calling me?

Is he/she dating someone else?

Why did he/she leave me?

Stealing/Lying:

Is _____ stealing from/lying to me?

Parents:

Why were my parents so mean to me?

Let me reemphasize that you should avoid phrasing your questions in a way that supports the victim in you ("Why did they hurt me?") or that focuses on getting into another person's psyche ("Why is Julie acting distant toward me?"). That is not the purpose of this tool. Until this practice becomes second nature, you have to remind yourself continually that you are looking for understanding and direction about how best to work with and through your Contract with a particular person or experience. Your goal is to come away from interpreting your Archetypal Wheel and working charts feeling empowered with a sense that all of your Contracts serve your growth, and that nothing that happens to you has a negative intent.

After you have phrased your intention as clearly as possible, you are ready to:

- Release your intention
- Cast your chart
- Begin your interpretation of the archetypal configuration that manifests

Scripting Your Game Plan
with Healing Mantras

Whether your intention is to heal or to plan the next step in a creative project, the working chart will give you information about what your next step will be. So you need to draw up a plan for action. Like an architect's blueprints, that plan allows you to deal with problems or difficulties as they arise.

To script a plan, begin at the first house of your chart, and write down a word or brief phrase that will help you put into practice the insight you have gathered from each house on the Wheel. This word or phrase will become your mantra for action. For instance, if your Actor archetype resides in your third house (self-expression and siblings), and you are seeking guidance about how to release the weight of past professional failures, your mantra could be "No repeat performances." Ideally the mantra you choose should relate in some way to the significance of the house, the archetype that falls into it, or both, as the Actor and the house of self-expression both relate to the mantra drawn from theater lingo. In one of the stories that follows, for example, Trevor had the Hedonist in his eighth house, which rules other people's resources and legal matters. He was looking for guidance about starting an e-commerce business that would help people find good restaurants via the Internet while traveling, and he felt that that combination reinforced his plans. And so he created "Pleasure and gain" as his mantra for that house, to remind himself that serving others' desires for pleasure could help him advance financially. Your mantras need not all be clever wordplays, of course, although having a sense of humor helps. The important thing is to establish some organic connection between the mantra and the archetype-house linkage.

Once complete, this game plan can be used as a spiritual reminder of how to stay committed to the choices you've made. It will help bring back your spirit into the present time, and it will help you consciously manage the way you invest your personal power. I recommend that you write down these mantras on a small card and carry it with you at all times so that you can refer to it in moments of trouble or indecision.

The following stories are examples of how three people used working charts for guidance in their very different life concerns. Karl was seeking insights into his struggle with depression and drug addiction. Trevor was eager to break through his block with finances. Fay was searching for guidance regarding a health problem.

Karl's Story: A Relationship Chart

I met Karl while I was sitting with friends around a hotel pool within sight of a lovely Caribbean beach. He and his buddy had just gotten off a boat and invited themselves to join us, and Karl immediately began acting the Fool. Within ten minutes of our meeting, for instance, he had rolled up one of his sleeves and was showing me a tattoo of his daughter's name. "That's the only true love of my life," he said. Clearly, Karl was in some pain. Still only in his late forties, his body had aged prematurely from an addiction to drugs and alcohol, which he also revealed to us.

Karl's personality was a fascinating mixture of bravado, self-pity, and roguish charm. Beneath his clowning, tough-guy demeanor, it wasn't hard to see a man at odds with himself and painfully in need of guidance. With very little prodding on my part, he agreed to let me help him cast a working chart seeking insight into his failed marriage and how he could be a better father. He had never found a way to get grounded in his life. Although he seemed casual at first about his addiction to heroin, which had destroyed his marriage and come between him and his daughter, he was nonetheless tormented by his inability to kick his habit. Karl was at a crossroads between wanting to heal himself and not being able to imagine that his life could be any different. When he spoke about his twelve-year-old daughter, he would almost break down and would have to stare out at the ocean until he could gather his emotions again. Karl desperately wanted to be a good father and wanted his daughter to respect him. Unfortunately, he went about trying to buy her respect by getting her anything she wanted, rather than working on the more difficult emotional issues between them.

The working chart we cast refers only to guidance that Karl was seeking about his broken marriage and his relationship with his daughter. He made a point of saying that in doing this exercise, he was making choices, not promises. He continually had to remind himself that he could not lie to his daughter and then run and hide, the way he did with his wife. His intention was to build a healthy and loving relationship with his daughter and this guided him in drawing up a game plan. Figure 10 shows Karl's working chart.

FIGURE 10: KARL'S RELATIONSHIP CHART

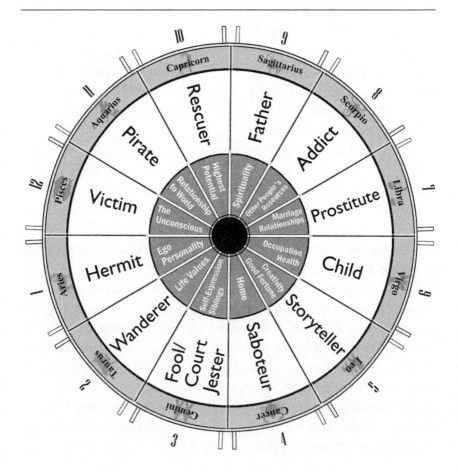

First House: Ego and Personality: Hermit

Karl said that his wife, Karen, always saw him as a Hermit, but in the beginning of their relationship that didn't bother her. This pattern became a serious concern for her, however, as his addictions became the focus of his life (he had the Addict archetype in his eighth house) and he withdrew from her more and more. "I didn't want to see Karen," he said. "She was always asking me if I was high, and I could never get away with lying to her. She could see it all over my face. All addicts lie—it goes with the habit. But you always think you can hide your addiction, that people can't see through you. She'd get a kick out of seeing the Hermit in the house of my personality, because she knew I was in hiding due to my drug habit."

It was the shadow Hermit that was ruling Karl's personality—withdrawing from society not to gather his reserves of strength but merely to avoid facing reality. Another interpretation of the Hermit archetype in his first house was that his feelings of shame at having lost his self-respect were so intense that he could not face his wife. "That's true," he said immediately. "I don't want my daughter to see me, either. I'm not proud of who I am today, believe me."

Karl thought that changing himself was nearly impossible, but he was willing to try anything. We asked what he could do that would help him become strong enough to face his daughter without feeling ashamed of himself. On reflection he said, "I would like to help my daughter realize the hell drugs lead to. I would like to be able to tell her the truth about myself so that she will never be tempted to use drugs. I'd like her to learn from my mistakes."

As part of the healing process, he decided to carry a small version of his mantras—his healing plan—in his wallet and refer to it like a map to guide his spirit. To remind himself of his commitment to recover his self-esteem, he used a phrase that his dad, whom he loved dearly, had used every morning when he would wake Karl up: "Look alive, Karl. It's a new day." So Karl chose the phrase "Look alive" as his first-house mantra, because it reminded him of his father and awakened in him his desire to recover his self-esteem. That became the first step in Karl's game plan.

Second House: Life Values: Wanderer

Karl said that he never could feel at home in one place. He longed to travel, but this became a problem as his marriage progressed. "Karen and I met when we were in our twenties. We were young and crazy, and we didn't have a kid. We went everywhere together. Problem is, once our daughter, Zoe, was born, Karen gave up the wandering—but I didn't. Between my drug problem and never being home, her life was miserable. I tried to settle down, but I would get to the point where I thought I was going mad. I guess I valued being away from home more than I did being with her."

The phrase he chose to help him heal this part of his life was "Zoe love." This represented that, no matter where he was, he was always sending his love to his daughter.

Third House: Self-Expression and Siblings: Fool/Court Jester

The Fool is an archetype that carries wisdom in disguise into places that would otherwise disdain such knowledge. Karl paused when he heard that, and then he said that feeling like a fool was familiar to him in his communication with his wife. "You know, I always had to cope with depression one way or another, and I wanted to talk about it to Karen," he said. "But she disregarded it most of the time. She said I was always wrapped up in what bothered me and never had time to listen to her."

Karl had a great deal of regret over the fact that he never acknowledged his pain because he never wanted to listen to his wife's pain—or her criticism. "I knew she was right, but I didn't want to hear it."

Karl chose the mantra "Listen" as his third-house guide.

Fourth House: Home: Saboteur

"I think I started sabotaging my marriage the day after we got married," Karl said. "It never occurred to me that anything in our lives would have to change, even if we had kids. Neither of us realized how important it would be for my wife to have a home." Karl described a number of incidents that took place either in his physical home or that related to the symbolic meaning of *home* as his wife saw it. He was apparently incapable of providing the kind of stable family life his wife wanted, much less living, in his words, as "good neighbor Sam." From a positive point of view, Karl acknowledged that "the Saboteur on this house could have been my best white flag, had I known about this stuff earlier—though I'm sure I wouldn't have listened anyway."

Not a day went by when Karl didn't long to wake up in his old bed. "How true it is," he said, "that you don't know what you've got till you lose it." And so Karl chose the mantra "Appreciate" for his fourth-house guide.

Fifth House: Creativity, Good Fortune: Storyteller

Karl gave out a yell when his Storyteller arrived in his fifth house, saying, "I was kind of expecting that archetype to land in my marriage house, because I sure told my wife a lot of stories. But actually I've told a lot of stories to a lot of ladies, so this archetype fits here maybe even more than in my marriage house. I stepped out on my wife, and she knew it. I would get into an argument with Karen, and in my mind that gave me permission to bed down with another woman. Believe it or not, I love my wife, and I would give anything for another shot at having a life with her. I know she wouldn't believe me if I told her I'd stay clean [from drugs]. More stories, huh? I'd have to have a lot of good luck behind me with that project, I can tell you that much."

Karl insisted that he would also like to create an open and honest relationship with his daughter, although he admitted that this would take work because of all the lies she had seen him tell her mother. He chose as his fifth-house mantra the single word "Honesty."

Sixth House: Occupation and Health: Child

Karl always struggled with being an adult, as is clear from his difficulties in settling down and being a responsible husband and father. The only occupations that he could handle were those from which he could come and go. A sailor and craftsman by trade, he was very good at woodwork, and he used this talent to keep up the repairs on the boats he was sailing. "I am someone who you hire for day or two to fix this or that. This drove my wife nuts, and that bothered me because, as much trouble as I had staying put, I always provided materially for my family. We had a nice home even though I wasn't there a lot. She worked too, and that helped keep the place running." Karl was like a Peter Pan, never wanting to grow up. Yet he also had a Pirate archetype and spent much of his time at sea. Karl's list of all that he had provided for his family, which to him proved that he had held up his end of a marriage partnership, referred only to material things. "You should see my home," he said. "I bought a great entertainment unit, a pool table that doubles as a Ping-Pong table. I got my daughter a great computer so that she could play all those computer games. Her friends were over all the time because there was so much stuff to do at our place."

As kindly as I could, I pointed out to Karl that children need more than just toys or material gifts in order to grow and mature. In response, he said that his sixth-house mantra would be "Emotional support," which represented his new commitment to give more of himself to his daughter.

Seventh House: Marriage and Relationships: Prostitute

The first thought that occurred to Karl when he saw the Prostitute in his seventh house was that his wife always thought of him as a street person selling everything he could get his hands on to make more drug deals. From his wife's point of view, Karl's true partners in life were his drug suppliers. "When you're an addict, you don't care about anything other than getting your next fix," he said. "So if your wife is in front of you, and the guy who's got your next heroin shot is standing next to her, chances are you're going to pick your supplier first. So what does that say about who you are really married to?"

Karl said that creating a seventh-house mantra was a no-brainer. "'Loyalty' is the one word that says it all. No matter what, my loyalty to my daughter comes first."

Eighth House: Other People's Resources: Addict

Karl said that having his Addict in the house of other people's resources was perfect. "I mean, all an addict does is rely on other people's resources—drugs, money, anything that works." Karl admitted that he would rifle through his wife's purse for cash when he ran short. "I would take her resources, if you want me to put it in this language." This behavior was just one more reason that his wife, after hanging in there with him for twenty-one years, demanded a divorce. "She gave it her best shot. I realize that now. I'm not sure I could have stayed with her that long if she was the addict who always strayed from home." And then he paused, "Yeah, I'd stay with her."

Karl realized that he had also drained his wife of all her inner resources during their marriage and that he did not want to do the same to his daughter. That desire inspired him to say that he wanted to create with his daughter a material and emotional investment rather than a withdrawal. His eighth-house mantra, then: "Invest not withdraw."

Ninth House: Spirituality: Father

Karl's Father archetype in his house of spirituality fit with his intention to discover how to be a better father to Zoe. He said, "My screwups in my marriage and as a father are the reason I started to pray."

Karl chose "Faith" as his ninth-house mantra.

Tenth House: Highest Potential: Rescuer

Karl said that this was the most obvious match on the entire chart for him. "Rescuing myself from my addictions and getting past the need to run away from my past is going to take everything I've got. I haven't been able to do that yet. If I thought I had half a chance of getting back with my wife, I'd sure give it a try. But that ain't gonna happen, so what's my motivation?"

His response came directly from the Child archetype in his house of health. Exhibiting a kind of perennial mother-child bond, Karl refused to heal himself unless someone more responsible, like his ex-wife, would help him out. Yet he knew that he had to rescue himself, and the only phrase that represented the seriousness of this dilemma was "Sink or swim."

Eleventh House: Relationship to the World: Pirate

Karl was a modern-day Pirate, with his long hair, tattoos, and manner of dress. He reminded me of Errol Flynn as the pirate Captain Blood, and it turned out, of course, that he was a great admirer of Errol Flynn and his pirate escapades. Karl loved the Pirate spirit and loved sailing the world. "I don't sail like a tourist," he said with pride. "I am a sailor. I've been in my share of barroom fights, and I've taken what's not mine when I felt 'inspired' to. But Pirates don't make good husbands. When I told my wife that I can't change who I am, she decided that there was no sense waiting around. I moved out of the house about a week after that conversation."

How did the Pirate affect his role as father? "Life is an adventure," he said, choosing those four words as his eleventh-house mantra. "I went about enjoying it too carelessly, but it's still an adventure, and I would like Zoe to believe that and experience that. I don't want her to be afraid of life because of the way I live."

Twelfth House: The Unconscious: Victim

At first Karl thought this archetype referred to his being victimized, which it could, but that interpretation did not resonate with him as much as his realization that he had victimized his own wife constantly. For all Karl's obvious flaws, he wasn't afraid to shoulder the blame for them. Because of him, she had lived in constant fear. There were times on drugs when his behavior verged on the psychotic. "I would have hallucinations [twelfth-house madness], and I would threaten her." Eventually she couldn't trust him at all, because she knew that he was cheating on her, stealing, using drugs, and disappearing for weeks at a time. "I drove her insane. I know it. She did feel like a victim of my disease. And I'm paying for it now. I am alone."

Karl struggled with depression now because he saw only an empty life ahead of him. "Getting my daughter back means the world to me. I only hope I can actually change enough to make that happen." For that reason he chose "Transformation" as his twelfth-house mantra.

Although Karl's grief over his situation with his daughter and former wife was sincere, and even though he participated in this exercise with the belief that we can receive divine guidance, he unconsciously offered a negative interpretation of almost every archetypal pattern in his chart. As soon as any option or new thought would emerge, his immediate response was "Aw, that wouldn't work," or "I could just see my wife's face if I told her that I've had an archetypal transformation." At one point his eyes filled with tears as he continued the exercise. Despite his pain he deflected all options for change that I offered him.

Karl's interaction with this tool is a classic example of a conflict in which the conscious mind reaches for guidance while the unconscious sabotages every effort to make changes. Karl's Saboteur archetype in his fourth house is of particular significance, because it revealed the area he most wanted to repair while underlining the danger of self-sabotage that he faced in that very realm. His working chart revealed the paradox that held his spirit in polarity—his desire to heal and his Pirate's fear of never being allowed the freedom of the waters again.

From a symbolic perspective—the third column—through this exercise in self-examination Karl was able to step outside of his shadow and chart a new passage for his life. He was ready to reevaluate what mattered most to him and retrieve his spirit from the guilt and shame of disappointing people. If Karl could muster the fortitude to follow his new game plan, the chances were still good that he could salvage a decent relationship with his daughter. At the very least, this exercise allowed him to articulate his inner demons. Once these forces are brought out of the shadows and into the conscious mind, we have a chance to heal and resolve them.

Trevor's Story: A Career Chart

Trevor was in his early thirties. An ambitious man who dreamed of creating an e-commerce businesse that held the promise of great and instant wealth, he had all the right pedigrees. Besides a master's degree in business, Trevor spent the previous ten years learning about business management at two corporations. During our work together on his chart, he struck me as having the ability to generate one creative idea after another. It was also apparent, however, that he was afraid to move forward on his e-commerce venture without some safeguard or guarantee that he would not fail—and this conflict between needing a safeguard and taking an intuitive risk is one of the most paralyzing of fears. We experience many Contracts through their shadow side as a result of repressing our intuitive instructions. In this way we manifest our creativity through the stress of what could be, hanging on to the dreams and visions that we could have expressed in the physical domain of our lives. These dreams or Contracts never evaporate. They remain an integral part of our lives, only we maintain them in the realm of possibility, and we experience them through regret.

Trevor said that he had to take all possible precautions because he intended to approach other people for funding his new venture. In casting his chart he asked to gain insight into his relationship with money and his need to be wealthy, which lay at the root of his insecurity about actually beginning his venture.

Together with the four survival archetypes—Victim, Prostitute, Saboteur, and Child—Trevor chose archetypes that he felt best represented not only his skills, talents, and ambitions but also his lifelong fears. He chose the Beggar archetype because he frankly felt that this pattern represented a controlling force that had been a part of his nature from his earliest recollections. Like so many people, Trevor's profile was rife with contradictions. Just as we are all made up of many voices and many opinions, Trevor believed in himself and was torn by doubts. He had faith in his ideas and none in God. Depending on what we are doing and when, we can be buoyed by confidence or devastated with fear.

Trevor's chart appears in Figure 11.

First House: Ego and Personality: Beggar

The Beggar archetype in Trevor's first house represented, in his words, his greatest fear: giving the impression that he was incapable of earning his own wealth. He was determined to present himself as successful, a goal that influenced not just his own persona but the persona of his environment. His car was a "spokesperson" for his ego, and therefore it had to be a BMW. He was impeccable about his dress and self-conscious about his manners. The Beggar-ego validated for Trevor that no amount of elegant clothing could hide his fear that people would not consider investing in his ideas, that they would think of him as a beggar asking for a handout. He realized that until and unless he believed in himself, no one would invest in anything he did. He decided that the question "Would I invest in me?" would be

FIGURE 11: TREVOR'S CAREER CHART

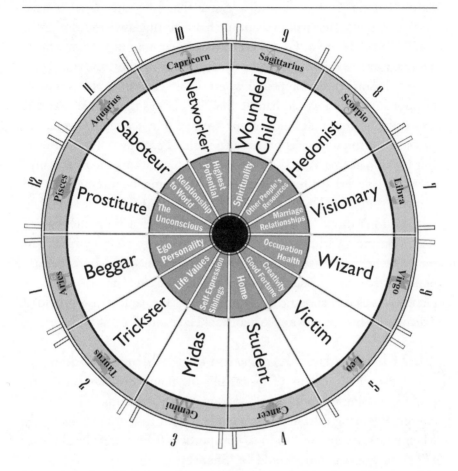

his mantra for this house, because it would help him keep his attention on his need to maintain his own self-esteem.

The positive aspect of the Beggar manifested itself for Trevor as generosity of spirit and financial sharing. He realized that he had been unsupportive of the creativity of other people who also held visions of getting ahead in life, and so he decided that he would confront his insecurities in part by applauding the work of his friends and co-workers.

Second House: Life Values: Trickster

Trevor chose the Trickster as one of his archetypal companions because it reflected his relationship to God. He always felt braced for

God to pull the rug out from under him unless he did everything right. "I don't trust God, and I realize that," he said, "so I behave myself, thinking that will prevent me from getting any attention from the Trickster nature of God. Part of why I fear jumping into my business venture is that I would be responsible for the funds of other people. If something happened where I lost control of my business, I'm not sure how I would handle that." This was more than a fear; it was a superstition that held Trevor hostage. He needed to overcome this shadow theology and try to have faith. "I already tell myself that. But looking at this Wheel, I don't believe God wants me to fail anymore. I believe that I have obstacles to overcome, beginning with the fact that I don't believe in myself. Not only do I not trust God," he said, "I don't think I trust anyone. I am afraid that no matter who I start a business with, they are eventually going to take my ideas and start a business of their own." This insight stunned Trevor as he recognized that his superstition about the Trickster nature of other people was as real an issue as his mistrust of Heaven. It also provided Trevor with his second-house mantra: "Have faith."

Third House: Self-Expression and Siblings: Midas

Trevor had a habit of discussing his plans with far too many people, sharing his ideas and visions, and exhausting his creative energy. Realizing this, he made a commitment to share his ideas only when necessary and not to look for approval from others by sharing. His third-house mantra would be "Silence."

Fourth House: Home: Student

The Student in Trevor's fourth house represented that he was never sure he knew enough to "leave home" and pursue life as an adult. Starting his own e-commerce business represented adulthood and independence. "I am always reading something more or thinking that I don't yet know enough. I think that's natural. A lot of people feel that they don't know enough to do what they want in their lives. And I realize that shouldn't stop me, but I guess it does."

At some point book learning has to take a backseat to experience. A fourth-house Student could be symbolic of the message to leave home now. Trevor decided to use that symbol in scripting a mantra for his fourth house: "Graduate."

Fifth House: Creativity and Good Fortune: Victim

This house represented everything Trevor needed and wanted as well as what he had already experienced. In spite of all his business fears, he also thought of himself as lucky and certainly believed himself to be a highly creative person. His fears about failing, he said, were not for lack of creativity or luck. Therefore he interpreted the Victim on this house as an ally, a voice that supported his intuitive instincts when it came to being able to count on himself to generate ideas. "I know from my work experience that I am excellent at taking charge of the projects at work," he said. "I'm good at managing people and I am dependable. I can sense when something is wrong, and I don't get taken advantage of at work. My problem is in seeking investment capital for my own ideas." Trevor decided to utilize his positive associations with his Victim archetype, scripting the guide phrase "Trust my instincts."

Sixth House: Occupation and Health: Wizard

Trevor interpreted his Wizard in the house of occupation and health as an omen validating his self-image and the nature of e-commerce in general. For him, the computer industry was a modern Wizard's laboratory, producing unbelievable results with its technological power. The positive qualities that he associated with the Wizard archetype, such as alchemy and magic, promised that interventions of good luck and the impossible would happen to him. His mantra for this house would be "Make the impossible happen."

Seventh House: Marriage and Relationships: Visionary

The Visionary in the house of relationships indicated that Trevor needed to find partners in his business project who could understand his vision and not just want to make money from it. His vision was as real to him as a person. He was in a partnership with his own idea of an e-commerce company, and he needed to recognize that he was highly emotional and protective of his project. Business partners who invested in his project for a fast return on their capital would be extremely difficult for him to cope with, so the Visionary archetype on this house indicated how intimately Trevor was linked to his vision. He decided on "Unity" for his mantra, because this word represented a quality that he would want in any person on his team.

Eighth House: Other People's Resources: Hedonist

The Hedonist in the house of outside resources applied specifically to the issue of Trevor's financial block. Trevor loved good food and wine and wanted to create a website where people could find restaurants in whatever city they were going to, based on the type of food, atmosphere, and wine they preferred. Trevor said, "My business is a Hedonist business. It is for people who enjoy the pleasures of life and have the ability to pay for them. The Hedonist in the house of money, which is a great partnership, tells me that my success will be enhanced if I cater to the right audience. I should emphasize pleasure and indulging the self when I finally have the site created."

Trevor felt the electricity of guidance kick in when he read this house. "This idea makes me feel that I have yet to come near all of the possibilities that lie beneath the surface of my e-commerce idea," he said. For those reasons, Trevor felt that the phrase "Pleasure and gain" contained the key ideas he had to keep in mind in relationship to this house.

Ninth House: Spirituality: Wounded Child

Trevor felt his Child was wounded by abuse that he had suffered early in his life. He also thought of God as a Trickster or bully who kicks down your sand castle. For him God and money were incompatible, and he could not associate earning a living with remaining spiritually clean. He realized that he had a great deal of thinking to do about the depth of this psychic wound, lest he end up sabotaging his efforts because of an unconscious fear that his desire for success was evil. Toward that goal Trevor created the guide phrase "Spiritually rich." Whenever he felt himself slipping into this particular fear pattern in the future, he intended to focus on this phrase and what it represented symbolically. Simultaneously he would invite his shadow associations with God and money to surface into his conscious mind so that he could take whatever steps were necessary to heal that wound, including seeing a therapist.

Tenth House: Highest Potential: Networker

The Networker is a contemporary archetype that, as noted earlier, is related to the Messenger or Herald, which can be traced back to the deity Mercury or Hermes. Trevor was thrilled that his Networker archetype was matched with his highest potential. Applied to his financial and business concerns, this archetype and house partnership symbolized the possibility, if not probability, of success. His future rested on his ability to trust his own vision and believe in himself, but the one archetype that represented his computer self now also represented his highest potential. In support of his highest potential, Trevor created the mantra "One in wine," which represented his vision of eventually being able to have business connections around the planet.

Eleventh House: Relationship to the World: Saboteur

Trevor wanted to make the Saboteur as much an ally in his business as his Victim archetype. He wanted to visualize his business as being able to compete and succeed with all the other e-commerce sites that were being started all over the world. Given the speed of e-commerce businesses and how many people get the same idea, he was aware that he needed to act on his inspiration as soon as possible. He decided on "Now" as his mantra.

Twelfth House: The Unconscious: Prostitute

The Prostitute represented Trevor's fear of money and its capacity to control and own him. He was afraid that wealth would be stronger than his character and that once the ball of success started rolling, he could not count on himself to act ethically. As Trevor considered under what circumstances he could be bought, he said, "It has not been difficult for me to maintain my values so far, but then, I've never had to fight to keep alive something that I have created. I think I am very much afraid of the Prostitute inside of me, and that my business has what it takes to make that part come out in me."

This house represented the beginning point of the work Trevor needed to do as a result of his initial question. He had to come to terms with his personal sense of honor, and he felt very deeply that once he connected with that, moving forward with his business venture would naturally unfold. For those reasons Trevor chose "Honor code" as his key phrase.

As a consequence of casting this Wheel, Trevor was able to reorganize his whole approach to business. He realized that his ambitions were going to manifest only if he believed in himself, but he also decided to challenge his determination that his plans should unfold exactly as he intended. His method of employing his commitments began with choosing three investors and arranging to meet them as soon as possible. "I am going to present my business plans to these three entrepreneurs," he said. "I recognized in doing this exercise that whether I arranged a meeting next week or next month would not really matter, because I would be just as nervous then as I am now. Ultimately there comes the moment when you just have to move on your dreams."

And with his twelve mantras now written on a single index card in his wallet, that's exactly what he did.

Fay's Story: Health and Healing

Illness can sometimes serve as a "time out" from our commitments in life, a chance to regroup and reevaluate where we are headed. Now forty-six, Fay had dedicated her life to environmental causes since graduating from college at age twenty-one. Although Fay loved her work as an administrator for a major nonprofit environmental organization and felt that it was beneficial to the world community, she went about her job in a military fashion. She hated the people who hurt the environment and wanted to destroy them on almost a physical level. Nobody else in the organization shared or endorsed Fay's fanaticism, and this lack of recognition by her peers added to her frustration. She felt that she never accomplished enough in defense of the environment, and that she had somehow failed to inspire her co-workers to rise to her pitch of fury.

Over the last twelve years of her life, Fay had also suffered from crippling depression and chronic fatigue syndrome. The combination of these two disorders left her unable to stay employed for more than two years at a time, and at one point she went on disability for nine months. Fay's uncompromising, militaristic attitude and her frustration with her colleagues clearly had contributed to her depression and the physical maladies that derived from it.

Fay had been on medication since her depressions began. Her health disorders also led to the dissolution of her marriage and difficulties with several family members, who she said withdrew from her because they felt that she was looking for caretakers, and they did not want to be responsible for supporting her. Now Fay wanted to get off her medication and find an alternative method for coping with her depression. She also wanted to heal from chronic fatigue but believed that her depression was the underlying reason for her exhaustion. Years of therapy had made her suspicious of conventional self-examination, yet she was willing to cast a working chart. Her aim was to gain insights into the root cause of her depression and into how to proceed with her healing process.

Fay needed to ask herself if she saw any benefits to remaining ill. Many people unconsciously build their lifestyles around their illness, and as a result the prospect of healing holds the same threat as the prospect of symbolically losing their home. In becoming comfortable with pain, in effect, you take up residence in a pill bottle.

As with Trevor and Karl, Fay's answers sometimes seem to contradict each other, but the relationship of intention to those contradictions alerts you to an important energy. Fay's open frame of mind helped her enormously in constructing an overview of her illness that incorporated her work and her background, her strengths and her fears. Her chart is shown in Figure 12.

First House: Ego and Personality: Servant

Fay interpreted the Servant in her first house as symbolic of the fact that, because she was passionately involved with healing the environment, she had to wear the illness of the environment on her person. In interpreting her chart she recognized her belief that, had she given the impression of being buoyant and attractive, no one would

FIGURE 12: FAY'S HEALTH CHART

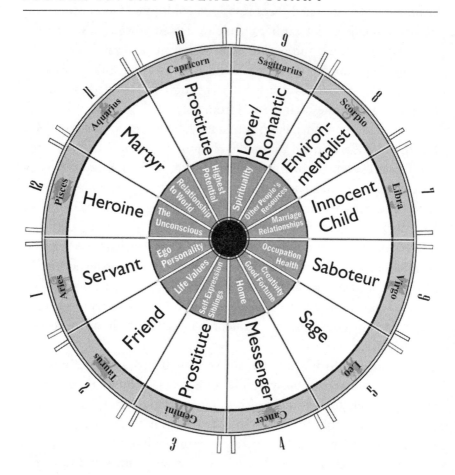

take her commitment to her work seriously. "I think I was afraid to appear too glamorous, because glamour and nature do not go together. I had to look intense and committed to educating people on how toxic the world was becoming." Fay said that she would have to rethink her self-image as it related to her work. She chose the phrase "Nature is beautiful" as her reminder.

Second House: Life Values: Friend

"The association that immediately comes to mind with my Friend archetype and my health experience," said Fay, "is that I have always believed that my spirit was my best friend but my body served little role in enhancing my relationships. I am a good friend to people. I am a good listener, and I am loyal and trustworthy and always ready to support my friends." Having said that, Fay admitted that she had not treated her body and spirit in the same way in recent years. "I feel that my body somehow has betrayed me. It has become a toxic environment, and I am angry with it." In response to that realization, Fay chose "Respect this friend" as her key phrase for the second house.

Third House: Self-Expression and Siblings: Prostitute

The Prostitute in Fay's house of self-expression represented anger. Fay's motivation to join the environmental movement was the anger she felt toward large corporations, industry, and society that turned a blind eye to the destruction of nature for the sake of profit. "Righteous anger was healthy anger to me back then. I felt immune to the consequences of this anger because it was expressed on behalf of a worthy cause. But obviously no anger is healthy, nor is it inspiring." Fay had come to this realization long before this chart, but upon seeing the Prostitute on this house she commented that she had never ceased to feel that way toward the industrial world. "I think I have a lot to heal in this house," she said, and toward that goal Fay chose "Release" as her mantra.

Fourth House: Home: Messenger

"This illness has kept me at home," said Fay, "and given this archetype, I need to find the message not just in the illness but in my having to stay at home as well." In our discussion of that point, Fay said that she would have to give thought as to how she was spending her time at home. "When you are in depression and have chronic fatigue, you just sit around all day, and in time feeling sorry for yourself becomes natural. My husband was great at helping me in the beginning, but then I started to reconcile myself to the idea that this exhausted state was going to be permanent. That's when our relationship started to disintegrate."

Fay said that she would make a positive effort to use her time at home as productively as possible. "The biggest obstacle for me has been that staying at home made me feel useless. Unless I was out in the field, I was unable to do anything of value." The Messenger on this house inspired Fay to think about finding alternative ways of communicating her work from where she was. "Just the thought of going back to work again, of finding that I can do something of value that continues my work from my home, makes me feel alive again." Fay took her key phrase for this house from the song in the movie *Snow White*, "Heigh-ho, heigh-ho, it's home from work we go," saying that introducing humor into her attitude would not be a bad idea.

Fifth House: Creativity and Good Fortune: Sage

Fay was strongly drawn to the Sage archetype. She had an obvious love for the wisdom of great thinkers and felt spiritually nurtured by their insights. "My association with the Sage in this house is that I need to make wiser choices about how I have been living and how sincerely I have been working to heal. I have to give some serious thought to how honest I am with myself." Fay said that, because she felt that she was "on the right side of the right cause," she was never wrong about her beliefs and judgments of others. In looking at the significance of this house, Fay said, "I have fallen out of touch with loving life. I am living on what's left from yesterday. I need to have a love affair with life again." In support of her Sage archetype, Fay chose "Love" as her mantra.

Sixth House: Occupation and Health: Saboteur

Fay took her time coming up with a response for this archetype in her sixth house. Finally she said, "I think that I have been sabotaging my healing because I want people to acknowledge how much I have put into my work. It's not easy to produce your accomplishments for people. I can tell them I've given a talk here and there, but that doesn't mean much to anyone." This particular archetypal connection was like a depth charge, causing Fay to think about whether she was trying to make some of her friends and family, as well as her ex-husband, feel guilty for not having taken her more seriously. Therefore she chose "Be honest, be wise" as her guiding mantra.

Seventh House: Marriage and Relationships: Innocent Child

Fay focused on partnership and specifically that she was in a partnership with her illness. This interpretation allowed her to change the terms of the partnership, indeed to break it off entirely. "I am realizing that we become intimately involved with our illness. We refer to it as 'my' illness, giving it a very personal status in our life. Dissolving this partnership represents my becoming impersonal and distant, withdrawing my emotions from this experience, and the very thought of that is empowering." Since Fay's goal was now to end her relationship with her illness, "Divorce" became her seventh-house mantra.

Eighth House: Other People's Resources: Environmentalist

The Environmentalist archetype is a modern extension of the Steward, who in ancient times was charged with protecting and conserving an estate. Native Americans and other indigenous peoples have expanded that concept to cover the entire natural environment in which they live, and today environmentalists apply the same sense to the earth as a whole. The Environmentalist in her eighth house inspired Fay to consider opening herself to her friends and to the suggestions and help they had offered her in the past few years that she had turned down. "I lost my belief that anything could make a difference," she said, "which is why I finally gave in to conventional medication. This was a very difficult decision for me, because using drugs represented everything that I have worked against. But I had gotten to the point where I felt that I didn't have much choice." Fay said that in addition to reconnecting with her friends' loving advice, she would once again investigate the resources in the field of alternative health. She wanted to remain, in the phrase that made up her eighth-house mantra, "Wide open."

Ninth House: Spirituality: Lover/Romantic

Fay was drawn to the Lover/Romantic archetype because being romantic balanced her Environmentalist. "I would have told someone in my situation that no matter what you have to go through, you need love to heal, because that's the way of the spirit," she said by way of interpreting this archetype in this house. "I need to return to that truth." And as a way of connecting this archetype with her spiritual impulses, she chose "God is love" as her guide for this house.

Tenth House: Highest Potential: Prostitute

Fay showed great imagination with her interpretation of this archetype. "I think that I will compromise my highest potential if I don't make a conscious effort to heal my attitudes and climb out of my reservoir of self-pity. I will have sold out my dreams and ambitions, because the outcomes I had anticipated when I was younger did not happen as soon or as dramatically as I wanted them to happen." Fay also needed to rethink the meaning of her highest potential. Basing its definition only on what she did for a living, she realized, was "not good enough and not God enough. A job is my ego's highest potential. I don't know what my soul's is, but I think I need to let go of my definition of highest potential and see what unfolds." For her guiding mantra, Fay chose "Emptiness," because it reminded her to clear out any negative thoughts or feelings immediately.

Eleventh House: Relationship to the World: Martyr

"Well, well," Fay said as we discussed her Martyr. "Who would've thought I would see the world through the eyes of a Martyr?" She laughed and said it was almost too obvious. "I always associated martyrs with causes. Where there was a worthy cause, there had to be a mighty martyr, or what else could possibly sustain the cause?" Fay said that she chose the image because *she* saw the *world* as a suffering, ill being, then paused and added, "I think that somewhere in me is the belief that I have to suffer for this cause. This archetype goes along with my belief that you have to look like an earthy environmentalist in order to be taken seriously. I could never show up at a rally in heels and makeup. I went in sandals and a T-shirt." Fay said that her key phrase for healing this part of her psyche would be "No need," as in, *No need to be a martyr just to help the cause.*

Twelfth House: The Unconscious: Heroine

Fay chose the Heroine as one of her archetypes because she always wanted to champion a cause. As a child she used to fantasize a great deal about who she would like to be and what it would feel like to be so able and sure of herself. "I think that I need this type of recognition more than I care to admit," she said. "I have to give some thought to how much of my depression might be connected to my feeling that I have failed as a Heroine. I have not succeeded in championing a cause, and I am not well known for my work. Even as I say this, I can feel the dark weight that fills my mind at night when I think about the fact that I've spent another day of my life doing nothing. This could be the failure that began my cycle with depression." Fay chose the phrase "Guide me" for this house, because releasing her own plans and ambitions into the hands of Heaven felt like the most powerful act she could do in support of her healing and her life.

As a result of this chart work, Fay decided to return to work, beginning with what she could do while she was home. She realized that she had lost her passion not just for doing her work but for everything. "I have to work at believing that everything a person does to help a cause is a positive contribution," she concluded. "I think I am going to make my spiritual path the study of the invisible self. This exercise has made me consider that perhaps I have been sabotaging my healing process out of anger at lack of recognition of my efforts, though I am not going to say that is the whole cause. But I do realize now that my attitude has not been an asset to my recovery."

The Choice Is Yours

Using these working charts to establish a system of guidance helps you explore your life through the symbolic realm. Interpreting archetypal information is like putting on a pair of glasses that brings everything into focus, allowing you to recognize your opportunities, your higher potential, and your mission. This clarity does not in itself provide courage. The choice to take action or not is always yours. You may or may not want to remind yourself of the archetypal significance of why a relationship ended or why you struggle with self-esteem. Still, you now have the option: you can cast a working chart. You can open yourself to inner guidance. The choice is yours, and everything in life ultimately comes down to choice.

CHAPTER II

Healing Challenges of the Archetypal Wheel

In the last three chapters you've learned to cast and interpret your Chart of Origin for an overview of your life, and to cast working charts for guidance on specific current issues. In our final chapter you'll consolidate both sets of skills in learning how to seek guidance about the root causes and attitudinal dynamics affecting an illness or ailment, or a psychological or emotional difficulty or condition. While this information will not be a medical diagnosis and is not meant to replace one, it can help you begin your search for ways to heal.

Our physical well-being is clearly influenced by our psyche. As a medical intuitive, I have often observed the links between certain psychological stress patterns and certain illnesses related to specific areas of the body. Emotional "heartache" usually affects the heart itself, for instance; financial stress or the feeling that you lack support in what you do often hits you in the lower back; and the pancreas is especially sensitive to issues related to responsibility. At their root many physical and mental ailments also represent an inability to respond appropriately to a challenge to one's personal power. Once you understand the connection between these power challenges and the resulting health challenges, you gain valuable insights into the energy causes of your ailment. As you explore the connections between specific ailments and their energy basis, you can use your knowledge of the archetypes and the Archetypal Wheel to devise healing strategies.

Since archetypes reside in the psyche, reviewing which of your personal archetypal companions may be involved in a specific health challenge can help you find clues to healing it. Simply knowing that a particular archetype is involved in your illness or ailment will give you some measure of comfort, just as reading a story or myth that describes the same journey that you are on gives you a model to guide your own life. People who lose everything in a catastrophe, for example, are experiencing the Death and Rebirth archetype. Perhaps their lives have been burned to cinders in order for them to rise Phoenix-like from the ashes. If they can recognize that they are in that pattern, they can take comfort in the stories of Osiris, Job, and Jesus, whose experiences with death and rebirth became the core of their identities. The resurrection story of Jesus gave birth to Christianity. Job's loss of all his earthly possessions, including his wife and family, portrays the archetype of Death as a force that can sweep through one's life and take with it all that is familiar. The myth of Osiris, one of the most significant and revered deities of ancient Egypt, shows the cycle of death and resurrection going back almost five thousand years. All these stories embody the need to die—either physically or to the things of this world—in order to be reborn in a higher state.

These archetypal stories, which are also archetypal promises—Contracts, in fact—hold the system of life together. They also offer us an opportunity to heal, if we can become alert to their presence within us and find a way to connect them to a physical ailment. At first, however, it may not be apparent just which of your archetypes is involved in a health challenge, so you will need to narrow the field.

The Alchemy of Timeless Healing

Change takes but an instant," goes the old Hebrew proverb. "It's the resistance to change that can take a lifetime." Within the energy fields of your mind, heart, and willpower, you can transform the lead of physical matter—the dense energy content of your memories, history, attitudes, beliefs, and life experiences—into gold. Just as the alchemists of old sought to find the touchstone that would allow them to convert base metals into precious metals, you can use your understanding of archetypal influences to plumb the deeper meaning and purpose of the events of your physical life. Forgiveness, for example, melts the "lead" of painful memories into the "gold" of understanding. Conversely, knowing that you should forgive, but choosing not to, adds lead to your psyche and spirit, which eventually accumulates dead weight in the cell tissue. Lead is any form of unfinished business, such as hatred, bitterness, unrequited love, or regret, that contributes harm to your body as well as to your spirit. The more unfinished business, or history, you have, the heavier your lead will be.

The energy weight of our history affects the density of our biology. Heavy cell memories act like lead to slow down the speed with which healthy cell processes normally work, increasing the potential for the development of illness. The way I express this rule is: *weight = wait.* All your psychic, emotional, and mental unfinished business adds to the density of the weight that you carry in your energy field. And the more weight you carry, the longer you have to wait for change to occur in your life, which could mean that you are inadvertently delaying an opportunity or even your own recovery from an illness.

One of the most graphic descriptions of what it feels like to be dragging our leaden past around with us appears in Charles Dickens's *A Christmas Carol.* In that familiar story Ebenezer Scrooge receives an ominous warning on Christmas Eve that he must change his ways or else. Scrooge's nightmare begins when he is visited by the ghost of his former partner, Jacob Marley, who is dragging behind him a great length of heavy fetters. Scrooge asks him about them. "I wear the chain I forged in life," the ghost replies.

> "I made it link by link, and yard by yard; I girded it on of
> my own free will, and of my own free will I wore it. Is its
> pattern strange to you?"
>
> Scrooge trembled more and more. "Or would you
> know," pursued the Ghost, "the weight and length of the
> strong coil you bear yourself? It was full as heavy and as long
> as this, seven Christmas Eves ago. You have labored on it,
> since. It is a ponderous chain!"

Marley had presumably forged his chain through the lack of generosity and compassion he shared with his partner, Scrooge, just as we forge our own chains of history link by link every time we choose to stay in the first column and create more lead. What Marley is offering Scrooge is nothing less than the chance to transmute his lead into gold. Dickens's story is itself an archetypal narrative of self-transformation from the Miser to the Divine Child. After Scrooge has his awakening experience with Marley's ghost, he goes into his inner laboratory, where he is visited by the spirits of Christmas Past, Present, and Future. They show him where he went wrong, how he got to where he is today, what will happen if he doesn't melt the lead of his past into gold, and the good things that can happen if he does. The spirits take Scrooge into transcendent time, where linear chronology is suspended and he is able to live past, present, and future in one extended, timeless moment. Having learned his lesson (for which he rightly declares his undying gratitude to the departed Marley), Scrooge says, "I will honor Christmas in my heart, and try to keep it all the year. I will live in the Past, the Present, and the Future. The Spirits of all Three shall strive within me. I will not shut out the lessons that they teach."

When Scrooge awakens from his "dream," it is Christmas Day. "I haven't missed it," he declares with Child-like joy. "The Spirits have done it all in one night. They can do anything they like!"

Indeed, they can. Pity the mortal that doesn't believe in such miracles.

Our own work resembles Scrooge's task: to stop creating more lead in the present and begin converting the lead we already carry into gold. Having recognized this rule, it is easier to understand, for example, why energy medicine and treatments sometimes have limited effects on illnesses. Energy medicine is a timeless method of healing. Its effectiveness in massage, aromatherapy, or acupuncture comes from activating or freeing blocked energy that has accrued over time. These healing methods seek to break down heavy energy from the past to facilitate the flow of current energy. By healing and releasing negative attitudes and beliefs and traumatic memories that are pulling your energy into the past, you return that energy into present time, where it enhances the vibration of your entire system. The more you remain in present time, the higher the frequency you attain on the scale of present-time consciousness. In that process your energy field plugs into cosmic electricity. When you are in present time, perfumes are transformed into healing scents through aromatherapy; massage becomes a discharge of cell memory through touch; forgiveness transforms the poisons of anger and resentment. The speed of your healing is increased, and any restrictions that the tribal mind has determined for an illness—such as that it takes six months to heal from one disease and five years from another—no longer apply. You have removed the weight of history, and with it the length of time you need to wait for results.

Yet to enter a timeless state, we have to surrender our will to the Divine and live according to that choice. Consider, for instance, the life of Jesus, the master most closely associated with acts of instantaneous healing. Jesus often admonished those who asked him for help to have faith and, in effect, to come into present time. For instance, the Gospels tell the story of a woman who had been suffering with a hemorrhage for twelve years (Mark 5:25–34). "She had suffered a great deal under the care of many doctors and had spent all she had, yet instead of getting better she grew worse." Sound familiar? But when she hears that Jesus will be passing by, she thinks, "If I can just touch his clothes, I shall be healed." The moment she makes contact with the hem of Jesus' garment, her hemorrhage dries up, and she feels completely cured. When Jesus senses that his energy field has been tapped, he asks who has touched him, and the woman confesses. "My daughter, your faith has returned you to health," he says. "Go in peace and be freed from your suffering."

In another instance Jesus is approached by the Jewish friends of a Roman centurion whose servant is near death (Luke 7:1–10). They explain that this Roman is sympathetic to their beliefs and ask in his behalf that Jesus go to heal his favorite servant. Before Jesus even arrives at his home, however, the centurion sends word that Jesus need not make the journey but can heal his servant simply by willing to. Jesus is astonished at the man's level of faith. "I tell you," he says, "not even in Israel have I found faith as great as this." And he then heals the man's servant at a distance.

Accounts of Jesus' healings show an intimate relationship between one's ability to receive a timeless healing and one's ability to release the linear, time-based world. They show how we can move from the first column of physical reality into the third or symbolic column, gaining insights that we then work with in our inner laboratory—transforming lead into gold. But we have to be willing to live according to the mysteries of timeless laws, to serve the spirit first, to give up the temporal perceptions of the first three chakras of physical survival. Jesus' surrender to the will of the Divine is apparent in the manner in which he constantly accepted what needed to happen next. In the garden of Gethsemane, as we saw, although he asked God to release him from what he saw coming, in the next breath he also accepted God's will. When he was brought before Pontius Pilate, the most powerful man in Judea urged Jesus to defend himself, saying, "Don't you realize that your life is in my hands?" Jesus knew that Pilate actually had no power at all but was acting unconsciously under Contract to fulfill his role by condemning Jesus. The life of Jesus was no more in Pilate's hands than was the power to make the Jews love Rome. But Jesus did not resist or argue against his divinely ordained destiny.

Cases abound of timeless healings and spontaneous remissions, sometimes referred to as miracles. In each instance what preceded the healing was a decision to release, to forgive, to agree to change, and in general to accept a different path for one's life. I have never heard of a timeless intervention after which the person returned to the same temporal life. People who have made timeless choices radiate that energy, or charism, drawing others into their field of divine protection, of faith made manifest.

Every one of your Contractual agreements is a temporal experience that contains a timeless potential. You can count on everything you do and every one of your relationships to become, at some point, uncontrollable. That is the point at which you would be wise to separate from your first-column perceptions and, as I tell people in my workshops, imagine yourself running up to your third column to focus into a timeless reality. You need to see whatever circumstance you are in as outside of time and space, as an archetypal story with a theme, characters, and lesson, and as an opportunity for you to surrender to the Divine in some way. Every act of surrender earns a timeless intervention: time is lessened and timelessness is increased in your energy field. Thought comes into form more rapidly when you are not dragging linear, chronological history, or time, in your energy field like Marley's chains. Your energy is increased, your aging slows, and your body creates health. This is pure divine mathematics.

Your Chart of Origin and Your Spiritual DNA: Lessons of Power and Health

Your Chart of Origin provides a profile of your spiritual DNA. By comparing your archetypes and their companion houses, you learn your spiritual strengths and vulnerabilities and their influence on your physical, emotional, and psychological energy systems. Each house of the Archetypal Wheel corresponds to certain tests of self-empowerment that manifest throughout your life. How you interact with the power challenges inherent in each house has a substantial effect on the quality of your health. Healing challenges are not only emotional, psychological, and physical vulnerabilities but also the stress that comes from not pursuing your talents or not opening up emotionally to the people who mean the most to you, allowing key relationships to disintegrate.

Healing challenges will help you to consolidate the fragments of your psyche, because clearing these hurdles demands that you gather the inner resources most vulnerable to those challenges. There is no simple one-to-one equation of an archetype to a specific disease, yet each house on your Archetypal Wheel has an area of "energy vulnerability" that corresponds to its specific challenges, a region of the body that is most susceptible to power imbalances in a particular house.

These vulnerabilities can make you susceptible to a range of physical ailments and psychological and emotional conditions. In the outline that follows, you will find a healing challenge for each house on the Archetypal Wheel, along with its corresponding area of energy vulnerability and the potential illnesses that may result. That an illness is listed for a particular house by no means implies that you will develop it if you have prolonged difficulty with its specific challenge.

It does, however, suggest a physical, mental, or emotional manifestation of the relationship between issues of power and your biological makeup. These illnesses are a representative sample rather than a complete listing.

Each challenge concludes with suggestions for healing appropriate to that house. These are merely examples of many potential healing strategies. By working with your symbolic understanding of the root causes of a particular energy vulnerability, you can come up with strategies of your own. The healing process has three steps:

1. Begin by consulting the listing of energy vulnerabilities and potential illnesses for each of the twelve houses on the Archetypal Wheel. These are the same for everyone. Determine which house most closely corresponds to the ailment you are seeking to heal.

2. Consult your Chart of Origin to find which of your twelve archetypal companions resides in that house. Using your intuition and imagination, combined with the insights you have already gained through interpreting your Chart of Origin, look for ways in which that archetype may be related to the root causes of your illness. Remember that when consulting your Chart of Origin, you are receiving guidance about a lifelong pattern rather than one specific, recent event or relationship.

Let's say, for example, that you are seeking healing guidance for colon cancer, which is a potential illness of the seventh house. Say the Actor is in the seventh house of your Chart of Origin. Many of the people I've read who have colon cancer have a driving need to control other people or their own lives, and so their relationships to others tend to have a controlling aspect to them. The seventh house rules one-on-one relationships, including marriage and business partnerships. Having the Actor in that house indicates that in your encounters with others you may present contrived rather than genuine emotion, perhaps based on your need to control them. Becoming aware of that pattern and taking steps to release your need to control others, especially through duplicity, would then be a good first step in your healing process.

3. Once you have learned as much as you can from your Archetypal Wheel, you can cast a working chart (called a "healing chart") to seek guidance about the psychological, emotional, and energy aspects

ment. Follow the directions in Chapter 10 for casting a
chart, using your same twelve archetypes, and phrase your
n like this: "I am seeking insight into the energies that are
g stress in my present life, and guidance for healing that stress."
(Once again, never ask for a *diagnosis* or *prognosis* of your ailment.) As
you cast your healing chart, most of the archetypes will relocate in
different houses, and you can then interpret the meaning of each
archetype within the power challenge of that house.

Continuing with the previous example, let's say that in your healing chart the Victim falls into your seventh house. You might begin by
asking yourself if you feel victimized by a marriage or business partner. Explore your need to control and compete with others as a result
of feeling like a victim. Learning to trust your Victim archetype as a
guardian that will alert you to the danger of actually being victimized
allows you to release your need for such obsessive control.

First-House Challenge: Birthing the Self

Energy vulnerability:
Skeletal system, spine, joints, autoimmune system, and skin
Potential illnesses:
Chronic pain, eczema, multiple sclerosis, Crohn's disease, and lupus

Throughout your life you will confront circumstances that cause
you to separate from the group mind. It is essential that you give birth
to your power of choice and personal responsibility. Without this separation, you will not gain access to your individual inner strength,
self-esteem, and gut instinct. You can certainly develop self-esteem
and strength living within a family unit, but "birthing the self" means
having the strength to follow the mature guidance that directs you to
begin your personal spiritual path. You are making the transition from
group consciousness to individual consciousness, thereby opening the
way for the higher potential of your Contract to reveal itself.

The first house rules the entire "self" or personality, and so its
health challenges involve the entire framework of the body. Although
all illnesses affect the body as a whole, immune disorders, structural
ailments, and skin diseases symbolically represent how safe you feel in
the "body" of your life and personality. Because birthing the self

requires breaking away from the family and developing self-esteem, it is influenced by both the first and third chakras.

Healing Guidance: Keep your attention in present time, and do not allow your vital life-force to slip into your history. Can you identify limiting and negative attitudes that you have inherited from your family or the social mind? Which of these specifically do not support your healing, such as "Cancer runs in my family"? Recast these in ways that are more positive and expansive—for instance, "My health is independent of my family history." Traditional forms of therapy can assist you, but I encourage you to seek out a therapist who is trained in archetypal traditions, such as a Jungian.

Second-House Challenge: Claiming of Values

Energy vulnerability:
Lower back, hips, and sexual organs
Potential illnesses:
Impotence, sciatica, ovarian or prostate cancer, lower back pain, slipped disk, endometriosis

Challenges to your sense of values make you aware of the polarity between your external and internal values, and between a choice and its consequences. Examine your ethics and morals, as well as your motivations and private agendas regarding your interactions with others, because these properties form your character and conscience. Then evaluate how you have ordered your values. Do you value material gain over generosity? Do you make your decisions based on your fears or on your faith? Are you able to follow intuitive guidance?

The illnesses associated with the second house are in energy alignment with the issues of the second chakra, which are connected to external expressions of power inherent in money, status, and sex. The struggle to maintain balance in a world in which values are continually tested generates survival-related stress that is connected primarily to the foundational area of the body. And so lower back pain, sciatica, or cancers of the genital area may be linked to your relationship with what you hold as having power.

Healing Guidance: Review the values by which you have been living. Where is your lifestyle incongruent with your inner self? It is vitally important to know the content, boundaries, and character of your conscience. Can you admit, if only to yourself, the standard by which you make your decisions? A spiritual director or a therapist skilled in personal development can be very helpful in this process of inner work, as can reading books and other material directed toward self-empowerment.

Choose one area in which you have a conflict that continually disempowers you. This could be a relationship with another person or even with yourself, for instance if you continually judge or second-guess yourself. Every time you become aware of feeling a loss of power, pause and remind yourself that you are now experiencing the power of a negative perception and not a reality. Then replace that perception with a positive thought, and continually refer to that thought as a marker. As you repeat the perception, use deep breathing to absorb it into your body and cell tissue. As with all shifts in consciousness, steady work is required to replace the old with the new.

Third-House Challenge: Facing the Fear of Truth and the Seduction of Deceit

Energy vulnerability:
Solar plexus, intestines, throat, thyroid, esophagus, and sinus cavities

Potential illnesses:
Ulcers, over- or underactive thyroid, laryngitis, chronic sinus problems

You explore the power of truth and deceit through your relationships, and the third house rules communication and the expression of who you are, including your honor and integrity and your ability to give and keep your word—an extension of your second-house values. Symbolically, giving your word means committing your energy to a process of creation, and the promise to keep someone's secret is a commitment to contain a thought within you on their behalf. Breaking such an agreement is an act of deceit.

Empowerment demands that we become strong enough to seek truth rather than run away from it. We prevent truth from entering our psyche through acts of deceit, such as denying how we feel or creating excuses for our disempowering actions. We also seduce or deceive others to protect ourselves from learning too much about ourselves too soon. For example, blaming someone else for the consequences of your own actions allows you to deflect your personal responsibilities for those consequences.

The potential illnesses of the third house are symbolic of how we represent ourselves through communication, honor, and integrity, which are related to our sense of self-esteem and personal power. If you lack these inner strengths, you are unable to protect your personal boundaries, and your solar plexus will be vulnerable to illness—just as it would be vulnerable to a punch or kick if you were unable to defend yourself physically. As a result, stress disorders such as ulcers and digestive ailments may develop. These areas of vulnerability correspond roughly to the third and fifth chakras (the solar plexus and throat, respectively), which regulate self-esteem and how you express that to other people.

Healing Guidance: This challenge demands that you review your moral and ethical codes of action, along with your ways of intellectualizing and rationalizing your behavior. Do you keep tabs on what others have done to you? Ask yourself what you have done to deceive others by breaking your word and other acts of dishonor. Make a list of your actions that fall into this category, and next to each experience write down how and why you rationalize your behavior in that instance. How do you imagine the other person involved perceived you? Write down your answer. Finally, how would you act in the same situation if given another chance? You may want to call on a spiritual director or someone who is skilled at objective listening to help you with this self-examination.

Fourth-House Challenge: Developing Loyalty and Coping with Betrayal

Energy vulnerability:
Respiratory, circulatory, lymph, and central nervous systems
Potential illnesses:
Asthma, allergies, and nervous disorders

Acts of betrayal are meant to teach us that we cannot control life according to our fears. We need to "fail" at creating a perfectly safe and controlled world for ourselves, because experiences of betrayal and/or failure are the means through which we are forced to examine the limits of our dependence on the rational order of the physical world. Although acts of betrayal can be excruciatingly painful to both the betrayed and the betrayer, the spiritual reason for these experiences is to get us to examine why we compulsively seek to maintain human order and gain physical power while mistrusting "divine chaos."

The illnesses associated with this house reflect a level of emotional stress that is panic-driven. If this is your challenge, then anxiety at extending control over everything that represents physical order and survival often captures the majority of your energy. This stress frequently settles in your nervous and circulatory systems because survival issues consume so much of your emotional and mental energies. Loyalty and betrayal are powerfully emotional issues that are also linked to survival. Because your home is both your link to your family and the seat of your emotional life, this house resonates with both first- and fourth-chakra energies.

Healing Guidance: Clear out your inner self, just as you might flush out your respiratory or circulatory system. What can you change about your daily routine that will nudge you to realign your priorities? If possible, go on a retreat, even just for a weekend. Alternatively, go on a cleansing diet accompanied by a daily practice of yoga and breath work. You may choose to seek professional help through yoga workshops or classes, but even incorporating five minutes of deep breathing every few hours, or as soon as you recognize that your body is entering into an anxiety zone, can immediately counteract the anxiety in your nervous system.

Fifth-House Challenge: Entering the Desert

Energy vulnerability:
Mental energy, intuition, creativity
Potential illnesses:
Physical and emotional fatigue, depression

The energy challenge of this house descends when your creative juices dry up and what once came so easily to you—whether in romance, the creative arts, or spiritual endeavors—now seems all but inaccessible. Part of the challenge of enduring the classic Dark Night of the Soul described by mystics, for example, is that you are no longer receiving energy from the world you have left behind, but you also have not yet established a flow of energy from the next stage of your life. That period of aridity—the desert—can be exhausting and depressing as you symbolically thirst for God. This challenge corresponds to the sixth chakra, the seat of the intellect and imagination. Its healing challenges may arise from an imbalance between rational and intuitive thought.

Healing Guidance: This challenge sets you up against the force of your willpower, making you aware of how much genuine authority you have to take charge of your own actions. Do you often feel as if you have no power over how you respond to crises? Are you often tempted to become passive and depressed in these situations? To counter those tendencies and generate new currents of energy in your psyche and body, get involved in something that is out of character for you. Initiate an exercise program, read books that open up a new area of interest, travel, or take up a new hobby.

Sixth-House Challenge: Establishing Self-Worth

Energy vulnerability:

Cardiovascular system, eyesight, hearing, taste

Potential illnesses:

Heart attack, cataracts, tinnitus

An essential step to establishing self-worth is to become someone who does not need the approval of others to feel good about him- or herself. Experiences of rejection accompany this challenge, because we all start off in life being taught how to please others and receiving negative feedback when their expectations are not met. Because this challenge of empowerment has to do with your occupation and values, it corresponds to the second chakra.

The sixth house rules occupation and physical health, a partnership of forces that assumes that we connect our self-worth to what we do, and that often leads us to value what we do above who we are. You must embrace the value of the Contracts to which you agreed, regardless of the fact that you know so little about their true value. Learn to let go of the negative practice of disliking, disapproving, or diminishing the value of your life.

We suffer deeply when we or the people we love are rejected or hurt by others, and the stress of that rejection strikes at the heart. The cardiovascular system and the five senses are especially sensitive to the stress generated by sixth-house experiences precisely because these are primarily emotional concerns.

Healing Guidance: You need to empower yourself by carrying out personal actions that make you feel good about yourself. Have you been eating or drinking too much, or watching too much television? Have you been pushing yourself too hard at work, or giving in to your anger? Changing those habits can have a positive effect on your self-esteem. Choose three habits that you know are limiting and have been a source of stress for you, and make a concentrated effort to break their hold over your psyche.

Seventh-House Challenge: Maintaining Personal Boundaries

Energy vulnerability:

Solar plexus, pancreas, colon and intestines, sexual organs, intuition

Potential illnesses:

Colon and intestinal disease, spleen and liver disorder, diabetes, obesity, and alcoholism

Your personal boundaries are the rules you choose for interacting with the power of other people. As infants, we have few boundaries, and in our early years we tend to remain within the mind-set of the family. As our passion grows stronger to experience life as individuals, we need to become strong enough to maintain our individuality and chart a spiritual course. The seventh house rules relationships, within which you encounter the emotional, psychological, and physical violation of your personal boundaries, just as you will violate others'.

Learning to define your boundaries is a natural stage in the process of self-empowerment. Without this awareness you run the risk of becoming co-dependent and incapable of engaging in healthy interactions. You become vulnerable to compromising yourself in any number of ways, from seeming to agree with people when you really don't to remaining in relationships that you know are not healthy.

The seventh house rules partnerships and marriage, and this combination of values and love resonates with the energies of the second and fourth chakras.

Healing Guidance: Identify the boundaries you need to feel empowered, and make a commitment to maintain at least one of them consistently. To pinpoint one boundary as your beginning step, think about where you feel most violated in interpersonal relationships. Do others make your decisions for you? If so, in what area of your life? Or do you violate the boundaries of another person in an effort to maintain your personal security? You must hold yourself as accountable for your actions as you hold others for theirs. It takes only one concerted shift in a boundary pattern to initiate an awareness that boundary maintenance is crucial to self-empowerment.

Eighth-House Challenge: Confronting Greed and Developing Personal Integrity

Energy vulnerability:

Lower back, liver, kidneys, and brain

Potential illnesses:

Migraine, disk problems, sciatica, cancer of the stomach or other central body organ, brain aneurysm

Your need for physical forms of power can involve a dispute over an inheritance, business dealings, or even lending money to friends. Through these experiences you learn which world your spirit serves, the physical or the spiritual. The illnesses associated with the eighth house reflect the mental stress generated by fear of the loss of powers tied to physical survival, such as financial savvy. The stresses listed for the second house (life values) that relate to your physical life are maximized in this house, because it represents the power values of *other* people interacting with your own. The two houses overlap in their concerns about survival, so many illnesses are common to both, but this house resonates with the energies of the second and sixth chakras.

Healing Guidance: You need to release your fear of money or the lack of it. How much authority does the financial domain have over your inner being? What causes you to feel vulnerable in the physical world? Once you recognize just one fear, evaluate how many of your decisions it motivates, and begin a daily discipline of visualizing yourself detaching from that fear. Continually hold the image of what your life would be like were you free of that fear.

Ninth-House Challenge: Enduring Faith Crises

Energy vulnerability:

The psyche

Potential illnesses:

Spiritual depression, manic depression, chronic fatigue

Questions about whether God is fair and whether we deserve what comes our way make us consider whether we have a Sacred Contract and a purpose to all that we do. The psychological and emotional dysfunctions related to the ninth house are similar to those experienced in the desert challenges of the fifth house. They reflect the soul's journey as it wavers between states of intimacy with and distance from the Divine. The emptiness that emerges from periods of spiritual isolation frequently produces deep depression and exhaustion that rarely seem to be rooted in a physical cause.

Unlike the fifth-house challenge, which is to experience the process of creation and contribute something of your own spirit to life, the ninth house corresponds to your need to pursue a spiritual life per se. Our deepest passion is to transform our physical life into a consciously spiritual journey. This passion, whether we are aware of it or not, continually directs our inner self through psychological and emotional passageways. We often feel a vague sense of meaninglessness long before we acknowledge intellectually that we are spiritually empty. Our spirit needs to feel that we have adjusted our sights so that the choice to connect all that we do to God becomes our primary focus. Because it involves our relationship with God, this house corresponds most closely to the energy of the seventh chakra.

Healing Guidance: You need to commit to a daily practice of prayer and meditation and vow to maintain it under all circumstances. How many times have you cycled through the faith-and-fear archetype? At those times how did resolution and guidance come into your life? Write your recollections in your journal, and summarize what you have learned from these repeated cycles. How has that learning changed your life? Finally, review your life, identifying what parts should now be released, and then cooperate with the process of letting go.

Tenth-House Challenge: Coping with Rejection and Failure

Energy vulnerability:

Overall physical tissue, willpower

Potential illnesses:

Skin cancer, bone marrow cancer, throat disorder or disease, eating disorder, TMJ, arthritis

The spiritual reason why you experience failure and rejection, and reject others, is that you must learn to trust in your own guidance and in the value of your Contracts. Until you release your need for approval, you will find it difficult to follow your intuition, because you will weigh the validity of your hunches according to whether others approve—and few will approve of your becoming more empowered or insightful than they are.

Tenth-house illnesses resonate with the vulnerability of pursuing one's dreams and ambitions without the support of others. The pursuit of your highest potential, whether in creative expression or in practicing compassion, is a challenge you face alone. When we compromise the spiritual expression of our contribution to life, we want to hide that truth from others. Since we do not want to be "seen" as having failed at our own lives, we symbolically wear this failure on our body—on our skin. Failing to uphold our spiritual framework can leave us vulnerable to diseases that attack our own framework, including the bone marrow. Repressing creativity can affect the throat and trigger eating disorders and TMJ. Finally, all forms of arthritis derive from the need to control change, including repressing opportunities for self-expression. Pursuing your highest potential requires willpower and engaging your spiritual perceptions, and so this house corresponds most closely to the energies of the fifth and seventh chakras.

Healing Guidance: Rejection and *failure* are the names we give to feeling disempowered. Until you can believe in yourself without the support of others, you will always be vulnerable to rejection and feeling like a failure. What makes you inclined to reject another person? The last time you rejected someone, what about that person made you feel disempowered? Identify what makes you reject others, and note how many of those reasons apply to you. Choose one characteristic, and commit to changing it.

Eleventh-House Challenge: Surrendering to the Divine

Energy vulnerability:
Vitality
Potential illnesses:
Parkinson's, Alzheimer's, and other neurological disorders; neurosis, paranoia, and other mental and emotional disorders

Reaching a point of surrender, sometimes referred to as "hitting bottom," is among our most frightening experiences. The stress of this journey to the bottom often manifests in emotional and psychological disorders. In these experiences none of your ambitions, decisions, or desires correspond to how you see your role. The spiritual purpose for these experiences is to allow you to accept opportunities that you would otherwise dismiss. The way you see the world colors how you see yourself within the world and consequently what you can offer the world. You may well be holding on to a vision of yourself that eclipses your talents. But most likely you have no idea what you are capable of doing or being. Once you are able to surrender yourself in hope and trust to a higher Source of wisdom, you open a passageway for a deeper process of empowerment. Because surrendering requires the coordination of your heart and mind, this house resonates to the fourth and sixth chakras.

Healing Guidance: Surrendering means letting go of your need to control everything and everyone at all times. Ask yourself how deeply you fear being out of control of your life. How much do you believe that you can determine the outcome of every event? Do you believe you should be able to get others to do what you want all the time? Choose one area that makes you especially anxious—financial security, marital stability, career direction—and every time your fears are triggered, practice the mantra "I surrender the outcome to the Divine."

Twelfth-House Challenge: Overcoming the Fear of Personal Empowerment

Energy vulnerability:
Balance of the psyche and spirit
Potential illnesses:
Panic attacks, bipolar disorder, schizophrenia

You are continually directed to confront the shadow within, returning like Persephone to the underworld to uncover your archetypes. But your fear of becoming whole by consolidating the fragments of your consciousness can lead you to sabotage your spiritual growth. Opportunities to forgive the past and move on, for example, are stifled by toxic pride or fear of change. We often resist change because we fear that an empowered life will demand more of us than we are prepared to give. The cycle of "knowing better but acting otherwise" is the most common form of psychological torment that we experience when we fight our own spiritual growth, and so the issues of this house are aligned to both the sixth chakra, which rules our intellectual and intuitive faculties, and the seventh, which regulates our spiritual development. Compromising what you know to be the truth, having a fear of confronting the truth, and using your intellect to deliberately distort the world around you, including the value of other people, is rooted in the shadow power of the twelfth-house psyche.

Healing Guidance: The only way to break the hold of the Saboteur is to face it head-on. What fears cause you to shut down? What symbolic imagery or truth can you use to melt down your fears? Patterns of fear are greater at night and smaller in the morning, so before going to bed, bring to mind what is limiting you the most. Remind yourself that this is an archetypal experience that you are meant to use to examine why you fear your own potential. Get as impersonal about your fears as possible. Read spiritually inspiring prayers with the intention of calming the spirit within. On waking, invoke your fear, however briefly; for example: "I am afraid that I will have to express my opinion in this meeting. I am afraid that I will be criticized." Then follow it with "I owe myself this opportunity. If I face a critical response, that only indicates that the power emerging in me is being witnessed. Above all else, I will represent the power of my spirit fully."

Your Chart of Origin and Your Spiritual DNA

The second step in healing a specific challenge is to examine the relevant archetype-house pairing in your Chart of Origin. Refer to your journal for the information that you recorded when selecting that archetype, and any subsequent data that you may have entered in response to questions concerning the archetype. You'll need to use your imagination and intuition to explore ways in which the relevant archetype may relate to your ailment, especially its psychological, emotional, and spiritual causes, before you move on to the final step of casting a working chart.

The people in the following stories began by relating their illness to a particular house of their Archetypal Wheel, then examined the role of the archetype residing in that house.

Parkinson's Disease and the Puppet Archetype

A happily married mother of two teenagers and a high school teacher, Francine developed Parkinson's when she was forty years old. Francine's health habits were admirable, and her illness could certainly not be blamed on a destructive lifestyle or emotions. Because the conventional explanations for the origin for her illness yielded no answers, Francine decided to investigate her archetypal patterns to see if they might help her understand its cause.

As I've said, you cannot use an archetypal pattern to "predict" an illness or a death. But the symbolic associations you hold with an archetype can sometimes release a resource of inner power that can help you heal yourself, even if you previously had no awareness of that pattern in your psyche. You may never have considered yourself to be a Hero or a creative Wizard, for instance, yet if you were to realize that you had a strong connection to these archetypes and their symbolic power, your self-image would go through a dramatic transformation.

Such was the case with Francine, who chose to work with her Puppet archetype because it resided in her eleventh house, which is associated with neurological disorders such as Parkinson's. She had originally chosen the Puppet as one of her support group of twelve because she loved working with puppets and had even taught her school guidance counselors to use puppets in therapy with students. Youngsters readily identify with the imagery of being controlled by someone else, and the students generally responded by expressing a broad range of emotions when they were "playing" with puppets.

Having witnessed the therapeutic value of working with puppets, Francine was able to work with the Puppet archetype in her imagination as an active way of drawing out her unconscious fears, along with any guidance that could help her heal her illness. As she entered progressively deeper states of relaxation, she imagined that she was herself a puppet. Instantly she made the association that Parkinson's causes your body to shake uncontrollably, like a puppet that has no power over its own movements. That insight led her to ask, "What part of my psyche feels like a puppet on a string?" Francine imagined that some aspect of her unconscious was pulling on her strings and controlling her, and that she needed to confront that aspect and cut the strings.

As Francine continued this visualization, she imagined that she was dialoguing with the puppeteer—her unconscious—and made notes of every impression. At first what she wrote made little sense because she was not accustomed to focusing within. As she learned to work with her Puppet image on a regular basis, however, she established a rapport with it that she felt spoke to her intuitively. That rapport eventually allowed her to expand from therapeutic analysis to a kind of spiritual self-examination.

Then one night Francine had a dream in which she managed to move her own puppet-self to look directly into the eyes of the puppeteer. She realized that she was looking into the energy of God. After that dream Francine felt that nothing in her life would ever be the same, and she had complete faith that she had been given a direction through which to begin her healing process. "My Puppet dream told me that I needed to become actively aware of what forces were influencing the choices and actions of my life," she said. "As in the story of Pinocchio, having redefined what it means to be honest with myself, I was being directed to move forward. That marked a major shift in the way I interact with people. I have always been extremely caring of others, and although this has not been a burden, perhaps it is simply not the way I am meant to proceed."

I explained to Francine that we often do not hear our own intuition, because the voices of so many other people are in our psyches. These voices are not necessarily negative, but they do tend to be "needy," especially if you are naturally inclined to care for others. And if you are filled with the concerns of others, you will have trouble establishing a resonance with your own intuition because you can't hear yourself. Francine was being led into another life cycle in which the next several Contracts would demand that she establish a more direct connection to her intuition. She needed to cut the strings that she had unconsciously placed in the hands of so many others and put her life purely in the hands of the Puppeteer she recognized in her dream as God. So it is that an illness can come into our lives not because of negativity but because Heaven is demanding more of us. Developing a serious illness can make you cut all unnecessary strings to the needs of those who should now be able to stand on their own. Armed with these insights, Francine made a major emotional turn-around. Her pessimism and feelings of futility were healed, and she is better able to face the changes in her body, even if a physical healing does not follow this spiritual breakthrough.

Pancreatic Cancer and the Patriarch Archetype

Now in his sixties, Ivan had emigrated from Russia with his family and a determination to create a life that was better than the one they had left behind. He had succeeded at that, but in the years since his arrival his health had suffered. When I met Ivan—he was "dragged" to one of my workshops by his daughter Elisa, who had taken charge of his healing—he had recently been diagnosed with pancreatic cancer and had begun chemotherapy. His daughter had introduced him to alternative healing methods, pointing out that his own grandparents would have recognized many of these treatments, such as using herbs and medicinal plants. That appealed to Ivan, but archetypes seemed beyond his comfort zone. Still, Ivan was open-minded and jovial and chose archetypes that he felt reminded him of himself, such as the Craftsman, Pilgrim, Beggar (how he saw himself in Russia and what he most feared becoming), and Patriarch. Because the Patriarch was in his seventh house, whose area of energetic vulnerability includes the pancreas, we chose to begin working with that archetype. Ivan acknowledged that the Patriarch not only gave him the most pride of all his archetypes but also reflected the sense of responsibility he felt toward his family.

As I noted earlier, the pancreas is sensitive to a range of issues related to personal responsibility. If you feel responsible for everyone else, to the exclusion of your own needs, that self-neglect will chip away at the health of the pancreas and its vital role of creating insulin. As a result, the rest of the body is eventually affected by the extreme stress. At the other end of the spectrum, abdicating all responsibility for yourself, finding ways for others to take charge of you, causes stress that also lodges in the pancreas. To contribute to the development of a serious illness, however, these patterns of stress must be chronic or acute. Bearing responsibility at reasonable levels does not in itself exert this extreme level of stress on the pancreas.

Ivan was certainly driven by an all-consuming sense of responsibility for his entire family and a determination not to fail them. The image of his elders begging in the streets in postwar Russia haunted him, and he had promised himself as a youth that this traumatic scene would never repeat itself in his life. I told him that such feelings were the symbolic voice of the Patriarch in him and that we now needed to let his inner Patriarch know that he had accomplished his goal. It was time to let the next generation take charge. The very thought of this filled Ivan with sorrow, but his daughter encouraged him to recognize that, because of him, his children had learned to make a place for themselves in the world.

To let go of his responsibilities would probably have proven impossible for Ivan without some guidance and support. So Elisa asked her father to tell her what he was most afraid of for each of his children and what he saw as their greatest strengths. She told him that the time had come for all of her siblings to reorganize the family in a way that could provide support for Ivan and her mother while respecting his self-image as the Patriarch. Elisa said she would gather the family and begin the distribution of his responsibilities immediately.

"Elisa," Ivan said, "are you preparing me to die?"

"You could die from this disease, Dad," she responded. "We have no way to know what lies ahead. But I do know that the pressures that have driven you all of these years must be shifted to us, and I also know that you need to see that we can handle our own lives now. Most of all, I realize that your healing is going to take all the energy you have always poured into us, and now you need that force for yourself. I think that maybe the new lesson that is facing you is one of self-responsibility, because you do not even know what it is to take care of your own needs."

As I parted with Ivan and Elisa, she had begun calling him "the Patriarch," and I could see that this would become his official family title. He would now live surrounded by loved ones who would recognize from that day forward all that he had done for them. About six months after the workshop, Elisa contacted me to report that because Ivan was now being "officially" addressed as the Patriarch, he was able to realize all that he had done for his children and how much they loved him for it. He was still receiving chemotherapy for his cancer, which had not metastasized throughout the rest of his body. "But however this works out in the long run," Elisa said, "I am so grateful that we have been able to recognize all this man has truly been to us."

On a psychological and emotional level, Ivan's healing had already begun. He had let go of his all-consuming sense of responsibility and was receiving the empowering love of his family. The energy boost to his system from releasing stress and receiving love and support could only improve his chances of survival.

Bone Marrow Cancer and the Hedonist Archetype

Intuitive healing guidance can go against the grain, against conventional wisdom. Don't be afraid to trust your own instincts and do what feels right, even when it seems questionable to your rational mind.

In a workshop some years ago, I met a woman named Josie, who had recently been diagnosed with bone marrow cancer. She had gone through radiation treatments and was completely involved in natural healing practices. In choosing her archetypes, Josie was drawn to the symbolic meaning of the Hedonist, because she loved "living the good life." Her attraction to wine tastings, gourmet cooking, fashion design, and an active sex life was a reaction against her puritanical upbringing. "I'm like the preacher's daughter," Josie said. "I wanted to get into everything I was told to stay out of."

Josie's core emotional issues involved coping with rejection and failure, which is the healing challenge of the tenth house. Because she was overweight as a young girl, she was rejected by her schoolmates, especially boys, and this early experience marked her emotionally. Although the conventional wisdom might propose that Josie had created her illness through her indulgent lifestyle, she sensed that her Hedonist archetype actually offered the best imagery for healing herself. Seeing the Hedonist in her tenth house confirmed for Josie that she should work with that archetype to heal her cancer. As a coping mechanism and as a reflection of her sense of humor, she followed the modern adage "Living well is the best revenge." "I refuse to give up the good life," she said, "and I need to rely on my determination, humor, and artistlike ability to break all rules in order to break the rules of this illness."

The latest scientific research tends to support Josie's intuitive hunch. In *Healthy Pleasures*, Robert Ornstein, Ph.D., a psychologist and brain researcher, and David Sobel, M.D., cite medical research showing that what pleases us—a wonderful view, beautiful music, delicious food and wine, appealing aromas, or the company of good friends—improves our health and helps us resist illness.

Josie began by interviewing her Hedonist about charting a course of action. She felt that the Hedonist would not fail in directing her intuition to discover the healing power of her highest potential. Entering a state of quiet thought, Josie would visualize her Hedonist archetype and repeat, "Tell me what to do to break the power of this illness in my psyche." She then wrote in her journal the thoughts that came to her, paying no attention to whether they made logical sense. One reply her unconscious gave was that she should study dancing. Josie, who loved to dance, interpreted this to mean that she needed to make dancing a spiritual discipline. "I wasn't about to do anything elaborate, like enrolling in ballet school," she said. "But I was being told to use my body in a way that makes me feel good, which dancing does. It was essential for me to keep moving."

Josie also got the impression that she was supposed to make use of her illness, to find some way of having it benefit her. She began writing a book she called *Becoming a Healthy Hedonist*, which took up much of her time. She went to cancer support groups and interviewed the members, asking them, among other things, what gave them the most pleasure, what they would love to do now, and what they always wanted to do but thought too out of character for them. Her intention was to write a book that could inspire people to love being alive. "I am learning that people are absolutely afraid of the good things in life," she said. "We are held captive by the fear of punishment, so no wonder we see disease as some form of retribution. I believe that one of the Contracts I have is to help break this toxic attitude."

To dialogue once with her Hedonist was not enough, and Josie continued to be in touch with the archetype on a regular basis. She felt inspired by her new project, and five months after the workshop I received a letter from her telling me that her cancer had gone into remission. Josie anticipated healing the disease entirely, because she had decided early on that it would not take away the relationship she had established with the pleasures of life. "I love living," she wrote, "and I knew that I had to continue to find a way to love life even though I had developed an illness. But even then, as I teach others, you have to find a way to appreciate each day, no matter how slight an act that may be. And above all, confront that horrible attitude that illness is a punishment from God. How can you heal if you feel you have done something to deserve your affliction?"

Casting a Healing Chart

Once you have cast your healing chart to explore your healing challenge, compare the houses where the one or two archetypes on which you are focusing intensively fall with their location on your Chart of Origin, and look for fresh insights that apply to the particular situation that you are confronting now.

A woman named Cynthia, for example, looked at two archetype-house links for insight into why she was having difficulty conceiving a child, which can sometimes have an emotional aspect. (Fear, for instance, can affect fertility.) She first examined the location of these archetypes on her Chart of Origin, then cast a healing chart and worked further with the same two archetypes.

Cynthia had the Queen in the first house of her Archetypal Wheel, where the challenge is Birthing the Self, and she had the Prostitute in her fifth house, whose challenge is Entering the Desert. Beginning with the Queen, she noted that every time she strove to give birth to her self by making choices independent of her family traditions, she faced a "battle" with her parents. Realizing that the attitudes and anger that emerged in her during such exchanges were connected to her Queen archetype helped Cynthia understand that her parents were fearful of her breaking away to establish her own "domain." Conceiving a child would clearly mark her as a woman with her own life independent of her family. Her values were quite different from those of her parents and her mother-in-law, as she rejected their rigid religious beliefs and racist attitudes.

These insights allowed Cynthia to release in a healthy way the emotional pressure that is created whenever one breaks free of group authority. The power struggle between Cynthia and her family was actually essential to her developing the strength and stamina that a Queen needs in order to rule, and this image and understanding allowed her to detach from the situation and indeed to see it as constructive for her. Had she lacked this reference point, she might have slipped into a toxic mind-set of resentment at her parents' lack of support and let bitterness color her interaction with them. Now she could see the exchanges symbolically, so that her reactions tended to be calmer—as if it were "nothing personal, just business."

The challenge of the fifth house involves the search for creativity and talents. Each of us must walk in the desert at some point, because only we can discover the gifts of our own spirit. Like walking through shifting sands, the feelings of emptiness that you encounter during this challenge make it difficult to maintain your balance without reaching out for help. If you had the Victim in this house, for example, you might respond to the challenge of the desert by feeling sorry for yourself or complaining about all the hardships you faced. Because

Cynthia had the Prostitute there, however, she was more inclined to negotiate or sell a part of her life to another so that the other person would complete the journey of discovering her inherent talents for her. But knowing that the Prostitute rules her fifth-house challenge alerted Cynthia that whenever she began to negotiate her power to another, she was giving away her power to be creative. She could then separate herself from the fears that emerged during these experiences and remind herself that she could not afford to allow another to direct or repress her creativity for her, because that would drain her of the power essential to maintaining physical health. Applying this insight to her difficulty conceiving, Cynthia realized that, because her parents and in-laws were constantly pressuring her to have a baby, she had begun to feel as though she would be conceiving a child for them rather than for herself and her husband, and that resentment might have inhibited her natural ability to conceive.

Cynthia then cast a healing chart to address the same health issue. In her healing chart her Queen archetype fell into her seventh house, where the challenge is Maintaining Personal Boundaries. Having her Queen in this house led Cynthia to see that becoming a mother would represent a dramatic shift in the power boundaries that she had established for herself. She had become known in her social circle for her strong opinions and her independence, while maintaining an intimate partnership with her husband—which baffled some of her friends, who were incapable of balancing intimacy and independence. Cynthia had broken free of the standard husband-wife convention, and having a child represented for her the undoing of that role. She feared that she would become dependent and that her image as the independent Queen would have to go "into retirement." Cynthia was also afraid that she would resent the restrictions that a child would inevitably bring into her life.

Cynthia's Prostitute now fell into her twelfth house, where the challenge is Overcoming the Fear of Personal Empowerment. She interpreted this union in connection with her inability to conceive in a very favorable light. She was passionate about her own empowerment and felt that one of the gifts she could offer a child would be to teach her how to strive to become fully empowered. "I would be a spectacular role model for a child, especially my own," she said. "The Prostitute in this house tells me that I have what it takes to lead my children into empowerment and not away from it."

This insight put Cynthia's mind at ease and, along with her new awareness of her emotional resistance to the responsibilities of motherhood and the demands of her family, allowed her to relax about the prospects of bearing a child. Within several months she did conceive and later gave birth to twins.

Keep in mind when working with your houses and archetypes that there is no single "magic bullet"—to use Dr. Paul Ehrlich's famous term—to heal your illness or disorder. You need to accumulate data and insights from many sources, then use your intuition to draw healing strategies from the combined information. The goal is to find the path that best utilizes your knowledge, wisdom, insight, and will to heal.

Keep Your Attention on Your Highest Potential

In working with thousands of people through the years, I've discovered that the sure way to find your path—whether by understanding your overall Contract, a particular relationship or event, or an ailment that you want to heal—is to keep your attention on reaching your highest potential. Once you have made this crucial decision, every other decision in your life, from what kind of diet to follow to the manner in which you nurture your spiritual life, takes on a distinctive shape.

Remember that your highest potential is not your job. We can't help thinking that the perfect job will provide us with self-esteem and financial security, assure us of personal health and romantic love, and guarantee us an electric social life and creative projects on our own schedule. We cling to this dream in order to cope with the ordinary life challenges that we would rather avoid.

Fulfilling your highest potential actually means acting on your highest or deepest truth each moment of your life. This involves your occupation, your relationships, your health, and maybe even what movie you want to see tonight. Weigh all your decisions against this one criterion: each choice either serves your highest good or detracts from it. Using that simple guide can take a lot of the mystery out of your everyday decisions.

We aren't meant to solve all the mysteries in our life, of course. Rather, we are meant to explore the mysteries and discover ourselves one piece of our spirit at a time. Gradually we become whole, more conscious, more aware that life is a spiritual journey and everything else is make-believe. Your archetypal companions are the guides of your unconscious. These patterns will surely get you where you are meant to go, because their role is a manifestation of how the Divine keeps up its end of your Contract. You will arrive where you need to be when you need to be there, and you will meet the people you are meant to meet, whether you know it or not. Knowing it, however— recognizing that everything in your life is organizing around your Contracts—awakens trust, and that is the first step toward making our final choice. Do we trust enough to allow the Divine to make our choices for us? Once we do, then our role in life is only to follow through with those choices. If you find yourself in a relationship that is hurting you deeply, you now have a reference point. Your highest choice is to forgive. You always have the option of understanding that this relationship may have come together to open your heart in just that way. You may not want to act on that insight, but at least you can see it. You have the option, as hard as it may be for your personality and ego to grasp, of appreciating the fact that you were meant to meet this individual. You have a higher perspective from which to view your life, to see that your part in all Contracts is to search for the divine intention hidden within the physical form, and to base your choices on those insights.

Remind yourself, when you need to, that a Contract is a guarantee that terms have been set. The other party or parties to your Contracts have as much interest in your spiritual growth as you do. Use the energy of that truth to create an extraordinary life in this physical world; don't just leave your spirit to wander on its own. Keep yourself in present time, in one place, in yourself.

Above all, remember that we are each following different routes along the same general path that leads us all to the same final task: surrender the self. Only through realizing the futility of spinning our wheels in the direction of personal control do we finally wake up to the truth that we are in control of nothing other than the moment when—or if—we can finally trust that our Sacred Contracts are governed by a force of wisdom much greater than our own. And that the agreements you made prior to your birth will lead your spirit back home again.

That is what surrender looks like.

APPENDIX

THE GALLERY OF ARCHETYPES

Space limitations make it impossible to list all of the most common archetypal patterns in detail. Many of these overlap to a large extent, and so I have included related archetypes in the heading of the dominant listing, e.g., Artist *(Artisan, Craftsperson, Sculptor, Weaver)*. If you relate to a variant not listed—say, the Photographer—then simply substitute it. I've tried to provide a few examples of each archetype, drawn from popular films, fiction, drama, myths, religion, folklore, or fairy tales. You can probably come up with many more on your own, a process that can be helpful in determining your connection to a given archetype. Volumes of information can be written about each archetype, as they are complex forces that cannot be fully represented in a brief entry. The descriptions provided are the result of the work I have done with people and my own observations of their patterns as expressed through their work with this tool, combined with their examination and interpretation of their life experiences.

Each archetype represents a fundamental learning experience or process that is meant to guide us throughout our lives. In evaluating whether a particular pattern is part of your intimate family of twelve, pay special attention to whether you can perceive a continuum of this learning process in your history, rather than just isolated incidents. Never evaluate your connection to an archetype by the obvious. You have to stretch your imagination and burrow into yourself to discover your life patterns, lessons, and gifts. This inner knowledge does not surface easily. If you feel that you have an archetype that is not listed here, describe the patterns of behavior that you identify as archetypal in nature and come up with examples from the arts or mythology.

Addict *(Conspicuous Consumer, Glutton, Workaholic—see also **Gambler**)*
Every one of us is touched by the Addict archetype. The only question is how much of our lives is consumed by it. Besides the usual suspects—drugs, alcohol,

food, and sex—one can be addicted to work, sports, television, exercise, computer games, spiritual practice, negative attitudes, and the kinds of thrills that bring on adrenaline rushes. In its positive aspect, this archetype helps you recognize when an outside substance, habit, relationship, or any expression of life has more authority over your willpower than does your inner spirit. Confronting addiction and breaking the hold that a pattern or substance has on you can impart great strength to your psyche. Discovering the empowerment that comes with perseverance has a lifelong impact, becoming a reference point for what you are able to accomplish. In the words of one former alcoholic, "I know now that if I can quit drinking, I can do anything."

From a symbolic perspective, the shadow aspect of the Addict represents a struggle with willpower and the absence of self-control. People who are extremely intellectual or emotional frequently have a close link to this archetype, because they struggle to balance these powers. Without this internal balance, the will may give up its power to an external substance that exerts authority, providing shadow order to your life. The shadow Addict compromises your integrity and honesty. Many addicts, for example, steal as a means of supporting their habits.

In evaluating your connection to the Addict, review how many of your life's challenges concern an external substance or a consistent, domineering pattern of trying to maintain order in your life. Although that challenge is a part of all of our lives, the degree to which an addiction controls you and your lifestyle determines whether the Addict is part of your intimate family of twelve. For instance, you can be inconsistent in your exercise program yet quite disciplined in your spiritual practice. Needing a substance or practice or person so intensely or regularly that you compromise relationships, finances, integrity, character, or emotional and psychological well-being, however, indicates that you should look very seriously at this archetype as a possible choice.

> *Films:* Jack Lemmon and Lee Remick in *Days of Wine and Roses* (alcohol); Ben Stiller in *Permanent Midnight* (heroin); Dom DeLuise in *Fatso* (food); Claire Bloom in *The Chapman Report* (sex).
>
> *Drama: A Long Day's Journey into Night* (morphine) by Eugene O'Neill.
>
> *Fiction: The Basketball Diaries* (heroin) by Jim Carroll; *Under the Volcano* (mescal) by Malcolm Lowry.
>
> *Religion/Myth:* Soma (Vedic god of intoxication, as well as the intoxicating drink itself and the plant from which it is made); Tantalus (a son of Zeus and king of Sipylos in Greece, he was invited to share the food of the gods but abused the honor and was punished by being "tantalized" for all eternity by food and drink he could not reach).

Advocate (*Attorney, Defender, Legislator, Lobbyist, Environmentalist*)
Coming to the defense of others is one manifestation of what Ram Dass calls "Compassion in Action." The Advocate embodies a sense of lifelong devotion to championing the rights of others in the public arena. People who

relate to this archetype have recognized early on a passion to transform social concerns, specifically in behalf of others. Symbolically, they are dedicated to inspiring the empowerment of groups or causes that are unable to be empowered on their own. By comparison, archetypes such as the Hermit are clearly more personal and lack the Advocate's fire for furthering social change. The Advocate needs public expression, even if only through writing or artwork.

The shadow Advocate manifests in false or negative causes or in committing to causes for personal gain. In evaluting your connection with this archetype, you should ask yourself how much of your life is dedicated to social causes and a willingness to take action.

> *Films:* Paul Newman in *The Verdict;* Spencer Tracy in *Inherit the Wind;* Julia Roberts in *The Pelican Brief* and *Erin Brokovich;* Robert Duvall in the *Godfather* trilogy (shadow).
>
> *Television: Perry Mason; L.A. Law; The Practice.*
>
> *Fiction: The Devil and Daniel Webster* by Stephen Vincent Benét.
>
> *Fairy Tale: Puss in Boots.*
>
> *Religion/Myth:* David (in the Hebrew Bible, the Jewish champion who slew the much larger Goliath); Hakuim (a pre-Islamic deity of southern Arabia who administers justice and oversees arbitration).

Alchemist *(Wizard, Magician, Scientist, Inventor)*

These archetypes share the common trait of converting some form of matter into an altered expression of itself. The Wizard and Magician produce results outside the ordinary rules of life, whether causing people to fall in love or objects to disappear. Whereas a Wizard is associated with supernatural powers, the Magician tends to be seen more as an entertainer. The Alchemist is associated with vain attempts to turn base metals into gold, but in its highest manifestation it seeks complete spiritual transformation. You may identify with this archetype if you are interested in a path of spiritual development that is aligned to the mystery schools or study of the laws of the universe. From this perspective, Nostradamus and Isaac Newton could both be classified as Alchemists.

The shadow sides of these archetypes are found in the misuse of the power and knowledge that comes through them. Seduction and trickery brought about through magic and wizardry play on the desires of many people to transform their lives.

For the Alchemist or Wizard to be one of your circle of twelve, it needs to be associated with your physical life in some significant way. Perhaps your work or living situation demands that you be especially inventive or interventionist on a regular basis. The shadow Wizard manifests either as the use of ingenuity for criminal or unethical purposes or as feelings of superiority based on high intellect.

> *Films:* Spencer Tracy in *Edison the Man;* Greer Garson in *Madame Curie;* Anthony Michael Hall as Bill Gates and Noah Wyle as Steve Jobs in

Pirates of Silicon Valley (HBO video); Fred MacMurray (or Robin Williams) in *The Absentminded Professor*; Katharine Hepburn in *The African Queen*; Jane Powell in *Seven Brides for Seven Brothers*; Jeff Goldblum in *The Fly* (shadow); Patrick Stewart and Ian McKellen (shadow) in *X-Men*.

Fiction: The Alchemist by Paulo Coelho; *The Mists of Avalon* by Marion Z. Bradley; the Harry Potter series by J. K. Rowling; *Alice's Adventures in Wonderland* by Lewis Carroll.

Drama: The Miracle Worker by William Gibson.

Religion/Myth: Merlin (wizard and prophet involved in every phase of King Arthur's life, from conception to rulership, who also counseled him as king); Cessair (magician who became the first Queen of Ireland); Tezcatlipoca (Aztec god of night and material things, whose black magic mirror made of obsidian or hematite reflected the thoughts and actions of humanity and could kill enemies); Paracelsus (sixteenth-century Swiss alchemist and physician who described humans as the microcosmic reflection of the macrocosm); Hermes Trismegistus (Greek mythic figure who served as messenger of the gods, but who in later esoteric thought became a master of reality manipulation able to travel freely between the various realms and dimensions); Simon (Samaritan magician in the Book of Acts, 8:9–24, condemned by the apostle Peter for offering to buy the power of the Holy Spirit from him); Suyolak (gypsy wizard said to know all medicinal cures).

Fairy Tale: Rumpelstiltskin (spun straw into gold).

Angel *(Fairy Godmother/Godfather)*

Angels exist in a category unto themselves because they are thought to be living beings of Light and messengers of the Divine. Almost every cultural and religious tradition on earth features angels of some description, including belief in a personal Guardian Angel in the Jewish, Christian, and Islamic traditions. Angels are typically represented as winged beings who intervene in times of great need or for the purpose of delivering a message of guidance or instruction from God to humans. Even though you probably aren't an actual Angel, you can acknowledge a strong connection to the angelic realm, as noted in people who have a dedication to representing the presence of angels. Artists who paint their images, for example, authors who write about their interaction with humans, and those whose lives in some way provide a channel through which their presence is physically manifested exhibit a rapport with the angelic realm. Some people are also referred to as "angels" because of the loving and nurturing qualities of character that they embody. One may also play the role of a Fairy Godmother or Godfather by helping someone in need either anonymously or with no expectation of any return.

The shadow side of this archetype manifests through people who make claims to be in touch with angelic guidance for the sake of control or ego enhancement, or who act innocent or angelic to mislead others about their true nature. From a biblical perspective, the shadow Angel is frequently associated with Satan or Lucifer, but the Devil or Demon should also be considered as a unique archetype.

> *Films:* Herbert Marshall in *The Enchanted Cottage;* Charles Coburn in *The More the Merrier;* Mary Wickes (Aunt March) to Amy in *Little Women;* the two angels in *It's a Wonderful Life;* Marlon Brando in *The Godfather* trilogy (shadow); Danny Glover and Kevin Kline in *Grand Canyon.*
> *Television: Touched by an Angel.*
> *Fairy Tale:* Glinda in *The Wonderful Wizard of Oz* by L. Frank Baum.
> *Religion/Myth:* Angiris (Hindu angels who preside over sacrifices); Uriel (in rabbinic lore, the angel who wrestled with Jacob); Gabriel (archangel who appeared to Mary in the Gospels and recited the Quran to the Prophet Muhammad); Sijil (Islamic angels overseeing the heavenly scrolls); Tenshi (Japanese angels who are messengers of the gods and helpers of humanity); Lucifer and Iblis (in medieval Christian and Islamic belief, respectively, evil angels who work to destroy human souls); Fravashis (ancient Zoroastrian guardian angels who guide the souls of the dead to Heaven); Ombwiri (tribal guardian angels and ancestor spirits in central Africa); Athena (goddess who frequently comes to the aid of Odysseus in *The Odyssey*).

Artist *(Musician, Author, Dramatist, Actor, Artisan, Craftsperson, Sculptor, Weaver)*

The Artist archetype embodies the passion to express a dimension of life that is just beyond the five senses. The Artist psyche is animated with the energy to express it into physical forms. The nature or relative grandeur of any form of expression is irrelevant; a chef can be as much of an artist as a painter or landscaper. The signature of artists is not in what they do but in how intense their motivation is to manifest the extraordinary. Doing what you do in such a way that you create an emotional field that inspires others also indicates the Artist energy at work, as does the emotional and psychological need to express yourself so much that your well-being is wrapped up in this energy.

The shadow Artist comprises many clichés, including an eccentric nature and the madness that often accompanies genius. The Starving Artist represents the fear of financial ruin or the belief that fame and fortune come only after death, which often causes artists to suppress their talents. In evaluating your relationship to this archetype, recognize that the need to bring art to others, such as dedicating part of the energy of your life to supporting artists, is as much an expression of the Artist archetype as actually holding a brush in your hand.

> *Films:* Ed Harris in *Pollock;* Alec Guinness in *The Horse's Mouth;* Isabelle Adjani in *Camille Claudel;* Kirk Douglas in *Lust for Life;* Gene Kelly in *An American in Paris.*
> *Drama: Amadeus* by Peter Shaffer.

Fiction: A Portrait of the Artist as a Young Man by James Joyce; *The Horse's Mouth* by Joyce Cary.

Fairy Tale: Gepetto in *Pinocchio* by Carlo Collodi.

Religion/Myth: Galatea (sculptor of Greek myth who brought the statue of Pygmalion to life); Shen-nung (one of the Three Noble Ones of Chinese mythology who invented the plow and taught humanity the art of agriculture); Basa-Jaun (in Basque lore, a wood spirit who taught humanity the art of forging metal); Sarasvati (Hindu patron of the Arts); Ptah (Egyptian creator god and deity of craftsmen, said to have molded humanity on his potter's wheel); Ambat (Melanesian hero-deity who taught the art of pottery); Ixzaluoh (Mayan water goddess who invented the art of weaving); Hiro (Polynesian hero who introduced humanity to the art of writing); Hephaestus (Greek god of the blacksmith's fire and the patron of all craftsmen).

Athlete *(Olympian)*

This archetype represents the ultimate expression of the strength of the human spirit as represented in the power and magnificence of the human body. Because the Olympian is so connected to spiritual as well as physical strength, a code of ethics and morality is associated with the archetype, which is an excellent example of the universal power of the "psyche" of an archetype. A link to the Athlete should not be evaluated by whether your physical skill is on par with that of professionals or whether your body is perfect in form and function. A person dedicated to transcending the limits of a physical handicap qualifies as much for this archetype as the professional or artistic athlete, because the development of personal willpower and strength of spirit is a requirement for the body to manifest its perfection.

The shadow aspect of athletics, however, may manifest as a misuse of one's strength against any sort of person or opponent in the world, even outside the field of professional athletics, such as a professional boxer who starts a bar fight; a false sense of invulnerability, like that of Achilles or Samson; dirty play; or colluding with gamblers (see **Bully**). The shadow may also appear as a lack of honor that compels you to cheat to win.

Films: Esther Williams in *Million Dollar Mermaid*; Burt Lancaster in *Jim Thorpe, All American*; Tom Courtenay in *The Loneliness of the Long Distance Runner*; Daniel Day-Lewis in *My Left Foot*; *Hoop Dreams* (documentary).

Fiction: The Natural by Bernard Malamud; *Hans Brinker and the Silver Skates* by Mary Mapes Dodge.

Folklore/Fairy Tales: The Tortoise and the Hare.

Religion/Myth: Atalanta (female athlete in Greek myth); Smertios (Celtic war-god portrayed as a bearded athlete); Nike (in Greek myth, feminine personification of victory who runs and flies at great speed); Samson (Nazarite strongman and biblical Judge); Achilles (Greek warrior known for his exceptional might, and the hero of *The Iliad*).

Avenger *(Avenging Angel, Savior, Messiah)*

This archetype and its related manifestations respond to a need to balance the scales of justice, sometimes by employing aggressive techniques. Attorneys who work for the impoverished or disadvantaged or who volunteer part of their time for pro bono work are modern Avengers. Bringing war criminals to trial or legally pursuing corporations that harm society are examples of the Avenger on a global scale, fueled by a sense of righteousness in behalf of society. One can also be motivated to avenge an injustice against oneself or one's family. The Avenging Angel is an expression of this archetype of mythic proportions that suggests that one is on a mission from God, as in the case of Joan of Arc.

On the global level, the shadow manifests as avenging perceived immoral behavior by resorting to violence, from acts of ecoterroism to bombing abortion clinics. The "rightness" of one's cause can never justify harming innocent third parties. (Gandhi countered the shadow of social vengeance by emphasizing passive resistance to illegitimate authority.) In evaluating your connection to this archetype, review your life for experiences in which your primary motivation was to defend or represent a cause on behalf of others. One instance is not enough. You need to relate to this archetype as a primary force through which many of the choices and actions of your life are directed. A burning desire to get even can be so forceful that you organize a lifetime around meeting that end.

> *Films:* Ingrid Bergman in *The Visit;* Jane Fonda in *Cat Ballou;* John Wayne in *The Searchers;* Antonio Banderas in *The Mask of Zorro;* Jane Fonda, Dolly Parton, and Lily Tomlin in *Nine to Five;* Vincent Price in *Theatre of Blood* (shadow—an actor who kills his critics); Al Pacino in *The Godfather* (shadow); Robert de Niro or Robert Mitchum in *Cape Fear* (shadow).
>
> *Television: The Avengers.*
>
> *Drama: The Oresteia* by Aeschylus; *Hamlet* and *Macbeth* by Shakespeare.
>
> *Fiction: To Kill a Mockingbird* by Harper S. Lee.
>
> *Religion/Myth:* The Furies or Erinyes (avenging spirits of Roman and Greek myth); Bastet (Egyptian cat-headed goddess who is the instrument of Ra's vengeance); Durga (vengeful warrior goddess of the Hindu pantheon); Kali (Hindu mother goddess and symbol of destruction who annihilates ignorance and maintains the world order).

Beggar *(Homeless Person, Indigent)*

Completely without material resources, the Beggar is associated with dependence on the kindness of others, living on the streets, starvation, and disease, whether in New York City or Calcutta. It is easy to believe that the archetype of the Beggar is solely a negative one, but that is an illusion. A person need hardly be starving for food to be considered a Beggar. People "beg" for attention, love, authority, and material objects. We "throw a dog a bone" to give a powerless being a "treat" of power. From a symbolic perspective, the Beggar archetype represents a test that compels a person to confront self-empowerment beginning at the base level of physical survival. Learning about the nature of generosity, compassion, and self-esteem are fundamental to this archetypal pattern.

Films: Patrick Swayze in *City of Hope.*

Fiction: Oliver Twist by Charles Dickens; *The Prince and the Pauper* by Mark Twain.

Nonfiction: Meeting the Madwoman by Linda Schierse Leonard, Ph.D.

Religion/Myth: Lazarus (the beggar in Luke 16:22–23, who is "carried by the angels to Abraham's bosom" after his death, while the rich man outside whose gate he begged went to Hades); Yeta (Japanese beggar who may be a disguise for Inari, the god of food or goddess of rice); Odysseus (who disguised himself as a ragged beggar when he returned home from Troy); Lan Cai-he (in Taoist myth, one of the eight immortals, who dresses in rags and roams the streets as a drunken beggar).

Bully *(Coward)*

The archetype of the Bully manifests the core truth that the spirit is always stronger than the body. Symbolically, our physical bodies can "bully" our spirits with any number of reasons why we should back down from our challenges, which appear to overwhelm us by their size and shape. Your relationship to this archetype should be evaluated within a framework far more expansive than evaluating whether you "bully" people. Consider whether on your life path you confront one experience and relationship after another that appears to have more power than you and ultimately leads you to ask, "Will I stand up to this challenge?" People are often called to take on bullies for the sake of others, as David did Goliath, and this is another criterion of your connection to this archetype.

Conventional wisdom holds that underneath a bully is a coward trying to keep others from discovering his true identity. Symbolically, the Coward within must stand up to being bullied by his own inner fears, which is the path to empowerment through these two archetypes.

Films: Matt Dillon in *My Bodyguard;* Jack Palance in *Shane;* Mel Gibson in *Braveheart;* James Cagney in *The Fighting 69th;* Bert Lahr in *The Wizard of Oz;* Jack Nicholson in *As Good as It Gets.*

Fiction: The Red Badge of Courage by Stephen Vincent Benét.

Fairy Tales: Jack and the Beanstalk; Jack the Giant Killer.

Child *(Orphan, Wounded, Magical/Innocent, Nature, Divine, Puer/Puella Eternis,* or *Eternal Boy/Girl)*

Everyone has expressions of each one of these aspects of the Child within his psyche, although one aspect is usually so dominant that it eclipses the energy of the others. The Wounded Child, for example, can be so needy that it is almost impossible for the Magical Child to manifest its qualities. At the same time, because every one of the Child aspects is present in various degrees of strength in every psyche, similar patterns often overlap, making it hard to distinguish which one you relate to most intensely. You may find that you relate equally to the Orphan and the Wounded Child, or to the *Puer Eternis* and the Nature Child. When this is the case, choose one and include the specific qualities that you relate to in the other archetype as you investigate the psyche of this archetype in your life.

Child: Orphan

The Orphan Child is the major character in most well-known children's stories, among which one could identify Little Orphan Annie, the Matchstick Girl, Bambi, the Little Mermaid, Hansel and Gretel, Snow White, Cinderella, and many more. The pattern in these stories is reflected in the lives of people who feel from birth as if they are not a part of their family, including the family psyche or tribal spirit. Yet precisely because orphans are not allowed into the family circle, they have to develop independence early in life. The absence of family influences, attitudes, and traditions inspires or compels the Orphan Child to construct an inner reality based on personal judgment and experience. Orphans who succeed at finding a path of survival on their own are celebrated in fairy tales and folk stories as having won a battle with a dark force, which symbolically represents the fear of surviving alone in this world.

The shadow aspect manifests when orphans never recover from growing up outside the family circle. Feelings of abandonment and the scar tissue from family rejection stifle their maturation, often causing them to seek surrogate family structures in order to experience tribal union. Therapeutic support groups become shadow tribes or families for an Orphan Child who knows deep down that healing these wounds requires moving on to adulthood. Identifying with the Orphan begins by evaluating your childhood memories, paying particular attention to whether your painful history arises from the feeling that you were never accepted as a family member.

> *Films:* Margaret O'Brien in *The Secret Garden;* Victoire Thivisol in *Ponette;* Hayley Mills in *Pollyanna.*
>
> *Fiction: David Copperfield* by Charles Dickens; *The Wonderful Wizard of Oz* by L. Frank Baum.
>
> *Drama: The Changeling* by Thomas Middleton.
>
> *Fairy Tales:* Snow White, Cinderella, Bambi, the Little Mermaid.
>
> *Religion/Myth:* Romulus and Remus (twins of Roman myth who were cast into the Tiber, miraculously rescued by a she-wolf, and went on to found Rome); Moses; Havelock the Dane (in medieval romance, the orphan son of Birkabegn, King of Denmark, cast adrift by treacherous guardians but found and raised by a British fisherman, and eventually made King of Denmark and part of England).

⸰ Child: Wounded

The Wounded Child archetype holds the memories of the abuse, neglect, and other traumas that we have endured during childhood. This may be the pattern people relate to the most, particularly since it has become the focus of therapy and accepted as a major culprit in the analysis of adult suffering. Choosing the Wounded Child suggests that you credit the painful and abusive experiences of your childhood with having a substantial influence on your adult life. Many people blame their Wounded Child, for instance, for all their subsequent dysfunctional relationships.

The painful experiences of the Wounded Child archetype often awaken a deep sense of compassion and a desire to find a path of service aimed at helping other Wounded Children. From a spiritual perspective, a wounded childhood cracks open the learning path of forgiveness. The shadow aspect may manifest as an abiding sense of self-pity, a tendency to blame your parents for your current shortcomings and to resist moving on through forgiveness.

> *Films:* Diana Scarwid in *Mommie Dearest;* Dean Stockwell in *The Secret Garden;* Linda Blair in *The Exorcist;* Natalie Wood in *The Miracle on 34th Street;* Leonardo di Caprio in *This Boy's Life;* Jon Voight in *Midnight Cowboy.*
>
> *Fiction: Native Son* by Richard Wright; *Oliver Twist* by Charles Dickens.
>
> *Religion/Myth:* The Amazons (warrior women of Greek myth who, as children, had their right breasts removed to facilitate the use of bow and arrow, their chief weapon).

Child: Magical/Innocent

The Magical Child represents the part of us that is both enchanted and enchanting to others. It sees the potential for sacred beauty in all things, exemplified by Tiny Tim in Dickens's *A Christmas Carol,* and by Anne Frank, who wrote in her diary that in spite of all the horror surrounding her family while hiding from Nazis in an attic in Amsterdam, she still believed that humanity was basically good. Her insights, offered at a time when most people were collapsing under the weight of war and persecution, continue to inspire people to seek out the wondrous side of life, even in a crisis.

One might assume from the name that this archetype refers to only the delightful qualities of children, but as demonstrated by Anne Frank and Tiny Tim, it also embodies qualities of wisdom and courage in the face of difficult circumstances.

Baudelaire wrote that "genius is childhood recaptured," and in that sense the Magical Child is something of a genius too. The Magical Child is gifted with the power of imagination and the belief that everything is possible. The shadow energy of the Magical Child manifests as the absence of the possibility of miracles and the transformation of evil to good. Attitudes of pessimism and depression, particularly when exploring dreams, often emerge from an injured Magical Child whose dreams were "once upon a time" thought foolish by cynical adults. The shadow may also manifest as a belief that energy and action are not required, allowing one to retreat into fantasy.

> *Films:* Drew Barrymore in *E.T.*; Margaret O'Brien in *Meet Me in St. Louis*; George du Fresne in *Ma Vie en Rose*; Shirley Temple in *Heidi* and *Wee Willie Winkie*.
>
> *Fiction: The Little Prince* by Antoine de Saint-Exupéry; *Pippi Longstocking* by Astrid Lindgren; *Alice's Adventures in Wonderland* and *Through the Looking-Glass and What Alice Found There* by Lewis Carroll.
>
> *Religion/Myth:* Merlin (in Arthurian legend, the "child without a father" who was about to be sacrificed when he saved himself by displaying magic greater than the king's sorcerers).

Child: Nature

This archetype inspires deep, intimate bonding with natural forces and has a particular affinity for friendships with animals. Although the Nature Child has tender, emotional qualities, it can also have an inner toughness and ability to survive—the resilience of Nature herself. Nature Children can develop advanced skills of communicating with animals, and in stories reflecting this archetype an animal often comes to the rescue of its child companion. Many veterinarians and animal-rights activists resonate with this archetype because they have felt a conscious rapport with animals since childhood. Other adults describe being in communication with nature spirits and learning to work in harmony with them in maintaining the order of nature.

The shadow aspect of the Nature Child manifests in a tendency to abuse animals and people and the environment.

A love of animals is not sufficient to qualify for this archetype, however. A life pattern of relating to animals in an intimate and caring way, to the extent that your psyche and spirit need these bonds as a crucial part of your own well-being, is your best clue in this direction.

> *Films:* Elizabeth Taylor in *National Velvet*; Anna Paquin in *Fly Away Home*; Claude Jarman in *The Yearling*; Kelly Reno in *The Black Stallion*; Tommy Kirk in *Old Yeller*; Jean-Pierre Cargol in *The Wild Child*.
>
> *Television: Rin Tin Tin; Flipper; My Friend Flicka; Lassie.*
>
> *Fiction: Tarzan of the Apes* by Edgar Rice Burroughs.
>
> *Song:* "Nature Boy."
>
> *Religion/Myth:* Persephone (in Greek myth, the daughter of Demeter, who was abducted to Hades and was associated with the agricultural cycles of growth and harvest); Saint Francis of Assisi (Catholic friar said to have communicated with animals).

Child: *Puer/Puella Eternis (Eternal Boy/Girl)*

Positive aspects of the archetype manifest as a determination to remain eternally young in body, mind, and spirit. People who maintain that age will never stop them from enjoying life are relying on the positive energy of this archetype to supply that healthy attitude. The shadow Eternal Child often manifests as an inability to grow up and embrace the responsible life of an adult. Like Peter Pan, he resists ending a cycle of life in which he is free to live outside the boundaries of conventional adulthood. The shadow *Puella Eternis* can manifest in women as extreme dependency on those who take charge of their physical security. A consistent inability to be relied on and the inability to accept the aging process are also markers of this archetype. Although few people delight in the ending of their youth, the Eternal Child is sometimes left floundering and ungrounded between the stages of life, because he has not laid a foundation for a functioning adulthood.

> *Films:* Tom Hanks in *Big*; Pee Wee Herman in *Pee Wee's Big Adventure*; Carroll Baker in *Baby Doll*; Thomas Hulce in *Dominic and Eugene*, and as Mozart in *Amadeus*.
>
> *Fairy Tale:* Peter Pan.
>
> *Religion/Myth:* Cupid (boy-god of Roman myth said to have been born from a silver egg); Harpa-Khruti (Horus the child); Harpocrates (Greek deity of silence and secrecy, represented as a naked boy sucking his finger).

Clown *(Court Jester, Fool, Dummling)*

The Clown archetype is associated with three major characteristics: making people laugh, making them cry, and wearing a mask that covers one's own real emotions. The Clown is generally male, with few women playing the role either in literature or the theater. This may well be explained by the social attitude that associates weakness and loss of control with a man who expresses emotions. Therefore, the man has to wear a mask, which often portrays a crying face. The Clown reflects the emotions of the crowd, making an audience laugh by satirizing something they can relate to collectively or by acting out social absurdities. In general, the messages communicated through a Clown's humor are deeply serious and often critical of the hypocrisy in an individual or in some area of society. Because of the mask he wears, the Clown is allowed— indeed, expected—to cross the boundaries of social acceptance, representing what people would like to do or say themselves.

The Court Jester or Fool is the manifestation of the Clown in a royal setting. Since no one can possibly take a fool seriously at the physical level, he is allowed entry into the most powerful of circles. While entertaining the king with outrageous behavior, the Fool is actually communicating messages that the king trusts. Political satirists often have dominant Court Jester archetypes, revealing the motivations of the highest officials in the nation in a manner that is generally granted freedom from the legal retribution that might be leveled against an ordinary citizen making the same comments.

Related to the Fool is the Dummling, the fairy tale character who, although often simpleminded, acts with a good heart and is usually rewarded for it. Modern film characters such as Forrest Gump and Nurse Betty embody this aspect of the archetype, which does not so much impart wisdom as foster living with kindness and simplicity.

The shadow aspect of the Clown or Fool manifests as cruel personal mockery or betrayal, specifically the breaking of confidences gained through knowledge from the inner circle.

In reviewing your relationship to this archetype, consider your use of humor in association with power. Since everyone is prone to jesting, you are looking for a connection to a pattern of behavior that is fundamental to your personal protection and survival. In distinguishing Clown from Fool, note that the Fool is connected to arenas of power, while the Clown does his best work as an Everyman, like Ralph Kramden on *The Honeymooners*. Reflect on whether "clowning" around is an essential channel for expressing your emotions over and above simple play. Ask yourself if, like the Fool, you carry truth into closed circles or closed minds.

> *Films:* Danny Kaye in *The Court Jester*; Buster Keaton in *The Navigator*, *Sherlock Jr.*, and *The General*; Charlie Chaplin in *The Circus* and *The Gold Rush*; Giulietta Masina in *La Strada*; Barbra Steisand in *What's Up, Doc?*; Renée Zellweger in *Nurse Betty*; Woody Allen in *Zelig*.
>
> *Drama: He Who Gets Slapped* by Maxim Gorky.
>
> *Opera: I Pagliacci* by Leoncavallo.
>
> *Literature: Don Quixote* by Miguel de Cervantes; *Gimpel the Fool* by Isaac Bashevis Singer; *Holy Fools and Mad Hatters* by Edward Hays; *The Autobiography of Henry VIII with Notes by his Fool, Will Somers* by Margaret George.
>
> *Religion/Myth:* Mullah Nasruddin, aka Hoja Nasredin (Sufi figure in Egypt, Iran, and Turkey, half saint and half fool, who acts like a ninny to teach wisdom); Sir Dagonet (the fool of King Arthur who was knighted as a joke, but who also performed bravely in tournaments); Heyoka (in Lakota Sioux lore, someone who does things backward to teach people not to take themselves too seriously); Coyote (in Native American lore).

● **Companion** *(Friend, Sidekick, Right Arm, Consort)*
The Sidekick's qualities of loyalty, tenacity, and unselfishness are the positive aspects of this archetype. A Sidekick/Companion provides a service, symbolically speaking, to a personality that often has a stronger nature or a role in life that carries more authority. Secretaries and personal assistants are examples of Right Arms, taking care of the day-to-day details of life. You might have an inner Companion that takes care of the details and allows another archetype to focus on work central to your mission. Companions are associated with providing emotional rather than sexual support. Platonic or friendship bonds are more in keeping with that particular archetype.

Betrayal is a common example of the shadow side of the Companion, which damages the soul.

> *Films:* Eve Arden in *Mildred Pierce, The Lady Takes a Sailor*, and *The Kid from Brooklyn*; Frank Sinatra and Montgomery Clift in *From Here to Eternity*; Susan Sarandon and Geena Davis in *Thelma and Louise*.

Television: My Friend Flicka; Lassie.

Fiction: The Adventures of Sherlock Holmes (Dr. Watson) by Arthur Conan Doyle.

Drama: Iago in *Othello* by Shakespeare (shadow).

Religion/Myth: Damon and Pythias (in Christian lore, two young men whose loyalty to each other won their freedom after Pythias was condemned to death); Enkidu (companion created by the gods for Gilgamesh, a natural man who proved a perfect match for the godlike hero king); Eris (Greek goddess of strife and constant companion of the war god Ares); Apis (holy bull worshiped in ancient Egypt as the companion of the creator god Ptah); Nike (Greek victory goddess and companion of Athena, goddess of wisdom and war).

Damsel *(Princess)*

The Damsel in Distress may be the oldest female archetype in all of popular literature and the movies. She is always beautiful and vulnerable and in need of rescue, specifically by a Knight, and, once rescued, is taken care of in lavish style. When disappointed, a Damsel must go through a process of empowerment and learn to take care of herself in the world. The shadow side of this archetype mistakenly teaches old patriarchal views that women are weak and teaches them to be helpless and in need of protection. It leads a woman to expect to have someone else who will fight her battles for her while she remains devoted and physically attractive and concealed in the castle. Many women still expect to marry a man who will give them a castle and take care of them. And some men are raised to expect to do this (see **Prince** and **Knight**).

The Damsel's fear of going it alone is holds the Damsel/Knight relationship together. It also often shatters the relationship when the Prince or Knight grows older and expects to have a perennially young, attractive Princess at his beck and call. The Princess inevitably grows older even if she remains helpless. Or she becomes more interested in the outside world, develops skills and competencies, and is unable to maintain the same old dynamic of dependency. Either way, most Damsel/Prince relationships ultimately find that they change or fail. The Damsel/Princess must ultimately learn to fight her own battles and evolve into a Queen.

The Princess is more often associated with romance rather than distress. She awaits a Knight who is worthy of her beauty and rank and will take her not to his castle but to a palace. The castles that Damsels are taken to have prisons, cold stone walls, drawbridges, and moats. Palaces are fantastically beautiful and charmed and are associated with ballrooms and elegance. The common (archetypal) expression "Daddy's little princess" implies an adoring father who brings up his daughter surrounded by beauty and abundance. There is no "Daddy's little damsel in distress." The Princess and the Damsel, however, both are taught to be helpless and do share a yearning for a Knight as a partner in life, the implication being that without a Knight, they are powerless in this world. The challenge inherent in these archetypal patterns, therefore, is to do for yourself what you expect the Knight to do for you—provide for and protect yourself.

The Princess archetype is also influenced by our colloquial use of the term and especially its heavy freight of antifeminist connotations of a woman who is overly demanding, as in "Jewish-American Princess" or in the story of the Princess and the Pea. Even when used positively, the word can imply an unreal, bland, or cosseted character, like the teenage daughter nicknamed Princess on the TV series *Father Knows Best*. But a genuine Princess looks out not for her own comfort and whimsy but for the welfare of those around her. In Asia, tales abound of clever and resourceful Princesses and of conflicts between schools of martial arts (for instance, a Prince and Princess battle it out in the Ang Lee film *Crouching Tiger, Hidden Dragon*). And Scheherazade bravely married the sultan who had decided to kill all his new wives at daybreak, and beguiled him with tales for a thousand and one nights until he rescinded his decree, thus saving all the women.

In reviewing your relationship to this archetype, return to your fantasies as a young girl and note what your expectations were in looking for a mate. Most significantly, were you (or are you) consciously or unconsciously awaiting the arrival of your "Knight in Shining Armor"? Did you think or behave like a Damsel? Were you hoping to be rescued? And if you are now coping with the consequences of a broken relationship, can you trace the reasons for the failed partnership back to being disappointed that your expectations as a Damsel were not met?

> *Films:* Pearl White in *The Perils of Pauline* silent films; Fay Wray in *King Kong;* Betty Hutton in *The Perils of Pauline;* Jean Simmons in *Young Bess;* Robin Wright in *The Princess Bride;* Carrie Fisher as Princess Leia in the *Star Wars* trilogy; Ingrid Bergman in *Anastasia;* Gwyneth Paltrow in *Shakespeare in Love;* Kate Winslet in *Titanic;* Jeff Daniels in *Something Wild.*
>
> *Fiction: Gone with the Wind* by Margaret Mitchell; *Emma* by Jane Austen.
>
> *Fairy Tales:* Snow White, Sleeping Beauty, Rapunzel, Cinderella.
>
> *Religion/Myth:* Ko-no-Hana (in Shinto belief, the Japanese Blossom Princess, who symbolizes the delicate aspects of earthly life); Io (in Greek myth, the princess daughter of a river god, who suffered continually as the object of Zeus' lust); Princess Aigiarm (strong, valiant daughter of Mongolian King Kaidu, who offered herself in marriage to any suitor who could wrestle her down but who, if he lost, had to give her a horse. She never married and won ten thousand horses).

Destroyer *(Attila, Mad Scientist, Serial Killer, Spoiler)*
Destruction and Reconstruction is another way of describing the Death and Rebirth cycle of life. Systems and structures must be dismantled so that new life can be born. Myths and legends about gods and goddesses bringing destruction to the earth are common to all traditions. Yahweh destroyed the

world through the great Flood and rained fire and brimstone on Sodom and Gomorrah. In the Hindu tradition, the goddess Kali, generally pictured wearing a belt made of dismembered arms and a necklace of human skulls, represents the positive power of destruction, annihilating ignorance and maintaining the world order. The god Shiva, Kali's male counterpart, destroys in order to create.

The impulse to destroy and rebuild is archetypal. We are bound to that cycle and therein lies the learning. Destruction also refers to releasing that which is destroying us, and, so, many therapists and other healers serve the role of the Destroyer by assisting others to release destructive emotions or behavior. The power of positive destruction is enormously healing and liberating.

In its shadow manifestation, destruction becomes an end in itself, and one becomes intoxicated with one's own destructive power and addicted to it. The Destroyer generates death, madness, and abuse and targets individuals and groups. It can manifest as a nation that destroys other nations or people who destroy the environment. To count this shadow archetype as part of your support group, you must be able to recognize a pattern within your psyche that destroys relationships or promotes attitudes and opinions that destroy others' dreams or potential.

> *Films:* Jack Palance in *The Sign of the Pagan;* William Holden in *The Wild Bunch;* Anthony Hopkins in *The Silence of the Lambs;* Ralph Fiennes in *Schindler's List;* Richard Baseheart in *Hitler.*
>
> *Religion/Myth:* Angra Mainyu or Ahriman (in Zoroastrianism, the eternal destroyer of good, personification of evil, and conveyor of death and disease); Kalki (in Hindu belief, the final incarnation of Vishnu, who will descend from the sky on a white horse to destroy the wicked, renew the world, and restore righteousness); the Furies or Erinyes (avenging deities of Greek myth who pursued and persecuted anyone who killed a parent, brother, or fellow clansman by driving the murderer mad); the Four Horsemen of the Apocalypse (allegorical figures in the New Testament Book of Revelation, or Apocalypse, who symbolize war, pestilence, famine, and death).

Detective *(Spy, Double Agent, Sleuth, Snoop, Sherlock Holmes, Private Investigator, Profiler*—see also **Warrior/Crime Fighter)**
Positive characteristics of the Detective include the ability to seek out knowledge and information that supports solving crimes and protecting the public. Detectives combine great powers of observation with highly evolved intuition to deduce the solutions to crimes. Whereas the Detective is public and often highly respected—especially its modern counterpart, the police Profiler—the empowered Spy is associated far more with the surreptitious and often illegal acquisition of secret information regarding politics, business, or national security. Our attitude toward spies often depends on whose side

they're on. Many Americans see Gary Powers as a heroic figure, while Double Agents such as Robert P. Hansson or British intelligence officer and Soviet spy Kim Philby are considered traitors.

The shadow side of these archetypes can manifest as voyerism, falsifying information, or selling out to the highest bidder. Parents who "spy" on their children with good intentions, such as uncovering their involvement with sex or drugs, are nonetheless flirting with the shadow Detective.

> *Films:* Humphrey Bogart in *The Maltese Falcon* and *The Big Sleep;* Richard Burton in *The Spy Who Came in from the Cold;* Kelly McGillis and Jeff Daniels in *The House on Carroll Street;* Kathleen Turner in *V. I. Warshawski;* Laurence Olivier in *Sleuth;* any James Bond, Sherlock Holmes, or Charlie Chan film.
>
> *Fiction:* Sir Arthur Conan Doyle; Dashiell Hammett; Agatha Christie; Rex Stout; Tom Clancy; John le Carré.
>
> *Television:* I Spy; Magnum, P.I.
>
> *Religion/Myth:* Sinon (in Greek lore, a spy who gained the trust of the Trojans by pretending to have deserted the Greeks, then convinced them to take in the wooden horse, leading to their downfall).

Don Juan *(Casanova, Gigolo, Seducer, Sex Addict)*

Sexual energy provides great power when properly channeled. Like the Femme Fatale, the Don Juan archetype can make us aware of falling into sex role clichés, misusing the power of romantic attraction and pursuit. Although associated with sensuality and sophistication, this archetype represents a man preying on women for the sake of conquest alone. Sex addiction is not about sex but about the need to gain control of someone. Don Juan radiates an attitude that all women need him far more than he needs them, and that he is invulnerable to their charms.

The positive aspect of this archetype is its underlying vulnerability and its power to open wide a heart that is capable of deep love. As many stories portray, once the gigolo meets his match, he has also found his mate. His match, however, in keeping with the profile of this pattern, must have emotional independence and the self-esteem to be immune to his manipulative skills.

> *Films:* Warren Beatty in *Shampoo;* Richard Gere in *American Gigolo;* Donald Sutherland in *Casanova;* Michael Caine in *Alfie;* Johnny Depp in *Don Juan de Marco;* Jude Law in *A.I.*
>
> *Fiction: Quiet Days in Clichy* by Henry Miller.
>
> *Religion/Myth:* Satyr (in Greek myth, a creature with a goat's tail, flanks, hooves, and horns, but otherwise human upper body, who drinks, dances, and chases nymphs. The Roman version is the faun, and in Slavonic culture, the Ljeschi); Priapus (Greek and Roman deity of gardens attributed with enormous genitals); Aka Manah (in Zoroastrianism, the personification of sensual desire).

Engineer *(Architect, Builder, Schemer)*
The Engineer is eminently practical and hands-on and devoted to making things work. The characteristics of the Engineer reflect the grounded, orderly, strategic qualities of mind that convert creative energy into a practical expression. This archetype also manifests as a talent for engineering everyday situations or designing solutions to common dilemmas. The shadow Engineer manifests as a master manipulator, designing and engineering situations to one's own advantage regardless of the needs or desires of others.

> *Films:* Alec Guinness in *The Bridge on the River Kwai*; Gary Cooper in *The Fountainhead*; Jeff Bridges in *Tucker.*
> *Drama: The Master Builder* by Henrik Ibsen
> *Religion/Myth:* Elen (in Welsh myth, the world's first highway engineer, who protected her land by magically creating highways so that her soldiers could defend it); Amenhotep (ancient Egyptian architect who later was venerated as the god of building); Daedalus (renowned Cretan architect who constructed the Labyrinth of the Minotaur and fashioned artificial wings for himself and his son, Icarus).

Exorcist *(Shaman)*
The ability to confront evil in the form of possession by destructive or antisocial impulses in oneself and others is as valuable today as it was in the time of Jesus, the master Exorcist. Just as modern biblical scholars suggest that the demons that Jesus cast out may have been forms of psychological illness, so we can see our own inner demons as arising from forces that we feel are beyond our control. Shamans, for example, conduct rituals for the release of negative spirits from a person's soul. To include this among your family of archetypes, however, you would have to find a lifelong pattern of exorcising the negative spirits of others or of social groups or society.

The shadow Exorcist attacks the evil in others without having the courage to face his own demons.

> *Films:* Jason Miller in *The Exorcist*; Bruce Willis in *The Sixth Sense.*
> *Religion/Myth:* Shoki (Shinto god of the afterlife and exorcism); Zhongkui (Taoist god of the afterlife and exorcism).

Father *(Patriarch, Progenitor, Parent)*
This archetype combines a talent for creating or initiating with the ability to oversee others, whether a biological family or a group of creative people. Although the Father has taken on negative connotations associated historically with paternalism and male dominance, we shouldn't lose sight of its primary characteristics of courage—think of Abraham leaving the home of his ancestors to father a new race in a strange land—and protectiveness. A true Father guides and shields those under his care, sacrificing his own desires when that's appropriate. The shadow Father emerges when that caring guidance and protection turns into dictatorial control or abuse of authority.

Being a biological father and family man clearly isn't enough to include this archetype in your intimate circle. You will need to uncover a lifelong attachment to the role of family patriarch, however you conceive of that family.

Films: William Powell in *Life with Father;* Spencer Tracy in *Father of the Bride;* Dustin Hoffman in *Kramer vs. Kramer;* Gregory Peck in *To Kill a Mockingbird;* Lamberto Maggiorani in *The Bicycle Thief;* Raymond Massey in *East of Eden* (shadow).

Television: Robert Young in *Father Knows Best;* Fred MacMurray in *My Three Sons.*

Fiction: All the Way Home by James Agee.

Religion/Myth: Most ancient cultures had at least one Father god, usually associated with the sky, who also functioned as creator and patriarch, including Uranus and Zeus (Greece); Jupiter (Rome); Indra and Brahma (India); the "Jade Emperor" (China); Izanagi (Japan); Ra and Ptah (Egypt); and Olorun and Obatala (Africa/Yoruba).

Femme Fatale *(Black Widow, Flirt, Siren, Circe, Seductress, Enchantress)*
The female counterpart of Don Juan sometimes adds the twist of killing her conquests as an expression of her ability to dominate, thereby reversing the conventional sexual stereotypes. As with Don Juan, the Femme Fatale represents highly refined skills at manipulating men without investing personal emotion. The Femme Fatale is both a sexual and a financial archetype and either comes from or is drawn to money and power. Seducing men with money and power and for the sake of personal control and survival is a classic part of this archetype, although the Femme Fatale is not looking for a home in the suburbs and the pleasures of family life.

As with the Don Juan archetype, the positive aspect of this pattern is the opening of the heart, which often occurs when the male object rejects the manipulations and dependency of the Femme Fatale, as Rhett Butler rejects Scarlett O'Hara at the end of *Gone with the Wind.*

Films: Barbara Stanwyck in *Double Indemnity;* Linda Fiorentino in *The Last Seduction;* Theresa Russell in *Black Widow;* Marilyn Monroe and Jane Russell in *Gentlemen Prefer Blondes;* Kathleen Turner in *Body Heat;* Elizabeth Taylor in *Cleopatra.*

Fiction: The Postman Always Rings Twice by James M. Cain.

Religion/Myth: Circe (in Greek myth, a sorceress/seductress who could turn men into animals with her magic wand); Potiphar's wife (in the Hebrew Bible, when her attempt to seduce Joseph failed, she had him thrown into captivity. Her name is Zeleikha in Islamic tradition); Tapairu (Polynesian nymphs who inhabit the waters that lead to the underworld; the goddess of death employs them to seduce men away from the earth); Lorelei (in Teutonic myth, a beautiful maiden who drowned herself after being spurned by her lover and was then transformed into a siren whose hypnotic music lured sailors to their death).

Gambler

The Gambler is a risk-taker who plays the odds. This archetype has many more aspects than are commonly considered, including not just card sharps and racetrack gamblers, but also drug addicts, entrepreneurs, and day traders. The Gambler is also active in the psyche of people who take risks in politics and other social activities that amount to gambling with one's reputation. From an energetic perspective, gambling is an attempt to outrun the speed at which ordinary change happens. Acquiring great wealth in a casino in one throw of the dice or by winning the lottery is a spectacular experience not only because of the money but because of the experience of the compression of time. The drama of trying to outrun the odds is the psychic lock on the Gambler within a person's psyche.

The positive aspect of this archetype manifests in following hunches and in the belief in one's intuition, even in the face of universal doubt. From real estate ventures to scientific research, hunches have often yielded fruitful outcomes. To assess whether you are a Gambler, review your ability to follow your intuition and what others might consider risky inner guidance. Ask yourself how many of your decisions are based on gut instinct rather than facts and figures.

You can evaluate your relationship to the shadow Gambler according to whether you have a compulsion. Some people who are obsessed with winning lotteries and striking it rich at casino tables—or in get-rich-quick or pyramid schemes—may spend relatively little money compared to professional gamblers, but their focus on finding ways to beat the odds is a central part of their life. A related form of gambling may affect the way you are focused on looking for lucky breaks in your relationships, rather than doing the hard psychic work needed to make them succeed.

Films: Steve McQueen in *The Cincinnati Kid* (shadow); Paul Newman, Jackie Gleason, and George C. Scott (shadow) in *The Hustler;* Woody Harrelson and Wesley Snipes in *White Men Can't Jump;* Edith Evans in *The Queen of Spades;* Clive Owen in *Croupier;* Roger Duchesne in *Bob le Flambeur (Bob the Gambler).*

Fiction: The Gambler by Dostoevsky.

Religion/Myth: Jason and Odysseus (heroic figures of Greek legend who fearlessly gambled against the odds, risking life and limb to achieve their goals); Cunawabi (Native American Paiute figure known as a gambler who takes many risky adventures and who also brings night and illness).

God (*Adonis*—see also **Hero**)

Whether a great worldly power or a great physical specimen, the God archetype represents the ultimate in male dominance. On the positive side, a God can be benevolent and compassionate, willing to use his powers to help others out of love for humanity. The shadow God easily becomes a dictator or despot, oppressing others with those same powers, or using his physical attractiveness to get what he wants without ever returning the affection he elicits. To claim this archetype among your support circle of twelve, you need to have a lifelong sense of great power, used either selfishly or selflessly.

You may feel a powerful connection to a particular deity, so here are a few from the Roman/Greek pantheon: Jupiter/Zeus: father god, head of the pantheon; Bacchus/Dionysus: wine and revelry; Mars/Ares: war; Neptune/Poseidon: the sea; Pluto/Hades: death and the underworld.

Films: Marlon Brando in *The Godfather* trilogy.

Religion/Myth: Like the archetype in human manifestation, mythic and religious Gods run the gamut from omniscient, benevolent deities to arbitrary destroyers. In addition to those listed above are Yahweh (Hebrew); Shiva, Vishnu, Brahma, Indra (Hindu); Allah (Muslim); Ra, Osiris, and Ptah (Egyptian); Baal (Canaanite); Marduk and Ishtar (Babylonian); Quetzalcoatl and Tezcatlipoca (Aztec); Enlil and Dumuzi (Sumerian); Osun and Olokun (Yoruba); Wakan Tanka (Native American).

Goddess *(Heroine)*

The oldest religious tradition on earth may well be Goddess worship, which some archaeologists trace back further than thirty thousand years. It was certainly natural to worship the archetype of woman as the Source of all life, especially in the age before male warriors replaced Her with their combative sky gods. The connection of fertility with exaggerated sexual attributes found in ancient statues of the Goddess survives in modern worship of screen goddesses such as Marilyn Monroe and Jayne Mansfield. The Goddess can be inspiring to women, embodying wisdom, guidance, physical grace, athletic prowess, and sensuality. This aspect is awakened by our relation to the goddesses of various spiritual traditions, including Kali, Durga, and Uma in India, Tara in Tibet, Quanyin in China, and the many manifestations of Mary, the Mother of Jesus, in Western belief, such as Our Lady of Guadalupe or the Black Madonna of Czestochowa.

The shadow side of the Goddess emerges from the exploration of the feminine power, including the exploitation or overindulgence of movie stars and fashion models.

Identifying with a goddess figure as a major archetype in your chart requires that you review lifelong associations with the image and personality associated with it. Athena is the able-bodied warrior woman as well as the classic "powerful woman behind the throne." Today we see this power reemerging in popular form in neomythic characters such as Xena the Warrior Princess and Buffy the Vampire Slayer—attractive women who are also strong and capable. The energy of Venus (Aphrodite) is prevalent in women who form their self-image strongly around their sexuality. Study the specific qualities of each goddess and evaluate how much of your sense of self is reflected in one of those patterns, beginning with a few of the most familiar names from the Roman/Greek pantheon: Venus/Aphrodite: love and fertility; Diana/Artemis: nature and hunting; Minerva/Athena: strength, clear thinking; Ceres/Demeter: motherhood; Juno/Hera: queenship and partnership; Proserpina/Persephone: mysticism and mediumship; Sophia: wisdom.

> *Films:* Kim Stanley in *The Goddess;* Ava Gardner in *One Touch of Venus;* Marilyn Monroe in *The Seven Year Itch;* Mira Sorvino in *Mighty Aphrodite.*
>
> *Fiction: She* by H. Rider Haggard.
>
> *Religion/Myth:* Every culture in the world has mythological stories portraying the power of the Goddess. Besides those mentioned above, you can choose from Tara and Quanyin (Tibetan and Chinese bodhisattvas of compassion); Amaterasu Omigami (Shinto sun goddess); Shakti (Hindu personification of energy as Divine Mother); Branwen (Celtic goddess of love and beauty); Oshun (East African Yoruba goddess of pleasure, love, and beauty); Pan Jin Lian (Chinese goddess of prostitution); Frigg (Norse goddess of marriage, motherhood, childbirth, and midwifery); Turan (Etruscan goddess of love, health, and fertility).

Gossip (see also **Networker**)

The Gossip archetype is associated with rumor-spreading, backbiting, and passing along information that is exaggerated and harmful and intended to disempower. On a professional level, the shadow Gossip manifests as publishing misleading information, creating damaging rumors, or hounding celebrities for their photos. Although everyone is prone to listening to and spreading gossip in some way, a Gossip archetype thrives on the power that is generated by passing around information that is secret or private. Most people would hesitate to choose this archetype because of its negative implications, yet many others make their living in the business of political, social, and entertainment gossip in a positive way. The archetype is connected to lessons of truth, integrity, and honoring the trust another has placed in you.

In assessing your connection to the Gossip, review how many of your life lessons have emerged from participating in gossip that has harmed another and then coping with the consequences. Do you measure the quality of a relationship by whether a person is willing to share secrets with you?

> *Films:* Rosalind Russell in *The Women;* Richard Hayden in *Sitting Pretty;* Burt Lancaster in *The Sweet Smell of Success;* John Malkovich and Glenn Close in *Dangerous Liaisons.*
>
> *Religion/Myth:* Ratatosk (in Norse myth, a squirrel whose name means "swift teeth," lives in the World Tree called Yggdrasil, and is a notorious gossip).

Guide (*Guru, Sage, Crone, Wise Woman, Spiritual Master, Evangelist, Preacher*)

The Guide takes the role of Teacher to a spiritual level, teaching not only the beliefs and practices that make up established religions, but also the overarching principle of seeing the Divine in every aspect of life. Clearly you do not have to be a professional preacher or guru to have this archetype, as we can all

learn to lead others spiritually by developing our own intuitive spiritual awareness and passing on whatever we have learned with genuine humility. To count
this archetype as part of your support group, however, you will need to discern
in your life a continuing pattern of devoting yourself to teaching others from
your own spiritual experiences. This presupposes that you have gained wisdom
through some combination of self-disciplined practice and study and perhaps
spontaneous spiritual experiences. Wisdom also comes with age, and so the
Crone or Wise Woman represents the ripening of natural insight and the
acceptance of what is, allowing one to pass that wisdom on to others.

The shadow aspect of the Guide is visible in many modern televangelists
and gurus of various traditions who are more interested in financial gain and
controlling their followers than in imparting genuine spiritual insight.

Films: Meetings with Remarkable Men; Robert Duvall in *The Apostle.*

Religion/Myth: Marpa (Buddhist master and guru of Milarepa who guided
him through arduous tasks to become the greatest yogi of Tibet).

Healer (*Wounded Healer, Intuitive Healer, Caregiver, Nurse, Therapist, Analyst,
Counselor*)
The Healer archetype manifests as a passion to serve others in the form of
repairing the body, mind, and spirit. It expresses itself through channels
other than those classically associated with the healing of illnesses, and so you
need to look beyond the obvious definition of what you "do." You can be
strongly guided by this archetype in any occupation or role in life. Some
people, by their very nature and personality, are able to inspire others to
release their painful histories or make changes in their lives that redirect the
course of their future. Essential characteristics include an inherent strength
and the ability to assist people in transforming their pain into a healing
process, as well as having the "wiring" required to channel the energy needed
to generate physical or emotional changes.

Religion/Myth: Rabbi Hanina ben Dosa (Jewish healer considered to
have been in the same class as Jesus); Ninkarrak (Babylonian/Sumer-
ian goddess who nursed sick humans); Bear Medicine Woman (American Indian healing spirit); Mukuru (creator god of the Herero
bushmen of Namibia, who sends life-giving rain, heals the sick, and
cares for the elderly).

Wounded Healer
The Wounded Healer is initiated into the art of healing through some form
of personal hardship—anything from an actual physical injury or illness to
the loss of all one's earthly possessions. Regardless of the shape of the wound,
the challenge inherent in this initiation process is that one is unable to turn to
others for help beyond a certain degree of support. Only the initiate can ultimately heal the wound; if it is an illness or accident, it will frequently be one
for which there is no conventional cure. The Wounded Healer archetype

emerges in your psyche with the demand that you push yourself to a level of inner effort that becomes more a process of transformation than an attempt to heal an illness. If you have successfully completed the initiation, you inevitably experience an exceptional healing, and a path of service seems to be divinely provided shortly after the initiation is complete.

The shadow of both the Healer and Wounded Healer manifests through a desire to take advantage of those who need help, including claims that you can heal any and every illness a person has.

Films: Ellen Burstyn in *Resurrection;* Louise Fletcher in *One Flew Over the Cuckoo's Nest* (shadow); Rosalind Russell in *Sister Kenny;* Barbara Stanwyck in *Miracle Woman* (based on Aimee Semple McPherson).

Fiction: The Citadel by A. J. Cronin; *Elmer Gantry* by Sinclair Lewis (shadow).

Religion/Myth: Asklepios (Greek hero who later become a plague god, then the god of medicine and healing); Aesculapius (Roman god of healing based on the Greek Asklepios); Garuda (great golden bird with an eagle's beak and wings and human body, the Indian symbol of medicine); Meditrina ("Healer," a Roman goddess of wine and health who was later syncretized into the cult of Aesculapius); Eeyeekalduk (Inuit god of healing); the Medicine Buddhas (most prominently, Bhaishajyaguru in Tibet and Yakushi-Nyorai in Japan, who symbolize the healing and transformative quality of buddhahood).

Hedonist *(Bon Vivant, Chef, Gourmet, Gourmand, Sybarite*—see also **Mystic***)*
This Archetype has an "appetite" for the pleasurable aspects of life, from good food and wine to sexuality and sensuality. As scientific research has shown, pleasure can improve our health and extend our lives and needs to be part of a balanced life. Indulging the self is central to the psyche of this archetype, whether treating oneself to a health spa or learning the nuances of lovemaking. That the Hedonist is generally thought of as someone who pursues extremes of self-indulgence is more a reflection of our Puritan heritage than of the archetype itself. In positive terms, it inspires creative energy in the psyche to embrace the "good" things in life. It also challenges in a positive way the collective archetypal fear of being seduced and losing control in the physical world. The shadow Hedonist may manifest as pursuing pleasure without regard for other people or one's own good health.

The search for physical ecstasy parallels the search for spiritual transformation, a truth that is apparent in the dual identity of the famous Greek icon of pleasure-seeking, Dionysus. Besides being a god of wine and fertility (later adopted by the Romans as Bacchus), Dionysus also represents the goal of mystery religions, like those practiced at Eleusis: ecstatic delivery from the mundane world through the physical or spiritual intoxication induced by secret rites. The sacrament of Soma (also a god of the Vedic pantheon) played a similar role in ancient Indian spirituality.

Films: Babette's Feast; Like Water for Chocolate; Big Night.

Fiction: Tom Jones by Henry Fielding; *The Unbearable Lightness of Being* by Milan Kundera; *Les Liaisons Dangereuses* by P. Choderlos De Laclos.

Religion/Myth: Oshun (Yoruba goddess of love and pleasure who is generous and benign); Bebhionn (Irish patron goddess of pleasure); Qadesh (Western Semitic fertility goddess and epitome of female sexuality and eroticism); Bes (Egyptian dwarf god originally associated with royalty and childbirth who became popular among the masses as a god of human pleasures of mirth, music, and dance).

● Hero/Heroine (see also **Knight, Warrior**)

Many of the gods of the world's ancient religions began their lives as heroes capable of great feats of strength or skill. The Hero is also a classic figure in ancient Greek and Roman literature, often portrayed as one who must confront an increasingly difficult path of obstacles in order to birth his manhood. Today this archetype holds a dominant position in the social mind as an icon of both male and female power, from the superheroes of comic books, such as Superman and Wonder Woman, to television and countless movies and popular novels. In the classic Hero's Journey, as defined by Joseph Campbell and others, an individual goes on a journey of initiation to awaken an inner knowing or spiritual power. The Self emerges as the Hero faces physical and internal obstacles, confronting the survival fears that would compromise his journey of empowerment and conquering the forces arrayed against him. The Hero then returns to the tribe with something of great value to all.

From a shadow perspective, the Hero can become empowered through the disempowerment of others. The manner in which the Hero uses his physical power is a reflection of the spirit of the Hero, represented through authentic acts of heroism.

Films: Sigourney Weaver in *Alien*; Dustin Hoffman in *Hero*; Jeff Bridges in *The Last American Hero*; Kevin Costner in *The Postman* and *Waterworld*; Debbie Reynolds in *The Unsinkable Molly Brown*; Seema Biswas as Phoolan Devi in *Bandit Queen*.

Religion/Myth: Ulysses (hero of *The Odyssey* whose most renowned trait was his supreme resourcefulness, the ability to find a way out of the most dangerous situation); Arjuna (in the Bhagavad Gita, his questioning of his Hero/Warrior role leads the god Krishna to instruct him in divine wisdom); Hidesato (in Japanese legend, a killer of many monsters, including the feared Centipede); Saynday (a hero-trickster of the Native American Kiowa tribe); Paul Bunyan (legendary hero of the lumber camps of the American Northwest, whose feats included creating the Grand Canyon by dragging his axe behind him); Theseus (Athenian hero who slew the Marathonian Bull and the Minotaur); Bernardo del Caprio (ninth-century Spanish hero credited with defeating Roland at Roncesvalles).

❖ **Judge** (*Critic, Examiner, Mediator, Arbitrator*)

The template for the Judge archetype in Jewish-Christian culture largely derives from King Solomon, who was notable for balancing justice and compassion. So thoroughly do we maintain this ancient template that Solomon's characteristic balancing is now the standard by which we measure all judges. Those who manipulate or disgrace justice or violate this creed are held to be social and moral criminals, having damaged the honor of the courtroom and the nation, and the archetype itself. For that reason, this archetype should be understood as one that has the vision to manage the fair distribution of power in whatever form it takes, from violating military codes to breaking marriage vows.

One need not be an attorney, judge, or critic by profession to identify with this archetype. If you are a natural mediator or involved in interventions between people, you may carry this archetype in your psyche. Personal qualities that inspire in you a commitment to lead a life with high standards related to justice and wisdom as well as the manner in which you interact with other people reflect a strong connection to this archetype. Prolonged suffering from having been misjudged—an experience that walks hand-in-hand with learning forgiveness—should also be considered an expression of this archetype in your life. But as with all other archetypal evaluations, you are not looking for one experience of having been misjudged or misjudging another, but rather a lifelong learning process that is centered around the learning of justice and compassion.

The shadow Judge manifests as consistently destructive criticism, judging without compassion or with a hidden agenda. Legal manipulation, misuse of legal authority, and threatening others through an association with the law are other expressions of the shadow. Such manipulation includes the misuse of business authority as well as conventional legal and criminal authority.

> *Films:* Spencer Tracy in *Judgment at Nuremberg;* Louis Calhern as Oliver Wendell Holmes in *The Magnificent Yankee;* John Forsythe in *And Justice for All* (shadow); Dominic Guard in *The Go-Between.*
>
> *Fiction: Billy Budd, Foretopman* (Capt. Starry Vere) by Herman Melville; *The Ambassadors* by Henry James.
>
> *Religion/Myth:* Skan (creator god of the Dakota Sioux who judges both gods and the souls of humans); Yama (Hindu and Buddhist god of death, judge of the dead, and ruler of death's kingdom or the Hell realms); Pluto/Hades (Roman/Greek god of the underworld and judge of the dead); Thoth (primarily the Egyptian patron deity of scribes, also known as a mediator among the gods); San-guan ("Three Rulers," collective name for three Taoist deities who keep a register of the good and evil deeds of people).

King (*Emperor, Ruler, Leader, Chief*)

The King is an archetype of major proportions, representing the height of temporal male power and authority. Both benevolence and cruelty in their extreme expressions are associated with this archetype. (Classic to the cruel

King is the collective hope of his kingdom that he should fall from his throne.) The King is associated more with the royal blood and inheritance, whereas an Emperor can arise from common society, as did Napoleon. The bloodline connects the King to the Prince archetype and to attitudes of "entitlement," one of the shadow characteristics of archetypes associated with rulership. A resistance to criticism, questioning, and challenges in decisions about controlling his kingdom is also part of the King's shadow.

Throughout history, the pendulum has swung from good Kings to evil, from benevolent, even saintly rulers to greedy, gluttonous criminals. King Louis IX of France—Saint Louis—combined the qualities of a just ruler, fearless warrior, and holy man. The thirteenth-century sovereign lived for the welfare of his subjects and the glory of God. Charlemagne, King David, and Akhenaton of Egypt were among earth's most enlightened, if occasionally all-too-human, rulers. And then there was mad King George III of England, who led the colonies to rebel; King Louis XVI of France, who was synonymous with decadence and excess; and Emperor Hirohito of Japan, who led his country into a devastating war.

This archetype maintains the same characteristics on an individual level, whether one's kingdom is a corporation, a community, or a family. The need to rule and exert control over a kingdom is key to this archetype.

> *Films:* Charles Laughton in *The Private Life of King Henry VIII*; Yul Brynner in *The King and I*; Richard Gere in *King David*; Paul Scofield in *King Lear* (1971); Christopher Walken in *The King of New York* (shadow extraordinaire).
>
> *Drama: Richard III, Henry IV, Henry V, Hamlet,* and *Macbeth* by Shakespeare.
>
> *Fiction: King of the Gypsies* by Peter Maas; *The Godfather* by Mario Puzo (shadow); *The Once and Future King* by T. H. White.
>
> *Religion/Myth:* Priam (king of Troy); Daibutsu/Daibosatsu (Japanese meditating buddha as world ruler); Sila or Silap-inua (divine ruler of the Eskimo seen as the air you breathe and the energy that moves both the entire universe and each of us individually); Amun (supreme Egyptian creator god, originally ruler of the air and the force behind wind and breezes); Chief Seattle (Native American leader); Haile Selassie (emperor of Ethiopia, later deified by the Rastafarian religion).

Knight (see also **Warrior, Rescuer, Hero**)

The Knight archetype is primarily associated with chivalry, courtly romance, protection of the Princess, and going to battle only for honorable causes. The Knight serves his King or Lord and so this archetype has spiritual overtones as well of service and devotion. Loyalty and self-sacrifice are the Knight's great virtues, along with a natural ability to get things done.

The Black Knight donning dark armor and riding a black horse represents the shadow characteristics of this archetype, especially the absence of honor and chivalry. Somewhat like the Warrior, the shadow Knight manifests as loyalty to a questionable ruler or principle. In its negative aspect, the Knight can also, like the Rescuer, fall into a pattern of saving others but ignoring his own needs. A true Knight, like the Mystic, walks the fine line between self-sacrifice and self-neglect.

Films: Harrison Ford in *Indiana Jones and the Last Crusade;* Tom Hanks in *Saving Private Ryan* and *Apollo 13;* Christopher Reeve in *Superman;* Kevin Costner in *Dances with Wolves, Tin Cup,* and *JFK.*

Drama: Man of LaMancha by Dale Wasserman.

Television: Have Gun, Will Travel.

Fairy Tale: Prince Valiant.

Religion/Myth: Knights of the Round Table (in medieval English lore, a semimythic group of 150 knights including Lancelot, Gawain, Kay, Mordred, Galahad, and others who served under King Arthur); Sir Percival/Parzifal (Knight of the Round Table who got to see the Holy Grail); Fabian (a good Knight turned into a forest spirit by his ex-lover, a sorceress, and now dwells in the hills near Prague); Damas (shadow Knight who trapped other knights so that his brother could fight them).

Liberator

We tend to think of Liberators as great military and political leaders who free an entire country or people from servitude, such as Mahatma Gandhi, Abraham Lincoln, Simón Bolívar of Venezuela, Nelson Mandela, and, depending on your politics, Lenin, Castro, and Che Guevara. In everyday life, however, any number of people can play a similar role on a smaller scale, helping to liberate us from the tyranny of self-inflicted negative thought patterns and beliefs, spiritual sluggishness, poor nutrition, destructive relationships, or addictive behavior. This archetype can be an invaluable ally in helping to free us from old, entrenched beliefs and attitudes that have been inculcated from without, much like occupying colonial armies. Jesus, Muhammad, and the Buddha were Liberators in this sense, offering options to the violence, suffering, and spiritual stagnation of their respective times and places. You do not have to be a charismatic leader to have this archetype, though. Thousands of people have taken part in long campaigns to win freedom from various kinds of oppression, from the Freedom Riders of the civil rights movement in the United States to the freedom fighters of the Hungarian revolution.

The shadow Liberator manifests in those who would liberate us from one tyrant only to impose their own tyranny over our lives—corporate, political, religious, and spiritual leaders who speak of freedom as a way to their individual aggrandizement.

In evaluating whether this archetype belongs in your circle of twelve, ask whether you have shown a lifelong pattern of helping to free others from injustices, from adverse economic or social conditions, or simply from their misconceptions.

Films: Anthony Quinn in *Zorba the Greek;* Rosalind Russell in *Auntie Mame;* Ingrid Bergman in *Joan of Arc;* Tom Selleck in *In and Out.*
Fiction: Siddhartha by Hermann Hesse.
Fairy Tale: Belling the Cat.
Religion/Myth: Dionysus and Eros (both bore other names meaning "the liberator").

❋ Lover

This archetype appears not only in those who are romantically inclined, but also in anyone who exhibits great passion and devotion. One can be a Lover of art, music, gardening, Persian carpets, nature, or needlepoint. The key is having a sense of unbridled and exaggerated affection and appreciation of someone or something that influences the organization of your life and environment. Although the Lover is present in everyone's life to some degree, as a personal archetype it needs to play a significant role in the overall design of your life and your self-esteem, which is its strongest link to your psyche. The Lover is connected to issues of self-esteem because this archetype is so strongly represented by one's physical appearance. Even if you have the Lover archetype prominently in your psyche, you may repress this pattern out of a lack of self-esteem, especially regarding your physical attractiveness.

The shadow Lover manifests as an exaggerated, obsessive passion that has a destructive effect on one's physical or mental health and self-esteem.

Films: Nicolas Cage in *Moonstruck;* Charles Denner in *The Man Who Loved Women* (Truffaut version); Ingrid Bergman and Humphrey Bogart in *Casablanca;* José Ferrer in *Cyrano de Bergerac.*
Drama: Romeo and Juliet by Shakespeare.
Poetry: Troilus and Cressida by Chaucer.
Fiction: Stealing Heaven by Marion Meade (Abélard and Heloïse).
Fairy Tales: The Princess and the Frog; Beauty and the Beast.
Religion/Myth: Pyramus and Thisbe (star-crossed Babylonian lovers, described by Ovid, who commit double suicide); Endymion (in Greek myth, a shepherd boy and mortal lover of the moon goddess Selene); Hasu-Ko (a Japanese girl who died of love for her betrothed, whom she had never seen); Freya (Norse goddess of love and fertility and a symbol of sensuality, a lover of music, spring, flowers, and elves); Guinevere and Lancelot (although Guinevere was married to King Arthur and Lancelot was one of his favorite knights, they pursued an affair that led to the eventual undoing of the Round Table).

Martyr

The Martyr archetype is well known in two arenas: as a classic political or religious figure, and in the self-help world of contemporary psychology. Within the self-help field, the shadow Martyr is viewed as a person who has learned to utilize a combination of service and suffering for others as the primary means of controlling and manipulating her environment. Ironically, in the social and political world, the Martyr is often highly respected for having the courage to represent a cause, even if it requires dying for that cause for the sake of others. Suffering so that others might be redeemed, whether that redemption takes a spiritual or political form, is among the most sacred of human acts. While people recognize this archetype in others, particularly when they are directly influenced by the individual sporting this pattern, they often cannot see it in themselves.

Films: Paul Scofield in *A Man for All Seasons*; Meryl Streep in *Silkwood*; Denzel Washington in *Malcolm X*; Ben Kingsley in *Gandhi*.

Drama: Saint Joan by G. B. Shaw.

Fiction: A Tale of Two Cities by Charles Dickens.

Religion/Myth: Many Christian saints, including the Apostles; Mansur al-Hallaj (tenth-century Sufi mystic martyred for his belief that God existed within him).

Mediator *(Ambassador, Diplomat, Go-Between)*

Smoothing relations between potentially antagonistic groups or individuals requires patience and skill, an ability to read people and situations with great acuity. If a good Advocate must empathize with those he is helping, a good Mediator must be able to see and respect both sides of an argument or cause, thereby bringing warring parties together. One member of a family often assumes this role, so you do not have to be a career diplomat to qualify for this archetype. But you must have a lifelong commitment to resolving disputes and bringing people together.

The shadow Mediator manifests as an ulterior motive or hidden agenda, working two sides of an issue for personal gain.

Films: Dominic Guard in *The Go-Between*.

Fiction: The Ambassadors by Henry James.

Religion/Myth: Thoth (Egyptian god of wisdom and mediator among the gods, who always sought his counsel); Genetaska (Iroquois woman so respected for her fairness and impartiality that all disputes were brought to her to settle); Mitra/Mithra (Vedic/Persian god of friendships and contracts and guardian of the cosmic order, regarded as a mediator between the gods and humankind).

Mentor *(Master, Counselor, Tutor)*

A Mentor is a teacher in whom you can place your implicit trust. The word comes from the character in *The Odyssey* to whom Odysseus, on setting out for Troy, had entrusted the care of his house and the education of his son, Telemachus. Today the role of Mentor is crucial in a surprising range of life situations, from many forms of art and artisanship to business and spiritual practice. Mentors do more than just teach; they pass on wisdom and refine their students' character. In its shadow aspect, however, the Mentor can take on an overbearing attitude that is more about imposing control than imparting wisdom. A characteristic of the shadow Mentor is an inability to allow the student to move on into the role of Master, maintaining control over the student's development of mind, body, and skills.

The distinction between this archetype and the Teacher is mainly one of degree. If you have shown a lifelong pattern of taking individual "students" under your wing and guiding many aspects of their life, this may be an appropriate choice.

> *Films (Mentor):* Alec Guinness to Mark Hamill in *Star Wars;* Takashi Shimura to Toshiro Mifune in *The Seven Samurai;* Yul Brynner to Horst Bucholz in *The Magnificent Seven;* Bette Davis to Anne Baxter in *All About Eve;* Paul Newman to Tom Cruise in *The Color of Money.*
>
> *Films (Teacher):* Bette Davis in *The Corn Is Green;* Sidney Poitier in *To Sir with Love;* Michael Caine in *Educating Rita;* Glenn Ford in *Blackboard Jungle.*
>
> *Television:* James Gandolfini to Robert Imperioli in *The Sopranos.*
>
> *Fiction:* Fagin to Oliver in *Oliver Twist* by Charles Dickens (shadow).
>
> *Drama: The Miracle Worker* by William Gibson.
>
> *Fiction: The Prime of Miss Jean Brodie* by Muriel Spark (shadow); *Hard Times* by Charles Dickens (shadow).
>
> *Religion/Myth:* Krishna (in Indian scripture, the spiritual mentor of Arjuna); Chiron (in Greek myth, a wise centaur who had extensive knowledge of the healing arts and tutored Asclepius, Theseus, and Achilles); Ninsun (in Sumerian legend, the mother of Gilgamesh who serves as his counselor).

Messiah *(Redeemer, Savior)*

This archetype is associated with the embodiment of divine power and being sent on a mission by Heaven to save humanity. For all of its Judeo-Christian significance, the archetype of the Messiah has also become associated with psychological behavior. The Messiah complex, for example, applies to a person who is convinced of his divine mission and, in almost all cases, becomes obsessed with his mission to the point of psychosis, reaching an extreme in which a person begins to hear voices directing him to take lethal action. Criminals such as Jim Jones and Charles Manson are evidence of the shadow Messiah in its extreme.

Its subtle expression, however, is far more common and more difficult to identify as a personal pattern. People can become obsessed about their spiritual purpose, convinced that God needs them to do something.

> *Films:* Reese Witherspoon and Tobey Maguire in *Pleasantville;* Jeremy Irons and Robert De Niro in *The Mission;* Marcello Mastroianni in *The Organizer.*

Religion/Myth: Mashiach ("the anointed one" in Hebrew, the descendant of King David who is expected to restore the Jewish kingdom); Jesus Christ ("the anointed one" in Greek, believed by Christians to be the promised redeemer); Adam Kadmon ("Primordial Man," in the Jewish Kabbalah, described as the most perfect manifestation of God that humanity could contemplate, later identified with the Messiah); al-Mahdi ("the guided one" in Arabic, awaited descendant of Muhammad who will herald the end of history and restore Islamic purity); Maitreya ("the loving one" in Sanskrit, the fifth and final earthly Buddha who will help all those who have not yet realized enlightenment); Kalki (in Hindu belief, a future reincarnation of Vishnu who will arrive on a white horse to liberate the world from strife); Tang (a Chinese messiah who saved mankind from a great drought by sacrificing his body in a mulberry bush, immediately inducing rainfall).

Midas/Miser

These two archetypes are so close that for practical purposes you can consider them together. Midas turned everything he touched into gold, including, tragically, his beloved daughter. The archetype is associated with entrepreneurial or creative ability. That Midas was a king symbolically implies that the Midas figure has the power to generate wealth for an entire kingdom, yet is interested only in his personal aggrandizement. Greed is his downfall. For that reason, lessons of generosity are a large part of the characteristics of this archetype. The shadow Midas or Miser creates wealth by hording money and emotions at the expense of others, and refusing to share them.

Although the desire to earn a living or become wealthy is not negative, this archetype also represents a need to control the forces around you for fear of losing your wealth. The challenges inherent in the Miser and Midas can go so far as to make a person confront what he is willing to do to create a mountain of wealth.

Films: Bette Davis in *The Little Foxes;* Michael Douglas in *Wall Street;* James Dean in *Giant;* Lionel Barrymore in *It's a Wonderful Life.*

Fiction: Scrooge in *A Christmas Carol* and Uriah Heep in *David Copperfield* by Charles Dickens; *Silas Marner* by George Eliot.

Drama: The Miser by Molière.

Religion/Myth: Midas (a king of Phrygia in Asia Minor who was given the dubious gift of the golden touch by the god Dionysus); Kukuth (in Albanian lore, the spirit of a deceased miser who cannot find rest).

Monk/Nun *(Celibate)*

The positive aspects of this archetype are fairly obvious: spiritual intensity, devotion, dedication, persistence, and perhaps wisdom. On the shadow side, the role of a religious recluse could be seen as being removed from the real world, overly pious, even privileged in the sense of not having to be concerned about earning a living or raising a family. Yet, historically, monks have been extremely industrious and involved in real-world enterprises, whether draining swamps and planting vineyards in medieval Europe, working the rice fields in Asia, building monasteries, teaching, or copying and preserving texts. Today the Monk archetype may show up in the ability to be single-minded, assiduous, devoted to a spiritual path or to any great achievement that requires intense focus. In this sense, novelists and entrepreneurs can carry the Monk as readily as spiritual adepts.

The Celibate reserves his or her energy for work and/or spiritual practice. Yet one can be a Monk, even a religious one, without being celibate, as is the case with some Tibetan lamas, yogis, and Islamic scholars. Then there were Abélard and Heloïse, the twelfth-century Monk and Nun who forsook their vows of celibacy out of passion for each other. Both were superior in their fields—Abélard as lecturer, debater, and philosopher, Heloïse as a radical prioress and founder of convents—and, although their passion caused them great suffering, it does not seem to have hurt their spiritual work.

> *Films:* Claude Laydu in *Diary of a Country Priest;* Audrey Hepburn in *The Nun's Story;* Yi Pan-Yong in *Why Has Bodhi-Dharma Left for the East?;* Deborah Kerr in *Heaven Knows, Mr. Allison;* Loretta Young in *Come to the Stable;* Lilia Skala in *Lilies of the Field.*
>
> *Television:* Derek Jacobi in *Brother Cadfael.*
>
> *Fiction: The Name of the Rose* by Umberto Eco.
>
> *Religion/Myth:* Friar Tuck (the mythical swordfighting monk of Robin Hood's Merry Men); Nennius (Welsh monk commonly believed to have compiled the *Historia Brittonum,* which was used by Geoffrey of Monmouth and others to reconstruct the history of King Arthur); Bernadette Soubiros (nineteenth-century French girl who at the age of fourteen claimed visions of the Virgin Mary).

Mother *(Matriarch, Mother Nature, Parent)*

The Mother is the life-giver, the source of nurturing and nourishment, unconditional fountain of love, patience, devotion, caring, and unselfish acts. This archetype is the keeper and protector of life, from children to the family to (in the greater Mother Nature archetype) the earth and all life. Mother Nature, also known as Gaia, is the Goddess of Life, the caretaker of the living environment of this planet. She is recognized as powerful, and when storms leave death and destruction in their wake, she may be referred to as wrathful. The power of compassion and the endless capacity to forgive her children and put them before herself are essential to the Good Mother. The Devouring, Abusive, Abandoning, and Working Mother each represent different aspects of this primal archetype within the entire human community.

Although Mothers have always worked, the contemporary archetype of the Career or Working Mother reflects the crises experienced by many women who seek also to be Devoted Mothers. Measured against the impossible mythic ideal of the Perfect Mother, the Career Mom is sometimes assumed unfairly to be a mother who puts her own needs before those of the children. This is an archetypal crisis for many women.

The Devouring Mother "consumes" her children psychologically and emotionally and often instills in them feelings of guilt at leaving her or becoming independent. The Abusive and Abandoning Mothers violate natural law by harming their own young.

Connections to the Mother archetype are not to be measured only by whether a woman is a biological mother. If you are intimately connected to nurturing and protecting the environment, including gardening or farming or supporting any life form, you should strongly consider whether your bond to Mother Nature is part of a lifelong devotion that defines you. You may also recognize a strong bond to the Mother archetype in the form of one or all of her shadows. While it is difficult to admit, some women may have to face the fact that their children see them through the shadow aspects of the Mother, including the Abusive or Abandoning Mother.

Just as women can have a real connection to the Father archetype when they take on the paternal role in the household, so some men may relate to being "Mr. Mom," yet another contemporary sculpting of the Mother archetype. The qualities that are associated with this archetype can be expressed in other than biological ways, such as giving birth to books or ideas or by nurturing others.

Films: Irene Dunne in *I Remember Mama;* Myrna Loy in *Cheaper by the Dozen* and *Belles on Their Toes;* Sophia Loren in *Two Women;* Sally Field in *Places in the Heart;* Anne Bancroft in *The Pumpkin Eater;* Rosalind Russell in *Gypsy* (devouring); Katharine Hepburn in *Suddenly Last Summer* (shadow); Faye Dunaway in *Mommie Dearest* (shadow); Angela Lansbury in *The Manchurian Candidate* (shadow); Gladys Cooper in *Now Voyager* (shadow); Alberta Watson in *Spanking the Monkey* (incestuous).

Drama: Mother Courage by Bertolt Brecht; *Medea* by Euripides; *The Glass Menagerie* by Tennessee Williams.

Religion/Myth: As with Gods, Goddesses, and Mystics, the Mother appears in all religious traditions and myths, usually as the Divine Mother. These are just a few examples: Lakshmi, Durga, and Kali (Hinduism); Mary/Miryam (Christianity/Islam); Sarai and Naomi (Judaism); Cybele (fertility goddess of ancient Anatolia, also known as the Great Mother); Demeter (Greek myth); Isis (Egyptian myth); Tellus (Roman Mother Earth goddess); Cihuacoatl (Aztec Mother Earth goddess, also patron of birth and of women who die in childbirth).

Fairy Tales: Mother Goose, Mother Hubbard.

Mystic *(Renunciate, Anchorite, Hermit)*
Perhaps no archetype is more coveted by my students or more misunderstood than the Mystic. Many want to believe that they have mystical inclinations, yet underestimate how arduous the genuine mystical path is. When

they find out, they're usually happy to let someone else have this role. The lives of the world's great mystics have often included extraordinary states of consciousness, such as prolonged ecstatic trances, and preternatural abilities of precognition or bilocation. Yet they also contained sometimes great physical as well as spiritual suffering, hard work, and mundane activities that made up much of their days. If you truly want to name this archetype as part of your sacred consortium, ask yourself if you are ready to pay the price in blood, sweat, and tears. If mystical consciousness is something you engage in once a day during meditation, or on a weekend retreat or a yoga workshop, you may be a spiritual seeker, but not a Mystic. The single-minded dedication of the Mystic carries over to the Renunciate, who relinquishes material desires and ambitions to pursue spiritual practice; the Anchorite, who withdraws from the world almost entirely to follow a similar path; and the Hermit, who withdraws from others to pursue a solitary life, although not always for spiritual purposes.

The shadow Mystic manifests as an egocentric concern for one's own spiritual progress to the exclusion of others, and an attendant sense of self-importance at having achieved "higher" states of consciousness. It may also emerge in behavior that takes advantage of admirers or students in base economic, emotional, or sexual ways. Since genuine enlightenment manifests as the desire to be of service, this is a pretty good indication that you haven't arrived yet.

Films: Catherine Mouchet in *Thérèse;* Richard Dreyfuss in *Close Encounters of the Third Kind;* Emily Watson in *Breaking the Waves.*

Drama: Agnes of God by John Pielmeyer.

Fiction: Lying Awake by Marc Salzman.

Religion/Myth: All the great traditions have produced mystics, of which the following are a small representative sample: Teresa of Ávila, Meister Eckhart, William Law, Hildegarde of Bingen (Christianity); Ba'al Shem Tov, Moses ben Nahman, and Abraham Abulafia (Judaism); Rabi'a, Ibn al-'Arabi, and Mansur al-Hallaj (Islam); Sri Ramakrishna, Anandamayi Ma, and Ramana Maharshi (Hinduism); Bodhidharma, Milarepa, Bankei, and Pema Chödron (Buddhism); Chuang-tzu and Wang-pi (Taoism); Padrinho Sebastão and Credo Mutwa (shamanism).

Networker *(Messenger, Herald, Courier, Journalist, Communicator*—see also **Gossip***)*
Although networking seems like a very modern skill tied to career advancement in the media age, it is actually quite ancient. Networkers expand their sphere of influence by forging alliances and making connections among vastly different groups of people and can be traced back to the intrigues of the Middle Ages, Greece, Rome, and ancient China. Networking would also have been an integral part of any military alliance as well as all social and clan

confederations in prehistory. In its positive aspect, this archetype helps us develop social flexibility and empathy that enables one to find commonality with others who might not at first seem to be potential friends, allies, or confederates. Like the related archetypes of Messenger and Communicator, the Networker has the skills to bring information—or power—and inspiration to disparate groups of people. The shadow Networker merely uses others for personal gain.

> *Films:* Peter Finch in *Network;* John Boles in *A Message to Garcia;* Stewart Peterson in *Pony Express Rider;* Jeff Goldblum in *Between the Lines.*

> *Religion/Myth:* Almost every culture on earth has or had a messenger of the gods who networks between the divine and human realms, including the angel Raphael (Judaism); Gabriel (Christianity); Jibril (Islam); Matarisvan (Vedic India); Eagle and Coyote (American Indian); Iris and Hermes (Greece); Mercury (Rome); Sraosa (Zoroastrianism); Nusku (Assyria); Nirah (Sumeria); Srosh (Persia); Paynal (Aztec); Savali (Samoa); Gou Mang (China); Narada (Java); Gna and Hermod (Norse).

Pioneer *(Explorer, Settler, Pilgrim, Innovator, Entrepreneur)*
The Pioneer is called to discover and explore new lands, whether that territory is external or internal. The passion to explore the South Pole is as much a pioneering endeavor as the passion to explore medicine or spiritual practice. Even initiating new fashions, art, music, literature, or business ventures may qualify as expressions of this archetype. The core ingredient is innovation—doing and creating what has not been done before. To consider this archetype seriously as one of your twelve, your life must be characterized by a need to step on fresh and undiscovered territory in at least one realm.

The shadow Pioneer manifests as a compulsive need to abandon one's past and move on, just as the Don Juan or Femme Fatale "pioneers" ever new conquests. Those who are forced out of their homeland and made into unwilling Pioneers—the Jews of the Diaspora, Africans bound into slavery, Tibetan Buddhists, or Native Americans—should not be included under the shadow, however.

> *Films:* Debbie Reynolds in *How the West Was Won;* Jean Arthur and Van Heflin in *Shane;* Judy Garland in *The Harvey Girls;* Jackie Robinson in *The Jackie Robinson Story.*

> *Television: Wagon Train, Bonanza, Little House on the Prairie.*

> *Fiction: Lost Horizons* by James Hilton; *O Pioneers!* by Willa Cather.

> *Religion/Myth:* Nana-Ula (seafaring pioneer who led his people on a voyage of 2,500 miles from Tahiti to Hawaii over a thousand years ago); Bodhidharma (Buddhist patriarch who carried the teachings from India to China and established the tradition that came to be known as Zen); Hagar (handmaiden of Abraham who brought her son, Ishmael, to the Becca Valley of Arabia and established the Arab people).

Pirate *(Swashbuckler, Buccaneer, Privateer)*
Pirates were traditionally the thieves of the open seas, pursuing rich treasures and burying them in caves, thus creating archetypal legends around buried treasures within the caves of our inner being. Although pirates were bandits, for the peasant population they symbolized freedom and the ability to strike back at the rich and aristocratic class who made their wealth from the labors of the poor. Modern Pirates steal everything from intellectual property to information via the Internet. It is tempting for us to steal another person's energy or creative wealth. The search for our own spiritual gold is a metaphor for coming of age in terms of spiritual awareness by finding our own value rather than pirating others' wealth.

> *Films:* Errol Flynn in *Captain Blood;* Walter Matthau in *Pirates;* Robert
> Stevens (as Henry Morgan) in *Pirates of Tortuga.*
> *Operetta: The Pirates of Penzance* by Gilbert and Sullivan.
> *Fiction: The Count of Monte Christo* by Alexandre Dumas.
> *Religion/Myth:* Formorians (in Irish-Celtic mythology, a race of demonic,
> prehistoric giants who pillaged Ireland from the sea).

Poet (see also **Artist**)
Closely related to both the Author and the Artist, the Poet combines lyricism with sharp insight, finding the essence of beauty and truth not only in the epic affairs of humanity, but also in everyday acts and objects. Classic poetry extols momentous events and great deeds, and also expresses wonder at the hidden joys and sorrows that most of us might overlook. And although you don't have to be a published poet to have this as one of your twelve archetypes, you do need to be driven by the need and the ability to discover beauty in the people and things around you, and express it in a way that helps others see that beauty too.

The shadow Poet turns his gift for lyricism to negative or destructive effect, as in songs or poems written in support of military aggression or genocide.

> *Films:* Glenda Jackson in *Stevie;* Philippe Noiret in *Il Postino;* Sean Con-
> nery in *A Fine Madness.*
> *Fiction: The Basketball Diaries* by Jim Carroll (shadow).
> *Religion/Myth:* King David (ruler of Israel credited with writing many of
> the Psalms); Orpheus (great musician and poet of Greek myth capable
> of charming wild beasts); Bragi (in Norse myth, the god of eloquence
> and patron of poets); Finn Mac Cumhail (legendary Irish hero and
> leader who was also greatly skilled as a poet).

Priest *(Priestess, Minister, Rabbi, Shaman, Evangelist)*
The ritual that establishes the unique role of the Priest is ordination, the official capacity to facilitate the making of spiritual vows—commitments made to divine authority. Ordination or similar rituals of initiation allow the Priest, Rabbi, Shaman, or Medicine Man to serve as a vehicle or spiritual channel

of energy for others. Many of those devoted to spiritual life, such as Monks and Nuns, do not facilitate the ritual exchange of vows and spiritual energy. Ordination also empowers the Priest to convey to the public the power of sacred teachings, rituals, wisdom, morality, and ethics of each spiritual tradition. Because of these profound spiritual responsibilities, the ordained are expected to represent the teachings through personal example. And, so, the shadow side of this archetype manifests through the inability to live according to those teachings, especially in lapses of personal morality. The breaking of vows while conducting vows for the community, or using ordained authority to control the population for personal gain, has always been the dominant expression of this archetype's shadow. From the corrupt temple priests of the ancient Egyptians to the scheming, power-hungry prelates and popes of medieval Christianity, shadow Priests have interfered in secular politics to gain church power; extorted money from people who need food and shelter, just to build larger temples and cathedrals; held back women's rights and gay rights; and misused the people's trust to satisfy their own sexual needs.

Films: Montgomery Clift in *I Confess*; Karl Malden in *On the Waterfront*; Don Murray in *The Hoodlum Priest*; Richard Todd in *A Man Called Peter*; Richard Burton in *Becket*.

Fiction: *Diary of a Country Priest* by Georges Bernanos.

Drama: *Mass Appeal* by Bill C. Davis; *Murder in the Cathedral* by T. S. Eliot.

Religion/Myth: Eleazar (first high priest of Israel); Pythia (priestess of Apollo's temple at Delphi who went into trance and made oracular pronouncements); Apotequil (high priest of the Incan moon god); Hungan (Haitian priest of vodun); Ishkhara (priestess of Ishtar and Babylonian goddess of love); Kokopelli (in Zuni lore, a priest who brings rain to the people); Utnapishtim/Ziusudra (in Babylonian/Sumerian myth, the priest-king of Shurrupak who is warned by the gods of a coming deluge and builds a large ark to preserve human and animal life).

Prince

The connotations of certain words is as significant as their literal meaning in determining the nature of an archetype. Our word *prince* comes from Latin roots meaning "first" or "chief," and the word was originally applied to the ruler of a principality or the son of a sovereign, but we often use the term today for anyone preeminent in his field, or for any generous individual. The adult fairy tale *The Little Prince* by Antoine de Saint-Exupéry further colored our image of the Prince as an innocent, awestruck explorer. Yet the true Prince is a ruler-in-training who is in service to the people he will rule, whether that is a literal kingdom or a figurative or spiritual one, as with Prince Siddhartha prior to becoming the Buddha. The shadow Prince can manifest as a young man with great feelings of entitlement, an heir apparent who uses his position solely for self-aggrandizement, or one who stands to inherit an evil empire and so takes on all the negative characteristics of the "king," like the character of Michael Corleone in *The Godfather*. Machiavelli's *The Prince* was a guide to using a ruler's shadow power purely to advance one's career and self-interest without regard for the needs of others.

> *Films:* Laurence Olivier in *The Prince and the Showgirl*; Henry Fonda in *The Lady Eve*; Joseph Cotten in *The Farmer's Daughter*; Paul Newman in *Cat on a Hot Tin Roof*; Robert Redford in *The Way We Were*; Anthony Perkins in *Phaedra*.
>
> *Drama:* Biff in *Death of a Salesman* by Arthur Miller.
>
> *Fiction: The Prince and the Pauper* by Mark Twain.
>
> *Fairy Tales:* Sleeping Beauty, Cinderella.
>
> *Religion/Myth:* Rama (the prince of Ayodhya, seventh incarnation of Vishnu, and the hero of the Hindu epic *Ramayana*); Shotoku (Japanese prince deified as the reincarnation of Siddhartha, the Buddha); Xochipilli (Aztec god of flowers, maize, love, beauty, and song, whose name means "Flower Prince"); Beelzebub (originally the patron god of the Philistines and Canaanites whose name meant "Prince Baal," demonized in the Judeo-Christian tradition as the Prince of Darkness).

Prostitute (see text for extended description)

The Prostitute archetype engages lessons in integrity and the sale or negotiation of one's integrity or spirit due to fears of physical and financial survival or for financial gain. This archetype activates the aspects of the unconscious that are related to seduction and control, whereby you are as capable of buying a controlling interest in another person as you are in selling your own power. Prostitution should also be understood as the selling of your talents, ideas, and any other expression of the self—or the selling-out of them. This archetype is universal and its core learning relates to the need to birth and refine self-esteem and self-respect.

> *Films:* Jack Lemmon in *The Apartment, Some Like It Hot, Save the Tiger, The China Syndrome,* and *Mass Appeal*; Judy Holliday in *Born Yesterday*; Fred MacMurray in *Double Indemnity*; Marlon Brando in *On the Waterfront*.
>
> *Drama: The Tragical History of Dr. Faustus* by Christopher Marlowe.
>
> *Religion/Myth:* Ochun (Yoruba Orisha of love, marriage, and motherhood, who was forced for a time to become a prostitute to feed her children); Temple prostitutes (in ancient Greece, Rome, Asia Minor, and India, women who engaged in public intercourse as a way of sympathetically activating the energy of fertility).

Queen *(Empress)*

Besides having a rulership position in a court, the Queen represents power and authority in all women. Symbolically, her court can be anything from a corporation to her home. The image of the Dark or Evil Queen has been largely represented by male authors of fairy tales and folklore as a wicked force. She may also be depicted as prone to hysteria and dark powers, influences, or plots, as in the story of Snow White. *Gulliver's Travels* presents a benevolent Queen who rules the Land of the Giants, but that is a rare exception.

The Queen archetype is also associated with arrogance and a defensive posture that is symbolic of a need to protect one's personal and emotional power. Queens are rarely portrayed as having a trustworthy support system; instead, they are lonely figures surrounded by a court filled with potential traitors, rivals, and back-stabbers. Women who have identified themselves as Queens in my workshops tend to have these qualities in common, suggesting that were it not for their aggressive personality characteristics, they would be vulnerable to others' control.

Challenges related to control, personal authority, and leadership play a primary role in forming the lessons of personal development that are inherent to this archetype. The benevolent Queen uses her authority to protect those in her court and sees her own empowerment enhanced by her relationships and experience. The shadow Queen can slip into aggressive and destructive patterns of behavior, particularly when she perceives that her authority or capacity to maintain control over the court is being challenged. The Ice Queen rules with a cold indifference to the genuine needs of others—whether material or emotional. The Queen Bee is a mixed image— she has the astonishing ability to power the entire hive without leaving her "chamber," yet at the cost of enslaving the rest of her community.

> *Films:* Joan Crawford in *Queen Bee*; Marlene Dietrich as Catherine the Great in *The Scarlet Empress*; Geraldine Chaplin in *The Three Muske-teers*; Greta Garbo in *Queen Cristina*; Judi Densch in *Shakespeare in Love*; Cate Blanchett in *Elizabeth*.
>
> *Drama: Antony and Cleopatra* by Shakespeare.
>
> *Religion/Myth:* Mary (Mother of Jesus; later elevated in Catholic tradi-tion to Queen of Heaven); Mab (Queen of the faeries and often a trickster who steals babies, possibly derived from the Welsh Mabb or Gaelic Maeve); Anatu (Mesopotamian queen of the sky); Antiope (in Greek myth, the queen of the Amazons); Marisha-Ten (Japanese queen of Heaven); Guinevere (King Arthur's Queen).
>
> *Fairy Tale:* Snow White and the Seven Dwarfs (shadow).

Rebel *(Anarchist, Revolutionary, Political Protester, Nonconformist)*
Our images of the Rebel may be too closely aligned with clichés of youth cul-ture to let us see the deeper significance of this valuable archetype. Whether politically inclined like Martin Luther King, Jr., Betty Friedan, or Lech Walesa, or an artistic innovator such as Van Gogh, Joyce, or Coltrane, the Rebel is a key component of all human growth and development. The Rebel in a support group can be a powerful aid in helping the group break out of old tribal patterns. It can also help you see past tired preconceptions in

your field of professional or creative endeavor. The Rebel can also lead you to reject spiritual systems that do not serve your inner need for direct union with the Divine and to seek out more appropriate paths. The shadow Rebel, conversely, may compel you to rebel out of peer pressure or for the sake of fashion, and so become mired in another manifestation of conformity. The shadow Rebel may also reject legitimate authority simply because it is asking you to do something you find difficult or unpleasant. Be especially careful in evaluating your rebellious impulses; even if the Rebel is not part of your intimate circle of archetypes, you probably have it to some extent and should pay attention to its urgings.

> *Films:* James Dean in *Rebel Without a Cause;* Marlon Brando in *The Wild One;* Kirk Douglas in *Spartacus;* Sally Field in *Norma Rae;* Meryl Streep in *Silkwood.*
>
> *Fiction: The Rebel* by Albert Camus; *One Flew Over the Cuckoo's Nest* by Ken Kesey.
>
> *Religion/Myth:* Iblis/Lucifer (in Muslim/Christian belief, a rebellious angel who refused to worship Adam or acknowledge the supremacy of God).
>
> *Folklore/Fairy Tales:* Jack and the Beanstalk; *Peter Rabbit* by Beatrix Potter.

Rescuer (see also **Knight**, **Healer**, **Hero**)

In its empowered profile, the Rescuer assists when needed and, once the rescue mission is accomplished, withdraws. A Rescuer provides an infusion of strength and support to help others to survive a difficult situation, crisis, or process that they lack the stamina or the inner knowledge to maneuver through themselves. Unlike the Knight, to which it is related, the Rescuer is more common among women, especially in its shadow aspect. The shadow Rescuer often surfaces through a romantic connection in which one party seeks to establish an intimate bond by lending emotional support, with a hidden agenda that assumes the rescued party will return the Rescuer's romantic feelings. Such romances are destined to fail, because the shadow agenda has to keep the "rescuee" in need of being rescued, lest the Rescuer lose her significance.

Healing and empowering the Rescuer within is a common emotional challenge, because being needed is essential to our nature. Most people can relate in part to the characteristics of this archetype, which somewhat parallel those of the Knight, Healer, Hero, and even Servant. If you feel drawn to this archetype be careful to compare the characteristics of those others before deciding to add the Rescuer to your family.

> *Films:* Sigourney Weaver in *Alien;* Tom Hanks in *Saving Private Ryan;* Jason Gedrick in *Iron Eagle.*
>
> *Television: The Lone Ranger.*
>
> *Religion/Myth:* Bidadari (in Javanese myth, a lovely nymph who uses her knowledge of magic to rescue a hero from a dangerous situation and marry him); Lancelot (Knight of the Round Table who rescues Guinevere—with whom he is having an affair—when King Arthur threatens

to execute her for adultery); Bran (in Welsh lore, a giant who rescued his sister Branwen from enslavement by her Irish husband).

❦ Saboteur (see text for extended description)

The Saboteur archetype is made up of the fears and issues related to low self-esteem that cause you to make choices in life that block your own empowerment and success. As with the Victim and Prostitute, you need to face this powerful archetype that we all possess and make it an ally. When you do, you will find that it calls your attention to situations in which you are in danger of being sabotaged, or of sabotaging yourself. Once you are comfortable with the Saboteur, you learn to hear and heed these warnings, saving yourself untold grief from making the same mistakes over and over. Ignore it, and the shadow Saboteur will manifest in the form of self-destructive behavior or the desire to undermine others.

> *Films:* Greta Garbo in *Mata Hari*; Angela Lansbury in *The Manchurian Candidate*; Woody Harrelson in *The People vs. Larry Flynt*; Judy Holliday in *The Solid Gold Cadillac*.
>
> *Drama: Amadeus* (Salieri) by Peter Schaffer; *The Madwoman of Chaillot* by Jean Giraudoux.
>
> *Religion/Myth:* Loki (in Norse myth, a Shape-shifter and Trickster who is crafty and malicious, but also heroic); Eris/Discordia (Greek/Roman goddess of discord, said to have caused the Trojan War); Bamapana (Aboriginal hero-trickster who causes discord and misunderstanding); Serpent (in many cultures, a figure who deceives humans, often sabotaging their only chance at immortality).

Samaritan

The Samaritan is closely related to the Martyr archetype, with the essential difference that Samaritans make sacrifices for those they might be least inclined to serve, as in the Gospel parable of the Good Samaritan. The act itself can be as simple as stopping in the street to give a stranger directions when you are in a hurry to get somewhere. The shadow Samaritan helps one person or group to the detriment of another, one's own family, or the greater good of society. A simple example is the driver who stops in traffic to let another driver make a turn against the flow, with the result of holding up many more drivers in the process. There seems to be implicit in such shadow Samaritan behavior a kind of self-importance that says others must adhere to one's own choice of who is most deserving.

> *Films:* Richard Dreyfuss in *Down and Out in Beverly Hills*; Gary Cooper in *Good Sam*; Jean Arthur in *The More the Merrier*; Liam Neeson in *Schindler's List*.
>
> *Religion/Myth:* Ninlil (Sumerian goddess of Heaven, earth, air, and grain who shows compassion to the unfortunate); Parzifal (Arthurian knight who heals the wound of Anfortas, the Grail King, by compassionately asking about it).

Scribe (*Copyist, Secretary, Accountant*—see also **Journalist**)
The Scribe differs from Author or Artist in one significant way: scribes copy existing works rather than create new ones. The Hebrew scribes were originally secretaries who wrote down the preachings of the prophets, but evolved into a priestly class charged with writing and maintaining the laws and records, copying previous scrolls, and committing oral traditions to paper. Medieval Christian scribes copied manuscripts and helped preserve learning. In India, the sages who compiled the Vedas are known as *vyasa*, a Sanskrit word that means "collector" but could be translated as "scribe." We can expand the definition to cover modern journalists, who also record the existing knowledge and information of their day and uncover secrets (investigative reporters). And we would also have to include that largely anonymous horde of copiers who are busy uploading everything imaginable onto the Internet in the hope of preserving it by distributing it to millions. What makes the Internet the modern equivalent of the medieval scriptorum is that so much information is transcribed onto it not for personal gain but for the sheer joy of preserving and sharing these artifacts with the rest of the world.

The shadow aspect of the Scribe can manifest in altering facts, plagiarizing, or selling information that belongs to others.

> *Films:* Dustin Hoffman and Robert Redford in *All the President's Men*; Sally Field in *Absence of Malice* (shadow); Kirk Douglas in *Ace in the Hole* (shadow); Nicole Kidman in *To Die For* (shadow); Holly Hunter in *Broadcast News*.
>
> *Fiction:* "Bartleby the Scrivener" by Herman Melville.
>
> *Religion/Myth:* Ezra (Hebrew scribe and priest, best known for collecting and editing the books of the Hebrew Bible, or Old Testament, in the fifth century B.C.); Imhotep (in Egyptian myth, an architect, physician, and scribe in the court of the pharaoh Zoser); Thoth (Egyptian god of wisdom, inventor of writing, and patron of scribes, often depicted as a man with the head of an ibis, holding a scribal tablet and reed pen).

Seeker (*Wanderer, Vagabond, Nomad*)
This archetype refers to one who searches on a path that may begin with earthly curiosity but has at its core the search for God and/or enlightenment. Unlike the Mystic, which has the Divine as its sole focus, the Seeker is in search of wisdom and truth wherever it is to be found. The shadow side of the archetype is the "lost soul," someone on an aimless journey without direction, ungrounded, disconnected from goals and others. The shadow emerges when seekers become infatuated with the trappings of a certain practice or guru—what Chögyam Trungpa so aptly called "spiritual materialism"—but never actually change their underlying egocentricity.

> *Films:* Tyrone Power in *The Razor's Edge*; Brad Pitt in *Seven Years in Tibet*; Peter Weller and Judy Davis in *The New Age* (shadow); Ellen Burstyn

in *Alice Doesn't Live Here Anymore;* Henry Fonda in *The Grapes of Wrath.*

Drama: A Doll's House (Nora) by Henrik Ibsen.

Fiction: Siddhartha by Hermann Hesse; *Lost Horizon* by James Hilton.

Autobiography: Bound for Glory by Woody Guthrie; *My Experiments with Truth* by Mahatma Gandhi; *Be Here Now* by Ram Dass; *Longing for Darkness* by China Galland.

Religion/Myth: Arjuna (he questions his role in life in the Bhagavad Gita); Siddhartha Gautama (before his enlightenment as the Buddha, Siddhartha undertook the classic path of the Seeker).

Servant *(Indentured Servant)*

We all serve someone or something. Because the spiritual path is essentially one of service to others, anyone can relate to this archetype. The Servant engages aspects of our psyche that call us to make ourselves available to others for the benefit and enhancement of their lives. This task can be done in a healthy manner only if the Servant is simultaneously able to be of service to the self. Without the strength to maintain your own well-being, the Servant becomes consumed by the needs of those around you and loses all focus of the value of your own life.

From a mundane perspective, the Servant is associated with money because servants are hired help. This aspect is witnessed within the psyche of the Indentured Servant, a person who sees himself bound by conditions of service that are not of his choosing or preference because of an inability to "buy his freedom," or symbolically coming into his own power. Therefore, the core challenge with this particular archetype is making choices that serve your highest potential. If this describes a substantial personal issue for you, then consider this archetype as a possibility for your own chart.

Films: William Powell in *My Man Godfrey;* Anthony Hopkins in *Remains of the Day;* Morgan Freeman in *Driving Miss Daisy;* Dirk Bogarde in *The Servant* (shadow).

Fiction: The Turn of the Screw (Mrs. Grose) by Henry James.

Religion/Myth: The names of many spiritual masters and teachers often contain a reference to service. The Sanskrit word *dasya,* for example, means "servant," and appears in the names of modern mystics such as Ram Dass, Bhagavan Das, and Lama Surya Das; Obadiah (Hebrew prophet whose name means "servant of God"); Ganymede (in Greek myth, the beautiful young boy who was one of Zeus' lovers and the cupbearer to the gods); Thialfi (Norse servant of Thor and the messenger of the gods).

Fairy Tale: Cinderella.

Shape-shifter *(Spell-caster—see also* **Trickster***)*

This archetype has long been known to shamans of the American Indian and other native traditions for having the ability to change appearances for a variety of reasons. The Shape-shifter can navigate through different levels of consciousness, both dream and waking states, and the astral plane. Somewhat related to the Trickster, it is more flexible and less tied to a specific goal. The shadow aspect emphasizes instability, fickleness, and lack of conviction, as can be seen in any number of modern-day politicians who reinvent themselves to appeal to the latest popular trends.

>*Films: Wolfen;* Lon Chaney, Jr., in *The Wolf Man;* Aaron Eckhart in *In the Company of Men.*

>*Religion/Myth:* Because most deities or mythological figures who have the ability to shape-shift are also Tricksters, many of them overlap with that archetype: Tezcatlipoca (Aztec god of night who changes shapes and uses his "smoking mirror" to kill his enemies); Estsanatlehi ("Woman who changes," the most powerful Navajo deity, a fertility goddess and shape-shifter associated with transformation and immortality).

Slave *(Puppet)*

The Slave archetype represents a complete absence of the power of choice and self-authority. Yet it is precisely the absence of willpower that gives the Slave its potential for personal transformation. The ultimate spiritual task is to surrender one's will to the Divine—in effect, to become a Divine Slave. The goal in many monastic practices is to release one's individual power of choice and become subject to the will of a spiritual mentor, trusting that individual to have your best interests at heart. This act of releasing your will to a higher authority is also witnessed within organizational hierarchies, such as in the military and corporations. One becomes a Slave to the system.

For tens of millions of African-Americans, the Slave archetype carries a level of historical freight that is impossible to overlook. If Slavery is part of your genetic history, you need to take a close look at the possible presence of the Slave archetype in your intimate family. Others who dismiss this archetype as having no role in their lives may discover that it is more prevalent than they imagine, because of its many different expressions. We don't think of a soldier armed with weapons as a Slave, yet following orders unconditionally is an aspect of the Slave—especially when these orders personally violate your integrity. The Puppet, for instance, may be manipulated by others, regardless of how this archetype manifests; however, its core learning is to understand the paradoxical truth that you are only truly free when you have surrendered all power of choice to the Divine.

>*Films:* Djimon Hounsou in *Amistad;* Ossie Davis in *Slaves;* Russell Crowe in *The Gladiator;* Yvette Mimieux in *The Time Machine;* Kevin Spacey and Annette Bening in *American Beauty;* Victor Mature in *The Robe;* Charlton Heston (Moses) in *The Ten Commandments.*

>*Television:* LeVar Burton in *Roots.*

>*Drama: The Emperor Jones* by Eugene O'Neill; *Ma Rainey's Black Bottom* by August Wilson; *Glengarry Glen Ross* by David Mamet.

Religion/Myth: Euryclea (in *The Odyssey*, the slave of Laertes, wet nurse of Odysseus, and the first to recognize the hero when he returned home from the Trojan War); Black Peter (medieval Dutch name for the devil, who was chained and enslaved by Saint Nicholas, who on December 4 made Black Peter drop candy and gifts down chimneys into the waiting shoes of the children); Sisyphus (in Greek myth, he chained the god of death, Thanatos, so the deceased could not enter the underworld, for which he was enslaved for all eternity to roll a boulder up a steep hill, only to have it tumble back down when he reached the top).
Fairy Tale: the flying monkeys in *The Wonderful Wizard of Oz*.

Storyteller *(Minstrel, Narrator)*

The classic Storyteller/Minstrel archetype relays wisdom and foolishness, mistakes and successes, facts and fiction, and tales of love and the impossible on a plane that is often exaggerated beyond ordinary life. Love is greater, power is more daring, successes are more astonishing, foolishness is more obvious. We have an archetypal need to be spoken to through stories because they bring us into contact with our inner being. We are, in fact, storytellers by nature. Those who have this archetype find that the Storyteller's voice and methods are essential to their way of communicating and perceiving the world. Some teachers are also connected with the Storyteller archetype, but not all Storytellers are teachers. Not all writers are Storytellers, but authors of fiction must be. A Storyteller communicates not just facts but also a metaphoric learning or experience. Storytellers abound in any walk of life, not just among professional writers.

The tradition of the Minstrel reveals how essential the Storyteller's role was in medieval culture, because Minstrels were expected to tell stories and sing stories as a way of entertaining a group as well as passing on the news of the day.

The shadow Storyteller is, in the extreme, a liar, and, in moderation, an exaggerator. The temptation always exists to misuse the skill of storytelling to your own advantage when sharing information. The shadow aspect manifests when we can't resist making up a story to conceal something we don't want to be truthful about. But the universal appeal of storytelling throughout history suggests some deeper connection of this archetype with the human soul. The oldest written works we possess, from the Gilgamesh epic to the Bible to *The Odyssey*, use storytelling to make their points. Maybe it's simply a reflection of the sense that each of our lives is a story worth telling, or a desire to impose order on what sometimes seems like a chaotic and random universe.

Films: Rod Taylor as Sean O'Casey in *Young Cassidy*; Laurence Harvey and Karl Boehm in *The Wonderful World of the Brothers Grimm*; Judy Davis as George Sand in *Impromptu*; Barbara Bel Geddes in *I Remember Mama*.

Fiction: Lord Jim by Joseph Conrad; *Beloved* by Toni Morrison; *Ulysses* by James Joyce.

Religion/Myth: Homer (combined history and mythology in the action adventures of *The Odyssey* and *The Iliad*); Blaise (Welsh storyteller who in Arthurian legend became Merlin's scribe); Thamyris (Thracian minstrel who won so many contests that he challenged the Muses themselves, and in return for his presumption was struck blind).

Fairy Tale: Arabian Nights (Tales of Scheherazade).

Student *(Disciple, Devotee, Follower, Apprentice)*

The student archetype suggests a pattern of constant learning, an openness to absorbing new information as an essential part of one's well-being. The Student archetype suggests an absence of mastery of any one subject but rather a continual pursuit of intellectual development. Within the spiritual aspect, the Student, Disciple, Devotee, and Follower imply that one has found a source of teaching, such as a guru or spiritual master, who becomes the instructor and spiritual guide.

The shadow Student usually manifests in tandem with the shadow Teacher or Mentor, avidly learning all the tools of the wrong trade or misusing the knowledge learned. This was graphically depicted in Walt Disney's animated imagining of Paul Dukas's "The Sorcerer's Apprentice" in *Fantasia*, in which Mickey Mouse portrays the Student Wizard who gets carried away with his own unperfected talent and wreaks havoc. The shadow can also show up as the eternal Student who never embarks on the sea of life in earnest, but manages to find new reasons to continue being schooled without ever putting that knowledge to the test. People who continually use the excuse that they are not ready or have not yet learned enough to advance with their dreams should take special note of this archetype and whether they have a shadow bond with it.

Films: Julie Walters in *Educating Rita;* Jean-Pierre Léaud in *The 400 Blows;* Matthew Broderick in *The Freshman.*

Drama: Pygmalion by G. B. Shaw.

Fiction: Tom Brown's School Days by Thomas Hughes.

Autobiography: The Education of Henry Adams by Henry Adams.

Religion/Myth: Dervish (Sufi term for the student of a sheik); Hunsi (Haitian term for a devotee of any African deity, derived from the culture of Dahomey); Telemachus (student of Mentor, who was assigned to care for and teach him by Odysseus); Medea (devotee of Hecate, Greek goddess of the crossroads, and a great sorceress); Ananda (renowned disciple of the Buddha); Peter (leading disciple of Jesus); Abu Bakr (one of the Prophet Muhammad's disciples, who were called *Companions*).

Thief *(Swindler, Con Artist, Pickpocket, Burglar, Robin Hood)*

The Thief is thought of as a nocturnal, hooded figure who slips silently into places and takes what he wants. In the hierarchy of thievery, the most

respected is the Jewel Thief, associated with glamour, class, and sophistication. The Good Thief steals on behalf of others, as in the case of Robin Hood.
He appears to be relieved of all wrongdoing because of his benevolent motive
to be of service to others, but often that is just a rationalization. The Bank
Thief maintains a degree of respect because the target is corporate and impersonal and the implication is that the thief has an intelligent and strategic mind.
The Street Thief and Pickpocket, on the other hand, rank lowest because they
rob ordinary individuals and their methods yield small gain.

Symbolically, theft can take many forms, including plagiarism and stealing ideas and even affection. Taking what is not yours because you lack the
ability to provide for yourself implies the need to learn self-respect. This
archetype prods you to learn to generate power from within. As with so many
archetypes that initially strike you as completely unrelated to who you are,
this archetype should be evaluated from its symbolic meaning. You may
never have stolen one thing at the physical level, but you also need to take
into consideration your emotional and intellectual arenas.

> *Films:* James Caan in *Thief*; Vittorio Gassman and Marcello Mastroiani
> in *Big Deal on Madonna Street*; Jean-Paul Belmondo in *The Thief of
> Paris*; Sabu in *The Thief of Baghdad* (1940); Steven Bauer in *Thief of
> Hearts* (shadow); Kevin Costner in *Robin Hood: Prince of Thieves*;
> Angelica Huston in *The Grifters* (shadow).
>
> *Fiction: The Adventures of Robin Hood* (various authors).
>
> *Religion/Myth:* Raven (among Northwestern Indians, a helpful thief who
> stole the moon and sun from the Sky Chief and placed them in the
> sky); Prometheus (in Greek myth, hero who stole the sacred fire from
> Zeus and the gods); Autolycus (a grandfather of Odysseus and
> renowned as a thief who stole the cattle of Eurytus); the Good Thief
> (in the New Testament, one of two men who were crucified with
> Jesus, repented, and asked for forgiveness).

Trickster (*Puck, Provocateur*)

Almost as far back as our earliest written records, the Trickster appears as a
key figure in the human drama. According to the great historian of religion
Mircea Eliade, a Trickster is a human or animal character that plays dubious
jokes or tricks, makes fun or is made fun of, and may be camouflaged as one
of the demigods of a religious tradition. The serpent who tempts Eve in the
Bible was based on similar characters in Sumerian and Babylonian mythology from the third millennium B.C., in which a serpent tricks humanity out of
the gift of immortality and assumes it for itself. (Observing snakes shedding
their skin led some to believe that the reptile was capable of renewing its life
indefinitely.) In many cultures, though, especially among Native Americans,
the Trickster can also be the Creator's helper or messenger.

Like the Prostitute and Servant archetypes, the Trickster seems at first to
have only negative connotations, but it can be a great ally in presenting you
with alternatives to the straight and narrow path, to people and institutions

who seek to hem you in through peer pressure and conformism. The best
modern illustrations of this dual role show up in the film work of Jack Nicholson and Groucho Marx. Although the characters they portray are often un-
savory or duplicitous on some level, their antics can also be liberating by
transcending convention, stuffiness, and predictable behavior.

Films: Barbara Stanwyck in *The Lady Eve*; Wilfred Bramble (Grandfather)
in *A Hard Day's Night*; Peter Cook in *Bedazzled* (shadow); Michael Caine,
Steve Martin, and Glenne Headley in *Dirty Rotten Scoundrels*.

Drama: *The Matchmaker* by Thornton Wilder.

Fiction: *The Witches of Eastwick* by John Updike.

Religion/Myth: Kaulu (Polynesian Trickster god); Blue-Jay (among
Pacific Northwest Indians, a Trickster who tries to outwit the other
animals); Spider Woman (Trickster among the Dakota Indian tribes);
Seth (ancient Egyptian god of chaos and adversity); Esu (West African
god of passage and Trickster who guards the home of the gods).

Fairy Tales: Little Red Riding Hood, the Fox and the Grapes, the
Gingerbread Man.

Vampire

The Vampire is a mythic creature associated with both bloodsucking and
eroticism. Vampires require blood, which they get by biting the neck of their
victims during a nocturnal visit. The female victim has been portrayed in the
paradoxical circumstances of wanting to repel the Vampire while at the same
time welcoming the erotic nature of the connection. The Vampire returns
every evening to his source of life until there is no more to be had. The parallels between human lust and vampiric blood-lust are rich: as the Vampire sat-
isfies his thirst for blood, his host grows increasingly helpless and submissive,
eventually being drained of any capacity for self-protection. Symbolically,
this relationship speaks of the power dynamics that frequently drive male-
female relationships, in which the male drains the power of the female for his
own psychic survival, and, once bitten, the female submits even though this
will eventually take all of her power. (In some relationships, of course, the
roles can easily become reversed.)

Beyond the sexual level, we sometimes form psychic attachments to others because we desire their energy, a desire that manifests through a need for
approval, a need to have the "other" take care of our survival, and a fear of
being abandoned. What has been defined as a co-dependent relationship
could easily fall under the Vampire template. You may find it hard to identify
yourself as a Vampire, yet it is essential to review this archetype personally.
Patterns of behavior such as chronic complaining, overdependency, holding
on to a relationship either emotionally or psychically long after it has ended,
and chronic power struggles are all indicators of Vampire patterns. Holding
on to someone at the psychic level is as real as holding on at the physical.

Interest in the Vampire archetype has reemerged through the literary and entertainment fields. It may well be that the archetypal opening of humanity's psyche during these past five decades has resurrected the Vampire, empowering it with a force on the psychic plane of consciousness that was not engaged prior to this time.

Films: Bela Lugosi in *Dracula;* Tom Cruise in *Interview with the Vampire.*

Fiction: Dracula by Bram Stoker; *The Vampire Chronicles* by Anne Rice; "The Vampyre: A Tale" by John Polidori.

Religion/Myth: Vlad Tepes, aka Vlad the Impaler (in fifteenth-century Wallachia—modern Romania—a bloodthirsty count who reportedly impaled and beheaded his enemies); Langsoir (Malayan vampire, a woman who died in childbirth and now assaults infants and children).

Victim (see text for extended discussion)

The negative traits of the Victim are self-evident. But when properly recognized, it can be a tremendous aid in letting us know when we are in danger of letting ourselves be victimized, often through passivity but also through rash or inappropriate actions. It can also help us to see our own tendency to victimize others for personal gain. In its shadow aspect, the Victim shows us that we may like to play the Victim at times because of the positive feedback we get in the form of sympathy or pity. Our goal is always to learn how to recognize these inappropriate attitudes in ourselves or others, and to act accordingly.

Films: Hillary Swank in *Boys Don't Cry;* Jodie Foster in *The Accused;* Meryl Streep in *Sophie's Choice;* Glenn Close in *Reversal of Fortune.*

Fiction: Dr. Jekyll and Mr. Hyde by Robert L. Stevenson; *Misery* by Stephen King.

Drama: Torch Song Trilogy by Harvey Fierstein.

Religion/Myth: Isaac (son of Abraham whom God orders Abraham to sacrifice); Heracles (seized by Busiris, a mythical king of Egypt who sacrificed all strangers to the gods to avert famine; Heracles avoided being victimized by using his great strength to break his chains and slay Busiris).

Virgin (See also **Celibate**)

This archetype is associated with purity, applied primarily to young girls. The Vestal Virgins of ancient Rome lived in service to a goddess and were often severely punished if they lost their virginity. The Virgin Mother of Jesus represents the purity of motherhood, bringing forth the perfect form of male life, a god. Your identification with the Virgin needs to be explored symbolically as a pattern that represents as association with purity as well as the beginning point of creation. To bring forth virgin ideas is as much an aspect of this archetype as is its application to maintaining virginal aspects of Mother Nature, as in virgin forests.

The shadow side of the Virgin is the prudish disgust with or fear of genuine sensuality. Resisting sex not to save one's energy for other endeavors, but because it seems inherently repellent, is not a virtue but a denial of an essential aspect of oneself. Celibate Monks or Nuns ideally learn to channel their sexual energy rather than merely repressing it.

Films: Sean Connery in *The Medicine Man;* Kirstin Dunst et al. in *The Virgin Suicides;* Jennifer Jason Leigh in *Fast Times at Ridgemont High.*

Religion/Myth: Parthenos (Greek for "Virgin," an epithet of the goddess Athena, who was the virgin mother of Ericthonius). Hestia/Vesta (the Greek/Roman virgin goddess of the hearth, and, by extension, domestic life).

Visionary *(Dreamer, Prophet, Seer*—see also **Guide**, **Alchemist***)*
The Visionary archetype lets you imagine possibilities that are beyond the scope of your individual life and that benefit all of society. The Visionary brings into view what could be if certain choices are made, or what is inevitable given choices that have already been made. The Prophet proclaims a message associated with divine guidance, as in the Hebrew prophets, some of whom also appear in the Quran. (Islam reveres both Jesus and John the Baptist as prophets.) Both the Visionary and the Prophet engage their abilities in behalf of humanity rather than for personal use, but while many Prophets are rejected by the group they were sent to enlighten, Visionaries tend to be celebrated for their capacity to read what is just over the horizon.

The shadow Prophet or Visionary manifests as a willingness to sell one's visionary abilities to the highest bidder, or to alter one's vision to make it more acceptable to society. In extreme cases, tainted visions may lead entire societies into murderous or destructive rampages; then the Destroyer archetype may supersede the Visionary, as in the case of Hitler, Stalin, and Mao.

Films: Eriq Ebouaney in *Lumumba;* Peter Finch in *Network* (shadow).

Religion/Myth: Hebrew Prophets (Isaiah, Jeremiah, Ezekiel, and others who often chastised powerful leaders while calling the people's attention to their own failings); Muhammad (the final Prophet of Islam, who directed God's message to the Arab people through the Quran); Baha'u'llah (nineteenth-century Iranian prophet who founded the Bahai Faith, spreading his vision of "one universal Cause, one common Faith"); Cassandra (in Greek lore, daughter of the king and queen of Troy who was given the gift of prophecy by Apollo in an attempt by him to seduce her; because she refused his advances, he made all her prophecies fall on deaf ears); Zarathustra (prophet and founder of Zoroastrianism).

Warrior *(Soldier, Crime Fighter, Amazon, Mercenary, Soldier of Fortune, Gunslinger, Samurai)*
The Warrior archetype represents physical strength and the ability to protect, defend, and fight for one's rights. Whereas the Knight is associated with

protecting Damsels, the Warrior is linked to invincibility and loyalty. Warrior energy is erotic for the male, representing the height of virility and physical power as well as toughness of will and spirit. To be unbreakable and to fight to the death is a large part of the Warrior archetype, which is also associated with the passage from boyhood to manhood.

The Mercenary and Soldier of Fortune are variations on the hired killer who sells his power on the open market, often with complete disregard for the buyer's cause. These archetypes are much like the Prostitute in that, although they appear negative, they warn us in their favorable aspect when we are in danger of aligning our might with an unjust or purely self-interested cause.

The Gunslinger and Samurai represent a double-edged sword (pun intended). They appeal to our fantasies of independence and the power to defend ourselves and right wrongs, yet they also carry the historic weight of savage, predatory evil. On one side are all the heroic characters portrayed by John Wayne, Gary Cooper, and others—standing up to injustice and holding off the forces of evil single-handedly. The Lone Ranger and the wandering samurai warriors in the films of Akira Kurosawa also epitomize this fiercely independent warrior that the American and Japanese pasts seem to share. And on the other side are all the evil, self-interested killers and thieves who embody our worst nightmares of lawlessness and unchecked male dominance. Somewhere in between are the ambiguous Crime Fighters and lone-wolf gunfighters epitomized by Clint Eastwood, whose heroism is often tinged with anger, vengefulness, and more than a little sadism.

The shadow Warrior distorts or abandons ethical principles and decency in the name of victory at any cost. What can be a virtue—heroic indifference to risk and pain—becomes contemptible when the indifference is directed not at oneself but at others.

The Warrior archetype is just as connected to the female psyche as to the male. Women have long been defenders of their families, and the Amazon tribe of Warrior Women has become legendary because of their ability to engage in fierce battle—even sacrificing part of their female physique to facilitate warfare. Loyalty to the family and tribe is among the Amazons' notable characteristics, along with nurturing their young and transmitting lessons of power and self-defense. In today's society, the Warrior Woman has emerged in her glory once again through women who liberate and protect others, especially women and children who need vocal and financial representation.

The concept of the spiritual Warrior has been pioneered by Dan Millman (*The Peaceful Warrior*), the Tibetan Buddhist teacher Chögyam Trungpa (*Shambhala: The Sacred Path of the Warrior*), Professor Robert Thurman, and others. They direct us to use the classic Warrior virtues of heroism, stoicism, and self-sacrifice to conquer the ego and gain control of our inner lives.

Films: Gary Cooper in *High Noon;* John Wayne in *The Searchers;* Clint Eastwood in *Pale Rider* and *Unforgiven;* Mel Gibson in *Road Warrior* and *Mad Max;* Barbra Streisand in *The Way We Were* (political activist); Shirley MacLaine in *Terms of Endearment* (fighting for better care of her terminally ill daughter); Denzel Washington in *Glory* (Civil War soldier); *The Seven Samurai.*

Television: Buffy the Vampire Slayer; Xena the Warrior Princess.

Drama: A Soldier's Story by Charles Fuller.

Fiction: In Dubious Battle by John Steinbeck (migrant workers).

Religion/Myth: Bhima ("the Terrible One"), warrior hero of the *Mahabharata,* known for his great strength; the son of the wind god Vayu and a brother of Arjuna, he became a Hindu warrior god); Oya (woman warrior of Yoruba myth, goddess of fire, wind, thunder, and the river Niger); Andarta (Celtic-Gallic warrior and fertility goddess, patron of the Vocontii); Popocatepetl (Aztec warrior who, with his consort, was transformed by the gods into a mountain after they both died of grief for each other); Brunhilde (female warrior, one of the Valkyries, in the German epic *Niebelungenlied*); Alyosha Popovitch (epic hero and mighty warrior of Russian folklore); Durga (warrior manifestation of the Hindu Mother goddess).

NOTES

INTRODUCTION
1. Quoted in Sam Keen, *Fire in the Belly* (New York: Three Rivers, 1997).

CHAPTER 1
1. See Roger Woolger, Ph.D., *Other Lives, Other Selves: A Jungian Psychotherapist Discovers Past Lives* (New York: Doubleday, 1987), and Brian Weiss, M.D., *Through Time into Healing: Discovering the Power of Regression Therapy to Erase Trauma and Transform Mind, Body, and Relationships* (New York: Touchstone, 1993).
2. Gregg Levoy, *Callings: Finding and Following an Authentic Life* (New York: Three Rivers, 1997).
3. John O'Donohue, *Anam Cara: A Book of Celtic Wisdom* (New York: HarperCollins, 1997).

CHAPTER 2
1. Clarissa Pinkola Estés, Ph.D., *Women Who Run with the Wolves: Myths and Stories of the Wild Woman Archetype* (New York: Ballantine, 1997).
2. D. Jason Cooper, *Mithras: Mysteries and Initiation Rediscovered* (Tork Beach, Me.: Samuel Weiser, 1996).
3. Anthony F. Aveni, "Other Stars than Ours," *Natural History*, April 1, 2001.
4. Plato, *The Republic*, Book 10, online at http://ball.tcnj.edu/pols270/plato/republic.htm.
5. James Hillman, *The Soul's Code: In Search of Character and Calling* (New York: Random House, 1996).
6. Harold Kushner, *How Good Do We Have to Be? A New Understanding of Guilt and Forgiveness* (Boston: Little, Brown & Co., 1996).
7. Joseph Campbell, *The Hero with a Thousand Faces* (Princeton, N.J.: Princeton University Press, 1968).

8. For further discussion of this question, see Bruce Chilton, *Rabbi Jesus: An Intimate Biography* (New York: Doubleday, 2000); John Shelby Spong, *Born of a Woman: A Bishop Rethinks the Birth of Jesus* (San Francisco: HarperSanFrancisco, 1992); and John P. Meier, *A Marginal Jew: Rethinking the Historical Jesus* (New York: Doubleday, 1991).

CHAPTER 3

1. Baba Ram Dass, *Be Here Now* (San Cristobal, N.M.: Hanuman Foundation, 1971).
2. Evelyn Underhill, *Mysticism: The Nature and Development of Spiritual Consciousness* (Oxford, England: Oneworld, 1993).
3. Thomas Cahill, *The Gifts of the Jews: How a Tribe of Desert Nomads Changed the Way Everyone Thinks and Feels* (New York: Nan A. Talese, 1998).
4. Richard A. Horsley and Neil Asher Silberman, *The Message of the Kingdom: How Jesus and Paul Ignited a Revolution and Transformed the Ancient World* (New York: Grosset/Putnam, 1997).
5. Dr. A. Zahoor and Dr. Z. Haq, *Biography of Prophet Muhammad* (1990), online at http://users.erols.com/zenithco/muhammad.html.
6. Martin Lings, *Muhammad: His Life Based on the Earliest Sources* (Rochester, Vt.: Inner Traditions International, 1983).
7. Hilda Charlton, *Hell-Bent for Heaven: The Autobiography of Hilda Charlton* (Woodstock, N.Y.: Golden Quest, 1990).
8. Lings, *Muhammad*.
9. Richard H. Robinson and Willard L. Johnson, *The Buddhist Religion: A Historical Introduction*, 3d ed. (Belmont, Calif.: Wadsworth, 1982).
10. For a fuller account of Glassman's career, see Peter Occhiogrosso, *Through the Labyrinth: Stories of the Search for Spiritual Transformation in Everyday Life* (New York: Viking, 1991), chap. 9.

CHAPTER 4

1. Richard Tarnas, *The Passion of the Western Mind: Understanding the Ideas That Have Shaped Our World View* (New York: Harmony Books, 1991).
2. Ibid.
3. Jung did, however, acknowledge correspondences with previous work by other researchers in the fields of mythology, animal psychology, and comparative religion, including Lucien Lévy-Bruhl and Adolf Bastian. "From these references," he wrote, "it should be clear enough that my idea of the archetype—literally a pre-existent form—does not stand alone but is something that is recognized and named in other fields of knowledge." See *The Archetypes and the Collective Unconscious*, vol. 9 of *The Collected Works of C. G. Jung*, edited and translated by G. Adler and R. F. C. Hull (Princeton, N.J.: Princeton University Press, 1970).
4. *The Portable Jung*, edited by Joseph Campbell, translated by R. F. C. Hull (New York: Penguin, 1976), xxi.
5. Ibid., xxii.

6. C. G. Jung, *The Structure and Dynamics of the Psyche*, vol. 8 of *The Collected Works of C. G. Jung*, edited and translated by G. Adler and R. F. C. Hull (Princeton, N.J.: Princeton University Press, 1970).

7. Marie-Louise von Franz, in Carl G. Jung et al., *Man and His Symbols* (Garden City, N.Y.: Doubleday, 1964), pt. 3.

8. Stanley Milgram, *Obedience to Authority: An Experimental View* (New York: HarperCollins, 1983). See also http://www.stanleymilgram.com.

9. L. Frank Baum, *The Wonderful Wizard of Oz* (Chicago: George M. Hill, 1900). Complete text online at http://www.bookvalley.com/collections/ozwizard.

CHAPTER 6

1. Aldous Huxley, *The Perennial Philosophy* (New York: Harper & Row, 1944), introduction.

2. Malcolm X, with Alex Haley, *The Autobiography of Malcolm X* (New York: Ballantine, 1992).

3. Lex Hixon, *Mother of the Universe: Vision of the Goddess and Tantric Hymns of Enlightenment* (Wheaton, Ill.: Quest Books, 1994), introduction. For the poems of Jelaluddin Rumi in modern translation, see *The Ruins of the Heart*, translated by Edmund Helminski (Putney, Vt.: Threshold, 1981), and *Unseen Rain*, translated by John Moyne and Coleman Barks (Putney, Vt: Threshold, 1986).

CHAPTER 7

1. *Egil's Saga*, translated by Hermann Pálsson and Paul Edwards (New York: Penguin, 1977).

2. Jung, *The Structure and Dynamics of the Psyche*.

SELECTED
BIBLIOGRAPHY

Angus, S. *The Mystery-Religions: A Study in the Religious Background of Early Christianity*. New York: Dover, 1975.

Baum, L. Frank. *The Wonderful Wizard of Oz*. Chicago: George M. Hill, 1900.

Cahill, Thomas. *The Gifts of the Jews: How a Tribe of Desert Nomads Changed the Way Everyone Thinks and Feels*. New York: Nan A. Talese, 1998.

Campbell, Joseph. *The Hero with a Thousand Faces*. Princeton, N.J.: Princeton University Press, 1968.

Castaneda, Carlos. *The Fire from Within*. New York: Pocket Books, 1991.

Charlton, Hilda. *Hell-Bent for Heaven: The Autobiography of Hilda Charlton*. Woodstock, N.Y.: Golden Quest, 1990.

Chilton, Bruce. *Rabbi Jesus: An Intimate Biography*. New York: Doubleday, 2000.

Cooper, D. Jason. *Mithras: Mysteries and Initiation Rediscovered*. Tork Beach, Me.: Samuel Weiser, 1996.

D'Alviella, Goblet. *The Mysteries of Eleusis: The Secret Rites and Rituals of the Classical Greek Mystery Tradition*. Wellingborough, England: Aquarian Press, 1981.

Egil's Saga. Translated by Hermann Pálsson and Paul Edwards. New York: Penguin, 1977.

The Encyclopedia Mythica: An Encyclopedia on Mythology, Folklore, and Legend. Online at http://www.pantheon.org.

The Encyclopedia of Eastern Philosophy and Religion. Boston: Shambhala, 1989.

Estés, Clarissa Pinkola, Ph.D. *Women Who Run with the Wolves: Myths and Stories of the Wild Woman Archetype*. New York: Ballantine, 1997.

Gaster, Theodor H. *The Oldest Stories in the World*. Boston: Beacon Press, 1952.

Hillman, James. *The Soul's Code: In Search of Character and Calling*. New York: Random House, 1996.

Hixon, Lex. *Mother of the Universe: Vision of the Goddess and Tantric Hymns of Enlightenment*. Wheaton, Ill.: Quest Books, 1994.

Horsley, Richard A., and Neil Asher Silberman. *The Message of the Kingdom: How Jesus and Paul Ignited a Revolution and Transformed the Ancient World*. New York: Grosset/Putnam, 1997.

Huxley, Aldous. *The Perennial Philosophy*. New York: Harper & Row, 1944.

Jordan, Michael. *Encyclopedia of Gods: Over 2,500 Deities of the World*. New York: Facts on File, 1993.

Jung, C. G. *The Structure and Dynamics of the Psyche*. Vol. 8 of *The Collected Works of C. G. Jung*. Edited and translated by G. Adler and R. F. C. Hull. Princeton, N.J.: Princeton University Press, 1970.

———. *The Archetypes and the Collective Unconscious*. Vol. 9 of *The Collected Works of C. G. Jung*. Edited and translated by G. Adler and R. F. C. Hull. Princeton, N.J.: Princeton University Press, 1970.

Jung, C. G., et al. *Man and His Symbols*. Garden City, N.Y.: Doubleday, 1964.

Keen, Sam. *Fire in the Belly*. New York: Three Rivers, 1997.

Kushner, Harold. *How Good Do We Have to Be? A New Understanding of Guilt and Forgiveness*. Boston: Little, Brown & Co., 1996.

Levoy, Gregg. *Callings: Finding and Following an Authentic Life*. New York: Three Rivers, 1997.

Lings, Martin. *Muhammad: His Life Based on the Earliest Sources*. Rochester, Vt.: Inner Traditions International, 1983.

Malcolm X, with Alex Haley. *The Autobiography of Malcolm X*. New York: Ballantine, 1992.

Milgram, Stanley. *Obedience to Authority: An Experimental View*. New York: HarperCollins, 1983.

Occhiogrosso, Peter. *The Joy of Sects: A Spirited Guide to the World's Religious Traditions*. New York: Image, 1996.

———. *Through the Labyrinth: Stories of the Search for Spiritual Transformation in Everyday Life*. New York: Viking, 1991.

O'Donohue, John. *Anam Cara: A Book of Celtic Wisdom*. New York: HarperCollins, 1997.

The Portable Jung. Edited by Joseph Campbell. Translated by R. F. C. Hull. New York: Penguin, 1976.

Ram Dass. *Be Here Now*. San Cristobal, N.M.: Hanuman Foundation, 1971.

———. *Still Here: Embracing Aging, Changing, and Dying*. New York: Riverhead, 2000.

Robinson, Richard H., and Willard L. Johnson. *The Buddhist Religion: A Historical Introduction*. 3d ed. Belmont, Calif.: Wadsworth, 1982.

Rumi, Jelaluddin. *The Ruins of the Heart*. Translated by Edmund Helminski. Putney, Vt.: Threshold, 1981.

————. *Unseen Rain*. Translated by John Moyne and Coleman Barks. Putney, Vt.: Threshold, 1986.

Shealy, Norman, M.D., and Caroline Myss. *The Creation of Health: The Emotional, Psychological, and Spiritual Responses That Promote Health and Healing*. New York: Three Rivers, 1998.

Tarnas, Richard. *The Passion of the Western Mind: Understanding the Ideas That Have Shaped Our World View*. New York: Harmony Books, 1991.

Underhill, Evelyn. *Mysticism: The Nature and Development of Spiritual Consciousness*. Oxford, England: Oneworld, 1993.

Weiss, Brian, M.D. *Through Time into Healing: Discovering the Power of Regression Therapy to Erase Trauma and Transform Mind, Body, and Relationships*. New York: Touchstone, 1993.

Woolger, Roger, Ph.D. *Other Lives, Other Selves: A Jungian Psychotherapist Discovers Past Lives*. New York: Doubleday. 1987.

Zahoor, Dr. A., and Dr. Z. Haq. *Biography of Prophet Muhammad*. 1990. http://users.erols.com/zenithco/muhammad.html.

INDEX

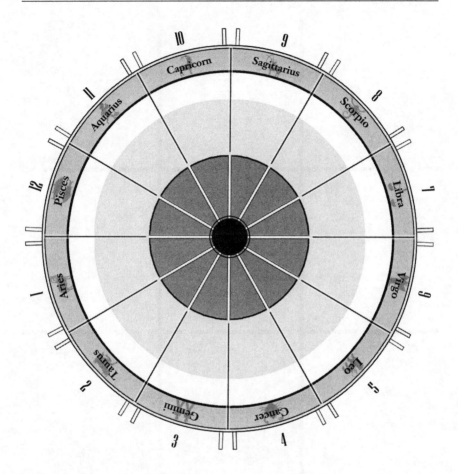

Photocopy the template above and use it to write in the names of your archetypes for your Chart of Origin and all subsequent working charts and healing charts.

Make two photocopies of the grid on the next page. On one set, write the numbers 1 through 12. On the other set, write the twelve archetypes you have selected for your personal support group.

ABOUT THE AUTHOR

Caroline Myss, Ph.D., is the author of the bestselling *Anatomy of the Spirit* and *Why People Don't Heal, and How They Can* and a pioneer and international lecturer in the fields of energy medicine and human consciousness. Since 1982 she has worked as a medical intuitive: one who "sees" illness in a patient's body by intuitive means. She specializes in helping people understand the emotional, psychological, and physical reasons why their bodies develop illness. She has also worked with Dr. Norman Shealy, M.D., Ph.D., founder of the American Holistic Medical Association, in teaching intuitive diagnosis. Together they wrote *The Creation of Health: Merging Traditional Medicine with Intuitive Diagnosis.* She lives in Oak Park, Illinois.